SAMS Teach Yourself

Adobe®
Photoshop®
Elements 2

in 24 Hours

Carla Rose
Jennifer Fulton

SAMS   201 West 103rd St., Indianapolis, Indiana, 46290 USA

Sams Teach Yourself Adobe® Photoshop® Elements 2 in 24 Hours

Copyright © 2003 by Sams Publishing

International Standard Book Number: 0-672-32430-X

Library of Congress Catalog Card Number: 2002104073

Printed in the United States of America

04   03   02   4   3   2   1

Trademarks

Warning and Disclaimer

ACQUISITIONS EDITOR
Betsy Brown

DEVELOPMENT EDITOR
Kate Small

MANAGING EDITOR
Charlotte Clapp

PROJECT EDITOR
George E. Nedeff

PRODUCTION EDITORS
Chip Gardner
Seth Kerney
Jennifer Lewis
Lindsey Rue
Matt Wynalda

INDEXER
Mandie Frank

PROOFREADER
Carla Lewis

TECHNICAL EDITOR
Kate Binder

TEAM COORDINATOR
Amy Patton

INTERIOR DESIGN
Gary Adair

COVER DESIGN
Aren Howell

Contents at a Glance

Contents

About the Author

CARLA ROSE started her photography career at the age of 8 with a Brownie Hawkeye. A graduate of the School of the Museum of Fine Arts in Boston, she worked as a TV news photographer and film editor, as well as an advertising copywriter and graphic artist, before discovering the Macintosh. She has written all or part of more than two dozen computer books, including *Sams Teach Yourself Photoshop 7 in 24 Hours*; *Maclopedia*; *Adobe InDesign for the Mac*; *Sams Teach Yourself Digital Photography in 14 Days*; *Sams Teach Yourself Photoshop 4 in 14 Days*; *The Whole Mac*; *Managing the Windows NT Server*; *PageMaker 6.5 Complete*; *Sams Teach Yourself Photoshop 4 in 24 Hours*; *Sams Teach Yourself Photoshop 5 in 24 Hours*; *Sams Teach Yourself Photoshop 5.5 in 24 Hours*; *Sams Teach Yourself Photoshop 6 in 24 Hours*; *Mac Online*; *The First Book of Macintosh*; *The First Book of PageMaker 4 for Macintosh*; *It's a Mad, Mad, Mad, Mad Mac*; *Turbocharge Your Mac*; and *Everything You Ever Wanted to Know About the Mac*. She is a contributing editor for *Photoshop User Magazine* and has also written for publications ranging from the *Atlantic Fisherman* to *Adobe Magazine* to the *New Yorker*. She lives near Boston, Massachusetts, with her husband, audio guru Jay Rose, and three large, friendly cats. She welcomes email addressed to author@graphicalcat.com but regrets that she cannot reply to every message.

About the Contributing Author

JENNIFER FULTON, iVillage's former "Computer Coach," is an experienced computer consultant and trainer with over 20 years in the business. Jennifer is also the best-selling author of more than 100 computer books written for both the education and retail markets, including *Sams Teach Yourself PaintShop Pro 8 in 24 Hours*, *Sams Teach Yourself Windows ME in 10 Minutes*, *How to Use Microsoft Publisher 2000*, *How to Use Microsoft Office XP*, *Easy Outlook 2000*, *Sams Teach Yourself Excel 2000 in Ten Minutes*, *Office 2000 Cheat Sheet*, and *The Complete Idiot's Guide to Upgrading and Repairing Your PC*.

Jennifer lives in the Midwest with her husband, Scott, who is also a computer book author, and her daughter, Katerina, an author-to-be. They live together in a small home filled with many books, some of which they have not actually written themselves.

Dedication

For Sebastian

Acknowledgments

No project this big could ever get started, much less completed, without help from a lot of wonderful people. I'd like to thank the folks at Sams, especially Mark Taber, Betsy Brown, and Amy Patton. Thanks to Kate Binder for a good technical edit, and Kate Small for a strong development, Matt Wynalda for copy editing, and George Nedeff for keeping it all on track.

Thanks also to the Adobe folks for providing beta software and for coming up with a wonderful product. Big thanks to the people who supplied photos and/or their own faces for use in the illustrations. As always, thanks to my friends in the ABCs for their moral support as I worked 20-hour days to meet deadlines. Thanks to Mary Roberts and David Arndt for more reasons than I can mention.

Apologies and a hug to everyone I had to ignore or chase away while I worked, especially the cats and the kids. And the biggest hug and deepest gratitude of all to my wonderful husband, Jay, who always does what needs to be done.

We Want to Hear from You!

As the reader of this book, *you* are our most important critic and commentator. We value your opinion and want to know what we're doing right, what we could do better, what areas you'd like to see us publish in, and any other words of wisdom you're willing to pass our way.

You can email or write me directly to let me know what you did or didn't like about this book—as well as what we can do to make our books stronger.

Please note that I cannot help you with technical problems related to the topic of this book, and that due to the high volume of mail I receive, I might not be able to reply to every message.

When you write, please be sure to include this book's title and author as well as your name and phone or email address. I will carefully review your comments and share them with the author and editors who worked on the book.

Email: graphics@samspublishing.com
Mail: Mark Taber
          Associate Publisher
          Sams Publishing
          201 West 103rd Street
          Indianapolis, IN 46290 USA

Reader Services

For more information about this book or others from Sams Publishing, visit our Web site at www.samspublishing.com. Type the ISBN (excluding hyphens) or the title of the book in the Search box to find the book you're looking for.

Introduction

There's something about software people. I guess it's a sort of heightened sense of per-fectionism. They create a wonderful program like Photoshop, and then say, "Now, how can we make it better? Easier to use? More fun?" Only a few months ago, Photoshop 7 was released to the high-end graphics market, to loud cheers from users and critics alike. Now, right on its heels, we have Elements 2, which provides most of the same improve-ments for the rest of us.

The fact is, for most users, Photoshop Elements 2 is all the graphics and image editing software we'll ever need. The big surprise for first-time users is that it's really not as dif-ficult to work with as it looks. If you have used any other Adobe software, the Photoshop Elements interface will be immediately familiar to you. If you're just getting started cre-ating digital graphics, you'll find the going easier if you work through the lessons in this book in order and don't skip the activities or exercises.

Please be aware that this book was written using beta versions of the software. As such, some of the screen shots may be slightly different from what you see on your screen. Nevertheless, every effort has been made to keep the book as accurate as possible.

I've provided many of the source images for the book's exercises on the Sams Publishing Web site. To download the images, point your Web browser to www.samspublishing.com and search for the book page by title, author, or ISBN (without hyphens).

Once the main book page has loaded, click the Downloads link to get to the files.

There's no way to become an overnight expert, be it in Photoshop or anything else, but *Sams Teach Yourself Adobe Photoshop Elements 2 in 24 Hours* will get you up and run-ning quickly. It's divided into two dozen one-hour lessons, rather than chapters. Each one should take you about an hour to complete. Please don't try to read the entire book in one day. The best way to learn is to take an hour or two between the lesson sessions to try out what you've learned. You'll want to simply poke around and see what's on the menus and what happens when you click here and there.

Here's an activity for you to start with: Open the About Photoshop Elements window by choosing Help, About Photoshop Elements, and wait for a minute. You'll see it start to scroll through the list of all the people who worked on the program. (Press the Option (Mac) or Alt (Windows) key to speed up the crawl.) Watch carefully for the very last name on the list. It's a pleasant surprise....

One last thing before we start. You may have already noticed the color plate section of gorgeous photos, located in the middle of this book. Keep a bookmark there, because I'll be referring to the color plate section throughout the book as I show you how to craft equally excellent photos yourself using Photoshop Elements.

Ready? Let's get to work.

PART I
Working with Elements

Hour

HOUR 1

Welcome to Photoshop Elements

Adobe Photoshop Elements 2 is an amazing digital graphics program. It has tools that let you do virtually anything you can think of to a photo or any other kind of bitmapped art. Whoa! Only two sentences in and you're already encountering what may be unfamiliar words. Bitmapped? Digital graphics? Don't worry. It's really easy, and you'll be creating beautiful pictures before you know it.

The term *digital graphics* refers to any kind of graphic image—a photo, scanned art, a squiggle of color—that you've created or placed on an Elements page. Bitmapped graphics are shown on the screen as a mass of little colored bits or *pixels*. Each bit has a coded description of its color and position. If you make a change in one pixel—or a whole screen full—the computer will update the pixel descriptions and change the screen so you can see what you have done. Depending on how complicated the change is, and how much random access memory (RAM) your computer has available to do the math, your change may take anywhere from a fraction of a second to a minute or more.

Essentially, Photoshop Elements is a program that juggles numbers. Changing the numbers in the computer memory changes what you see on the screen. If you're good enough at math to know which numbers change, and by how much, you could make all those screen changes by hand. Most people aren't. (Besides, it would be terribly inefficient to make all the changes manually.) That's where Elements steps in. Let's say you want to draw a red line about halfway down the page. You could figure out the positions of the pixels to change and change the color of each one from white to red. That's too much work. Let Elements do it. You just pick up a paintbrush, choose some red paint, and draw your line. There it is. The computer has taken all the math out of your hands and done the operation much faster than you could have on your own.

Now let's say you have a photo that's much too dark. If you were a photographer working in a darkroom, you would have to do some experimenting to find out how much lighter to print the photo. You'd probably find out that some parts need to be 15% lighter, some others 30% lighter, and some parts shouldn't change. You'd have to try to find a compromise and would probably waste several sheets of paper trying to get a good print. With Elements, you can look at the screen and lighten the image by moving a slider. More importantly, you can select and lighten specific parts of the picture without changing the rest. You've finally got control!

Photoshop Elements has two purposes: correction and creation. Use it to solve problems with pictures you've scanned or shot with a digital camera. Very few pictures are perfect right from the camera. You can recompose a picture by cropping away part of it. You can remove people or objects that shouldn't be there. You can make technical corrections for color, exposure, and even focus. Then you can get creative and have fun with it. Cure your kid's acne. Get rid of red eye. Change your lemons to limes, or your purple roses to sky blue ones. Liquify a clock face so it looks like one of Salvador Dali's dripping watches. Move your family group shot from the backyard to someplace more interesting. Add type to your pictures, remove backgrounds…. The only limit is your imagination.

Adobe Photoshop, despite being easy to understand, is a heavy-duty professional hunk of software. Each revision (version 7 is the most current) has added more tools and more bells and whistles for the pros. For its $600 price tag, you'll get a lot more features than most of us would ever use. Realizing that, the nice people at Adobe streamlined the software and created Photoshop Elements. They took out the more esoteric functions and added some nifty new ones, such as How To's: step-by-step recipes for all kinds of effects, tricks, and basic actions such as cleaning up a picture. They've given us almost the full power of Photoshop in a quick and easy-to-use program. Now there's no excuse for dusty scans, bad exposures, and other photographic sins. No more trees growing out of people's heads. No more faces too dark to see. Just picture after picture, better than you ever thought you could shoot.

In this hour you will

- Learn about the Elements help system
- Learn how to use tool tips, recipes, and more
- Learn about the Help button

Getting Help

The tools in Photoshop Elements are designed to make you feel as though you're dealing with the real thing, whenever possible. For instance, the paintbrush tools become pressure sensitive when you use a graphics tablet such as the Wacom Intuos2. *Dodging* and *burning*, which you might do in a real darkroom to lighten or darken parts of an image, are done in Photoshop Elements with tools that not only work the same way, but whose icons even look like their real-world counterparts. The Photoshop Elements desktop, which is far less cluttered than my own, has a toolbox, the usual menu bar, and a bar of shortcut buttons for actions, such as opening a new page, saving, and printing. The Shortcuts bar also has what Adobe calls a palette well.

When you first open Elements, you will probably notice several windows arranged along the right side of the screen. These are palettes. Each one has a particular function. Hints and How To are information palettes. The Layers and History palettes hold lists. History has a palette entry for each step you take in correcting your picture. It lets you choose an earlier step and revert to it, effectively giving you the ability to undo multiple changes. The Layers palette keeps track of whether each layer in a file contains type or an image, and in what order the layers should be displayed. The Color Swatches palette is a paint box. All of these are carefully designed to be user-friendly. You can generally guess what they do by looking at them, and if not, help is at hand.

Tool Tips

The most basic helper is one you should start to use immediately. (By the way, as I suggested in the introduction, it's really a good idea to sit in front of the computer, with Elements active, while you read this book. You need to be able to try things out as they come along.) Figure 1.1 shows some tool tips. They are like little yellow sticky notes that pop up on the screen if you hold the cursor over any tool, icon, or dialog box caption. They are extremely helpful if you're not sure what something does. A tip gives you either the name of the tool, or if that's obvious, its function.

FIGURE 1.1

*Tool tips pop up within
a couple of seconds.*

 If you don't see the tool tips popping up, open the General Preferences window (Select Edit, then Preferences, then General) and make sure that the Show Tool Tips option is checked.

Hints Palette

If the Hints palette is open, as soon as you hold the cursor over a new tool you'll see some suggestions on how to use that tool, effectively. (If the Hints palette isn't open, locate its tab in the palette well. Click and drag it away from the well, so it will stay open while you work.) When you're not a beginner anymore, you can put this palette away, but right now, keep it handy. It's a wonderful helper.

You'll notice a button labeled "More" on this and other palettes. *Always* click it to see what's there. It will take you to other options, put the palette away, and possibly give you access to additional commands.

Figure 1.2 shows the Hints palette for the Eraser tool. Frequently, there are additional relevant topics to check on, as well. When you click any of the underlined topics, you will be taken instantly to the program's comprehensive Help system, which runs in your Web browser.

FIGURE 1.2

*The menu pops up
when you click the
More button.*

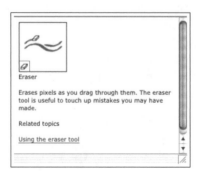

How To's

If hints just don't tell you enough, or if you want some step-by-step directions, open the How To palette. Here you can find lists of "recipes" for common Photoshop functions such as "Change an Object's Color," or "Rotate an Object." Figure 1.3 shows an example of such a recipe.

FIGURE 1.3

Recipes are reduced into simple steps.

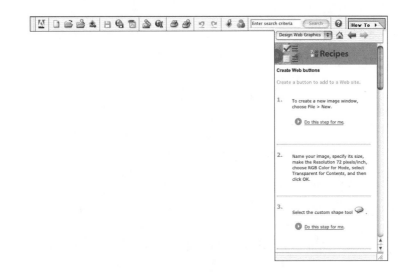

As you can see, the recipe steps even have Do This Step for Me buttons, so you can make the task absolutely foolproof. If you're in a hurry or feeling lazy, just use the recipes that Elements provides.

If you don't see exactly what you're looking for, or if you just want to keep up to date, open the pull-down menu at the top of the palette and choose Download New Adobe How To Items. You'll be connected to Adobe's Web site, where you'll find a list of all the latest recipes and How To's.

The Help Button

When all else fails, and you don't even know what it is that you don't understand, click the big question mark icon on the Shortcuts bar. It will take you to the beginning of the program's excellent Help manual. Enter a topic if you know what you're looking for, or just scroll through until something looks relevant. Check out Elements-friendly Web sites, such as www.PlanetPhotoshop.com and www.PhotoshopUser.com. And, of course, you can try writing to me (author@graphicalcat.com). I don't promise to answer every question that comes in, but if your question's a good one, I'll give it my best shot.

Summary

You are starting to learn your way around the Photoshop Elements screen, and you have learned how to open a new page. You've looked at the toolbox and the palettes, at least a little bit. You know about the Shortcuts bar and the Options bar. Most important, you know where to look for help.

Q&A

Q This looks as if it's going to be complicated. Are you sure I can do it?

A Of course you can. There's a lot to learn, but none of it's difficult.

Q What's the most important thing to know?

A The more you work with Photoshop Elements, or any other software program, the better you'll get at using it. In other words, practice. I try to take a few minutes a day, no matter what else I'm doing, to try a new way of combining filters, a different blending mode for combining two layers, or something else I haven't done lately.

Q Is Photoshop Elements going to be enough, or do I really need to upgrade to Photoshop?

A You'll know the answer to that after you have worked with Elements for a while. If you really need access to color channels, Bézier curves, and so on, you may need to upgrade. For most of us, most of the time, Elements has every tool and trick you need to rescue a bad picture or make a good one great.

Workshop

Do you know how to get help? Prove it with this quiz. And then try the activities.

Quiz

1. Does Elements have more than one kind of help system?

    a. Yes

    b. No

2. What are the two main uses of Photoshop Elements?

    a. Correction and creation

    b. Media management and analysis

    c. Retrieval and redistribution

Quiz Answers

1. a. Yes. Actually, help is everywhere.
2. a. Use Elements to repair whatever went wrong with a picture, but don't stop there. There's no limit to what you can do, whether you're starting from an existing photo or scanned art, or starting from a blank page. Go for it!

Activities

1. Think of this as recess, and have fun. Open Elements and try some of the help sources. Click the question mark on the Shortcuts bar. Hold the mouse over different tools and tool bar items. Explore. You're not going to break anything.
2. If you have an Internet connection, click the Adobe logo at the top of the toolbar. Visit Adobe Online and see what's there.

Hour **2**

A Tour of the Desktop

Luckily for us, the Elements working environment is a desktop, rather than a smelly, messy darkroom. It used to be that going into the darkroom was the only way you could do much of anything with a photo. That's why there are so many shoeboxes full of bad photos in so many attics, basements, and forgotten closets. Begin now to think about where they are. Pretty soon, you'll want to find them and fix them.

In this hour you will

- Tour the Photoshop Elements environment
- Learn about the tools in the Toolbox
- Familiarize yourself with the program menus and commands
- Adjust program preferences as desired

Finding Your Way Around

Let's start by looking at the Elements desktop shown in Figure 2.1. As with most other programs, there is a menu bar at the top. Next, there's a Shortcuts bar and beneath it, an Options bar. At the left is the toolbox and on the right end of the Shortcuts bar is the palette well. Rulers may or may not be displayed in the image area as shown here; their display is controlled by a command on the View menu, which is discussed later in this hour.

FIGURE 2.1

Your desktop should look something like this.

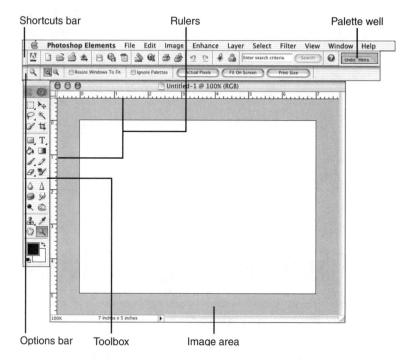

There may or may not be palettes open on the right side of the screen. As you learned last hour, a *palette* is a kind of window that gives you information about your project or lets you choose from a display of colors or styles. We'll look at the menus and tools in a moment. For now, let's jump ahead a step to the Shortcuts bar.

Understanding the Shortcuts Bar

The Shortcuts bar, shown in Figure 2.2, simplifies your workflow by providing buttons that correspond to the most common functions located on other menus. If you've used other software with similar button bars (Microsoft Word, PowerPoint, and Excel have them, to name just a few) then these buttons will be very familiar. The icons on the buttons should help you remember what's what. Starting with the first icon on the left and moving right, the Adobe logo opens your browser and takes you to www.adobe.com. The blank page icon, of course, means New image, and the partly open file folder icon stands for Open. The same folder icon plus a magnifying glass initiates a search by opening the File Browser. The last icon in this group, with a tilted image window and a right-pointing arrow, is used to import an image from a scanner, digital camera, or other source.

FIGURE 2.2

The Shortcuts bar, shortened to fit the page.

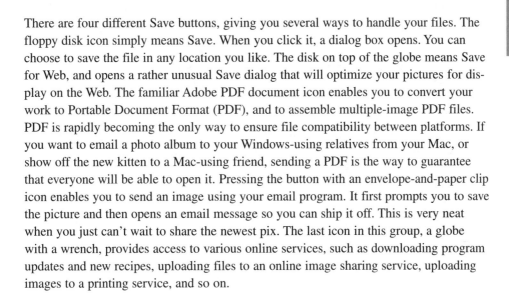

2

There are four different Save buttons, giving you several ways to handle your files. The floppy disk icon simply means Save. When you click it, a dialog box opens. You can choose to save the file in any location you like. The disk on top of the globe means Save for Web, and opens a rather unusual Save dialog that will optimize your pictures for display on the Web. The familiar Adobe PDF document icon enables you to convert your work to Portable Document Format (PDF), and to assemble multiple-image PDF files. PDF is rapidly becoming the only way to ensure file compatibility between platforms. If you want to email a photo album to your Windows-using relatives from your Mac, or show off the new kitten to a Mac-using friend, sending a PDF is the way to guarantee that everyone will be able to open it. Pressing the button with an envelope-and-paper clip icon enables you to send an image using your email program. It first prompts you to save the picture and then opens an email message so you can ship it off. This is very neat when you just can't wait to share the newest pix. The last icon in this group, a globe with a wrench, provides access to various online services, such as downloading program updates and new recipes, uploading files to an online image sharing service, uploading images to a printing service, and so on.

The next two icons are a printer and a printer with a magnifying glass, and they represent Print and Print Preview, respectively.

The Step Backward and Step Forward buttons are equivalent to the Undo and Redo buttons you may have used in other programs, such as Microsoft Word. With them, you can undo the last action, and then redo it if you don't like the result.

Clicking the Quick Fix button (with the lightning bolt) displays a dialog box that provides fast access to several image correcting tools. With the Color Variations icon (the three colored circles), you can access several color correcting tools instead. The next section of the toolbar contains the Search box and the Help button (labeled with a large question mark). Search finds specific help topics. Enter a word and click Search, and Elements will search through its entire Help file for it.

At the far right of the Shortcuts bar is what Adobe calls the palette well. (It looks like a set of file folder tabs.) It serves as a docking station for your palettes. You can decide how many palettes you want to keep there, how many you want open, and whether there are some you can just ignore. If palettes accidentally get lost, don't panic. You can restore them from the Windows menu.

Task: Starting a New Image

In a little while we are going to need a blank image file to try some of our tools on. Let's create one now, using the Shortcuts bar. We'll work with other kinds of images and other ways to create them in the following hours.

1. Point your cursor to the New button.
2. Click once to open the New dialog box shown in Figure 2.3.
3. Click on the Preset Sizes drop-down list and choose Default Photoshop Size.
4. Check to see that the White option in the Contents area of the dialog box is selected.
5. Click OK or press Return and the new page will open.

FIGURE 2.3

Your dialog box should look like this.

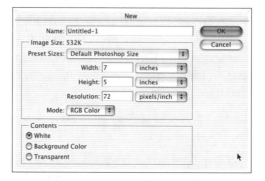

Now you have a blank image on your desktop, and we're about to look at the tools.... Go ahead and try them out. You can't break anything. Select something. Draw something. Paint a heart and move it around the screen. Try some colors. When the image gets too full, press Cmd+A (Mac) or Ctrl+A (Windows) to select everything. Then delete it by pressing Delete and start over again.

Using the Tools in the Toolbox

Our next stop is the toolbox, at the left side of the screen. For reference, it is shown in Figure 2.4. It's like an artist's work table or paint box that holds all the tools you'll use to draw, paint, erase, and otherwise work on your picture. There are sets of tools to select, to draw and paint, to blur and sharpen, and to place type in the picture.

FIGURE 2.4

You must first click on a tool to select it.

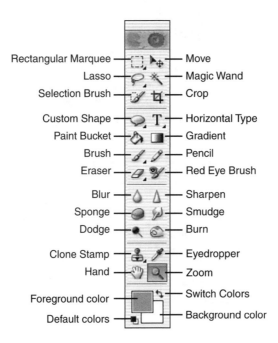

Rectangular Marquee — Move
Lasso — Magic Wand
Selection Brush — Crop
Custom Shape — Horizontal Type
Paint Bucket — Gradient
Brush — Pencil
Eraser — Red Eye Brush
Blur — Sharpen
Sponge — Smudge
Dodge — Burn
Clone Stamp — Eyedropper
Hand — Zoom
Foreground color — Switch Colors
Default colors — Background color

2

The toolbox has additional tools hidden wherever you see a black arrowhead. Click and hold on any tool with an arrowhead, and the additional tools associated with it will pop out on a short menu. Figure 2.5 shows the tools that are normally hidden in the Type tool menu.

FIGURE 2.5

You will learn about working with type in Hour 6, "Adding Type."

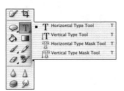

The colorful icon at the top of the toolbox takes you, by way of the Web, to www.adobe.com. Once there, you can find and download program updates, advice, and excellent tutorials. Check this site frequently.

Selection Tools

The first section of the toolbox contains a group of tools called Selection tools. They are used to select all or part of a picture. There are four kinds: the Marquees, the Lassos, the Selection Brush, and the Magic Wand. When you select an area of the screen with the Marquee tools, a blinking selection border surrounds it. (The Marquee tools are named after the lights on movie theater marquees that flash on and off.) The Marquees make their selections as you click and drag the tool over the part of an image you want to select, drawing a box or circle.

The Lasso tools—three in all—draw a line as you click and drag the tip of the lasso across the page. Draw part of a free-form shape, and Elements will complete the shape automatically with a straight line from where you stopped back to the start. There are also Lassos to select by drawing straight path segments instead of a free-form line, and to select "magnetically" by separating an object from its background. Figure 2.6 shows the selections that result from using these tools.

FIGURE 2.6

Each Lasso tool makes a different kind of selection.

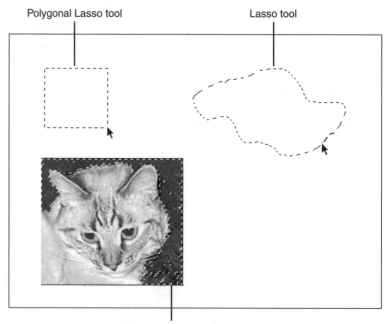

Polygonal Lasso tool

Lasso tool

Magnetic Lasso tool

The Selection Brush simply selects anything you paint over. Given that there are hundreds of standard paintbrushes, plus any you design yourself, this tool can be enormously flexible. Select it and drag your paintbrush over anything you want to turn into a selection. This tool doesn't exist in the "big" Photoshop program. I wish it did. You can use it to create masks over areas you want to protect when you're changing another part of the image. For instance, say you're working on a portrait of a lady, and you need to lighten her hair without bleaching out her face. Paint around the hair, or if it's easier, paint only the hair and then invert the selection so you've selected everything *but* the hair. If that sounds a little confusing, don't worry. We'll work more with selections in Hour 5, "Making Selections and Using Layers," and again when we get into photo repair.

The Magic Wand tool selects by color. You can set the amount of similarity it demands, and just click to select all pixels of that color, or all adjacent pixels that match.

The final tools in this section of the toolbox are the Move tool and the Crop tool. After you have made a selection, use the Move tool to drag the selected area to another place on the image. The Crop tool works just like the rectangular Marquee tool, in that you drag a *bounding box* to surround the part of the picture you are keeping. When you do so, the area outside the box turns gray. You can drag a side to make the bounding box bigger or smaller. When you're done adjusting the box, double-clicking in the box removes everything outside it.

Painting Tools

Elements has an impressive set of Painting tools: Brushes, a Pencil, an Eraser, and Paint Bucket and Gradient tools. These all apply color to the screen in one way or another, just like the real tools they imitate. You can change the width and angle for the Pencil and Brush tools. The Brush tool and the Impressionist Brush share a space in the toolbox. The latter simulates different kinds of brushstrokes. Though there isn't a lot of use for it in photo correction or enhancement, it's fun to play with. The Red Eye Brush simply finds the odd color and replaces it with the correct eye color. Two clicks and your "devil eyes" photos can be pictures of saints. Many of these tools are covered throughout this book, in hours that discuss how to make specific types of repairs on photos. You'll learn how to use other tools to create an image from scratch in Hour 20, "Making Composite Images."

There are also various erasers that, as you might expect, take away part of the picture. You can use a block eraser, or erase with any of the paintbrush or airbrush shapes. There are two special-purpose erasers, the Background and Magic Erasers. Use them to automatically erase a selected part of the image. The Paint Bucket, also called the Fill tool by some people, pours paint (the Foreground color) into any contiguous area you select. (If no area is selected, it'll fill the whole image.) The Gradient tool lets you create backgrounds that shade from one color to another, or even all the way through the color spectrum.

Lastly, there is a vector tool that draws shapes (the Custom Shape tool) and another that places type (Horizontal Type) as *vectors*—shapes defined by their outline rather than as bitmaps (tiny dots that form a shape). When you use these tools, you don't get the jagged effect you otherwise would when building an object from individual pixels because a vector image can be resized and its resolution adjusted without any effect on the clarity of the image. Figure 2.7 shows the difference between bitmapped and vector text and drawn lines. As you can see, the bitmapped text is ragged around the edges, especially when it's enlarged. Look closely at the curves of the *b*, *t*, *m*, *a*, *p*, *e*, and *d* to see this effect. The bitmapped line shares the same fate—it has bumps along its sides. The vector text and line, on the other hand, is quite smooth, regardless of the size at which you view it.

FIGURE 2.7

Vector type versus bitmapped type.

Toning Tools

Toning tools are tools that move, blur, and change the intensity of the image. The Blur, Sharpen, and Smudge tools change the level of focus and the Dodge, Burn, and Sponge tools change the degree of darkness or lightness of selected pixels. These tools will be covered in detail in Hour 14, "Repairing Black-and-White Pictures and Scans," and Hour 15, "Making Color Repairs."

Viewing Tools

There are two Viewing tools: the Hand tool and the Zoom tool. The Zoom tool is shaped like an old-fashioned magnifying glass, and the Hand, not surprisingly, like a hand. The Zoom tool lets you zoom in by clicking the tool on the canvas to see a magnified view of your picture, or zoom out by pressing Option (Mac) or Alt (Windows) as you click the image. You can also click and drag the Zoom tool to enlarge a specific part of the image. When you zoom in, the picture is usually too big to see all at once. The hand moves it within the window and is helpful after you use the Zoom tool to enlarge the picture. Use the hand to slide the part of the picture you want to see or work on into a convenient spot.

Special Tools

There are two tools that don't quite fit into any category. The Clone Stamp tool copies a piece of the existing picture and pastes it somewhere else. The Eyedropper picks up a sample of color, which you can make the active color or add to your Swatches palette. We'll talk more about these when we use them for photo correction in Hours 11 and 14.

Colors

Finally, there are two large blocks of color displayed at the bottom of the toolbox. They are your foreground and background colors, and by default they are black and white, respectively. Change them by clicking once on the appropriate square to open the Color Picker. There, you can click to select any color you like. The foreground color (logically, the one on top) is the color you'll apply when you paint a brushstroke, place type, or do anything that leaves a mark on the page.

Tool Shortcuts

You can select any of these tools by clicking its icon in the toolbox, but Elements gives you another, even easier way to access the tools. Instead of clicking the tools you want to use, you can type a single letter shortcut to select each tool. To toggle through the available tools where there are pop-up menus, press Shift plus the shortcut letter until you reach the tool you want. Table 2.1 lists the tools with their shortcuts. Dog-ear this page so you can refer to the table until you have memorized the shortcuts.

TABLE 2.1 Tools and Their Shortcuts

Tool	Shortcut	Tool	Shortcut
Marquee	M	Move	V
Lasso	L	Magic Wand	W
Selection Brush	A	Crop	C
Custom Shape	U	Type	T
Paint Bucket	K	Gradient	G
Brush	B	Pencil	N
Eraser	E	Red EyeBrush	Y
Blur	R	Sharpen	P
Sponge	Q	Smudge	F
Dodge	O	Burn	J
Clone Stamp	S	Eyedropper	I
Hand	H	Zoom	Z
Switch Colors	X	Return to Default Colors	D

Understanding the Options Bar

Every tool in the toolbox has many settings. For example, you're not stuck with a tiny little pencil and a big fat brush as your only drawing tools. You can make the exact tool you want by simply changing the way it behaves using the options bar. You can change a tool's degree of *opacity* (the degree to which the tool obscures the part of the image you use it on) and *blending mode* (the degree to which the tool's color blends with the existing colors in the image), and select from libraries of shapes and textures and styles. You can also save and store your own brushes and reach them via the Options bar. Note that the options bar changes with each different tool you select. For example, Figure 2.8 shows the Shape tool Options bar with a drop-down menu. This one displays the entire library of shapes included with Elements.

FIGURE 2.8

There are all sorts of pop-up menus and pull-out menus on each Options bar. Be sure to explore.

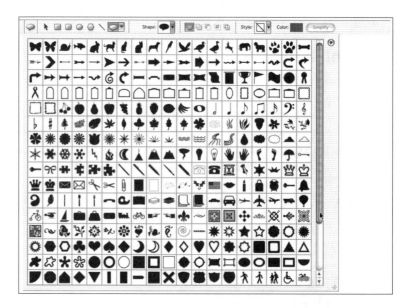

Typically, these drop-down menus will also have a submenu attached. To open it, click the right-pointing arrowhead at the top of the menu. As you explore Elements, try clicking arrows or buttons whenever you see them to find out what they do.

Using the Menus

If you have used *any* kind of computer software written in the past 20 years, you have used menus. The menus across the top of the Elements screen contain the commands that enable you to open and manipulate files. Access them by clicking the name of the menu to open it, and then selecting the desired command from the list. Whenever you see an arrow or an ellipsis (…) to the right of a menu command, it indicates that there is something more than just that command available. A right-pointing arrow indicates that there's a submenu. An ellipsis means that the menu item leads to a dialog box. Figure 2.9 shows the Elements File menu.

FIGURE 2.9

The Elements File menu. Note the arrows and ellipses.

2

It's no coincidence that you'll find the same set of commands, more or less, on any File menu, and that the Mac and Windows cut, copy, and paste commands are the same. One of the things that makes computers easy to use is the notion of a universal user interface. That's a fancy way to say that you do the same things the same way in all programs. Cmd/Ctrl+N always starts a new page. Cmd/Ctrl+Q always quits, and so on. This makes learning a new program simpler. Adobe's taken that even further, in that all Adobe graphics software uses the same tools and working methods. If you master using layers in Elements, as I am sure you will, you'll also know how to use layers in InDesign or Illustrator. As you work your way through this book, you will get a head start on learning the rest of the Adobe software. Similarly, if you already use Illustrator or PageMaker, or even Premiere, you'll find that you already know a lot about Elements. Of course, there's always something new to learn.

Taking a Look at the File and Edit Menus

The first two Elements menus are File and Edit. The File menu lets you work with files: opening, closing, saving, importing, exporting, and printing them, and, of course, quitting the program. Here's where you can select several sequential shots to stitch together a panoramic photo. Here's where you can choose to email a picture to your friends.

The New option opens a blank screen on which you can paint or drag images from other open windows. Open will bring up a dialog box that lets you locate any specific graphics file and open it. Finding these files isn't always easy, however (especially if you're like me and forget what you called the shot the first time you saved it). That's why there's a browser.

Using the File Browser

You can open the File Browser by selecting Browse from the File menu or File Browser from the Window menu, by using its key shortcut (Cmd+Shift+O [Mac], Ctrl+Shift+O [Windows]), or by clicking its tab in the palette well. You can also open the File Browser by clicking Browse for File in the Welcome Screen. Use it to locate and open your photos and other images. When you open the File Browser, you can search any of your graphics folders by selecting them. After you've selected a folder, thumbnail-sized views of all its pictures will appear as if they were slides on a sorting table. Figure 2.10 shows the setup. To open a picture, just double-click on it. If you select a picture and don't double-click, you'll also see all the information available about the picture, including its size, color mode, date and time it was shot, make and model of camera used, flash enabled or not, shutter speed, and a lot more than you'll ever need to know. Slide the partitions to make the information window smaller, and then you can see more thumbnails at once.

You can change the order in which the images are sorted by clicking the Sort By button and making a selection from its menu. To change the size of the thumbnails, click the View By button and make a selection. You'll learn more about the File Browser in Hour 3, "Starting and Saving Your Work."

Elements will also display disk icons, folders, applications, and whatever else it sees in the folder you select. Use the folder hierarchy to navigate down to the level where your picture is. The nice thing about the File Browser, as opposed to other image-indexing methods, is that when you find the image you need, you can just double-click, and you're ready to work.

2

FIGURE 2.10
You can find any photo you need with the File Browser.

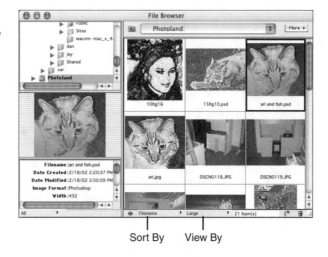

Sort By   View By

Taking a Look at the Image Menu

The Image menu has the commands to do what I'd consider "physical" things to the picture. Turn it sideways, flip it, rotate a single layer or the whole image, distort it, make it bigger or smaller…. You get the idea.

Duplicate Image

The Duplicate Image command *does not* save a copy of the image. I want to be very clear about that. If you want to keep a copy of your picture, use Save As and check Save a Copy. Duplicate Image puts a temporary copy of the picture into RAM and in a window on the screen. (See Figure 2.11.) Use it to save a "before" version, so you can compare the updated image to the original as you retouch a badly damaged photo or experiment wildly. When you're done, you can save the copy or not, as you wish.

FIGURE 2.11
You can tell that the picture on the right is just a working copy. It has no file type attached, so it's not saved as a file.

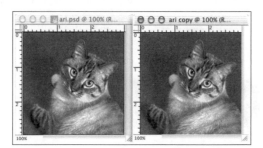

Rotate

Cameras and monitors are designed to work with horizontal rectangular images, or pictures that are wider than they are tall. But not all pictures have that shape. Suppose you are visiting New York and want a shot of the Empire State Building. First, you find a spot where you can see the whole building. If you hold your camera normally, you'll have to step backwards all the way to New Jersey before you'll be able to see the top of the building, and of course, you will have several blocks worth of other stuff on either side. Instead, if you turn the camera sideways, you change the format to vertical, and you can see a lot more of the tall building with a lot less of the neighborhood. Of course, when you get the photo back home and open it up in Elements again, it's sideways. It's not very practical to rotate the monitor. For one thing, it weighs a lot more than a camera. That's why you'll use the Rotate commands shown in Figure 2.12.

FIGURE 2.12

Rotate the entire image or rotate one layer at a time.

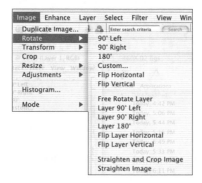

As you can see, there are many Rotate options. For Custom, enter a number of degrees and choose left or right. You need to be aware of the difference between rotating and flipping. When you rotate, you move the picture around its center point. Flipping draws a midline axis and flips the image relative to it. The difference is depicted visually in Figure 2.13.

FIGURE 2.13

Flipping crosses an axis. Rotating travels around a center point.

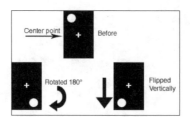

Transformations

Transformations occur within the theoretical perspective of a bounding box and are used to warp an object or selection. A bounding box is very much like a marquee. It's a rectangular selection box placed over the object to be transformed. Each corner and the center point of each side of the box has a small square called a handle. When you drag a handle, only the lines connected or related to it will move.

The Transformation options available in Elements are

- Free Transform—Apply multiple transformation techniques at one time, including skew, distort, and perspective

- Skew —Tilt the image horizontally or vertically

- Distort —Pull the image in any direction

- Perspective —Push the image backward or pull it forward along the third dimension

Figure 2.14 shows some examples. You can see in the bounding box at the bottom left that we're using perspective. The two side lines are of equal length, and the two angles on each side are complementary (they add up to 180°) .

FIGURE 2.14

The shape at the bottom left still has its bounding box in place.

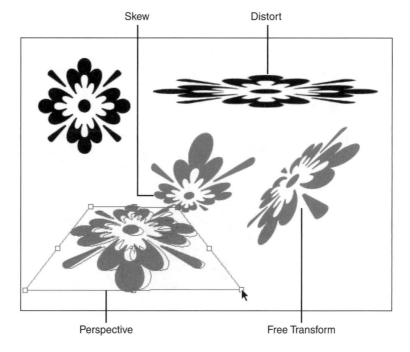

Skew   Distort

Perspective   Free Transform

Crop/Resize

Cropping is usually the single most important thing I do to a photo. You can't always stand where you should when you take a picture, so you may not be able to compose your shots in the camera. Cropping gives you a chance to correct them. It also lets you reshape a picture to emphasize a different part. We'll talk more about the theory and uses of cropping in Hour 9. Resizing is the process of changing the size of the image. There are many things you have to consider when you do this. Will your picture be seen in print or on the screen or both? Screen resolution becomes a factor here. There are right ways and wrong ways to resize. You can also keep the image the same size and in effect add more space around it by resizing the canvas. In Hour 9, we'll deal with shrinking and stretching the canvas.

Adjust

The items on the Image Adjustments submenu are mainly used for special effects. Invert and Posterize are easily the most useful. Invert takes a positive image in black and white and coverts it to an artificial but correct negative. It also does strange and amazing things to color by rotating the color wheel 180°. Posterize reduces the image from full color to a given number of colors, based on the sum of the average number of colors being converted. All the fancy math can often result in a beautiful picture. Figure 2.15 shows 4 levels of posterization (four levels of brightness for each color channel, such as red, green, and blue). Reducing the levels of brightness for each color creates large areas of a single color, removing the subtleties of color from an image and making it appear flatter. Be sure to see this in the color section. You'll learn how to use posterization in Hour 21, "Going Wild with Effects."

FIGURE 2.15

The lower the number of levels, the more simplified the drawing becomes.

Histogram

Were you ever into math or statistics? If so, you can probably explain a histogram better than I can. Simply put, it's a graph. In Elements, it's a graph that shows the distribution of pixels throughout the color/tonal range of the image. You can look at a histogram like the one in Figure 2.16 and know whether there's detail in the highlights and shadows and how to make corrections to bring them out. Shadows (blacks) are graphed on the left, midtones in the middle, and highlights (whites) on the right. Quite simply, if there are only a few lines that are very short, you may not be able to raise the picture from the dead. If you do have a lot of data, even though you're not sure what it means, there's hope.

FIGURE 2.16

The picture from which this histogram was generated has few real whites (on the right), but a lot of light grays and beiges (middle), and few true blacks (on the left).

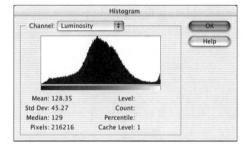

Modes

The four color modes available in Elements are Bitmap (which is 1-bit black and white), Grayscale (256 grays), RGB, and Indexed Color. When you work in color, as you will most of the time, stay with RGB. Indexed Color is for Web use, and since the adoption of JPEG compression, it isn't often used except for line art (simple drawings of one or two colors) or spot color (a method of identifying the exact color desired in a section of a graphic image, typically by selecting a Pantone color from a chart).

Taking a Look at the Enhance Menu

As the name of this menu suggests, these tools will improve your pictures. A little brightening here, a more intense shadow there…. But that's not all. You will find yourself doing a lot of your photo corrections from this menu, too. The kinds of problems solved here are mainly things that went wrong inside the camera or scanner—bad exposures, dull colors, the wrong colors—and these are all things that you can fix with a few clicks. Appropriately, the first item on the menu is Quick Fix.

Quick Fix

Quick Fix opens a window, shown in Figure 2.17, that suggests what problems exist in the picture, and tells you exactly how to fix them. The sliders are right there in the box, and you can watch Before and After images as you work. This is great for learning what the tools do and for making overall fixes.

FIGURE 2.17

Click the other tool buttons to run through the entire list of repairs.

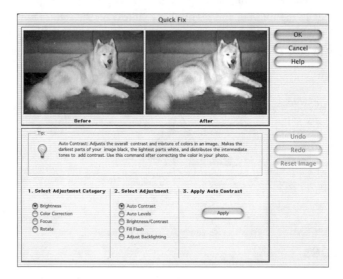

Also on this menu, you'll find a couple of "auto" settings for adjusting levels and contrast. If you're not too fussy, these are usually okay. Elements studies the picture, does some esoteric math, and tries to bring everything up or down to an ideal set of numbers. Well, sometimes ideal isn't what you want, and sometimes the program's idea of perfection isn't yours. Try these settings, but be prepared to undo them. You can make the same changes yourself to the degree that *you* think right.

Color adjustments and lighting adjustments can be a big help, both when you are trying to rescue a badly lit photo, and when you are trying to create a scene from several composite photos or from scratch.

Color Variations

We'll come back to this option a lot. The Color Variations command on the Adjust Color submenu is the best way to train your eye to really see color and to analyze what's wrong with it. It shows you the results of applying different color corrections to the same picture. Suppose you have a picture that has an orange cast. You know you want to add more of whatever color is the opposite of orange on the color wheel. But is that blue, green, or cyan? The Color Variations tool displays your picture with samples of each of the colors added to it. Choose the one you like best. It's that simple. You can vary the amount of color correction to apply. You can also look at samples of increased and decreased *saturation* (intensity of color) .

Taking a Look at the Layer Menu

Layers are useful, so much so that they have an entire menu and a half hour of this book devoted to them. That's plenty. If you have burning questions, jump ahead to Hour 5. You won't hurt my feelings.

Taking a Look at the Select Menu

You've already used the Selection tools. The Select menu (shown in Figure 2.18) has commands that will make them easier to work with. The Inverse command is especially useful, as it lets you make a selection and then invert it, selecting everything *but* the originally selected object.

FIGURE 2.18

The Select menu allows you to select elements of an image in various ways.

The ability to invert a selection can save you tons of time when you need to select a complicated object on a plain background. Instead of lassoing the object, click on the background with the Magic Wand tool. That selects it. If you need to combine several selections, press and hold the Shift key as you work. When everything but the object is selected, press Cmd+Shift+I (Mac) or Ctrl+Shift+I (Windows).

Taking a Look at the Filter Menu

This is the fun menu. Expect to spend at least two of this book's hours (Hours 17 and 19) and many hours of practice time on the contents of the Filter menu, especially if you also add on some third-party filters. If you count the different kinds of Liquify, there are over 100 filters on the Elements menu. You could learn one a week for the next two years and not run out of things to do.

The Hints palette can display examples of each of the filters applied to a typical image. If you forget what a particular filter does, take a look here. You can also shop here for the filter look you want.

In addition to the Elements filters, there are hundreds more. Some are shareware or freeware. Others can be bought from a computer store or online software vendor. After you have installed them, they also show up at the bottom of this menu.

Taking a Look at the View Menu

You can't do much if you can't see what you're doing, especially in photo repair. Fortunately, you can zoom in and out on your pictures with a mouse click or a key combination. It's not an infinite zoom. Each mouse click enlarges or shrinks the image to a certain percentage of its original size. You can view at 25%, 50%, 66.7%, 75%, 100%, and so on up to 1600%. The menu also has a command to fit the picture to the screen, even though that may not be a precise percentage enlargement.

Grid and Rulers are also included in the View menu. The Grid has a "snap-to" feature that you can toggle on and off from the menu. When it's on, if you try to align a line of type to a certain point, the grid will move it to the closest vertical and horizontal lines. Depending on where you want the type, that may or may not be helpful. Turn it off if it's a nuisance.

Taking a Look at the Window Menu

The Window menu, shown in Figure 2.19, actually tells you what all those windows and palettes and things on the screen are. Images, the topmost item, shows you a list of the images you have open. Selecting one brings it to the top of the pile.

Next, you have the option of toggling the toolbox and the Shortcuts and Options bars on and off. I suggest leaving them on, unless you have a good reason for not wanting them to clutter up the scenery.

In the next section of the Window menu, there's a list of all the palettes available in Elements. Because they are also conveniently docked in the palette well, you needn't come here to open a palette. You can just drag the desired palette tab from the well onto the desktop and the palette will remain open as long as you need it.

2

FIGURE 2.19

The Window menu allows you to display, hide, and arrange screen elements.

Taking a closer look at the Swatches palette in Figure 2.20 (which you can display by choosing Window, Color Swatches), you can see that there's more to it than a child's box of watercolors. Open the Swatches menu to display a list of all the color libraries currently available to Elements. (The menu on the left in this figure is available only to Mac users.)

FIGURE 2.20

The Swatches palette displays the swatches of color in the current palette.

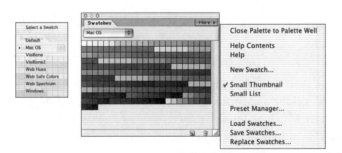

Clicking the More button opens a menu that can name a particular swatch of color, or add one that's not part of the original set. If your company's logo has a particular shade of blue, for instance, you can scan the logo and then use the eyedropper to copy the color and add it into the swatch palette.

At the bottom right of the palette is a trash can, for deleting unwanted swatches, and a New Page icon. You can add the current foreground color as a new swatch by clicking this icon. Although each palette has its own menus and lists and icons, they all do roughly the same things in relation to the function of the palette. For instance, the New Page icon on the Layers palette makes a new layer.

To prevent desk clutter, only open the palettes you need. I like to keep Undo History, Layers, and Swatches available, and leave the rest docked. I recommend leaving Hints open when you're just beginning, but it's entirely up to you.

Setting Preferences

You can get to the Preferences dialog boxes either by selecting Preferences at the bottom of the Edit menu or by pressing Cmd+K (Mac) or Ctrl+K (Windows). Once you're there you'll find eight different sets of options relating to everything from using smart quotes to changing the color of the grid lines. Figure 2.21 shows the first in the series: General.

Figure 2.21

Too many choices?

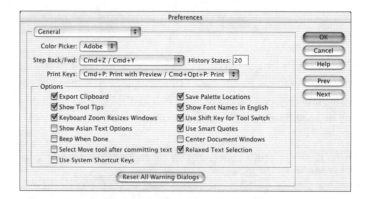

Some of these truly are common-sense preferences. And as long as Show Tool Tips is checked, holding the cursor over any tool or button will display a short explanation. My suggestion is to look through the Preferences screens and take note of what's there. If you prefer to think metric rather than measuring in inches, that's an easy change. If you'd rather see your grid in a different color, go ahead and change it. But leave the options you don't understand on their default settings. As you learn more about working with Elements, you can come back and adjust the Preferences to suit your needs.

Summary

In one dizzying hour we have covered everything on the desktop. You looked at the tools, and probably tried them out on the page you opened. You then learned about the Options bar and how its options can affect the way a tool functions. Finally, we discussed menus. (And it's a good thing—I'm more than ready for a snack break.) The Elements menus lead you to more menus and submenus and dialog boxes that contain everything you need to work with your pictures.

Q&A

Q I was sure I saw a tool for drawing rectangles. Now it looks like a blob. What happened?

A All the Shape tools share a single section in the toolbox. Clicking on that little black triangle in the bottom-right corner of the tool button will show you the rest of your options. Choose the one you want.

Q What's the Welcome Screen?

A It's a shortcut dialog box for opening a new image or getting to the help screens. You see it when you first open Elements and again if you choose Welcome from the Window menu. If you're starting a new image, however, the New button is a more efficient shortcut.

2

Workshop

Take a few moments to tackle the short quiz on the Elements environment below and check your answers to see how you did. Then work on the activities for extra credit.

Quiz

1. The Magic Wand is a _____.

    a. Drawing tool

    b. Filter

    c. Selection tool

    d. Eraser

2. The default colors are

    a. Red and blue

    b. Black and white

    c. The foreground and background colors

    d. Whatever you choose

3. How do you find the dialog box to open a new image?

    a. Go to the File menu and select New

    b. Press Cmd+N (Mac) or Ctrl+N (Windows)

    c. Click the New button on the Shortcuts bar

    d. All of the above

Quiz Answers

1. c. It selects pixels by color.

2. b. The foreground and background colors default to black and white, respectively.

3. d. You undoubtedly already have a favorite way to start a file in your word processor or other often-used programs. It's almost certainly one of these. Use what's familiar, provided that it works.

Activities

1. Display the palette of your choice. Dock it in the palette well, then move it into the work area. Display the commands on the palette's More menu. Resize the palette to display more information.

2. Start a new image file. Take a brush full of red paint and draw a heart. (It doesn't need to be perfect.) Select it and move it to another part of the page. Select it again with a different tool. Move it back to more or less where you started. Use the Rotate command to turn it over. Erase it, and repeat the process with a blue heart. Your goal is to practice with the tools and menu commands. Have fun!

Hour 3

Starting and Saving Your Work

Last hour, you learned a couple of ways to open a blank image file. I sneaked it in ahead of this hour so you could try out some tools. But in this hour I'll review that task and add some details about how to save what you create.

In this hour you will

- Create a new image file
- Browse for an image file to work on
- Save a new image
- Save changes to an image
- Undo changes to an image
- Change an image's resolution
- Prepare an image for use on the Web

Starting a New Image File

Let's take another quick look at the New dialog box before we move on. Here it is again, in Figure 3.1, just to refresh your memory.

FIGURE 3.1

The New dialog box is used to create a new image file.

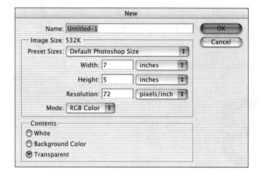

Starting at the top, you have the option of immediately naming your image, or leaving it untitled until you save it. Because I am almost always in a hurry, I skip that step and immediately consider page size. In this version of Elements and in the recent release of Photoshop 7, this dialog box has been modified to add a pop-up menu of possible page sizes, shown in Figure 3.2. The default is horizontal, 7×5 inches.

FIGURE 3.2

Most of the standard American and European page dimensions are included.

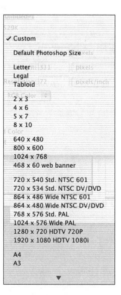

Choose a page size that's appropriate for what you want to do, remembering that screen formats are horizontal, while magazine covers and illustrations are more likely to be vertical. Landscapes and portraits dictate different orientations because of the shape of the subject.

If you have something on the clipboard that's waiting to be pasted into your new image, the dialog box will open with that item's dimensions in place of whatever other numbers might be there. You can still override it and choose a larger size, if you want.

Resolution is a tricky issue that we'll discuss in depth in the section, "Adjusting Resolution." Meanwhile, if your art project is to be viewed on the screen, perhaps as part of a PowerPoint slideshow or on the Web, or if you are just playing, as we are now, use 72 pixels/inch as the resolution.

You have only three choices for mode in this dialog box. If you're working in color, you must choose RGB Color as the mode. Grayscale lacks color, and Bitmap means simply black or white pixels, with no grays at all. If you want to use Indexed Color mode, you'll need to select that option from the Image, Mode menu after creating the file using RGB Color or Grayscale.

The Contents options refer to what appears on the first layer of the image when it's created for you. White is the usual choice. Background applies whatever color is the current background color in the toolbox. (By default, it's white.) Transparent backgrounds are indicated by a sort of gray and white checkerboard effect. (You can change its color in the Preferences.) Transparent backgrounds are extremely useful when you are creating Web graphics.

When you're ready, click OK or just press Return to open the new image.

Browsing for a File

Most of the time, though, you won't be starting with a blank image. Instead, you'll have a photo that you want to work with. If you know where it is, you can press Cmd+O (Mac) or Ctrl+O (Windows), click on the Open icon, double-click the file, or do whatever you generally do to open a file.

If you don't know where on the hard drive your picture is, or what it is called, opening it becomes a little harder. That's one of the times when you'll turn to the File Browser. Another is when you've shot and downloaded a bunch of similar pictures and want to find the best of the bunch. You really need to be able to see what you've got.

Open the File Browser by clicking its tab in the palette well, by choosing it from the File menu or the Windows menu, or by typing Cmd+Shift+O (Mac) or Ctrl+Shift+O (Windows).

You can select the thumbnail size from the More menu or by clicking the View By button. The File Browser can also show you the file hierarchy and the creation data or camera file info, as well as a larger thumbnail of a selected image, as in Figure 3.3. Normally, all information about a file is displayed in the info window; to display only camera/scanner information, select EXIF from the menu on the lower right. As I mentioned in Hour 2, "A Tour of the Desktop," you can change the sort order using the options on the Sort By menu.

FIGURE 3.3
The info window includes creation date, camera used, and so on.

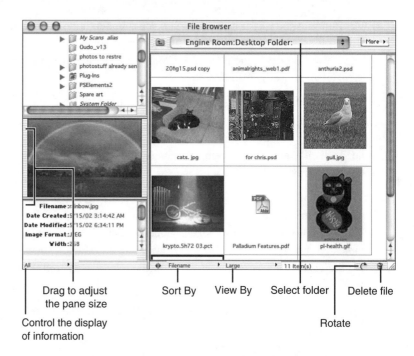

Use the top pop-up menu to locate the disk and folder you think the file is on, and just start scrolling through the folder list on the left until you find it. Drag it into an Elements window or double-click it, and it will open its own.

To rotate the selected image 90 degrees to the right, click the Rotate button. To delete the file from your computer, click the Delete File button.

Task: Browsing and Opening an Image

Time for a little practice…. The following steps will walk you through the process of browsing for some picture files on your hard drive:

1. Go to the palette well and locate the File Browser tab. Click it once. If you don't see the File Browser in the palette well, choose Window, File Browser to open it.

2. After the window opens, use the scrollbar to review what's on the desktop.

3. Use the pop-up menu at the top of the browser to navigate to a different hard disk, disk partition, or other external storage device. Again, scroll through to see what's there.

 If you can't find a graphic file, try the Samples folder, located in the Photoshop Elements folder.

4. The top-left browser window shows the file hierarchy. Scroll down until you locate the folder where a photo you'd like to select lives. Then click the file when it appears in the list on the right. It should be highlighted.

5. Read through the image information in the bottom pane. If it is a digital photo that you've shot and saved to the computer, you can find out a lot about it. What was your shutter speed? Did you use a flash? If you scanned it in, when did you do so? What's the resolution?

6. Double-click the file to open it, or drag it into the Elements window.

7. Notice that the File Browser remains open. If you like, explore your hard drive(s) and locate more pictures you want to come back to and work on later. When you're done, close the File Browser.

Saving Your Work

Saving is the most important step in any project, but you probably don't realize how important it is unless you have had a computer crash while you're working. It happens to everyone, and eventually most of us learn to save our work often, work on a copy of the original, or learn other tactics that end up saving our sanity as well as our words and pictures.

Elements has a couple of different Save options. You can save the image in the format of your choice with the File, Save As command, or you can save it optimized for the Web by choosing Save for Web from the File menu. The first time you save any file, you'll be asked to give it a name (if you didn't already do so when you created the file or imported the scanned or camera image).

Figure 3.4 shows the Save As dialog box. It looks a lot like the Save dialog boxes in other applications, with a few minor differences.

FIGURE 3.4

Be sure to use a name that will help you remember what the picture is. Raw camera filenames, like the ones shown here, don't tell you much.

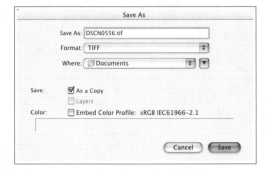

Choosing a File Format

The Format pop-up menu, which will indicate the current file format, lists about 17 different file formats you can use. How do you choose? That will depend on the kind of image you are working on, and what you intend to do with it. Web browsers can only display images in three formats: GIF, PNG, and JPEG. You must choose one of the three if your picture is for Web use. If you are going to place the picture into a page of text, such as a newsletter, advertisement, or brochure, you will need to save it in a format compatible with the word processing or desktop publishing program you plan to use. It must also be compatible with the printing system you'll be using. Finally, you must consider whether your image will be printed in black and white, in full color, or using "spot color."

Spot color refers to individual accent colors applied by an artist, as opposed to *full color*, as in a photograph. Spot color is printed with a separate offset plate and a precisely compounded colored ink for each color. Spot color is often used by graphic designers in places where a specific color must appear, such as on an official logo. Full color, also called process color or CMYK color, is printed with overlapping dots of cyan, magenta, yellow, and black inks.

The file format determines how the information in a file is compressed (if in fact it is compressed) and whether it contains data for multiple layers of the image as well as the color management system used and other important details. Elements can work with files in any of the types shown on its menu, but there are some you will probably never use.

Let's take a quick look at the formats available and what they actually do (the three-letter combination in parentheses after each format name is the file extension for that format):

- Photoshop (.psd)—This is the native format for both Photoshop and Elements documents. It saves all possible data about the picture, and is compatible with Adobe Illustrator and Acrobat as well as Photoshop itself. This is the best format to use while you are working, or if you intend to return to this image some other time.

- Bitmap (.bmp)—Bitmap is a standard graphics file format for Windows. Because it must describe each pixel on the screen, a bitmap file can be quite large.

- CompuServe GIF (.gif)—GIF stands for Graphical Interchange Format. It was first used (prior to the Internet) by the CompuServe online network to enable members to view each other's graphics. It is still in use as one of the three common graphics formats for Web publishing. It compresses file size by limiting the number of colors. Because it is a compressed format, files are smaller and take less time to transfer.

- Photoshop EPS (.eps)—EPS stands for Encapsulated PostScript, a format developed by Adobe to go transparently cross-platform to many graphic, page layout, and illustration programs. For best results, use it when your work will be printed on PostScript-enabled printers.

- JPEG (.jpg)—JPEG stands for Joint Photographic Experts Group, the group that developed this format, which relies on 8-bit color (RGB only) and a "lossy" compression system (a system that selectively removes data from the file). It is a popular format for Web publishing because it can produce small files, but each save results in further compression and files will deteriorate quickly. Use JPEG as a Web format, but never as a working format.

- PCX (.pcx)—PCX is a common graphics format for IBM-compatible PCs.

- Photoshop PDF (.pdf)—Adobe's Portable Document Format is a system for creating documents that can be read cross-platform.

- Photoshop 2.0 (.psd)—This is an early Photoshop format for the Macintosh that doesn't support layers and flattens your image. Use this format only if your files must be opened by a very early version of Photoshop.

- PICT file (.pct)—This is mainly a Macintosh format, and is equivalent to PCX.

- PICT resource (.rsr)—This format is used by Macintosh for icons, sprites, and other graphic resources.

- Pixar (.pxr)—Pixar is the proprietary format used by high-end Pixar graphics workstations.

- PNG (.png)—PNG stands for Portable Network Graphics. It's a newer and arguably better format for Web graphics than GIF or JPEG. It combines GIF's good compression with JPEG's unlimited color palette. However, older browsers don't support it.

3

- Raw (.raw)—This format saves image information in the most flexible format for transferring files between applications and computer platforms.
- Scitex CT (.sct)—This is another proprietary format for a brand of graphics workstation.
- Targa (.tga)—Another proprietary format, this one works with a specific kind of Truevision video board used by MS-DOS machines.
- TIFF (.tif)—TIFF stands for Tagged Image File Format. Files in this format can be saved for use on either Macintosh or Windows machines. This is often the preferred format for desktop publishing applications, such as PageMaker and QuarkXPress. Enhanced TIFF is a similar format that supports saving layers.

Photoshop format (.psd) is the default format in Elements, and is the best choice for saving a file that you intend to keep working on. As noted, it saves layers, layer style information, and color management information.

If you are opening a file in Elements that was created in Photoshop, you will not have access to unsupported features such as clipping paths or layer sets, but the data will remain with the file if you later reopen it in Photoshop.

Choosing Other Save Options

If you select the Save: As a Copy option in the Save As dialog box, Elements will save a (closed) copy of the current image and allow you to continue working on the open one. Save: As a Copy is especially useful for making a backup copy before you try a drastic change, such as reducing color depth or increasing JPEG lossiness (sacrificing clarity to reduce file size), or for saving the file in a different format. Suppose that you create a logo for your business and want to use it in print and on the Web. You should save it as a TIFF or EPS file to print from, and save a copy as a JPEG, GIF, or PNG file for your Web page. The word *copy* is automatically added to the filename.

If you select the Save: Layers check box, your file format options are limited to the file types that can save layers separately. The ICC Profile (Windows)/Embed Color Profile (Mac) option will save a color profile with the image file if you choose particular formats that use them. Use Thumbnail (Windows)/Image Previews Options (Mac) to save a thumbnail of the image in the file. Choose Use Lower Case Extensions (Windows)/File Extension Options (Mac) to save the file with a lowercase extension, which makes it compatible with Web/network servers that use Unix.

Adjusting Resolution

Resolution is an important concept to understand and can be just a little bit complicated because it means different things in different situations. Resolution is what determines the quality of what you see on the screen and what you see in print. You already know that your Elements images are bitmaps. A bit, in this case, is a pixel, an individual picture element. You can enlarge a piece of your image enough to take a good look at individual pixels. Figure 3.5 shows an image of flowers in various stages of enlargement up to 1600%. At that size, you can see that the image consists of little squares in different colors or shades of gray.

FIGURE 3.5

A pixel is a pixel, how-ever large or small it is.

100%

200%

800%

1600%

3

When you shrink the squares down to a smaller size, let's say 1/72 of an inch, they are too small to be seen individually. What you do see at that resolution is the picture as it appears on your monitor. Typical monitor resolution is either 72 or 96 dpi (dots per inch). (72 dpi is the traditional resolution of older Mac screens. New monitors are more likely to use 96 dpi resolution for a clearer picture. However, most people still think in terms of 72 dpi screen resolution. So will we.) In the case of 72 dpi, a square inch of picture has 72 pixels, squared, or a total of 5,184 pixels per square inch.

When you go to print a picture, you'll see that your printer most likely has a much higher resolution than your screen. So an image displayed in a 1:1 ratio on your monitor will appear smaller when printed because the dots of ink per square inch are more numerous and therefore smaller than screen pixels. Also, an image saved with a low resolution setting will not suddenly become more clear when printed with a high-resolution printer.

Of course, if you have a higher resolution image, you have a lot more data and a much sharper, clearer picture to work with. That also means a bigger file to store and work on. Your hard drive fills up faster. With a larger file, any operation you attempt in Elements will take longer. If you're applying a filter, for example, you're telling the computer to make a specific set of adjustments to each pixel. If the resolution is set to 72 dpi, the computer has to change a little more than five thousand numbers per square inch of image. If it's at 300 dpi, it has to make the same changes an additional 85,000 times per square inch. That adds up.

So, the problem lies in deciding whether you want to work slowly on a large file with high resolution that will print well, or quickly on a smaller file that will look fine on the Web. If you already have plans for the picture, your choice is simple. If it's only going to be seen on the screen, you might as well work at 72 dpi. If you are placing the photo into another document at something close to or smaller than snapshot size, or printing small copies at home on your inkjet printer, you can get away with using 150 dpi as a working resolution. For more flexibility or larger prints, keep the resolution at 300 while you are cleaning it up, cropping, retouching, and so on. You can always save a low-res (lower resolution) copy later. For instance, if you're saving a copy of the picture for a Web page, you can reduce the resolution when you convert it to a JPEG, and end up with a clear *and* very small file.

Most printers do a fine job of adjusting resolution, particularly if the printer's resolution is a close or exact multiple of the file it's printing. Typically, a home/office inkjet printer will have a resolution of 300, 600, or even as much as 1,200 dpi. If you send a picture that's an exact multiple (for instance, 200, 300, or even 150 dpi), the printed result should have nice even tones with smooth transitions from one color to another. You shouldn't see jagged edges or obvious blocks.

There are times when you have to change the image resolution, even though it may mean losing some image quality. If you have access to a high-end digital camera or scanner, it will present you with very large files at a very high resolution. You may find that you have to reduce the resolution of the image before you can work on it, especially if your computer is an older, slower one or doesn't have enough RAM to work on a large file.

Photoshop Elements does a pretty good job of changing resolution by *resampling* the image. When you *downsample* (decrease the number of pixels in an image and thus decrease the image's size), you can reduce the size of the image, or the resolution, or both. Suppose you have a picture that's six inches square. You want it to be three inches square. You open the Image Size dialog box by choosing Image, Resize, Image Size, shown in Figure 3.6, and change the numbers to make the image size 3"×3" instead of

6"×6". You don't change the resolution. When you click OK, the image shrinks to half the size it was on the screen. Because you haven't changed the resolution, the file size shrinks to a quarter of what it was.

FIGURE 3.6

You can change the size and/or the resolution in this dialog box.

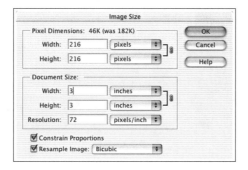

3

If you change the resolution while keeping the image the same size, the screen display will double, because you are now looking at an "inch" that's twice as long (144 pixels instead of 72) .

Downsampling condenses the file information into a smaller spread of pixels, so you won't lose detail in the image as you might when upsampling. When you increase the resolution, Elements has to invent new values for the pixels you're adding. There are three different ways it can do this, and you can choose which of the three to apply by selecting it from the Resample Image pop-up menu at the bottom of the dialog box. Your choices are

- Nearest Neighbor—This is the quickest method, because it essentially copies what's there, assigning a value to the next pixel based on the average of the ones on either side of it. It works best on edges that are not *antialiased*. (Antialiasing is a technique that's applied to artificially produced edges such as the curve of a letter or a drawn line. It adds bits of gray along the edge to smooth it out and make it less jagged in appearance.) It will also produce a smaller file. It may, however, result in lines that appear jagged because of the lack of antialiasing.

- Bilinear —This method, considered better than the nearest neighbor method, is based on averaging the four pixels above, below, and to the sides of a target pixel and assigning it the resulting value.

- Bicubic —Instead of taking an average of four pixels, the bicubic method takes an average of eight, surrounding the target pixel on all sides and corners. This method produces the best results but takes a longer time to complete.

Figure 3.7 shows the differences between these three methods.

FIGURE 3.7
This is approximately, but not mathematically, the way it happens.

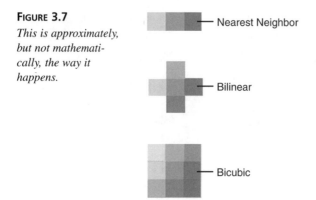

Remember, too, that the program goes through the entire set of calculations for each pixel in the image. When one is changed, all the ones around it must also change slightly.

Saving for the Web

The full-blown version of Photoshop ships with a second program called ImageReady, which is used to prepare images for the Web. It helps you find the best combination of file format, image size, and image quality to place the image on a Web page so it will load quickly and look as good as possible. Elements has a similar feature, which is simply called Save for Web and is found on the File menu. Figure 3.8 shows the Save for Web dialog box.

FIGURE 3.8
The two views of the image compare the original to the optimized version. It's often hard to see a difference.

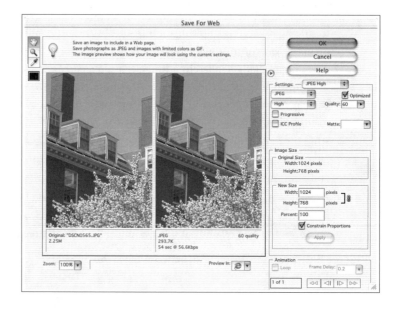

Choose PNG or JPEG for full color art and photographs. Choose GIF only if you are working with something that has a limited number of colors, such as a company logo or a drawing, graph, or chart. There's no need to include information on 256 colors if you are only using a handful. Be sure to watch the changes on the screen at different quality settings. You want to find the best compromise between quality and file size. If a file is large, it will load very slowly on an older, slower modem. Most people don't yet have a superfast Internet connection. In some parts of the country they're not even available. As a good cybercitizen, you want to make your pages as accessible as possible for all, and part of that is keeping the download time to a minimum.

On the File menu, you will also see an option called Attach to E-mail. Use this when you want to send a copy of the picture you've been working on. You'll be prompted to save the picture, if you haven't already done so, and then Elements will locate your email program and will open a blank email message with the photo already attached to it. The file will not be modified in any way—its file type, size, and resolution are preserved as they were when you selected this command. Add a message and send it off.

Exporting a PDF

If you have ever read Douglas Adams's *Hitchhiker's Guide to the Galaxy*, you already know about babelfish. As the story goes, if you stick one in your ear, it acts as an automatic translation system, so you can understand what's being said in any given language from Abyssinian to Vogon. Too bad babelfish don't actually exist; software file formats could use such a device. Adobe's PDF format comes close. PDF files can be passed back and forth from PC to Mac to SGI workstation to Palm and Pocket PC devices.

There are generic PDFs and Photoshop PDFs. Photoshop creates single-image PDF files. Generic PDFs (which can contain multiple pages, pictures, and text) come from Adobe Acrobat, or from Illustrator, or from other programs that make use of the Acrobat Distiller. You can save a single-image PDF file using the regular Save As box. To save an image using Generic PDF format, you'll need Adobe Acrobat, Illustrator, or a similar program.

As an alternative to creating a single-image PDF file, you can create a PDF slideshow. The slideshow will run on any computer system that has Adobe Acrobat or a similar PDF reader. The slideshow starts automatically when opened and displays the images you selected when you created the file, one at a time. To start, assemble a group of images in a folder, and then choose File, Automation Tools, PDF Slideshow. The PDF Slideshow dialog box is shown in Figure 3.9.

FIGURE 3.9

Be sure to check out the Transition pop-up menu. There are 18 possibilities, ranging from Blinds and Wipes to Glitter Down.

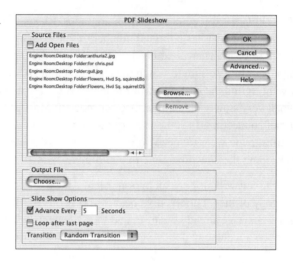

Click Browse and navigate to the folder you assembled. Select the files you want to use in the slideshow, and click Open to add them. Click Choose and type a name for the slideshow file, then click OK. Choose the length of time that you'd like each slide to stay on the screen, and decide whether you want the show to run once and stop or to loop and run continuously. Finally, choose a transition. If you like surprises, choose Random Transition. When you're ready to create the file, click OK. Anyone with a PDF reader on any platform can open and enjoy your show.

Undoing and Redoing

Before I got my Apple keyboard, I had a third-party model that was cheaply made. The paint started to wear off the letters. As a writer and an artist who works mainly in Photoshop, I use the keyboard a lot, particularly the Cmd+Z combination. That's why the Z was one of the first keys to fade to black.

Mac users know that Cmd+Z means Undo. Windows folk know this combination as Ctrl+Z. Same deal. It undoes the last thing you did. To be able to undo with just a keystroke is a wonderful thing. It gives you the freedom to make mistakes, to experiment; and that is how you learn. (I often wish life came with an Undo key.) If the Shortcuts bar is displayed, you can also click the Step Backward button to undo the last action. To redo any change you've undone, click Step Forward or press Cmd+Y (Mac)/Ctrl+Y (Windows). To undo multiple changes, click Step Backward as many times as needed, or press Cmd+Z (Mac)/Ctrl+Z (Windows) multiple times.

You can also find Undo at the top of the Edit menu, but the keystroke combination or the toolbar buttons are really easier to use.

Using the Undo History Palette

For those people who like to undo changes to their graphics, Adobe provides an Undo History palette, which makes it easy to back up step by step or jump back to an earlier state with just one click. (In regular Photoshop, and in the first version of this program, it was simply called History.)

In Figure 3.10, you can see a typical Undo History palette. To display the palette, choose Windows, Undo History, or click its tab in the palette well if it's displayed there. The Undo History palette lists all the tools I have used on the image so far. It reflects each use of a tool. If I select a brush and paint several lines, each line shows up as a history step because I have to press and release the mouse button in between lines. If I were to paint one very long continuous line without releasing the mouse button, there would be only one history step to show for it.

FIGURE 3.10

Changes I've made to an image are stored on the History palette.

If I select a step that's several steps back on the palette, all the subsequent steps will be undone. They'll appear dimmed on the palette and will be kept in memory until I do something different to the image. At that point, a new step will replace the ones I backed out of. Figure 3.11 displays a picture of the History palette before and after some changes are undone.

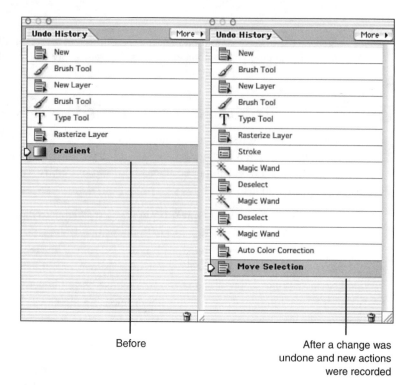

FIGURE 3.11

I was going to use the Gradient tool to make a change, and then changed my mind.

Before

After a change was undone and new actions were recorded

If you go to the General panel of the Preferences dialog box, you can enter a number of steps for the Undo History palette to remember. The default is 20 steps. Depending on your working style, you might find that 10 steps are enough, or you may need as many as 50 if you like to draw with short pencil or brush strokes. The limit is 100. You can clear the history, if you are about to start a complicated revision to your picture and want to make sure you'll have enough space on the palette to keep track of the steps. Clear Undo History is on the pop-up menu that appears when you click the More button at the top of the palette.

Summary

In this hour, you learned about page sizes and background colors, and practiced using the File Browser to find your favorite images. We talked about the importance of saving your work, and how to do so. We listed the file formats Photoshop supports and what each one does, and covered file resolution and how it can be changed. You found that Web images are saved differently than print images and learned how to find the most efficient way to save a Web graphic. Finally, we covered undoing and redoing, and the Undo History Palette, which lets you retrace your steps backward as you work on a picture.

Q&A

Q Is there a way to change the default image size?

A Unfortunately, no, but here's a workaround. Create a new image that has all the specifications as you want them: page size, color, resolution, and so on. Call it something like "New Image" and put an alias or shortcut of it on your desktop. Then, whenever you need an image that size, open it. Just be sure to save it with a new name so the original stays clean.

Q What does Open Recent do?

A It keeps a list of the last ten images you closed in Elements and reopens the one you select.

Q Why are there so many ways to open the File Browser?

A I think it's just part of the Adobe philosophy. For anything you want to do in any of Adobe's programs, there are usually several ways to do it. Try them all once and settle on the one that's easiest for you.

3

Workshop

Take a few moments to tackle this short quiz on file formats and opening/saving files, and then work on the activities for extra credit.

Quiz

1. GIF stands for _____.

   a. Good Information Format

   b. Government Image Files

   c. Graphics Interchange Format

   d. Genie Image Format

2. When you select Save a Copy in the Save As box, you save a *closed* copy of the current image.

   a. True

   b. False

3. If you open a file with a transparent background, you'll see _____.

   a. Nothing

   b. Your desktop

   c. A checkerboard pattern

   d. A plain white page

Quiz Answers

1. c. The format was developed for CompuServe users.
2. a. True. The file will have the word *copy* appended to its name.
3. c. It's normally gray, but you can change it in Preferences.

Activity

Using the File Browser, find a half dozen pictures you like. Move them into a separate folder and turn them into a PDF slideshow.

HOUR **4**

Importing Source Images

You've learned how to start blank images in Elements, and it's something you'll find yourself doing whenever you need a quickie Web graphic, like a button or a logo. But the real reason that Elements exists, just like Photoshop, is to clean up, retouch, edit, color correct, and work with photographs and scanned images in general. (That's why it's bundled with many of the better cameras and scanners.)

In this chapter you will

- Import a scanned image
- Import an image from a digital camera
- Capture still images from video
- Change the image size
- Change the canvas size

Using a Scanner

A basic desktop scanner is a device that looks and works something like a photocopier. It contains a lens and a glass platform that holds the original while you scan it. The lens is attached to a moving bar that slides up and down beneath the glass platform, "reading" the image one line at a time, and saving the data in a form the computer can reproduce on its screen. The scanner also has a built-in light that is color balanced to give you its best approximation of daylight. This helps assure that the color you see in the scanned image is accurate compared to the original. Some scanners have an additional carrier, drawer, or backlight on the cover so they can scan negatives and slides as well as prints. Most current scanners connect to the computer via a USB port or SCSI. At the time of this writing, only a few can use FireWire. Figure 4.1 shows a typical scanner.

FIGURE 4.1

This is a Microtek ScanMaker 5700.

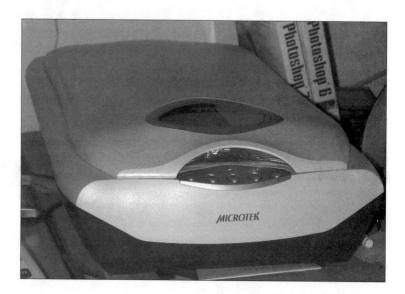

There are also high quality drum scanners. They have very high resolution, and consequently large price tags. You can have your photos scanned on one of these at a service bureau or print shop like Kinko's for a reasonable fee. Whether you only need an occasional scan, this may turn out to be more cost effective than purchasing a less expensive (but less capable) unit for home use. There are multipurpose combination scanner/fax/printer/copiers that will handle all your office chores. "Jack of all trades, master of none" certainly applies here. They do everything more or less okay, but nothing well.

Scanners typically come with several different pieces of software included. The first thing you need to install is a driver. This enables you to "drive" the scanner using the computer to control it. The makers of the scanner supply drivers for both Mac and Windows platforms. Even if your scanner is a couple of years old, you will be able to find updated versions of the driver that will work with recent software such as Elements 2 on the manufacturer's Web site (provided that the company is still in business).

Most scanners also come with Elements or with a simple graphics program and with *Optical Character Recognition (OCR)* software. OCR is an exceptionally clever and useful application that scans pages of text and identifies each character, punctuation mark, and space. After identifying them, it puts the text into an open word processing document so you can edit and patch as needed, and then save the scanned page as a text document.

Installing the scanner and software can't be much easier. The scanner has two cables. The first is the power supply, most likely one of those little black cubes that plugs into an outlet and into the scanner on the other end. The other is the USB or SCSI cable that connects to the computer.

If you have used up all your USB ports, you may need to purchase an expansion hub. It's a small box with a half dozen or so extra USB outlets. The hub shown in Figure 4.2 is typical. Plug it into one of the computer's USB ports and fill up the ports with as many USB devices as you have.

FIGURE 4.2
This is 7-port Entrega Mac hub.

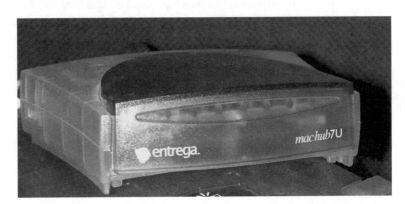

4

Making a Scan

The first step in scanning a picture is to put it into the scanner face down. Until you've actually made a scan, you may not know what end of the scanner is up. Quite often, you can't tell by looking, or with logic. My last scanner started its scanning at what I considered the "top"; the back end of the scanning platform, close to the cover hinge. My current one scans backward from the bottom, or open end, closest to me. It really doesn't make much difference, except that I need to remember to orient the photo correctly, or take the time to flip it before I start to clean it up. Of course, if your picture doesn't fill the scanner screen, you may choose to place it sideways to shorten the scanning time, as I have in Figure 4.3. Turning the image 90 degrees on the screen is probably quicker than scanning a correctly oriented portrait. However, you'll do yourself a favor and save a ton of time if you learn to place pictures in the scanner straight against an edge. Sure, you can always rotate it back, a half degree at a time, but why should you, when you can be a little careful and get it scanned right to begin with?

FIGURE 4.3

The picture as shown on the left will take about 1/3 longer to scan.

Okay, now what? Do you push the button on the scanner, or do something else? Because we're scanning into Elements, it makes sense to start from Elements. In the File menu, select Import and choose your scanner, as in Figure 4.4. You can also click Connect to Camera or Scanner from the Welcome window, and then choose your scanner from the Import list and click OK. If you're using Windows, your list of choices will look different. PICT is a Macintosh format, so you won't see it. You will probably see TWAIN as one of your choices. The TWAIN interface works cross-platform and handles images from scanners, digital cameras, and frame-grabbers (it takes a single frame from a video camera). If you can identify the scanner's own plug-in, use it. Otherwise, TWAIN is generic and will work with most scanners. If you use Windows ME or Windows XP, you'll probably see WIA (Windows Image Acquisition) instead. It's a good choice if you don't see your actual scanner listed. Oh, and be prepared to jump out of your skin when the scanner starts up. Most of them make a strange series of chirps and beeps and burps as they're starting up.

FIGURE 4.4

Scanning is done through the Import submenu in the File menu.

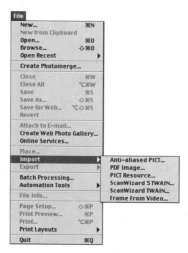

Selecting the scanner opens a window, which may or may not look like the one in Figure 4.5. There are, of course, dozens of different brands and models of scanner on the market, and each uses its own drivers. Unless you use the same model of Microtek scanner that I do, your screen will look different because your software is different—but that's okay. The elements in each are similar. At the very least, you'll see the scanner window, and the buttons for preview and scan. Preview gives you a quick, low-resolution version of the scan, mainly for positioning. Scan is the real thing.

FIGURE 4.5

Your scanner window may look different. See if you can identify the Preview screen and button, and the Scan button.

You probably also have a set of buttons or a drop-down list with choices similar to the ones at the right of the Microtek window. These help you set up the scanner by having you identify what you are scanning and what you want to do with it. I'll review the choices I have available on my Microtek scanner, with the hope that our choices are similar. The Original option seeks to determine the probable resolution of what you are scanning and gives you these choices:

- Photo—Any size black-and-white or color photograph
- Text Document—A page to which you will apply OCR
- Illustration—Drawn or painted art, regardless of the number of colors used
- Printed Material

    Magazine—Any standard-quality printed magazine such as *Newsweek*, *People*, or *Good Housekeeping*, or a laser-printed newsletter or pamphlet

    Art Magazine—A very high quality printed magazine such as *Art News* or *Architectural Digest*

    Newspaper—Lower quality (low resolution) printing

- Film

> Positive—Kodachrome or other 35mm colored slides, any size film positives
>
> Negative—Either black and white or color

This covers most of the items that you're scanning, but what if you're copying your coin collection or other small objects? Think about it. If you classify them as illustrations, you'll get the best combination of quality and resolution possible. If you don't much care what you get, call them newspapers. The scan will be much faster and still legible.

Scan Type refers to the number of colors to be scanned. Your choices are True Color, Web Color, Gray or Black and White. True Color allows all the millions of colors available. Web Color limits the scan to the 216 "Web-safe" colors. Gray gives you 256 shades of gray, and black and white is just that: one-bit b/w "color."

> If you are scanning type for OCR, always choose b/w. It doesn't try to inter-
> pret smudges or spilled coffee on the page.

Purpose affects the output resolution. If the picture's only going to the Web or for onscreen viewing, there's no point to giving it high resolution. Therefore, Onscreen Viewing outputs at 72 dpi. Inkjet printing, in search of a reasonable compromise for all kinds of inkjet printers, outputs at 200 dpi. Laser Print, Standard and Fine give you respectively, 100 and 150 dpi. Faxes are sent off at 200 dpi. OCR, which requires the most accurate scan of any, will output at 300 dpi. Finally, you can elect Custom and set any number between 10 and 9600 dpi. Remember that you don't need to go to the highest possible resolution. As long as your printer can print to a *factor* of the resolution supplied, you should end up with a nice clear picture.

The reason for this is easy to understand. Let's say you have an inkjet printer that outputs at 9600 dpi. You can scan and save the file at 9600 dpi. The scanner can handle that, but the resulting file is so big you'll probably choke the computer in the process. Whether you have enough RAM to handle all that, you'll still be limited by the speed. Handling that amount of data, as you learned last hour, takes a long time even with a fast computer. However, you can divide the 9600 dpi by any *factor*, which is to say, any number that divides in evenly with no remainder, and have a guaranteed good result. 200 pixels goes into 9600 pixels 48 times. You can also use 300, because 9600/300 = 32, and so on. The computer and printer agree on this very simple math and make the interpolation from 200 up with no trouble at all.

Scale Output or Adjust Output Size enables you to shrink or enlarge the output of the file by a percentage, maintaining the same aspect ratio. Increase to 150 or 200%, or decrease size to 75 or 50% of the original, precisely and with no loss of resolution.

The Adjust button gives you access to a panel of sliders, shown in Figure 4.6, which can correct obvious color and or exposure problems while scanning the image. It's good for fixing major flaws, like a photo that's turned purple from sitting in the sun. Because you can't really see what you're doing close up, it's not good for subtle adjustments.

FIGURE 4.6

Your scanner may do this differently, but the same kinds of sliders are somewhere in the interface. Look on the menus for them, too.

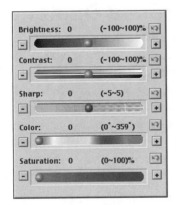

4

The last button (almost), Reset, puts every setting back to where it was originally. Use it if you're starting a new scanning job unlike the last one, for instance going from scanning a photo of Great-Uncle Hector to copying his typewritten love letters to Great-Aunt Sue.

Finally, you're ready to click the Scan button or a similar one. Because you've initiated the scan from Elements, you don't need to deal with other options. The scanned image will appear as any other image in the Elements window. Be sure to save it before you start working because it is only a temporary file at the moment.

Task: Scanning

If you don't have a scanner, please consider buying one. It will be very useful as you continue in computer graphics. Assuming you have a scanner available, try this:

1. Make sure the scanner is connected to the computer and that you can find it under the Import submenu of the File menu.

2. Find an old family photo in grayscale.

3. Place it in the scanner and choose File, Import to begin the import process from Elements.

4. Elements initiates the scan. Drag the sides of the selection box so it just fits the image. This will prevent scanning more area than necessary.

5. Check the settings. You should scan at 200 dpi, in 256 grays.

6. When you're ready, press the Scan button to send the image back to Elements.

7. Be sure to save your scanned picture with a filename such as Old Family Photo.psd. We'll use it later on.

Importing Images from a Digital Camera

Digital cameras and scanners have a lot more in common than digital cameras and film cameras. Film cameras rely on light and chemistry to produce an image. Digital cameras use a device that collects image data much like the scanner does. Scanners send the data directly to the computer. They don't have any storage media. Cameras have memory. They may have an internal memory and/or a removable memory card, stick, or floppy disk. When you fill up a card and need more memory, you remove the full card and pop in an empty one. Memory cards (and for our purposes, Sony's Memory Sticks are also considered "cards") are intended to be reused. They're not for data storage. So, at some point, you need to get the data off the card or out of the camera and into the computer. There are several ways to do this, depending on the make and model of camera you use.

USB Connection

The first and by far the easiest way to import data is from a camera that uses a standard 3 1/2" floppy disk. If you have one of these, simply remove the disk from your camera and stick it in the computer's disk drive. However, most digital cameras do not use floppy disk drives, so we'll talk about other options.

The next easiest method for importing digital pictures from a camera is to connect the camera to the computer with a USB cable. If your camera is capable of this, it will have come with the appropriate driver on a CD-ROM. After you install the driver and connect the two devices, you'll probably see your camera as an icon sitting on the computer desktop, as it is in Figure 4.7. If you don't see a desktop icon, connect the camera via USB and start the camera's software if it doesn't start up on its own. If you use Windows, the camera may show up as a "drive" in My Computer. Be sure you have set the camera to play....

FIGURE 4.7

Other brands of camera have their own icons. Some cameras do not display an icon on the desktop.

The connectors on the USB/camera cables are very delicate. Be sure you are inserting them right side up, and don't use force. You can replace a damaged cable, but getting either the camera's or computer's USB port replaced is expensive and time-consuming.

With the camera mounted this way, you can use it like any other hard drive. The Nikon software creates a page of thumbnails you can view and a folder with all the raw pictures. (See Figure 4.8.) The first thing I always do with my pictures is to copy them into a folder in the computer labeled with date and subject. Then I immediately back this folder up onto a CD-ROM and check it to be sure everything transferred correctly.

FIGURE 4.8

My Nikon lets me browse through thumbnails or open the folder containing the images.

That's the easiest way to import batches of pictures at the same time. If you simply need to locate and open a single photo, let your camera pretend to be a hard drive. Use the Open command in Elements to locate and open the picture you want. Then save it to the hard drive. Be sure you turn the camera off when you're done copying pictures. Leaving the camera on, even if it's "asleep," will eventually drain the batteries.

Card Reader

A third way to download images that's nearly as easy requires that you purchase a card reader. If you have an older camera, you've probably already done so. USB connectivity is fairly recent. Probably the next new thing will be image transfer via infrared light, the same way cordless mice and keyboards talk to the computer.

The card reader is a small box that plugs into SCSI or USB. Figure 4.9 shows a typical one. When you place a memory card into it, it acts like an external drive. Depending on your camera and its particular card reader, you may or may not need a card adapter. Older cameras used the larger PCMCIA memory cards, which slide right into the card reader, or if it's available, into a card slot in the computer. (My Windows laptop has one; my iBook does not.) Newer cameras use smaller "SmartMedia" or "Compact Flash" cards that slide into a frame that makes them fit the PCMCIA slot. Sony, always a step off to the side, uses a long, thin card it calls a Memory Stick. Naturally, only a Sony Memory Stick reader can read these. Older Sony digital cameras used regular floppy disks, which can be inserted into any computer that read floppies. For some people, these floppy disks don't hold enough data to be useful—only about 5 or 6 images at high resolution. But given their ease of use and the fact that you probably won't have to buy any disks specifically for your camera, these cameras are remarkably versatile.

FIGURE 4.9

Card readers, of course, also need drivers.

Plugging the card into the reader, just like attaching the camera to the computer, places it on the desktop so you can copy the pictures onto your hard drive, store a copy, and work on them as much as you like. In Windows, you'll probably find the camera's files listed as a "drive" in My Computer. It's always a good idea to put the card back into the camera and reformat it, rather than simply erasing it by dragging the pictures to the trash. Reformatting clears the entire disk, not just the directory.

If you use the disk in more than one camera, whenever you switch cameras, reformat the disk for the camera with which you will be using it. Drivers for different cameras may be quite different, and they may collect picture data in a different order or format. You can shoot a card full of pictures and then not be able to open any of them.

After you have the card reader icon on your desktop or in My Computer, you can proceed as you did previously, treating it as an auxiliary drive and copying the pictures from it to a folder on the hard drive and/or to a backup CD-ROM.

Importing Still Frame Captures

If you have a digital video camera, you can work with single frames from your favorite video. Save your video in a compatible format such as AVI, WMV, MPEG, or QuickTime, and choose File, Import, Frame from Video, as I've done in Figure 4.10. Click Browse to locate your video. It will open in the window in the dialog box. Use the video controls to steer to the frame you want to use, and click Grab Frame as it goes by. It will be copied into an Elements window, ready to work with and already labeled with a name similar to the video file. Continue grabbing as many frames as you like, then click Done to close the window.

FIGURE 4.10

This is a frame from a TV commercial my husband worked on. (Used by permission.)

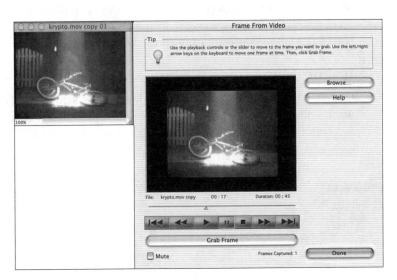

You should be aware that the quality of a single digital frame won't be very good, but you can still use it as a basis for filters and other tricks.

Changing Image and Canvas Sizes

The size of the image you import from your digital camera or digital video system is directly dependent on the file resolution. My favorite camera, a Nikon CoolPix 990, gives me the same number of pixels per image, regardless of the resolution I use. It just makes the picture correspondingly larger or smaller. If I shoot an image at my usual 1260×980 resolution, when I open it in Elements, it can be 17.7×13.3 inches at 72 dpi, or it can be 4.2×3.2 at 300 dpi, depending on how I have chosen to save it. Because I hardly ever need a picture as big as 17 inches, I can reduce the size of the original to something more reasonable and increase the resolution as needed with no loss of quality.

Remember that the amount of detail you see in an image depends on its pixel dimensions, whereas image resolution controls the amount of space the pixels are printed over. The difference between a 72 dpi image and a 300 dpi image that are both the same printed size is that the latter has smaller dots and more of them, hence greater detail.

If you change the resolution of the picture, without changing anything else, you will change the printed size. Increasing the resolution makes the picture smaller. If you want to keep the picture the same size as before, and still increase the resolution, you need to resample the image. You learned about resampling methods in the last hour. It simply means that Elements re-computes the data for each pixel based on adding or subtracting some of them. If you increase the resolution from 200 to 300 dpi, Elements has to add 100 extra pixels per inch, jamming them in between the existing ones. What color they will be depends on the color of the pixel they are next to.

Image Size

Changing the image size happens in the Image Size dialog box, shown in Figure 4.11. To display this box, choose Image, Resize, Image Size. As you can see, you can learn a lot from this dialog box. First, it tells you how large the current file is. (The file size will change as you add layers to the picture.)

FIGURE 4.11

This dialog box is located under the Resize submenu of the Image menu.

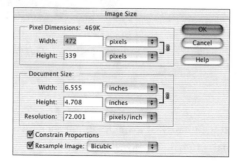

You can change the width and height by typing new numbers into the boxes. To be sure that you keep the proportions as they were, and to avoid doing all the math yourself, check Constrain Proportions and only enter one dimension. Elements will take it from there. Remember to use Bicubic, if you need to resample the image. It's the most accurate method.

Canvas Size

Sometimes you don't need to make the image bigger, you just need to add blank space around it. That's when you use the Canvas Size dialog box shown in Figure 4.12. To display it, choose Image, Resize, Canvas Size. Use the grid to indicate where to "anchor" the current image inside the larger one. Leave the anchor square in the middle if you are adding space all the way around the image or move it to the appropriate side or corner to add space at the opposite sides.

FIGURE 4.12

The old image is anchored in the corner so I can print the page as letterhead.

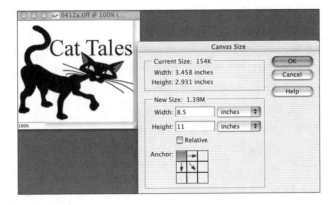

Summary

Your work in Elements is mainly based on photos and scanned images, but before you can start working on them, you have to get them into the computer as files. In this hour, you learned about scanners and digital cameras and how to import images from both. You also learned to capture a frame from a movie. Finally, you learned how to make the image larger or smaller using the Image Size and Canvas Size dialog boxes.

4

Q&A

Q Why don't they use real USB connectors on digital cameras?

A They're too big. The tiny plugs they do use enable them to put both USB Out and Video Out in the space that will otherwise fit only USB.

Q What is Video Out?

A Shorthand for Video Output. If your camera came with a video cable, plug it into the back of the TV set, and you can see your photos on the TV screen. Just scroll through them as you would if you were looking at them on the camera's LCD screen.

Q My old family pictures are printed in brown ink. Should I scan them in color or in grayscale?

A Try both, and see what you think. Generally, you'll pick up better contrast if you scan in grayscale, because you're forcing the image to compress from millions of grays to just 256. You can always put the brown back. By the way, the brown tone is called sepia, and it's a dye applied to the paper to stabilize the image. The brown color was simply a side-effect.

Workshop

Take a few moments to tackle the short quiz on importing images and check your answers to see how you did. Then work on the activities for extra credit.

Quiz

1. You can't use your scanner without special software.

    a. True

    b. False

2. The only way to copy pictures from a digital camera is to remove the memory card and read it in a laptop.

    a. True

    b. False

3. If your scanner has an 8.5×11 bed, and you are scanning a 3×4 photograph, how big will your scanned image be?

    a. 8.5×11

    b. 3×4

    c. 9×12@400 dpi

Quiz Answers

1. a. It needs a driver to work with Elements or some other graphics program.

2. b. You can connect the camera directly into the computer, or use a card reader.

3. b. There's no need to scan the whole surface. Just fit the preview box around what you want to copy.

Activities

1. Scan a handful of pocket change or other small objects.

2. Scan a fabric or other substance with an interesting texture. (Paper towels are good). Save it where you can find it again—use a filename such as papertowels.pdf. You'll learn how to make it into a texture in Hour 23.

3. Take your digital camera for a walk and shoot a half dozen pictures. Download them to a folder called Future Reference. Put the scanned coins and the interesting texture file in there, too.

HOUR 5

Making Selections and Using Layers

Now we're getting into the real nitty-gritty business of working with Photoshop Elements. The ability to make selections and add extra layers to your page gives you some very powerful tools. Instead of making a change to the entire picture, you can work on pieces of it, segregating them, so that the rest is preserved as it was. You can, for instance, clean up or remove a background while leaving the subject of the picture intact. You can make subtle changes, such as fixing the skin tones of a woman in a pink dress without changing the color of the dress. You can move parts of the picture around, stack things on top of each other, and control the amount that the bottom one shows through the top. If you only read one chapter in this book, this is the one to read.

In this hour you will

- Select a portion of an image
- Modify a selection
- Save and reuse a selection
- Work with multiple layers

Using the Selection Tools

The selection tools are conveniently located in the top section of the toolbox. You have four kinds of selection tools:

- Marquees—rectangular and elliptical
- Lassos —regular, polygonal, and magnetic
- The Magic Wand
- The Selection Brush

The Crop and Move tools are also in the same section. From a philosophical point of view, these last two tools really do belong there. After all, you need the Move tool to move selections, and cropping is the ultimate selection. By the way, you may have noticed that you can only see one Lasso and one Marquee. The others are on a pop-up menu that will appear when you click the small black triangle, as in Figure 5.1.

FIGURE 5.1

I wish that I could find the hidden tools on my real desktop this easily.

Making Selections with Marquees

Using the Marquees is quite simple. Select the proper tool for the job—either the rectangle or the circle—and position it at the start of the selection. Press the mouse button and drag until your selection is complete. By adding selections to an existing selection, you can build quite elaborate shapes, as I have in Figure 5.2.

FIGURE 5.2

It's not the Taj Mahal.

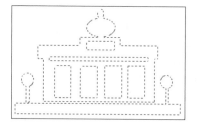

To constrain the shape to a perfect square or circle, press the mouse button and as you start dragging, press and hold the Shift key. This gets tricky, because pressing the Shift key *after* you have made a selection allows you to continue to add more pieces to the selection. If you have trouble with these, don't worry, you can accomplish the same thing by using the buttons on the tool Options bar, shown in Figure 5.3.

FIGURE 5.3

Use the key commands or these buttons; it's your choice.

From the left, choose either the square or circle as the Marquee shape. Then choose from the set of four small icons according to what you need to do: New Selection, Add to Selection, Subtract from Selection, or Intersect with Selection. Or else, press the Shift key to add, and the Option key to delete part of a selection.

Instead of pressing the Shift key as you drag to constrain proportions, you can choose a Style, such as Fixed Aspect Ratio and enter 1:1 for a square or circle or any other pair of numbers for constrained rectangles and ovals. To drag a marquee from its center out, press and hold Alt (Windows) or Option (Mac OS) after you begin dragging.

Task: Drawing a Donut with the Marquee Tool

Start a new image.

1. Select the Elliptical Marquee tool. Starting near the top left of the image, drag the crosshairs down and to the right, pressing the Shift key as you drag. This will give you a perfect circle. Make this circle whatever size you wish.

2. Holding down the Option/Alt key, draw a smaller circle inside the first. You can also click the Subtract from Selection button and draw the inner circle if you like.

3. Select the paint bucket tool, and pour paint into the area between the two circles.

4. Press Command/Ctrl+D to deselect and chase away the marching ants. Enjoy your donut.

Selecting with the Lasso Tools

Marquees are great when you have to select something with nice neat edges, or if you want to draw and fill a shape. For selecting small bits of a picture or pulling one flower out of a bunch, they're not the best tools for the job. That's when you need a Lasso. Use the Lasso to draw a selection line that is a single pixel wide around any object. As long as you're dragging the mouse while holding down its button, the Lasso tool will draw a line where you want it. As soon as you release the mouse button, the two ends of the line automatically connect, giving you a selection box in the shape you've drawn.

In addition to the "regular" lasso, you have two others, the Polygonal Lasso and the Magnetic Lasso. The Polygonal Lasso tool Options bar is shown in Figure 5.4.

Hour 5

FIGURE 5.4

I've selected the Polygonal Lasso.

The Polygonal Lasso is useful both for selecting objects and for drawing shapes to be filled or stroked. To use it, first select it from the tool Options bar. Place the cursor where you want to start drawing, and click once. Move it and click again. You've drawn a straight line between the two points where you clicked. Each time you move and click you add another line to the shape. When you're ready to place the last point to join the ends of the shape, the cursor changes to the one shown in Figure 5.5, adding a small circle to the right of the lasso. You can close the shape yourself, or double-click to draw a line between the point where you double-click and the beginning of the shape.

FIGURE 5.5

The next click will join the ends of the selection together.

The Magnetic Lasso is one of the tools I use most often. It's very useful when you **need** to make a specific or detailed selection of something that's not all one color. The tool detects the edge of an image near the spot where you click or drag, based on the degree of sensitivity you select. If the area you're trying to select contrasts well with its surroundings, you can set a large Width (click/drag area) and a high Edge Contrast value and drag quickly and quite roughly around the image, and Elements will select it. If the area does not contrast well with its surroundings, set a smaller Width and a lower Edge Contrast value, and click or drag more carefully around the selection. In Figure 5.6, I'm using the Magnetic Lasso to trace around the seagull. Each time I click, Elements places a square box to anchor the line in place. After the entire object is selected, the line will change to the familiar marching ant marquee.

FIGURE 5.6

This tool works by looking for differences in pixels. Contrasting objects are easiest to select.

Making Selections with the Magic Wand

The Magic Wand is, in many ways, the easiest of the selection tools to use. It selects by color, and can be set to select all pixels of a particular color or range of colors in the entire image, or only those pixels that qualify and are adjacent to each other. It's the perfect tool for tasks such as selecting the sky, prior to turning it from gray to blue, and for what I'm attempting in Figure 5.7, which is to select the big red tulip, without selecting the smaller one tucked in back, or any of the yellow ones.

FIGURE 5.7

Selecting the red tulip took about eight clicks, because there were many shades of pink included. Here, I'm almost done.

The Magic Wand's tool Options bar has check boxes for Antialiased and Contiguous selections, and for selecting through all layers or just the top one. These are obviously going to be useful, but the truly important option is to set a degree of tolerance for the wand. With zero tolerance, you'll select only the few pixels that are identical to the one you clicked the wand on. (If Contiguous is checked, the selected pixels must also be touching each other.) If you set a very generous tolerance, perhaps as much as 100, you will find yourself selecting much of the image with just one click. That's probably not what you wanted to do. Try a tolerance between 10 and 35 for tasks such as picking up the red tulip. After setting the options you want, simply click on a pixel of the color you wish to select. Don't forget that you need to keep the Shift key pressed to add to your wand selections, just as you do when drawing multiple marquees. When you accidentally select more than you wanted, Undo or Cmd/Ctrl+Z will immediately subtract the last pixels you selected.

You can combine selection methods, too, with the help of the Shift key. If you use the Magic Wand and get most of your red flower, but not the black seed pod in the center, you can circle that part with the Lasso while keeping the Shift key pressed, and add it right in.

5

Using the Selection Brush Tool

If you have a steady hand, and possibly a drawing tablet and pen instead of a mouse, you might find the easiest selection method, at least for some things, is to paint over them with the Selection Brush tool. It looks like a paintbrush, and in some circumstances works like one. To understand what it does, you need to think of making a selection as a way of isolating the part of the picture you're working on, from the parts you don't want to change. With the Selection Brush, you can either select the area you want to work with, or select the area you don't want to use by covering it with a mask.

Using the Selection Brush is like using any other brush. You have a choice, however, as to whether you are painting to mask the area around an object, or to select the object itself. The Options bar for the Selection Brush is shown in Figure 5.8. If you choose Selection from the Mode list, the area you drag over adds to the selection. If you choose Mask instead, the area you drag is subtracted from any existing selection (adding to the mask, or the area you don't wish to affect). What this actually means is that, when you choose the add icon, with your first brush click the image completely covers it with a layer of mask. Each subsequent brush stroke adds to the selection by erasing some of the mask. Select the brush type, size, and hardness of the edge from the lists on the Options bar. Then drag to select or mask part of the image.

FIGURE 5.8

Select the options you want to use with the Selection Brush.

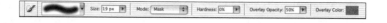

 Red isn't always the best choice for a mask, especially if you're working on a picture that has a lot of red or pink in it. Change the mask to a different color or opacity by clicking the swatch on the tool Options bar, and use the Color Picker to find a more effective color. Change the opacity by entering a different percentage. Higher numbers are more opaque.

In Figure 5.9, I have changed the mask color to blue for better contrast with the red flower, and I'm in the process of selecting it with the paintbrush. It's very easy to make an accurate selection this way, especially if you enlarge the image and work with a small brush.

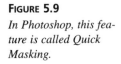

FIGURE 5.9

In Photoshop, this feature is called Quick Masking.

Selecting and Deselecting All

In addition to the selection tools, there's another quick and easy way to make a selection. To select the entire image, rather than dragging a marquee around it, or clicking the Magic Wand repeatedly, just type Cmd/Ctrl+A to select all. To deselect whatever is selected, use Cmd/Ctrl+D. If you want to clear the image and start over, select all and press Delete. To erase part of the image, draw a marquee the size and shape you want to erase, and press Delete. Memorize these commands. They will save you tons of time.

If you reach a point at which Elements seems to freeze or doesn't do what you want it to, try pressing the deselect keys. You may have accidentally selected a single pixel, and not noticed it.

Modifying Selections

After making a selection, you may want to modify it somewhat, expanding or shrinking it, or softening its edge. You'll learn how to do all this and more in this section.

Inverting a Selection

There are many ways in which you can modify your selections. Take a look at the Select menu in Figure 5.10. You've already learned to select all and deselect. Adding the Shift key to the deselect combination (Cmd/Ctrl+Shift+D) will reselect your last selection in case you accidentally dropped it.

Inverse is an incredibly useful command. Suppose you have something with very complicated edges on a simple background; perhaps a baby lying on a blanket, or a sunflower on a table. You can use one of your Lassos and trace around it. You can use the Selection Brush and paint neatly around the edges. Or, you can use the Magic Wand once or twice to pick up the entire, plain background, and then select Inverse, or press Cmd+Shift+I. Rather than selecting the background, you've inverted the selection and gotten the baby or flower, or whatever it is instead.

5

Feathering a Selection

Feathering a selection makes it have a fuzzy edge. This isn't something you will want every time you drag a marquee, but under the right circumstances, it's very useful. The right circumstances can be anything from making a portrait vignette, so that it fades into the background, to copying some grass to paste over the trash in a park picture. Figure 5.11 shows the vignette effect, one of the more obvious uses for feathering. In this case, I drew the oval selection marquee where I wanted it, and then feathered it by 20 pixels. (The original photo is quite large.) How much you should feather a selection is going to be something to experiment with. It depends on the size of the image, and on what you're planning to do with the result. Just a couple of pixels of soft edge may be all you need to make something fit into its new background.

FIGURE 5.11

*Feathering the edges
of a portrait is called
vignetting. (Photo
courtesy of D.
Maynard)*

Apply feathering after you have made the selection. Choose Select, Feather and type an appropriate number into the dialog box shown in Figure 5.12.

FIGURE 5.12

There's no right or wrong number of pixels to choose for feathering.

Changing Your Selection with Modify, Grow, Similar

Selecting Modify from the Select menu gives you four ways to modify your selection. Each requires entering a pixel value in the dialog box. Your choices include the following:

- Border—Places a second selection line outside of the first, at a distance you specify, making the selection into a border or frame.
- Smooth—Evens out lumpy lasso and brush selections.
- Expand—Adds as many pixels outward from the selection as you specify, enlarging it.
- Contract—Subtracts the pixels you specify, shrinking the selection.

Choosing Grow from the Select menu expands the selection outward to pixels of similar color. Similar locates and selects pixels located anywhere in the image that are similar to the ones already selected. Prior to choosing these commands from the Select menu, set the tolerance level for matching similar pixels by clicking the Magic Wand tool first and changing its Tolerance value.

Saving and Loading Selections

After you've gone to the trouble of making a complex selection, it seems a shame to lose it, especially if it's something you might want to work on again later. If you stroke the selection outline or fill it with color as explained in the next section, that information is saved as well. Fortunately, you can save your selection with the file, and use it whenever you want it. At the bottom of the Select menu are two commands called Save Selection and Load Selection. Selections are only saved with images stored in Photoshop (.psd) format.

To save a selection, select Save Selection to open the Save Selection dialog box. Give the selection a name, and click OK. To open and reuse it, use the Load Selection box, shown in Figure 5.13, to locate and activate your selection. To display this dialog box, choose Select, Load Selection. Remember, you can also start a new image with just the selection if it's something you expect to use often.

5

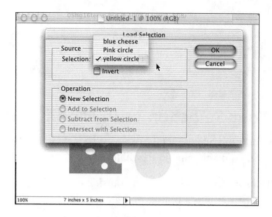

FIGURE 5.13

Save unique selections so you can reuse them.

Stroking and Filling Selections

No matter how you've made your selections, you have the option of filling or stroking them to make them objects in their own right. Let's say I need to draw some abstract shapes to use as part of a logo. I can use any of the selection tools to select a shape, and then Elements can turn the selection into an object by filling it with color or pattern, or stroking it with a colored line.

The Stroke and Fill commands are both found under the Edit menu. Filling places your choice of color, gray, or a pattern into the selected shape. Stroking places a line, of whatever color and thickness you determine, over the selection marquee. In Figure 5.14, I'm preparing to fill a complex shape with gray. Create a selection using your tools of choice. If you want to fill the selection with a particular color, click the Foreground or Background icon at the bottom of the toolbox, and select a color from the Color Picker. Then choose Edit, Fill.

FIGURE 5.14

Create a shape with a selection tool, and fill it with a color or pattern.

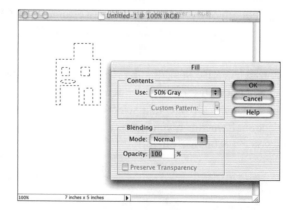

Select the color (foreground, background, white, black, or 50% gray) or pattern you want from the Use list. If you choose Pattern, you can select the exact pattern you want from the Custom Pattern palette. When you open this palette, it displays a small selection of patterns. To display a different selection, click the right arrow and choose a set of patterns from the list. Choose a blending mode and a level of opacity if you like. Because blending is a pretty advanced concept, I'll spend more time on it in Hour 20, "Making Composite Images." As for opacity, it's pretty easy to grasp. Basically, it's the strength of the fill—with a low percentage of opacity, the color or pattern already within the selection (if any) will show through the fill color or pattern you're applying. A higher percentage of opacity creates a more solid fill, with less of the original color/pattern within the selection still apparent. If you choose 100% opacity, you'll completely replace any color/pattern in the selection with your new choice. You can use the Paint Bucket instead of the Edit, Fill command to fill a selection—I'll discuss this tool in a moment.

To stroke the outline of your selection, choose Edit, Stroke instead. Select the width of the border you want. To choose a color, click the Color box and select one from the Color Picker. Next, choose the location for the line—on the inside, outside, or centered over the selection marquee. Once again, you can change the blending mode and opacity.

Stroking a line isn't necessarily a one-time event. You can build some very interesting designs by using different colored strokes, and placing narrow ones over wider ones. Figure 5.15 shows a few of the possibilities. These were all drawn with the selection tools, and then stroked and filled. To create the first object, I used the Rectangular and Elliptical Marquee selection tools, and filled and stroked the resulting compound selection. To create the second object, I used the Polygonal Lasso selection tool to create a star, then filled it with a pattern and stroked it several times with lines of varying widths, positions, and colors. To create the third object, I used the Selection Brush tool with the Dry Brush pattern, then filled and stroked the resulting compound selection. For the fourth object, I created a rectangle with the Rectangular Marquee selection tool and filled it with a dark color. Then I created a series of stars with the Selection Brush tool, star pattern, and stroked them with a medium color. I created more stars and stroked them with a lighter color. How many of these can you re-create?

5

Figure 5.15

It's easy to get carried away.

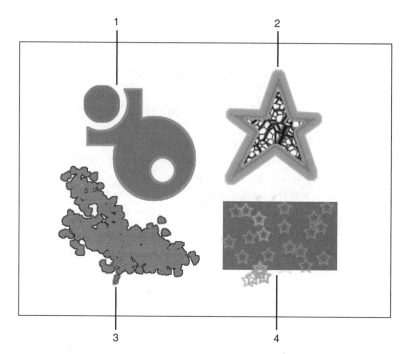

Using the Paint Bucket Tool to Fill a Selection

Earlier, I mentioned that you could fill a selection with the Paint Bucket tool. Using the tool is fairly simple: first select the tool, then from the Fill list on the Options bar, choose either Foreground or Pattern. If you select Foreground, the current foreground color will be used. If you don't like the current foreground color, you can change it. If you choose Pattern, you can select the pattern you want from the pattern list. As before, you can display additional patterns by clicking the right arrow and selecting the set of patterns you want to view. Select the blending option from the Mode menu (to learn about blending, see Hour 20), and set the opacity level you want.

The rest of the options are the same as those described earlier for the Magic Wand tool. The Tolerance option defines the type of pixel to be filled—a low tolerance tells Elements to fill only pixels within the selection that are very close in color to the one you click with the tool. A high tolerance is not as picky. The Antialiased option softens the edge between the filled selection and its background. The Contiguous option has no effect unless you have made at least two non-contiguous selections. Then, if you choose Contiguous, only the applicable pixels within the selection you click will be changed. Turn this option off to fill pixels in all selections. The All Layers option allows you to fill the selection within all layers; we'll get to layering in the next section.

After setting options for the Paint Bucket tool, click on a pixel within the selection. The pixel you click may or may not affect the outcome, depending on the selections you've made.

Working with Layers

Layers sound complicated, but they're not. They're really quite simple, if you've ever seen an animated cartoon. Animators work with two kinds of materials, sheets of white Bristol board, or something similar as backgrounds, and sheets of heavy transparent cellophane, called cells. The background holds the things that don't change: trees, grass, Marge's kitchen walls, Homer's couch. There are up to four or five cell layers for each character. Hands and feet move more than heads and trunks, so that the bodies are dismembered and placed on different layers. If Homer is to wave, for example, three or four drawings will be done of just his arm in different positions, from down to up. Then the sequence will be photographed with a different arm in each frame of film. It's layers that make it possible to see this movement.

Working with layers enables you to build up multipart collages of many images, paint over an original photo without destroying it, make color corrections that you can apply selectively to parts of the picture, stack picture elements behind others, and...I can go on and on.

When you open a new image in Elements, it has a background layer. No others. If you then paste something you've copied to the Clipboard, you'll automatically make a new layer. You can use the Layers palette to keep track of your layers. Think of it as a sort of command center for layer management. You can add and remove layers from the palette itself and manage them with its menu.

In Figure 5.16, I've assembled a page with a bunch of different layers. Type goes on a separate layer. Adjustment layers enable you to correct color and exposure, with the advantage of letting you also control how much of the correction you want to apply. A layer can change both opacity and blending mode as needed.

You can start a new layer in any of several ways. Whether you're pasting something in, or dragging it from another open file, the new part of the image will automatically be placed on a new layer. As soon as you position the Type tool on the picture and start entering letters, you've created a type layer to set them on. Because they are on their own layer, you can move the words around, correct spelling, even erase them and try different words or a different font, without risking the rest of the image. However, if you want to paint on a new layer over your image, create a new layer manually by selecting New from the Layer menu, or by clicking on the small New Layer icon at the bottom of the Layers palette.

5

FIGURE 5.16

A variety of layers.

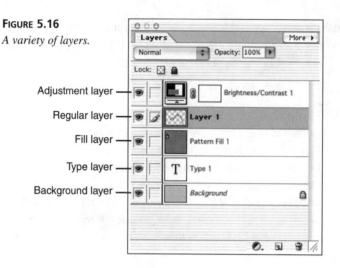

As you add more and more layers to your document, you'll probably need to give them more descriptive names, so that you can easily identify their content. To change the name of a layer, double-click the layer to open the Layer Properties dialog box. Type the name of the layer in the text box, and click OK. You can also simply double-click the name in the Layers palette, and type the new name right there. Press Enter when you're done.

Task: Experimenting with Layers

1. Start a new image (default size is fine). Open the Layers palette and drag it away from the palette well, so that it stays open on the screen.

2. Click the New Layer icon at the bottom of the palette. Now, you have Layer 1 on top of the background.

3. Go back to the background for a moment by clicking on the word "Background" on the Layers palette, and pour a color into it. To do this, set the foreground color to something light by first clicking its swatch and then choosing a color from the Color Picker. Select the Paint Bucket and click on the background. (Yes, you can use the Paint Bucket to fill a layer with color just as you can use it to fill a selection marquee or drawn object. You can also use the Edit, Fill command to fill a layer.)

4. Notice that, on the far left, the palette shows a brush on the active layer, and each layer has an open eye, indicating that both layers are visible. Click Layer 1 again, and see the brush move up to it.

5. Draw a large star with the Polygonal Lasso tool and fill it with a color that is darker than your background. To do this, click the arrow on the Lasso tool and select the Polygonal Lasso tool. Click once in the layer to establish the first star point. Click to draw each side of the star and double-click to complete the last side. To fill it with color, select a darker foreground color, click the Paint Bucket, and then click inside the star. At this point, your screen and Layers palette will look something like Figure 5.17.

FIGURE 5.17

Layer 1 is active, because that's where the brush is.

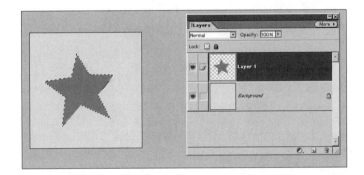

6. Click the eye next to the Background thumbnail. The background disappears, being replaced by a gray checkerboard indicating transparency. That happens because Layer 1 is transparent until you put something on it. If you look closely at the thumbnail, you will see the star you painted. Click the eye again to bring back the background. Save and close your star image.

Managing Layers

The Layers palette has a very helpful menu (you can access it by clicking the palette's More button), shown in Figure 5.18. Use it or the Layer menu, also shown, to add and delete layers, rename them, group and ungroup them, and eventually merge them and flatten the image.

Although the Layer menu and the Layers palette menu provide access to all the commands you need to manage layers, you can perform most of the more common tasks by simply clicking buttons and manipulating items in the Layer palette, shown in Figure 5.19. If your image has multiple layers, you can see and manipulate them here. As I mentioned earlier, the eye icon on the far left means that the layer is visible, and the brush icon tells you which layer is active. You can have all of your layers visible—or invisible, if you want—but only one layer can be active at a time.

5

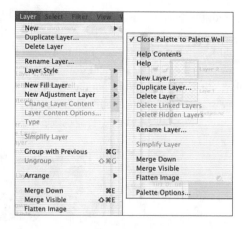

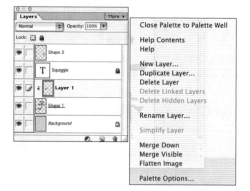

Adding a New Layer

There are, of course, several different ways to create a new layer. Whenever you copy and paste an object into your picture, it comes in on a new layer. If you add text using one of the type tools (covered in Hour 6, "Adding Type") or add a shape with a shape tool (which you'll do in Hour 19, "Creating Art from Scratch"), a new layer is created automatically.

You can also add layers manually when needed. When you click the New Layer button at the bottom of the palette, you create a new layer above the current layer. Objects placed on the new layer can obscure objects placed on lower layers. If you click the black-and-white circle icon at the bottom of the palette, you have the choice of opening a fill layer (solid, gradient, or pattern) or an adjustment layer (a layer in which adjustments such as brightness or color changes reside, without permanently affecting the image itself—you'll learn more about adjustment layers in Hour 20). When you choose Layer, New,

Layer, or select New Layer from the palette menu, or type Cmd/Ctrl+Shift+N, you open a dialog box that gives you access to some extra settings for the new layer. This box is shown in Figure 5.20.

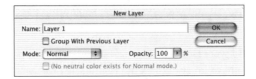

If you use the dialog box, you can name the layer, adjust its opacity and blending mode, and group it with the previous layers as you're creating it. We'll discuss grouping in a moment.

If you don't display the New Layer dialog box when creating a new layer, you can access most of those functions from the palette. You already know how to rename a selected layer. You can make changes to its opacity or its blending mode at the top of the Layer palette.

Moving or Removing a Layer

Layers play an important role in the final image, because objects on one layer can obscure all or part of an object on a lower layer. If needed, move layers up or down in the stack. The easiest way to move a layer on top of another is to grab it on the Layers palette and drag it to its new location.

In a perfect world, file size wouldn't matter because we'd all have fast computers with unlimited memory. Well, we're not quite there yet. Layers add to the size of the file, and with a lot of layers you can end up with a file big enough to choke computers with modest resources. So you need to use layers wisely. Good layer management means discarding layers you aren't going to use, and merging the rest when you are done using them. This will happen automatically and unexpectedly unless you're careful; not all file formats can handle layers. As of now the only formats that do are TIFF and the native Photoshop format. If you save your image for the Web, it will be flattened as part of the process. To remove a layer manually, drag it to the trash or click the Delete Layer icon after selecting the layer you no longer want.

Grouping Layers Together

When you group two or more layers together, they work in concert with each other. If you place an object such as a star on the bottom layer, then place a photo such as a flower on a higher layer and then group them, the flower image will appear to be star-shaped. In other words, the flower will show only within the star outline.

5

Grouped layers must be in succession. You can group a new layer with the previous one, or ungroup them, using either key commands or the Layers menu. To group a layer with the one directly below it, select the top layer and press Cmd/Ctrl+G or select Layer, Group with Previous. To ungroup, press Cmd/Ctrl+Shift+G or select Layer, Ungroup. You can also press Cmd/Alt and click on the line separating the two layers in the Layers palette to group them.

The base layer (lowest layer) is preceded by a bent, downward-pointing arrow. Its name is also underlined. The base layer defines the boundaries for what's displayed from the upper layer(s). Upper layers in the group are indented above this base layer in the list. If you look back at Figure 5.19, you can see that Layer 1 is grouped with the Shape 1 layer; the Shape 1 layer is acting as the base layer. This base layer controls the opacity and mode settings for the group.

You can also link layers together in order to treat them as a group for purposes of moving, copying, pasting, and applying transformations in a single step. To link layers, select a layer, then click in the first column to the left of the layer you want to link to this active layer. A link icon (a chain) appears in front of the layers you select. Later, if you select a layer that's linked to others, the other layers will be highlighted by this link icon, reminding you that they are linked. To unlink a layer, click any other layer in the linked group, and click its link icon to turn if off.

Changing Layer Opacity

Being able to control the opacity of individual layers gives you enormous flexibility, especially as you start to get into multilayer, multi-image composites, as we will in later hours. Opacity adjustments are also useful for making minor color changes. Suppose you have a landscape with a pale blue sky that you'd like to be a little more intense. Select the sky and copy it to a new layer. Then choose Layer, Fill Layer, Solid Color. (If you instead click the icon at the bottom of the layer palette, you won't have the option of linking the fill layer to the sky copy layer, and this is something you need to be sure to do. If you don't, the color correction will apply to the whole picture.) Type a name for the layer, and select the Group with Previous Layer option. You can guess at the opacity level now, but it's best to adjust it later when you can see the result. Click OK to open the Color Picker, so you can select an appropriate sky color. Click OK. In the Layer palette, use the Opacity slider to bring in just enough of the additional color that it looks right. Figure 5.21 shows the Layers palette with a color fill applied only to the sky.

FIGURE 5.21

You can also use this technique to apply gradients and pattern fills.

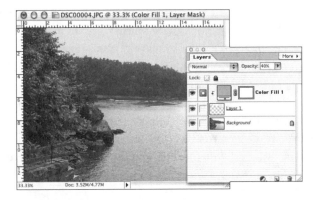

In the figure, the photograph is located on the Background layer. I selected the sky and copied it to Layer 1. You can see its white outline at the top of the thumbnail. The solid color fill layer, which is linked to Layer 1, is just above it. I could have used a pattern or gradient fill instead to create a strange sky effect.

Summary

It has been a long hour, and a useful one. First you learned about the selection tools, and how to use them not only to select an object, but as drawing and mask making tools as well. You learned about Marquees, Lassos, the Magic Wand, and Selection Brush. You learned how to add to a selection and to remove parts of one. Stroking and filling were covered in this hour, along with inverting, expanding, and feathering selections. Then, you learned about the importance of layers and how to create, delete, copy, link, and group layers as needed. You also learned how to adjust a layer's opacity, and how to use a fill layer to control the color of an object in another layer.

Q&A

Q Help! There are too many selection tools. Which one should I use?

A The one that makes the job the easiest. Think for a minute. What are you selecting? Does it have a clear outline? Is it differently colored from its background? Will it be easier to trace around it or select it by color? Do you need it exact, or will a rectangular marquee be close enough? Practice with all the selection tools. There's one that's right for the situation. Don't forget about selecting the inverse of what you want. That's often the easiest way to get there.

5

Q **I'm trying to paste a hunk of grass on a new layer over a picture of the back-yard to hide bad spots. Is there an easy way to make it blend in?**

A Try feathering the selection by about 5 pixels (more if necessary).

Q **I have trouble remembering what's on each layer, and the icons aren't big enough to see. What can I do?**

A Two things. You can rename your layers with something more descriptive. The easiest way is to click the layer name on the Layers palette, and then type in a new one and press Enter. Also, you can enlarge the icons by choosing Palette Options from the menu. Choose the largest of the three icons for better visibility.

> While you're there, press the Option/Alt key and choose Palette Options again. The funny little guy is Merlin, one of many "Easter eggs" or hidden goodies the Adobe programmers dropped in for us to discover and enjoy.

Workshop

Take a few moments to tackle the short quiz on layers, and check your answers to see how you did. Then work on the activities for extra credit.

Quiz

1. Adding a new layer doubles the size of the file.

   a. True

   b. False

   c. Depends what's on the layer

2. How many layers can be active at one time?

   a. All of them

   b. Just one

   c. No more than four

3. Grouping layers enables you to _____.

   a. Move them more easily

   b. Control what's displayed on a higher layer

   c. Fill a layer with a pattern

Quiz Answers

1. c. If it's just a spot of color, it won't add much.

2. b. Click a different layer to activate it.

3. b. The base layer contains the shape that defines the limits of what's displayed from the other layers in a group. You can use this technique with text as well, to display the stars and stripes within the abbreviation *USA*, for example.

Activities

Go to the Sams Web site at www.samspublishing.com. Navigate to the page for *Sams Teach Yourself Photoshop Elements 2 in 24 Hours*. Download the file called cheeseburger.zip, and extract its contents into a new folder so they'll be easy to find.

1. Start a new image (the default size at 72 dpi is fine). With the Elliptical Marquee tool, drag a circular marquee big enough to just fit comfortably on the page. Fill it with light blue paint. Choose light blue as a foreground color by clicking on the foreground swatch and using the Color Picker to find a nice pale blue. Then click with the Paint Bucket tool to fill the selection with pale blue paint. This is the plate for your cheeseburger.

2. Open the file called Bun 1.psd. Type Cmd/Ctrl+A to select all. In this case, you'll select the bottom of the bun. Copy it to the Clipboard and paste it onto the middle of the plate.

3. Open the Lettuce.psd file. Be sure you can see the window showing the bun on the plate. Use the Move tool to drag the lettuce from its window onto the bun. Slide it around until it's centered.

4. Use File, Place to locate and open the tomato. (Tomato.psd) It will appear with a white background. Select the white edges with the Magic Wand and delete them.

5. Click the New Layer icon on the Layers palette. Use the Lasso tool to draw a hamburger shape on top of the bun. Using the Paint Bucket tool, fill it with a nice beefy brown color.

6. To add some texture to the hamburger, create a new layer that's grouped with the burger layer, and fill it with the Red Rocks pattern (You'll find it in the Rock patterns). Set the opacity for the texture layer to around 50%.

7. Add another new layer, by pressing Cmd/Ctrl+Shift+N. This time, you'll be asked to name the layer. Call it Cheese. Draw a square marquee and fill it with "American Cheese Orange" or whatever color you think cheese ought to be. If you like Swiss, drag some holes with the Elliptical Marquee while pressing Option/Alt, before you fill the square with color. At this point, your picture should look like Figure 5.22.

5

FIGURE 5.22

*Swiss or American—
it's your choice.*

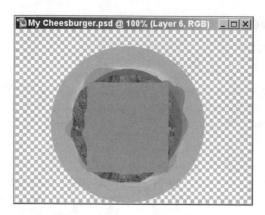

8. How about some mustard? First, let's get rid of some of these layers. Go to the Layer menu and select Merge Visible. Notice how the file size drops.

9. Add a new layer and choose the Selection Brush tool. Choose a nice fat brush, such as the Soft Round 27-pixel. style. Make sure the Mode is set to Selection, and draw a nice squirt of mustard all over your burger. Use the Paint Brush tool to fill your selection with a bright mustard yellow. Now, you've got a cheeseburger worthy of Jimmy Buffett. Save the file with the name "My Cheeseburger" and enjoy!

HOUR **6**

Adding Type

When Photoshop first appeared many years ago (at least "many" by software standards), it didn't do much with type. You could choose a color and a font and size and put the type more or less where you wanted it on the page, but that was all. For some, that was enough. Other users demanded more flexibility. And bit by bit, we've gotten it. The good news for you as an Elements user is that most, if not quite all, of big brother Photoshop's type capabilities have been brought over intact.

Your type can be set horizontally or vertically. You can fill the letters with a picture, or cut them out of a picture, using the Type Mask tool. You can stretch and distort your lettering, as well as apply any of the 100 filters Elements provides. Elements has a set of tools to warp type into waves, flag shapes, or even fish.

In this hour you will

- Add horizontal and vertical type to an image
- Fill type with an image
- Add special effects to type
- Warp your text

Using the Type Tools

The Type tool is actually four tools in one. As you can see in Figure 6.1, the toolbox holds both horizontal and vertical Type tools in both letter and mask modes. The masks allow you to do some very cool tricks with type and photos.

FIGURE 6.1

There are four Type tools.

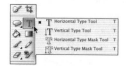

To use the Type tool, simply select it and click on the page where you want the type to begin. Before you do, however, you'll probably need to adjust the settings on the Options bar (see Figure 6.2).

FIGURE 6.2

Set your type options before you begin typing.

The first choice on the bar, which kind of type to set, is the same as in the toolbox: horizontal or vertical, masked or not. Next, a drop-down menu offers type styles. This will change according to the font you have selected, but generally you can choose from regular and italic, and often light, bold, or demibold, as well. The next drop-down menu displays a list of fonts installed, and the one after that offers a selection of point sizes. If you don't see the size you want, enter numbers into the window.

The next button, which looks like two *a*'s, is important. It determines whether to antialias the type. Antialiasing smoothes out jagged type. It's important to apply antialiasing if your work will be seen onscreen. Few things look worse, or less professional, than jagged type. Figure 6.3 shows the difference.

If your type is to be printed, however, turn off antialiasing. The same process that makes it look better onscreen adds a blur when the page is printed.

FIGURE 6.3

Notice the curves in the nonantialiased type. They appear lumpy, as if made of bricks.

I am anti-aliased.

I am not anti-aliased.

The next four choices give you false (or *faux*) bold, italic, underlined, and strikethrough type. The bold and italic options can be used to enhance a plain font or to increase the boldness and/or slant of already bold or italic faces. Strikethrough and underline have very limited uses, as far as I can see. Underlining was a way of indicating emphasis, back in the days of the typewriter, but it was always understood to be read as italic. Since you now have lots of options for italics, underlining isn't typographically correct. Nor is strikethrough, since the invention of the Delete key. Use them if you think you must, but don't tell me about it.

The little stacks of lines indicate alignment: flush left, centered, or flush right. Justified type, set flush left *and* right, is unfortunately not an option in Elements. Elements isn't a word processing program, after all. Its type functions are mainly intended to add a few words to a picture, not to typeset a newsletter or advertisement.

The color swatch, black by default, lets you choose a type color independent of the foreground and background colors. Just click it to open the usual Color Picker.

The sort of twisted letter with the curved line under it takes you to one of the more interesting aspects of setting type in Elements: warped type. I'll come back to it later in this hour. But first, let's finish off the Options bar. The final button lets you change horizontally set type to vertical type, or vice versa. It's most useful if you tend to use type as a design element rather than a means of communication. Simply click it to change a selected string of letters or symbols from reading left-right to up-down.

Adding Horizontal and Vertical Type

Horizontal type is what we're used to seeing in the English-speaking world. Other cultures use different alphabets and different typographic styles. Outside of short words on neon signs, we rarely see English, French, or similar horizontal languages intended to be read vertically. It's unnecessarily difficult, which doesn't mean you can't do it—just that you might want to think before you do.

To set type vertically, follow these steps.

1. Choose a legible font. Decide on a size and color, and make the settings on the Options bar. Be sure to click on the vertical type option.

2. Position the cursor where you want the first letter.

3. Start typing. If your word(s) runs off the image, try a smaller font.

6

To set type horizontally, do the following:

1. Make the appropriate settings as you did when placing type vertically, choosing the horizontal type option.

2. If you've chosen flush left justification, position the cursor where the type starts. If you've chosen flush right, position it where the type ends. Position it at the mid-point if you want the type centered.

3. Start typing.

Type is always set on its own layer. Each time you position the cursor and start typing, you create a new type layer. You can edit the type and apply layer commands to it. You can change the orientation of the type, apply or remove antialiasing, and warp the type into a variety of shapes. You can move, copy, and change the position or layer options of a type layer just as you would with a normal layer. To change the type's font size or color, or to edit the message, activate the type layer and click within the type to edit, or select all the type by dragging over it, then make your changes. You can also select all the text in the text layer by clicking on the layer in the Layers palette, and double-clicking the T thumbnail icon. After editing text, be sure to click the check mark button on the Options bar to let Elements know you're done.

Edits involving distortion or perspective (found on the Image, Transform menu) can't happen until the type is *simplified*, or rendered in bitmap form. In addition, you can't apply filters to text until that text has been simplified. To simplify text, click the type layer in the Layers palette, and choose Layer, Simplify Layer. Once simplified, text is no longer editable.

Choosing Fonts

Literally hundreds of thousands, if not millions, of fonts are available. And, that's before we start adding styles and special effects to them. But when you install Elements, the only fonts you'll see are the ones you've already installed. You can find fonts all over the Internet, as well as in your local computer store, catalogs, and so on. Some you can get for free; others cost money. I've found several CDs full of useful fonts advertised in the back pages of computer magazines, at very reasonable prices. And of course, there's Adobe, with everything from the classics to fonts made of bones or kids on skateboards. Figure 6.4 shows a few of the stranger examples.

FIGURE 6.4
Not all of these are right for all occasions.

Hello from STRANGE THINGS AND SILLY ONES Hash House Graduate Phooey Handsprings ORIENT Sailor knots

How many fonts do you need? That depends on what you intend to use them for. Certainly, you already have some useful ones, including classic serif fonts such as Palatino or Times New Roman. (*Serifs* are short lines that finish the ends of letters, like this: T. They make it easier to read small type.) You probably have one or two sans serif faces such as Helvetica or Arial. (*Sans serif* means *without serifs*, and looks like this: T.) You have something like Courier, which imitates a typewriter, and you probably have one or two script fonts, such as Chancery or Dom Casual. Beyond that, why not wait and see what you need? Adding dozens of fonts can actually make your computer run more slowly.

Tasteful Typography

With all those fonts waiting for you, it's hard not to get carried away and lose sight of the real reason for the type. Words mean something. You're putting type into your picture for a reason, and most of the time it's to help communicate an idea. Maybe it's a title. Maybe it's the headline for an ad, or the greeting on the greeting card. Whatever it is, you want people to be able to read and understand it. Otherwise, why clutter up the art?

Using bizarre fonts and too many special effects gets in the way of communication. If the words are hard to read, only the most devoted readers will even try. If the message is "Get Well," but the font came from a circus poster, there needs to be a reason. Otherwise, you've just given the reader one more thing to make his headache worse.

Keep the type in proportion to the picture, sizewise as well as stylistically. Don't let one element overpower the other, unless you have reason to do so. However, don't make the type too small to read, either. Print a copy and see if you can read it from five feet away without your glasses. If so, other folks probably can, too.

6

Using the Type Mask Tools

Photoshop's Type Mask tools are fun to use and can create some really cool effects. Unlike the horizontal and vertical Type tools, which create type that you can fill with color, the Type Mask tools create a selection in the shape of the type, which you can fill with an image or pattern. You can also use the Type Mask tools to punch type out of a picture (leaving a blank area in the shape of the type) or to mask the rest of the picture (leaving nothing but letters filled with the picture). Half the battle is finding a picture to work with. The other half is finding a nice fat typeface that leaves plenty of room for your picture to show through. Let's try filling some type.

To use the Type Mask tool, first select it. Set your font, size, and any other options you like. Faux Bold is often useful here, as big bold letters work best as cutouts. When you position the cursor and start to place the letters, something surprising happens. The screen goes into Mask mode and turns pink. As you enter the letters, they appear to be in a contrasting color, but when you finish typing and deselect the Type Mask tool, they turn into paths and the temporary mask goes away. Figure 6.5 shows how this looks onscreen. Don't forget that this is essentially another selection tool, rather than a Type tool, so you won't be working on a type layer. Your letters appear on whatever layer is selected.

FIGURE 6.5

Now you have the letters as selection outlines.

What you do with your text selection from this point on is up to you. You can fill it with a pattern or stroke it just like any other selection (see Hour 5, "Making Selections and Using Layers"). You can use the selection to cut the letters out of the image on which it was typed, essentially "punching out" the letters. You can invert the selection and cut the image away from the text, leaving the text filled with a portion of the image (assuming that you typed the text onto an image layer). Regardless of how you fill the selection, you can add some layer effects as I have in Figure 6.6. I applied the Wow Chrome, Shiny Edge layer effect and the Drop Shadow, Hard Edge layer effect to the top text, the Drop Shadow, High and Complex, Molten Gold effects to the middle text, and Bevel, Simple Pillow Emboss and Drop Shadow, Soft Edge to the bottom text. Be sure to check these out in the color plate section, too. (You can also add layer effects to horizontal or vertical type, by the way.)

FIGURE 6.6

Don't be afraid to experiment.

You can group two layers (one with the type mask, the other with an image) and cut out letters to reveal a picture that's actually on the layer behind them, as I have in Figure 6.7. I placed the image on one layer, and the text or a text selection on another, and then grouped them as described in Hour 5. By using two layers instead of typing the text directly on the image with a Type Mask tool and cutting it out, I gave myself a bit more room in which to grab the exact portion of the image I wanted to cut into letters. After cutting out the text, I applied an Outer Glow, Simple layer style to them. Again, please see this in color. If you're thinking, "Wow! I want to try that!" don't worry—you'll get your chance in an upcoming task.

6

FIGURE 6.7
I added a glow to help define the letters.

Working with Layer Styles and Text

Layer styles might not have been exclusively meant for working with type, but they do it so well that I nearly always use at least one, and sometimes more. That's why, although I intend to come back to using layer styles in Hour 20, "Making Composite Images," I want to tell you a bit about them here.

A layer style is a special effect such as a shadow or glow that affects all the objects on a layer. You can combine layer styles, such as an outer glow and chrome, to create a complex effect. If you want to use a layer style to format just the type in an image, that type must be on its own layer. With the horizontal and vertical Type tools, that's not a problem, since Elements creates a new layer whenever you use the tool. But if you use the Type Mask tools to create a type selection, make sure you first create a new layer to put it on.

Once you have some type or a type mask on a layer, to apply a layer style, open the Layer Styles palette. If it's not in the palette well, you can display it by choosing Window, Layer Styles. Open the drop-down list and select a category such as Drop Shadow. The palette displays a list of layer styles for that category. Click a style to apply it to the text on that layer.

When you apply a style, it shows up in the Layers palette as a cursive letter *f* to the right of the layer name, as shown in Figure 6.8. Because the Undo History palette only tells you that you've applied a style, and not which one, you'll need to pay attention to what you are doing. Also, if you select another layer style, it's added to the first style. Thus, it's easy to get confused about which styles you've added. To remove all styles from a layer, click the Clear Style button at the top of the Layer Styles palette. (It looks sort of like an aspirin tablet.)

FIGURE 6.8

I suppose it's meant to be a "stylish" f.

The most effective layer styles to use with text include Drop Shadows, Bevel (which provides bevel and emboss styles), Wow Chrome, and Wow Neon, to name a few. For example, you can improve the appearance of most type with a drop shadow, which adds dimension. Just don't overdo it. In Figure 6.9, you can see what a difference a simple shadow makes.

FIGURE 6.9

This is the preset shadow, called Low.

The Shadow Knows...

The Shadow Knows...

6

You can vary the effect of these layer styles by changing the blending modes and varying the opacity. As always, the best way to see what they do is to experiment with different settings.

Editing Layer Styles

If a layer style gives you almost, but not quite what you want, you can go back and edit the settings. You can reach the Style Settings dialog box either by choosing Layer, Layer Style, Style Settings, or by double-clicking on the style symbol (the cursive *f*) on the Layer palette. The Style Settings box is shown in Figure 6.10. You can change the position of the light, which determines the direction in which shadows are dropped, glows are cast, textures are lit, and so on.

FIGURE 6.10

Items that don't relate to a particular setting are grayed out and can't be changed.

You can also apply global light, which is a very clever way of keeping your shadows in line. Global light dictates that the light setting (in degrees) that you make here, or in any of the other dialog boxes that deal with light or shadow direction, will remain constant. If you put type with a drop shadow on another layer, the new shadow will match the old one. If you add a shape with a reflected glow, it will be lit from the same source. This is more important than it sounds at first. We live on a planet that has a single sun as its main light source. One light source produces one shadow, and that's what we are used to seeing. When you come inside and turn on a couple of lamps plus maybe the overhead fluorescent bulb, you've complicated things. Now there are several possible directions in which the shadow can go. The strength of the brightest light determines what you actually see. Designating a global light in your composition forces all the shadows you apply to fall in line. With the Style Settings dialog box, you can also change the height and size of a bevel, glow, or shadow.

Task: Applying Layer Styles to Text

1. Start with a new image. Use the default size, with a white background and RGB color.
2. Click the Horizontal Text tool. Using the Options bar, select a serif font and set the point size to 128. Set the font color to blue by clicking the color swatch at the end of the Options bar and choosing blue from the Color Picker.

3. Click along the left side of the image and type your name. Click the check mark button to indicate when you have finished typing. (If your name is too long to fit, change the text size using the Options bar.)

4. Open the Layers palette. Notice that Elements creates a new text layer for you, as indicated by the T thumbnail on the left.

5. Make sure that the text layer is active, then open the Layer Styles palette. Select Drop Shadow from the list. Click the Soft Edge icon to apply a soft shadow.

6. Select Glass Buttons from the list, and click the Yellow Glass icon. Notice how the text changes to green when the yellow color is placed on top of blue. Some layer styles completely override the text color, while others add to it.

7. Click the Clear Style button to remove all layer styles.

8. Select Outer Glows, and click the Heavy icon. Hmmm. Nothing seems to have happened.

9. Open the Layers palette, and change to the background layer. Use the Paint Bucket tool to fill the layer with red paint. Ahhh. Now we can see the glow. It just needed something to contrast with.

10. Open the Layers palette and change back to the text layer. Choose Layer, Layer Style, Style Settings. Reduce the Outer Glow Size to 10.

11. Save the image with the filename Glowing Name.psd and close it.

Warping Text

One of the major complaints about Photoshop used to be that you couldn't set type on a path within the program. If you wanted, say, a wavy line of text, you could either position the letters one by one or set the type in Illustrator or something similar and import it into Photoshop. It was a nuisance, at best. Photoshop, and now Elements, have finally added a feature called warped type. You can find it on the type Options bar.

It's not totally flexible. Rather than drawing your own path, the Warp Text dialog box allows you to select from 15 preset paths. You can also warp and distort the paths as necessary. Figure 6.11 shows a list of the presets. The Arch, Wave, Flag, and Rise presets are typically the best ones to choose when you have multiple lines of text, although any of the presets will work.

6

FIGURE **6.11**

Select a warp path.

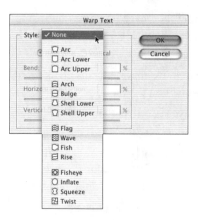

The dialog box settings, shown in Figure 6.12, are a bit tricky at first. Use the sliders to increase the amount of Bend applied to the path. Moving to the right bends words up; to the left (negative numbers), bends them down. Distortion makes the line of type appear to flare out on one end (Horizontal Distortion), or from top to bottom (Vertical Distortion).

FIGURE **6.12**

Move the sliders left or right to change the set-tings.

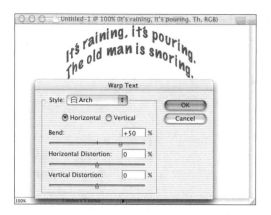

In Figure 6.13, I've applied some of the warp styles to various bits of type. The best way to master this tool is to play with it. Set a line or two of type and try the different kinds of warp on it. Try it with and without layer styles added. Move the settings sliders around. You can't break anything.

FIGURE 6.13

The only thing to watch out for is that the type stays legible.

Summary

Elements doesn't have all the type capabilities of a more traditional desktop publishing program, but it can handle most of your typographic needs, whether producing a single headline or a small block of text precisely placed over a photo. Of course, getting the letters into the picture is only the beginning. You can warp the text, punch it out of a graphic, or make the letters out of a picture. With Elements, your words can come alive. However, don't lose sight of your goal. Type is more than just a word or two pasted on your picture. It's there to communicate. Even though you can go completely wild with Elements and a few dozen fonts, try to resist. If you can't read the words, why put them there?

Q&A

Q Where's the spell checker?

A Sorry, not in this edition. You'll have to look up the words you don't know how to spell in the dictionary. However, Photoshop 7 has a spell checker now, so maybe we can look forward to it in the next edition of Elements.

Q How can I tell exactly where I'm putting the type?

A When you first click the I-beam cursor, the small horizontal line across it indicates the baseline of your type.

Q I've typed in the text I want and have simplified it. The problem is, I found a typo and when I try to go back and edit the text, I can't. What can I do?

A After you simplify text, it's converted from an editable text layer to a graphic that can't be edited by any of the Type tools. Ensure that you have the type you want and that it's all spelled correctly before you render it. To save your project, you might be able to go back in the Undo History palette to work from a state before you rendered the type.

6

Q **What's the difference between serif and sans serif? I know sans means without, but what's a serif?**

A Serifs are the little crosscut marks at the ends of strokes in some styles of letter.
Times and Century Schoolbook are examples of serif fonts. The strokes represent
chisel marks from the days when letters really were carved in stone.

Workshop

Take a few moments to tackle the short quiz on text below and check your answers to see
how you did. Then work on the activity for extra credit.

Quiz

1. Elements can set type horizontally or vertically.

    a. True

    b. False

2. Every piece of type needs a drop shadow.

    a. True

    b. False

3. Elements places type on

    a. The Background layer

    b. Special type layers

    c. Regular layers

    d. The top layer

Quiz Answers

1. a. Choose either one in the Options bar.

2. b. It's a matter of taste.

3. b. They are editable until "simplified" or rendered. If you use a Type Mask tool to
   create a selection in the shape of type (instead of actual text), the selection is
   placed on the current layer.

Activity

Find a nice photo of a family member and caption it appropriately. (Sally at age 3, or
whatever.) Experiment with placing the type in different parts of the picture. See if the
type works better with or without a drop shadow, and try it in different fonts and colors.

HOUR 7

Printing Your Pictures

By now, you've completed a quarter of the book, and although we haven't talked much yet about how to improve your photos, you know how to import them into Elements and make a few changes, so you're probably eager to print them and show them off. In this hour, you'll learn everything you need to know about printing.

In this hour you will

- Learn about color systems and how they relate to preparing and printing images.
- Select the best printer for printing your images
- Get your image ready for printing
- Create picture "packages" of a single image
- Print contact sheets to catalog folders of files

Understanding Color Systems

When it comes to printing color, there are many models you can use to specify the colors to print. Naturally, because there are thousands of colors visible to the human eye, it's difficult for any color system to accurately reproduce them all. If printing a color photograph is your goal, your result will depend on the color system you choose to display, save, and ultimately print your image with.

RGB

RGB (short for Red, Green, Blue) uses a system that defines a particular color by the amount of red, green, and blue it has in it. If you mix all three colors in equal amounts, you get white. If you don't add any of them, you get black. Computer monitors, television sets, and Photoshop Elements use the RGB system to define and display the colors you see onscreen.

Typically, a scale from 0 to 255 is used to specify the amount of each color (red, green, and blue) that exists in a particular color you're looking at. You may have noticed that when you open the Color Picker, instead of clicking on the color you want, you can define it by typing in the appropriate formula—the amounts of red, green, and blue in the color.

CMYK

Closely related to the RGB color system is CMYK, short for Cyan, Magenta, Yellow, Black. When you mix cyan, magenta, and yellow in equal amounts, you get black. If you don't add any of them, you get white. You might say that this color model should be called CMY, and you'd be right. The addition of black ink is required in the printing process, because when cyan, magenta, and yellow inks are mixed in equal amounts, they actually produce a dark brown, and not the pure black that you might expect.

CMYK is also known as the four-color process, and it's used by many computer printers and professional four-color printers. For that reason, it's also supported by a lot of software programs. Unfortunately, Elements is not one of them—but that shouldn't matter too much, because if you want to print in four colors (which is expensive) it's probably because you want to produce a nice-looking color brochure, sales catalog, or similar project, and the program you use to create such a project (such as PageMaker) will certainly support CMYK.

In the four-color process, four different plates are made, one for printing cyan, one for magenta, and so on. After a page is printed with each of these plates, the combination of the inks produces the final color desired.

HSB

The Hue, Saturation, Brightness (HSB) model is mathematically similar to the RGB model—it produces the same number of colors, but in a different way. The hue value specifies the color, such as red. The saturation value specifies the purity of the color—a lower saturation value gives you a more grayed-out version of your hue—in this example, a more grayed-out red. The final value, brightness, specifies the amount of whiteness in the color; in other words, how light or dark the red is. Brightness is sometimes also called luminance, value, or intensity. You might have noticed the Hue, Saturation, and Brightness boxes in the dialog box for the Color Picker. You can use these values rather than the RGB values to specify the exact color you want.

Pantone Color Matching System

With the Pantone Color Matching System, values are not needed. Instead, the system uses a series of color charts and accompanying print formulas to assure a designer that the color he or she chooses from a chart will be reproduced exactly. This system is often used to recreate colors critical to a printout—typically, a signature or logo color. All a designer has to do is select a color from a Pantone Color chart, and then specify the number of that color on the order form, or within the software program generating the image (assuming the program supports the Pantone system). If needed, you can use this system as well—Elements provides a place in the Color Picker dialog box for entering the Pantone color desired.

Hexachrome

This system is a variant of the CMYK color system that incorporates two more ink colors, Pantone Hexachrome Orange and Pantone Hexachrome Green. The two additional colors increase the color range and accuracy of this color system immensely. The CMYK system can accurately reproduce only 50% of the more than 3,000 colors in the Pantone system, while Hexachrome can reproduce more than 90%.

Choosing a Printer

The brand of printer you use can and should influence how you work in Elements to prepare your image, because you want to create an image whose use of color is best suited to your printer. If you're shopping for a new printer, or have recently purchased one, this hour might be especially important for you.

By the way, when I talk about *printers*, I mean the machines that put the image on the paper, not the people who run them. Some printers sit next to your computer; others reside in commercial print shops or service bureaus.

7

An entire book could be written about all the varieties of printers. In this section, we'll make do with a snapshot of what's available: inkjet printers, laser printers, dye-sublimation printers, thermal wax printers, and imagesetters.

Inkjet Printers

At the inexpensive end of the spectrum are home and office inkjet printers, almost all of which can deliver acceptable quality color printing. Examples of inkjets include HP's Deskjet series, Canon's Bubble Jets, and Epson's Stylus printers.

Not all inkjet printers support PostScript, the page description language that enables images to be printable at any resolution or color setting. Only certain models are capable of interpreting this language and reproducing images saved with this language. Most Elements images should not be saved in Photoshop EPS (Encapsulated PostScript) format unless you plan to import them into a page layout program such as Adobe PageMaker, and then send the results out to a commercial print shop that has a PostScript-friendly printer.

Inkjet printers work by spraying microscopically small dots of colored ink onto a sheet of paper. The most common four-color inkjet models utilize a time-proven process of blending cyan, magenta, yellow, and black inks to reproduce most colors in the spectrum—in other words, they use the CMYK model explained earlier. Higher-end printers refine this model by adding light cyan and light magenta, for better, smoother rendition of sky, skin, and other pale and pastel tones. With the standard four-color process, large patches of a bright pastel hue—for instance, the sky—might not appear solid. Instead, the dots of cyan and magenta that compose such patches are visible. In other words, when limited to just four colors of ink, bright pastel colors may not reproduce well. The addition of the two lighter shades of ink (light cyan and light magenta) refines the appearance of brighter, blended tones, making the sky look like the sky, for example, and not a dotted mess.

Kodak and Epson have introduced printers that use the Hexachrome system described earlier. The ENCAD division of Kodak has also introduced its own eight-color process, Octachrome, that couples Hexachrome's additions of orange and green with the pastel inks (light cyan and light magenta) of the older six-color process. These newer processes aren't common yet, but in the computer world, everything gets smaller, faster, smarter, and less expensive practically overnight. Naturally, a six- or eight-color printer will give you a better print than a four-color printer, all other things being equal. But all things are *never* equal, and you can get surprisingly good results from even the less expensive printers if you're careful about preparing the picture for printing. Figure 7.1 shows the inner workings of a typical inkjet printer.

FIGURE 7.1

The print head glides back and forth, spitting inks as it goes.

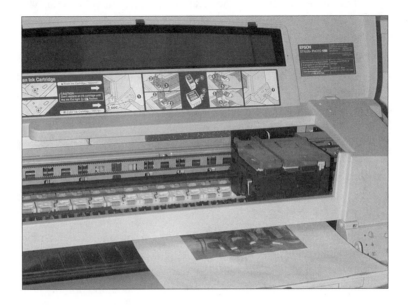

For your very best work, consider looking for a service bureau with an Iris printer. In the art world, Iris prints are very highly prized. (Art dealers may also call them giclée prints—*giclée* is French for "squirted.") High-end inkjets, such as the Iris, can cost tens of thousands of dollars but are perfect for graphics professionals. Iris and similar art-quality printers are sometimes found at service bureaus or art studios. They can produce very large prints, up to 33"×46", with remarkable detail and quality. You can have an Iris print made of your work, but prints tend to be expensive. Prices average around $150 for a single 16×20 print, but this is money well spent if the picture deserves the extra expense and effort. Some do.

Laser Printers

The laser printer is the professional standard and a good balance of price, quality, and speed. Laser printers abound from well-known companies such as Hewlett-Packard and Xerox.

Most laser printers produced today output 600 to 1200 dpi, and are particularly good with halftone and grayscale images. Some can subtly alter the size of the printed dots, thus improving quality. Laser printers are generally faster than inkjet printers, but they tend to be more expensive.

7

Laser printers work by heat-fusing powdered toner to the paper. Color lasers use a four-color toner cartridge. Color laser prints can be very good if you like bright colors and don't mind the shiny surface that you're likely to get in areas where the toner is quite dense.

Dye-Sublimation Printers

Dye-sublimation printers are expensive photographic-quality printers. You get what you pay for; image quality is superb. These printers use special ribbons and paper. You can't use ordinary paper with them, and the specially coated paper is expensive. You can often find these printers at a service bureau, where you can get a single dye-sub print for a modest fee. If you're satisfied with small but perfect prints, look into the new desktop dye-sublimation printers. Several companies make them at reasonable prices. The drawback is that they only make 4×6 prints.

Imagesetters

Imagesetters are printers used for medium- or large-scale commercial printing jobs. These large, expensive machines burn the image onto photographic film or paper. That film is then developed and used to make printing plates that are used for the actual printing. We're talking high resolution here: 1,200–2,400 dpi, or even better.

Imagesetters don't print in color, per se. Instead, you have to create a separate image for each color you want printed. These are called *separations*.

Preparing the Image

Professionals know the value of having color-compensated monitors and color-printing profiles, which guarantee that what you see on the screen is as close as possible to what you will see on paper. Because the process of mixing colors for a screen is inherently different from the process of mixing colors for print, what seems to be just the right color for an object when you chose it onscreen may appear altogether wrong on paper. Likewise, if you're designing graphics for use on the Web, the proper colors for one brand of monitor or even one resolution may appear completely wrong when seen on another monitor or at another resolution.

Elements solves this problem by giving you the power to invoke a background process called *color management*. This process translates the color you see when you're creating your image into a color that's as close to the original as possible for the finished product. For color management to work, you first have to turn it on. Doing so is a one-time process that is very simple and applies to all your work in Elements from that point on—or at least until you turn color management off. Here's how to turn it on:

1. Choose Edit, Color Settings.

2. In the Color Settings dialog box, select a color management option:

   Limited Color Management enables Elements to translate the colors you see for Web users with high-class monitors. This option slows down the program somewhat.

   Full Color Management is your best choice. This gives Elements the clearance it needs to optimize the colors you use for the printer that will render your image. This option slows down the program even more.

3. Click OK.

With that done, you can set up any image you edit for optimal printing or display on a wide variety of media, including your own printer. But first, let's talk about some other issues such as choosing the right paper, selecting your page setup options, and previewing an image.

Choosing a Paper Type

What you print on makes almost as much difference as how you do the printing. You can get various types and weights of paper for all kinds of printers. There are special papers for inkjet and laser printers. If you want your picture to resemble a photograph, consider investing in a pack of photo-weight glossy paper. It's a thick paper with a glossy surface that really does help make your inkjet- or laser-printed picture look like something that came out of a real darkroom rather than a computer.

You can get coated papers for printing color on inkjet printers. These give you photo-quality prints with a matte surface, rather than a glossy one. Transparency paper is clear acetate film, specially treated to accept the inks. Use it to make overhead projection slides and overlays.

You can also get art papers for some kinds of inkjet printers. These are heavy rag papers, much like artists watercolor paper. One place to find these is http://www.inkjetmall.com/store. I've had very good luck printing on Somerset Smooth and Somerset Velvet with the Epson Photo 750 and 1200 printers. These fine art papers are ideally suited to printing pictures that you've converted to imitation watercolors, pastel drawings, and so on because they are the same papers generally used for those techniques. If you use a heavy art paper, feed in one sheet at a time and set the printer for thicker paper (if it has such an option). Inexpensive drawing papers from the art supply store can also work quite well. I bought a pad with 24 sheets of Academie drawing paper for less than $2, and am quite happy with the prints it makes.

7

For some kinds of art projects, printing on canvas or foil is ideal. You can find treated pieces of thin canvas with a paper backing that will go through the printer very well at many art or office supply stores. There are also foils treated to accept inkjet ink. You can even buy sheets of rice paper or sugar wafers and edible inks, and put your photos on cakes or cookies. These might be suitable for birthday parties or other celebrations; I'm sure you've seen photos on cakes at your local grocery store bakery. (Check out http://www.icingimages.com for these materials, or for preprinted versions of your photos that come ready to apply and eat.)

Iron-ons have been around for quite a while now, and are good for all kinds of craft projects, not just T-shirts and mouse pads. If you have an object that's hard to decorate, such as a hat or something else that's not flat, iron your design onto plain white cloth, and glue or sew it on by hand. Follow the instructions that come with the paper and don't forget to flip any text in the image before you print it so that it reads correctly.

I used to use inexpensive photocopying paper for most of my work. Such paper is fine for printing a quick proof to see how a picture comes out. For serious proofing, though, you need to use the same paper that you'll use for the final print. Otherwise, you aren't proving that the combination of color and paper works. For work that a client will see, I use a coated inkjet paper such as Weyerhaeuser Satin because the colors are brighter and don't bleed into each other. If I want the picture to look more like a darkroom photo, I'll pay the high price per sheet to print it on special glossy paper.

Selecting Page Setup Options

You can make minor changes to your printed output from the Page Setup dialog box. Choose File, Page Setup to display it. Figure 7.2 shows a typical Page Setup dialog box.

FIGURE 7.2

Your dialog box will look different unless you use the same printer I use.

Page Setup
Settings: Page Attributes
Format for: Any Printer
Paper Size: US Letter
8.50 in. x 11.00 in.
Orientation:
Scale: 100 %
Cancel   OK

Each printer's Page Setup dialog box looks a little different, but they all provide the same basic functions. Here's a list of some of the more typical options:

- Printer—The name of the printer may appear at the top of this dialog box. If it's wrong, or if you don't see it listed, select the printer you want from the Printer list, or click the Printer button.

- Properties—On Windows machines, you can click this button (located near the Printer list) to access a dialog box that enables you to change things such as paper size, layout, printer resolution, and halftone settings. On the Mac platform, you can make these changes here or in the Print dialog box.

- Paper Size—Choose the size of the paper on which you're printing.

- Source—If your printer has two paper trays or gives you a choice of tray or single-sheet feed, you can choose the paper source that you want the printer to use.

- Orientation—Choose how you want the printed image to be placed on the page: portrait (the narrow edge of the page at the top) or landscape (the wide edge at the top).

- Reduce or Enlarge—If you see these options, use them to adjust the size of the image by a percentage.

- Margins—Use these settings if they're available to adjust the space between the image and the edge of the page.

When you actually print the image (we'll get there soon, I promise), you might run into a problem with files that are especially large. If the image dimensions are larger than the dimensions of the paper you're printing on, Elements will warn you. You can then choose to print anyway, resulting in only part of the image being printed, or you can cancel and adjust the Reduce or Enlarge value so that the whole image fits on the page.

Previewing an Image

After making page setup adjustments, if any, it's time to preview your image as it might look when printed. Take a look at the Print Preview dialog box in Figure 7.3. To display a similar box on your screen, choose File, Print Preview or click the Print Preview button.

7

FIGURE 7.3

Notice the options in my Print Preview dialog box.

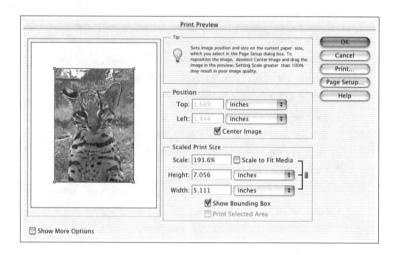

The first option here is Position. If you uncheck Center Image, which is checked by default, the image will print wherever it appears on the page in the preview window. If you then turn on the Show Bounding Box option, you can slide the picture around on the page, placing it wherever you want. If you drag a corner of the image, you can rescale it. The Scaled Print Size values will change accordingly. You can also scale the image by typing a percentage into the Scale field. Scaling is done relative to the original image size. If you have a photo that's 6 inches wide and you want it to print 9 inches wide, scale it to 150%. You might also be able to change this setting through the Page Setup box. To scale the image to fit the size of your page, select the Scale to Media option.

If the Print Selected Area box is checked and you have a rectangular area currently selected in your Photoshop image, you can print just that area. This works only with rectangular selections created with the Marquee tool, and it doesn't work for feathered selections.

When you click Show More Options, you can choose between Output options and Color Management options. In Figure 7.4, I've added crop marks and a caption line to my photo. By default, the caption is the file title. Here's a list of the Output options:

- Background—If you want to print a background color around your image, click the Background button and you'll be greeted by the standard Color Picker. Whichever color you pick is used only for printing and does not alter your actual image file. (If you're printing from Windows, be sure to turn this off after you use it. Otherwise, you'll print the background around the next picture as well.) Be careful about using this feature. It eats up a lot of ink!

- Border—Similarly, if you'd like a border around your printed image, click the Border button. In the resulting dialog box, you can set the width of the printed border in inches, millimeters, or points. The border is always black; you can't change the color. (As with Background, using this feature doesn't affect the actual image file.)

- Caption—Check this box, and on the printed page you'll see the text that appears in the Caption area of the File Info dialog box for that file. (To get to this dialog box, choose File, File Info and make sure that Caption is selected in the top pull-down menu.) This can be helpful for providing contact info or details next to your image. If there's nothing entered here, the filename will be the default caption.

- Corner Crop Marks—Corner crop marks appear around each corner of your image, defining where it should be trimmed. They're simply horizontal and vertical lines.

FIGURE 7.4

A picture ready to print, showing various crop marks, a border, and a caption.

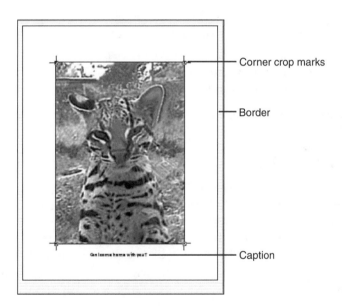

Corner crop marks

Border

Caption

Earlier, I explained how to turn on color management within Elements. But to get it to work with the current image, you must select a *profile* for your image. The profile instructs Elements with regard to how it should translate colors for output on its intended medium. To display the Color Management options, click Show More Options in the Print Preview dialog box, then choose Color Management from the drop-down list.

The area marked Source Space lists the native color management profile in use by the current image. Generally, there is none, so it will most frequently show something like "Untagged RGB." From the Profile list, choose the profile that best suits your printer, or

7

the device you intend to use to render the image. Toward the bottom of this list, you'll see dozens of printers and monitors—some branded, some generic. You may very well find your printer in this list. In any event, here's generally what you should choose, and why:

- Choose your printer model (if available) when you intend to print your image on your own printer.

- Choose your monitor model if you intend for your graphics to be used over the Web and seen on your monitor.

- Choose a generic monitor for everyday Web graphics, or a high-end monitor (such as a Trinitron) for highest-quality Web graphics.

- Choose Printer Color Management (second in the list) to have your own printer driver handle the job of color management. Most major brands of color inkjet printers sold today include their own color management options, which are accessible through their drivers' Print dialog boxes.

  Leave this option set to Same As Source if your image is saved using a newer format that includes its own print profiles. You can find out whether your image uses such a format by checking the Source Space area for the name of this profile.

After selecting your options and previewing your image, you're ready to print.

Printing the Page

Okay, now we're finally ready to print the image. I told you there were a lot of variables involved in printing, didn't I? One more thing before you print—consider making your image file smaller before sending it to your printer. This not only speeds up printing, but also reduces the chances that the printer will quit halfway through the print job. To reduce a file's size, flatten all the layers into one by choosing Layers, Flatten Image. You can also reduce the resolution and the image size by choosing Image, Resize Image. When you're ready to print, choose File, Print or click the Print button.

The Print dialog box for my Epson printer is shown in Figure 7.5. This dialog box's appearance varies depending on the printer you have, the platform you're running on, and the mode of the image. Select the number of copies to print, set other options as available, and click OK to print the image.

So that's how to print from Elements. But as you'll probably discover, printing directly from Elements doesn't happen as often as you might expect. Most of the time, images created here are put into another application for final placement and output. Most often these are page layout applications, such as Adobe PageMaker and QuarkXPress.

Elements images can even be put into other image-editing, painting, or drawing applications, such as Procreate Painter and Adobe Illustrator, and printed from there.

FIGURE 7.5

The ultimate dialog box: Print.

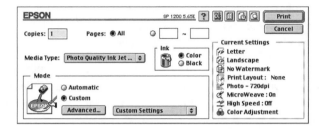

The main thing to watch for when you're printing Elements images from other applications is the format of your file. Make sure that it's compatible with the program you're putting it into. If it's not, believe me, you'll know! Other than that, any settings related to the image, such as custom colors or dithering options, are brought with the image automatically. (Dithering is a method of simulating the colors in an image by mixing colors actually stored in the file. When you reduce the colors in an image, you reduce its size, and dithering helps you make up for that loss.)

Making Contact Sheets and Picture Packages

In this automated world, it's only fair that our computers should provide ways to automate some of the more mundane tasks that we must occasionally do, such as making contact sheets and picture packages.

When you start to really use your digital camera, or to scan and store lots of regular photos on your computer, it's time to invest in a good photo organizer. For the Mac, I recommend iPhoto. For Windows, you might want to try a shareware program such as FotoArchive, Photo Organizer Deluxe, or BR's PhotoArchiver.

Contact Sheets

If you have a background in darkroom photography, as I do, you're already used to making contact sheets of every roll of film you process. When you download images from a digital camera, you might use a transfer program that displays your photos as slides in a sorter, or you might simply copy them from your card or camera directly to your hard

7

drive. If you follow the latter course, you really can't tell what you have until you open each picture in the Elements Browser and study it. That takes time. Fortunately, Elements enables you to simply scan thumbnails of your pictures and choose the ones you want to use without having to decipher the cryptic filenames from the camera or open each picture separately. Better yet, it lets you print these pages and index them to the hundreds of CDs full of photos you've taken. Much easier? You bet.

All you need to do is save the images for the contact sheet into a folder. You can even place several subfolders inside one main folder. Then select File, Print Layouts, Contact Sheet to open the dialog box shown in Figure 7.6 and select the folder you want to make contacts of.

FIGURE 7.6

Click Include All Subfolders if you want their contents to be included in the contact sheet.

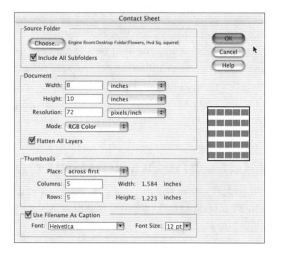

If you're going to print your contact sheets, be sure that the document size is no larger than the paper in your printer. Low resolution (72 dpi) is usually good enough to see what's going on, and saves time and space. The Flatten All Layers option has to do with the finished thumbnail file, not your images. It's typically best to select this option, unless you plan to manipulate the individual thumbnails for some reason.

Decide how many thumbnails you want per page, and arrange them across or down as you prefer. Finally, if you want their filenames to appear on the contact sheet (which I strongly recommend), click the Use Filename As Caption check box and select a font and size for the caption. When you click OK, Photoshop will automatically open your files one at a time, create thumbnails, and paste them into a new document. You can then save and print this contact sheet just like any other page. Figure 7.7 shows a typical contact sheet. Note that the pictures are in alphabetical order. Filenames, if too long, will be truncated.

FIGURE 7.7

Each little photo has its filename as its title.

Picture Packages

Remember school pictures? You got a page with one 5×7 print, a couple of "stick-on-the-fridge"-sized pictures for the grandparents, and several wallet-size photos for mom and dad. Around the holidays, your local discount store or department store offers similar deals. You don't need to bother with them. You can do your own and save a bundle.

Use File, Print Layouts, Picture Package to open the dialog box. There's a menu in the Source area that lets you locate the photo you want to package, or you can use whatever's already open. Choose a paper size based on what your printer can handle. In Photoshop Elements 2, you have options for 10×16 and 11×17 paper as well as 8×10. Figure 7.8 shows the dialog box with a layout selected.

Label your photos, if you want to, with the name of the subject, your studio name and copyright notice, date, proof warning, or whatever else you want. Choose a font, size, color, and opacity for this type, and decide where on the page it should go. Unfortunately, you are limited to only a few fonts, most of which are more suitable for copyrighting or captioning than for adding an elegant title.

Set the resolution as appropriate for your printer, and click OK. Elements will assemble the package for you in a new file, just as it does with the contact sheets. When you're ready, save and/or print it.

7

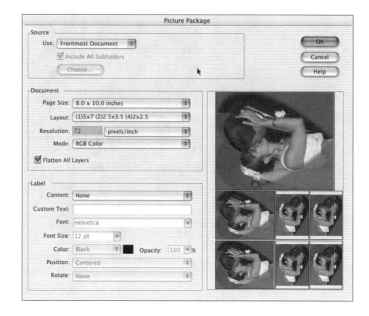

FIGURE 7.8
Portrait sizes, wallet sizes, even passport sizes—what more could you want?

Summary

In this busy hour, you learned about the process of printing your pictures. You learned about the various color systems in use, and whether or not they are supported by Elements. You worked through the relevant dialog boxes, from Page Setup to Print. You learned about the different kinds of printers and how they work. You learned to select between landscape and portrait orientation, and to set paper size and kind. Finally, you learned how to create contact sheets for picture collections, and to print picture packages with a single image.

Q&A

Q I get a lot of emails about cheap printer inks. Are they really just as good?

A Not if you're creating art prints. They are more prone to spattering and to fading. Almost any ink will fade in direct sunlight, so be careful where you hang your best pictures.

Q Is it okay to use ordinary copy paper to print proofs before I print the whole job?

A Ask yourself exactly what it is that you're proofing. Ink reacts differently to different paper surfaces. If you're checking position and spelling, print it on whatever is handy. If you're doing a critical color check, use the paper you plan to use for the final result, but consider making a half-sized print.

Workshop

Take a few moments to tackle the short quiz on printing below and check your answers to see how you did. Then work on the activity for extra credit.

Quiz

1. RGB stands for

    a. The initials of Roy G. Biv, inventor of ColorSync

    b. Raster, Gray, Black

    c. Red, Green, Blue

2. You should set your printer for the kind of paper you intend to use.

    a. True

    b. False

3. You can print on all of the following except

    a. Sugar wafers

    b. Artists paper

    c. Iron-on transfers

    d. Jello

    e. Canvas

Quiz Answers

1. c.

2. a. That's how it knows how much ink to apply.

3. d. But somebody may invent a way….

Activity

Go to a good stationery store or computer store and investigate the papers available. Buy a pack of glossy paper and a pack of matte inkjet paper. Print the same photo on both types of paper and study the differences. Look at color and ink density as well as sharpness and overall quality.

7

Hour **8**

Posting Your Work on the Web

Ever since the Web got started, ordinary people as well as multinational conglomerates have made it their own. Why not you? Service providers typically offer a reasonable amount of Web storage space for free, so why not use it to post your own Web page, share photos, or advertise your business? If you plan on using images on the Web, however, there are some things you should do first to prepare them, and in this hour, you'll learn how.

In this hour you will

- Convert images for publication on the Web
- Deal with problems caused by reducing file size
- Create Web buttons and other graphics for use on Web pages
- Arrange photos you want to share in a Web gallery
- Share an image through email

Internet Limitations and What They Mean to You

You've surfed the Web with your favorite browser—Internet Explorer, Netscape, or one of the lesser known programs, like iCab or Opera. You have email and probably even your own home page. But, do you know what's really going on out there in cyberspace? First of all, although the Web is what you might call a *virtual space,* meaning that it creates the illusion of space and distance, it also exists in a physical space. It is made up of computers called *servers* that send files to programs that request them (such as your browser), across networks that stretch around the world. The server computers can be anything from supercharged SPARC stations to minis and mainframes—or a machine not unlike the one sitting on your desktop. These machines run software that can talk with your computer via what are known as *protocols*. A protocol is a set of rules that define the exchange of information—in this case, the downloading of Web pages, files on a server, email messages, and so on.

Thus, when you type a URL (uniform resource locator) into your browser to access a Web site, a message made up of electronic pieces of information called *packets,* goes out to these remote machines. These machines then send back the files for which you have asked. The files that make up all the sounds, pictures, and text of the Web then have to travel across phone lines or down a cable TV line or other connection.

This creates a problem that you have to keep in mind as you create pages for your Web site. Phone lines are slow, and only so much information can travel through them at a time. If you are lucky enough to have a fast connection, such as a cable modem or an ISDN, DSL, or T1 connection, you have nothing to worry about regarding speed. If you use a dial-up modem attached to an ordinary phone line, you have a much slower connection. Web pages, even your own, will take longer to load. Because most ordinary people are still using dial-ups rather than high speed connections, it's a courtesy to keep the files that make up your Web pages small so they will load reasonably fast. Fortunately, there are ways to optimize your Web graphics so that you get the most bang for the bit, so to speak.

To optimize a graphic is to adjust the image size and number of colors to get the best quality possible with the smallest file size.

Putting together a Web page is more than just assembling graphics. You need a concept. You need a reason to have the page up, even if it's only to post pictures of the new baby,

8

or to sell your hand-knitted potholders and tea cozies. After you have a purpose in mind, you can start to think about what goes on the page(s) and how to put them together.

The most popular language used to publish documents on the Web is still HTML (Hypertext Markup Language). HTML isn't really a computer programming language, so relax. It is, as its name suggests, a *markup* language. A series of relatively simple *tags* enables you to specify how text appears in the browser, as well as images, and links to other sites. HTML isn't difficult to learn, but you really don't need to. (If you decide to get into it, look for *Sams Teach Yourself HTML and XHTML in 24 Hours* by Dick Oliver. It's an excellent reference.)

There are programs, including desktop publishing programs, Web browsers, and word processors you might already own, that can translate your pages into HTML with just a couple of mouse clicks. All you need to do is lay out the page the way you'd like it to look with your Elements pictures pasted in. You do have to make sure that they're in a Web-compatible format, though. Because Web pages can be viewed on all kinds of computers, the graphics have to be in a format that's common to as many as possible.

And don't forget: Some people surf the Web from a Palm, cell phone, or other low-bandwidth devices. Cell phones will soon get faster, but some older models still present a special problem, because their users won't see your pictures at all, and some cell phones that *do* display graphics do not show them in color. To avoid confusing cell phone surfers, or the many thousands of blind or low-vision Web surfers, add a line of text (which can be hidden under the picture) explaining what it is. This is especially important if your graphic is a title or logo.

Optimizing Images for the Web

Elements makes optimizing a photo or a graphic easy and almost automatic. Instead of saving your work in the usual way, choose File, Save for Web or click the Save for Web button. You'll open a dialog box like the one in Figure 8.1.

Here you can try out different ways of saving your picture, and see which method gives you the smallest file with the least degradation to the image. Yes, degradation—every time you save a picture as a file smaller than it was originally, you lose some data. If you save the same picture several times in the compressed format, you can end up with so much loss—and so little data remaining—that your photo starts to look like a seventh generation photocopy, barely visible. This is *not* a good thing to do. Always save the original in a noncompressed format like PSD. When you convert it for the Web, compress it and save it only once.

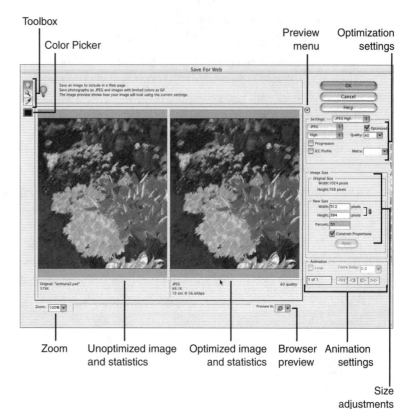

FIGURE 8.1

You can see how your changes affect the quality of the art, and decide what's acceptable.

There are three formats that all Web browsers can open automatically: JPEG, GIF, and PNG. If your browser has a QuickTime plug-in installed, it can also open TIFFs, but there's no guarantee that everyone with whom you want to share your pictures has QuickTime available.

After displaying your image in the Save for Web dialog box, Elements suggests a suitable image format compatible to the Web. You can change to a different format if you don't like the displayed results. I'll get to those formats shortly, but first let me explain a bit more about the dialog box.

The left pane shows your unoptimized image. On the right is your image as it might appear after optimization. Your considerations don't stop there, however. By clicking the right-pointing arrow and opening the Preview menu, you can change to various modes that simulate how your graphic will look when optimized and then displayed on a generic Windows monitor, a Mac monitor, or with its color profile. (You might select this if you are using a profile and you want to see how the image will look when printed.)

8

See Hour 7, "Printing Your Pictures," for more information on color profiles and the role they play in preserving color information for printing. Notice that the file size for both the original and optimized images is displayed underneath each pane. From this same menu, you can adjust the download time to match what you think most of your visitors will be using. By default, 28.8Kbps modem speed is used to calculate the download times shown below the optimized image.

You can zoom in or out of the image using the Zoom list at the bottom left. You can also zoom in by selecting the Zoom tool from the toolbox in the upper left and clicking with it on the image. Press Cmd/Alt and click with the Zoom tool to zoom out. You can move the image within the frame by dragging with the Move tool, to view hidden sections of it. If you have more than one Web browser installed (which you might, if you are seriously testing graphics for the Web), you can switch from one to another using the list on the lower right.

Finally, after adjusting the view, you're ready to change from one optimization type to another. Select the type you want, such as JPEG Medium, from the Settings list. The options displayed in the Optimization Settings area have been set to values that typically provide the best quality image for that setting. However, you can still adjust the individual options as needed. In the following sections, I'll explain each of these options.

JPEG (Joint Photographic Experts Group)

JPEG is the most commonly used Web file format. Depending on your needs, JPEG is probably the best file format for you, too. It is great for photographs and other *continuous tone* (full-color) images, primarily because it lets you use 16 million different colors. (Of course, some Web browser programs, and some older monitors, can't handle that color depth. Instead, they display a reasonable approximation of your artwork.) JPEG maintains color information, but does however employ a *lossy* compression scheme, which means that you can adjust and reduce the file size—at the expense of the image quality. It does this by examining adjacent pixels and averaging them against those closest.

When you select JPEG High, JPEG Medium, or JPEG Low format from the Settings list, the options shown in Figure 8.1 appear. The differences between high, medium, and low relate to the quality of the result, and thus, the amount of lossy compression. With Low, you'll get a smaller file, but with a greater loss of clarity. If your image will only be seen in a very small format, that may not be a big deal, and with some graphics, even Low compression results in a nice looking image.

After selecting the JPEG format you want from the Settings list, you can change other options as desired. You can choose Optimize to compress the file as much as possible in that format; however, you should be aware that some older browsers do not support this extra-optimized JPEG format. Adjust the quality level (compression level) by opening the list and dragging the slider. Choose Progressive to display the image in a browser, first at low quality, then gradually improving until the image is displayed in its saved format. Select ICC Profile to save the color profile (assuming you're using one) with the image; some browsers can use the profile to do simple color corrections for the user's monitor on the fly. If your image includes areas that are transparent, they must be filled with some color because JPEG format doesn't support transparency. Open the Matte list and select a color that closely matches your Web page background.

GIF (Graphics Interchange Format)

If you save an image as a GIF file, you lose color information. The millions of colors present in a photograph are reduced to a palette of only 256 colors. That's how GIFs shrink files. If your picture happens to have relatively few colors—for instance, if it's a drawing rather than a photo—you won't lose any quality. In fact, if you know that there are only six colors, you don't even need to save the other 250. Obviously, GIF is not as good as JPEG for continuous tone art, but it's great for line art, logos, and anything with limited color. GIF also lets you save files with transparent backgrounds, which is extremely useful when you are creating Web buttons or other round graphics and you want the background of the Web page to appear around their edge. Furthermore, you can animate a GIF.

Even though GIF supposedly uses 256 colors, the reality is that there are only 216 of them that Mac and Windows computers have in common. These are said to be "Web-safe" colors, because they'll look the same on both kinds of machines. So in the process of converting to GIF, a color table of the most common 256 colors in the image is generated. When a color exists in the image but not on the table, a close color is chosen.

When selecting GIF from the Settings list, your first consideration is whether or not to use dithering. *Dithering* was what my dear Aunt Celia used to do whenever a decision was required. "Should I? Shouldn't I?" She wobbled back and forth until the lines of the situation were so blurred that it didn't really matter what she decided. And that's essentially what dithering is all about.

In Elements, and in other graphics programs, dithering mixes colors so that when you convert an image to a GIF or to an 8-bit PNG, you don't notice the missing colors. When you select a GIF that uses dithering (or PNG, as you'll see in the next section), you can select the dithering method and the dither amount. A higher amount dithers more colors, but might increase file size. After selecting a GIF dithering option from the Settings list,

8

you can select the following dither options from the drop-down list in the Optimization Settings area:

- None—Does not dither, but instead uses a color from the color table that comes as close as possible to the missing color. This tends to result in sharp transitions between shades of the same color, rather than the gradual ones achieved through dithering.

- Diffusion—Uses a method that produces a more random dither than the Pattern option. By applying a less patterned dither to an image, it softens the effects over an area. To protect colors in the image that match those in the color table from being changed, select Preserve Exact Colors. You'll want to use this option if your image contains text or fine lines, which you quite naturally wouldn't want "fuzzified."

- Pattern—Uses a variation of a halftone pattern to simulate colors not found in the color table. Halftone is a process of dithering that uses circles of various sizes to simulate the intensity of a color—the more intense the color, the larger its dot. The Pattern option uses squares rather than dots, but the principle is the same: the more intense the color, the larger the square. Halftone dithering is used a lot in newspaper photos, because it's effective in images with larges patches of the same color.

- Noise—Uses a random pattern to dither, like the Diffusion option, but without dithering adjacent pixels. Instead, it dithers pixels in the "neighborhood." This dithering method reduces the "seams" that sometimes appear in the Diffusion method, especially along the edges of image slices. An image slice is just what it sounds like: a slice or section of an image saved in a separate file. You can slice an image into various color regions and save them each as GIF files, and each file can have its own 256-color table. Thus, more colors are saved from the original image. Place each of these slices in an HTML table, and they can be reassembled into a single cohesive image. Choose this option if you plan to slice the image for placement in an HTML table. (You can't do this in Elements, but you can in other graphics editors such as Photoshop and Paint Shop Pro.)

After selecting a GIF with or without dithering, adjust the individual options if desired. Select Interlaced to display a lower-resolution version of the image quickly, while the higher-resolution version is downloading. Choose a method for generating the list of colors for the color table from the second drop-down list. You have these choices:

- Selective—This is the default. This option adds Web colors (the 216 colors shared by Windows and Mac operating systems) to the table over other colors that may be present. Colors that appear in large patches are added to the table over other colors as well.

- Perceptual—Chooses colors for the table that the eye normally sees with the greatest accuracy.
- Adaptive—Looks for the most commonly occurring hues, then adds a proportionate sampling of those colors to the table.
- Web—Uses the 216-color palette common to Windows and Mac operating systems.
- Custom—Saves the current palette of colors, and doesn't update it even if you change colors within the image.

In the Colors box, you can enter a number lower than 256 and reduce the number of colors in the color table, and thus, the file size. The Web and Custom color table methods allow you to select Auto from this list, in order to have Elements tell you the optimal number of colors that provides the best quality in a small file size. To preserve transparency in your image, you must turn on the Transparency option; otherwise, transparent and semitransparent pixels are filled with the Matte color you select. Turning on Transparency creates jagged edges on round objects, so you might consider leaving it off, and instead selecting a Matte color that closely matches your Web background color. For animated graphics, make sure the Animate option is selected. You'll learn how to create your own animated images in Hour 24, "Animated GIFs and other Cool Tricks."

PNG (Portable Network Graphics)

There are two kinds of PNG: 8-bit and 24-bit. The PNG-8 format uses 8-bit color, which means that each image can contain only 256 different colors. Like GIF, PNG-8 compresses solid areas of color very well while preserving sharp detail, such as that in line art, logos, or illustrations with type. Because PNG-8 is not supported by older browsers (although it is supported by the not-so-old versions of those same browsers), it might be a good idea to avoid this format for situations in which your image must be accessible to as much of the Web-viewing audience as possible. The PNG-8 format uses a *lossless* compression method, with no data discarded during compression. However, because PNG-8 files are 8-bit color, optimizing an original 24-bit image—which can contain millions of colors—as a PNG-8 will degrade image quality. PNG-8 files use more advanced compression schemes than GIF, and can be 10%–30% smaller than GIF files of the same image, depending on the image's color patterns.

The PNG-24 file format uses 24-bit color and is suitable for continuous tone images. PNG-24 also uses a lossless compression scheme. However, PNG-24 files can be much larger than JPEG files of the same image. The PNG-24 format is recommended only when working with a continuous tone image that includes multilevel or variable transparency, such as you'd have in an antialiased image on a transparent layer—an image whose edges are blurred with varying levels of transparency so that the edges are smoother and less jagged. You might also use varying levels of transparency to blend the edge of an object with its background, again smoothing out the transition. (Multilevel transparency is supported by the PNG-24 format, but not the JPEG format.)

If you'd consider GIF for an image, consider PNG-8 as well. It might give you a smaller file, and can do the job well. If you're thinking about JPEG, consider PNG-24 if your picture has multilevel transparency. If it's a straight image, JPEG will probably give you a smaller, more efficient file.

If you select PNG-8 from the Settings list, you'll be presented with options similar to those described in the GIF section. If you select PNG-24 instead, you'll see only some of those options listed. Choose Interlaced to display a lower-resolution version of your image as the higher-resolution one is downloading. Select the Transparency option to preserve transparency in your image, or select a Matte color with which to fill them.

Task: Optimize a Graphic

In this task you will optimize a simple graphic for the Web.

1. Either open a graphic from your own collection, or to work on the same graphic as I am working on, you can download Healthcat.psd from the book's Web page at www.samspublishing.com.

2. Make sure the picture is ready for "prime time." Crop, adjust colors, retouch…. Do whatever is necessary to make it as good as you can. You'll find step-by-step directions for making image improvements in upcoming chapters, so you don't have to try them out now, but you won't harm anything if you play around. If you'd rather just optimize the picture right now, choose File, Save for Web, or click the Save for Web button in the shortcuts bar. That opens the window shown in Figure 8.1.

3. The dual windows show both the original and optimized images in the Save For Web dialog box. Thus, you can compare the two images and decide which optimization settings work the best. If the whole picture isn't visible in the view area, use the Hand tool to move the rest the image into view. You can also use the Zoom tool to magnify or reduce the view.

4. Decide which format to use. In a limited color environment like this one, GIF is the obvious choice. Use the Settings pop-ups to select GIF and 8 colors (because there are obviously no more than that used in the picture). See Figure 8.2.

FIGURE 8.2

*The changes you make
in the Settings box
determine how your
picture will be saved.*

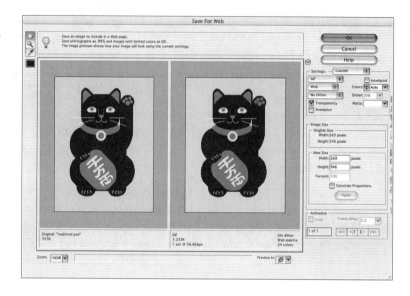

5. Now look at the information in the box at the bottom of the pictures. The notes for the original image show the file name and file size. The notes for the optimized image show the optimization options you chose, the size of the optimized file, and the estimated download time using the selected modem speed. (You can select a modem speed in the Preview pop-up menu.) In this case, we've reduced the file size from 355K to 3K, or by nearly 100%. It will load in considerably less than a second, no matter what the estimate says.

6. If you think you've found the right combination, check it out for yourself by clicking on the Preview In tab at the bottom of the screen. The pop-up menu will detect all the browsers installed on your computer. Choose one from the menu and open it by clicking on the browser logo. You'll see your full-size picture, along with the HTML tags to place it on the page. Figure 8.3 shows an example.

You can simply copy these lines of HTML code and paste them into the text version of your HTML page, after you add the image to the appropriate folder and upload everything to the Web host, or you can use your favorite Web page editor and let it do all the work.

FIGURE 8.3

If you're concerned about color accuracy, check your picture on both Mac and Windows platforms, if possible.

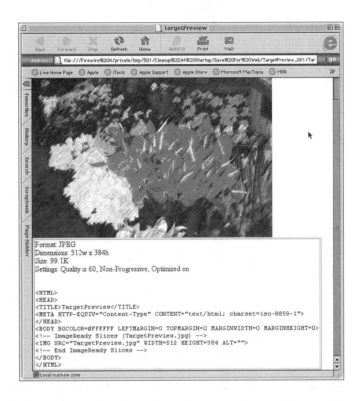

8

Preparing Text for the Web

You searched high and low and finally found the ultimate font that expresses the essence of *you*. Or maybe you had a custom font made up of your handwriting. What could be more personal than that? (You can do it at www.execpc.com/~adw/ for just under $100.)

So, naturally, you want to use your favorite font on your Web page. Well, guess what? Only the handful of folks who have that particular font installed will see your words your way. Worse yet, if it's your very own big buck custom font, *nobody* will see it. Instead, they'll see whatever their browser decides is a close match to the font you selected. Can you do anything about this? Sure. Set your type in Elements. Convert it to a GIF, and then paste it into the page. Because it's now a graphic instead of text, it'll look like your original. But it will take longer to load than regular text, so use it for titles rather than for entire pages. (If it's your actual handwriting, or a very funky font, be sure it's readable.)

Figure 8.4 shows an example of a logo I made up and converted for one of my Web pages, combining type and a drawing. I also tried this with a photo of a cat in approximately the same position, but the line drawing turned out easier to read as well as being a smaller file.

FIGURE 8.4

Because the colors are very limited, I saved it as a GIF. It loads faster than you can blink.

Preparing Backgrounds

I admit that I have mixed feelings about backgrounds on Web pages. They can really add personality to a Web site, but they can also make reading the text of your site difficult and frustrating. To quote Web designer David Siegel, "Gift-wrap makes poor stationery."

That said, however, if you use backgrounds with discretion, they can add to a site's presence and look. Because HTML includes the capability to tile any image as a background, your background file can be quite small. You just have to make sure that it doesn't have obvious edges or pictures/shapes that end abruptly at the edges, unless that's what you want. In Figure 8.5, I've created a simple tile for a Web page background. After creating the simple pattern, I saved it as a GIF file optimized for the Web using the Save for Web dialog box in Elements.

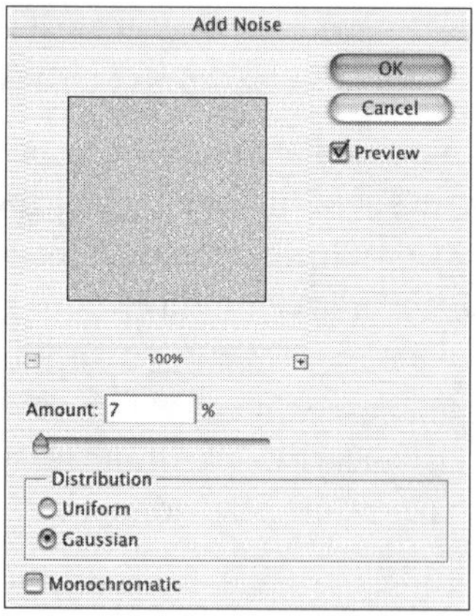

FIGURE 8.5

Simple backgrounds are less distracting.

8

This pattern was very easy to achieve. First, I filled a square with pale blue, and then added a small amount of noise (Filter, Noise, Add Noise). After trying both, I found the Gaussian distribution worked better than Uniform, and that Monochromatic noise just looked muddy. You'll learn how to apply the Noise filter yourself in Hour 17, "Using the Improvement Filters."

Converting the single tile into a background is easy. You simply open a page in your favorite Web page layout program, and import the image. Depending on the program, you can import it as an image and click a check box in the dialog box to make it a background. Some other Web page layout programs have a specific dialog box for placing backgrounds. Netscape's is called Page Colors and Background, and is shown in Figure 8.6.

FIGURE 8.6

The background will tile smoothly because the edges are no different from the middle of the square.

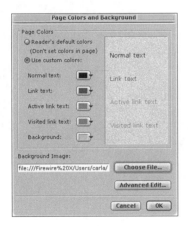

You can also use the tiling feature to create a background with one or more vertical stripes or other designs. Make the tile as many pixels high as necessary, but the full width of the page. The browser will have no problem at all tiling in only one direction. Figure 8.7 shows a background tile that will produce a multicolored background accent stripe down the left side of the page. I created it in less than a minute by applying brush stripes of related colors from the Swatches palette (a palette of the colors in an image; choose Window, Color Swatches to display it) and then using Liquify (Filter, Distort, Liquify) to blur them in only one direction. Be sure to see this in the color section, too. We'll play with the Liquify filter in Hour 21, "Going Wild with Your Images."

You can also use a photo as your Web page background, if you're willing to make a few changes to make it a better backdrop for text and to reduce its file size. First, resize or crop the graphic to fit the size of a standard Web page: It should be about 680×800 pixels wide by 480×600 pixels tall. Next, colorize your image—reduce it to a single hue (color) such as blue. To do this, choose Enhance, Adjust Color, Hue/Saturation, and turn on the Colorize option. Turn on the Preview option so you can see how your adjustments will look on the final image, then move the Hue slider until the image is the color you want. Adjust the Saturation and Lightness values to wash out the image so that your text will be easy to read on top of it. Finally, optimize your image by choosing File, Save for Web. For a photo such as this, JPEG is typically the best choice. You can use JPEG Low since you don't need a high quality image as your background—after all, the focus should be on the text in front of the image.

FIGURE 8.7

Choose colors that harmonize so they won't distract the reader from the real message of the page.

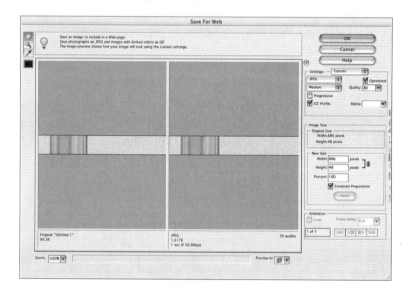

Making Transparent Images

If you've designed a custom background for your pages, or even just assigned them a color, the last thing you want is to paste down a graphic and have it show up in a white or colored square instead of on your page background. Figure 8.8 shows what this looks like.

To make a transparent GIF, follow these steps:

1. Place the object on a transparent background by selecting and deleting the current background, using an eraser to remove the background, or selecting the object and copying it to a new image file or a new layer that you have set up with a transparent background. (If you copy the object by itself to a layer that has a transparent background, you can remove the other layers in the file.) You'll know it's transparent when you see the gray checkerboard pattern. See Figure 8.9.

A graphic on a
nontransparent
background

8

FIGURE 8.8

This is one of biggest problems beginners face, and it's also one of the easiest to solve.

The same graphic
with transparency added

FIGURE 8.9

I copied this image to a new page with a transparent background.

2. Save the transparent version of the image as a GIF or PNG file using the File, Save for Web command, and then apply whatever tool your page assembly program uses to locate and place the image. In Netscape Composer, it's simply Insert, Image.

Making Pages Load Faster

The bottom line for making Web pages load faster is—you can't. The page will load only as fast as the server can send it and the recipient can receive it. Those are both factors beyond your control.

What you can do, though, is make sure that your page is arranged so that there's something to see while your graphics load. Bring up a Welcome headline first, and then add the background. If there's a graphic that will take some time to load, bring up a block of text before the graphic appears. The load time for the picture will seem much shorter if the person waiting has something else to read or think about. You can make these changes and others using your Web page editor.

Keep your images small or put up thumbnails and link the full-size pictures to them, so visitors have the option of waiting to see the big picture. Remember some people use text-based Web browsers or cell phones and don't see images at all. If the content of your picture is important, put a text description of it on the page, too. If you learn HTML, you can use the `alt` tag to place an image description in place of the image.

Creating a Web Gallery

Elements has an easy and elegant method of converting your stacks of photos into a Web-ready gallery that will display thumbnails of your pictures. Visitors clicking on a thumbnail will open up a full-page view of the image to appreciate it more fully. There are 14 different styles you can choose from, ranging from simple to elaborate. Bears is great for kid pictures, while Office is more businesslike, and Antique Paper is ideal for scanning in the old family album. Figure 8.10 shows a typical gallery page, as viewed from my Web browser. I chose the Horizontal Frame style, and selected pink for the background to best suit these little princesses.

To access this feature, choose File, Create Web Photo Gallery. You'll see the dialog box shown in Figure 8.11. First, though, make sure your pictures are all in one folder. Because they will be listed in alphabetical order by default, if you'd prefer some different arrangement, add numbers to the front of their filenames. Choose a gallery style from the Styles list and then click Browse and select your folder. Choose whether or not to include subfolders as well. Click Destination, and tell Elements where to place the completed gallery.

FIGURE 8.10

A photo gallery fit for a princess.

FIGURE 8.11

Select the gallery style and set other options from this dialog box.

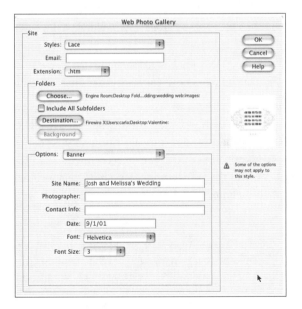

Some gallery styles have options; others do not. Here's a list of the options you may be able to set by selecting their category from the Options list:

- Banner—Enter information that will appear in the text banner at the top or bottom of the gallery. The site name appears in the browser's title bar.

- Large Images —Set the size of the images when they are selected from the home page, which displays the images as thumbnails. You can establish a size used for all images, or select a height or width, and allow the other dimension to be set proportionate to the image's original size. You can also select the JPEG quality used in the large displays. Add a border around the large version of each image by entering a value in the Border Size box. Select what you want to display as the title of the large image pages from the Title Use list.

- Thumbnails —Set the options for the home page, where images are displayed as thumbnails. Select a size for the thumbnails, add a border around each thumbnail with the Border Size box, and select a title for the thumbnail page(s) from the Title Use list. If you select the Simple, Table, or Web gallery style, choose the number of columns and rows for each thumbnail page.

- Custom Colors —Select the colors you want to use for each element of the gallery by clicking the appropriate color swatch and choosing a color from the Color Picker.

- Security —Protect your images from unauthorized use by selecting an option from the Content list. If you choose Custom, enter the text you want to use.

If you select the Table gallery style, you can choose your own graphic to use as the background if you like, by clicking the Background button. Click OK after choosing all your options to create the gallery. The home page opens in your browser so you can try out your creation. The destination folder you select will contain folders with the thumbnails and larger pictures, plus the HTML code to go into your Web page editor. Follow the usual procedures for adding pages to your Web site.

I find it easier to work with a folder that has only a few images in it, and to preview the results in my Web browser. Because Elements only has to prepare a few images, this process doesn't take very long. If I want to change some of the options after viewing them, I return to Elements and perform the steps again, making the changes I want to try out. Elements will ask you if you want to override your files, so click Yes to proceed. Repeat this process until you've created the perfect gallery, then copy all your images into the folder and perform these steps one last time to convert all the files.

Emailing a Picture

8

You might not want to share a ton of pictures with everyone on the planet. You just have one that you'd like to send to one special person, attached to an email. Elements can do this for you, without even making you open up your mail program yourself. Just open the picture you want to send, and then choose File, Attach to E-mail, or click the Attach to E-mail button. If the file isn't currently saved as a JPEG, you'll be asked whether you want it converted. You probably do, unless you're quite sure the recipient has the software to see it in whatever format you are sending.

Next your usual message window will open. The file is already attached, so all you need to add is the address, subject, and a message. Then click the Send button to send it off.

Summary

In this hour, we have taken a look at what we can do with pictures to make them ready for the Internet. You learned how to prepare images of all kinds for Web use, from photos to drawings to type. You learned about the formats that are compatible with Web browsers, and how to optimize an image for efficient Web use. You learned about custom backgrounds, and how to create and tile them. You learned about Elements' Web galleries, and finally how to attach a picture to your email. There's a lot more you can learn about Web graphics and Web design, and many good books from Sams Publishing to help you.

Q&A

Q I uploaded a bunch of pictures to my Web page, but they aren't showing up, not even as broken icons. They're all in a folder, and I added the name of the folder to the index page, but nothing happens. Why?

A Do you have placeholders for the images, and links to each picture by name? Probably not. Use the Web Photo Gallery to make up your page. Then use your Web page editor to add it to the site.

Q If I want to put my pictures on the Web, but only for my friends to see, can I protect them?

A There are lots of ways to do this. The easiest is to put them on a hidden page. This is a secondary page on your site, not linked to the first. Instead it has a separate address, such as `http://home.myservice.net/mypage/hidden.htm`. Give your friends the direct URL to this page. No one who doesn't know it's there will be able to reach it. However, "security through obscurity" is never a recommended policy for truly sensitive information or images. If you want to be more secure, you can learn enough JavaScript to password-protect the site. Look for

Sams Teach Yourself JavaScript in 24 Hours from Sams Publishing. It provides a good introduction to JavaScript.

Q If I'm emailing a file to a friend who has Photoshop, do I have to send it as a JPEG? I want her to be able to look at different layers.

A If you know she can read a native Photoshop file, go ahead and send one.

Workshop

Take a few moments to tackle the short quiz on Web formats below and check your answers to see how you did. Then work on the activity for extra credit.

Quiz

1. What do I have to do to a native Photoshop format file before I can put it on the Web?

    a. Attach a copyright notice

    b. Flatten the image and save it as a JPEG, GIF, or PNG file

    c. Get a model release on any recognizable people

2. HTML stands for

    a. Hypertext Markup Language

    b. Hand-coded Type Meta Language

    c. Hyperlinking Text Master Lookup Tables

3. It's legal to download other people's pictures and then change them around to make them mine.

    a. True

    b. False

Quiz Answers

1. b. (a. and c. are also a good idea.)

2. a.

3. b. You're violating copyright when you copy someone else's work, no matter what you then do to it.

Activity

Go Web surfing. Find some good graphics, and open your browser's View Source window to see how they were saved, as GIFs, JPEGs, or PNGs. If you find animated graphics, check out the source codes for these, too.

PART II
Simple Corrections

Hour

Hour 9

Cropping and Resizing Your Pictures

It would be pretty unusual to have your pictures come out of the camera perfectly composed, showing nothing more than the subject as you visualized it. Even the fanciest cameras, with the biggest and best zoom lenses can't always give you what you want. Maybe you're standing on a cliff, about to slide into the Grand Canyon, as I was in one of the examples that follow. Maybe there's something in the way of where you needed to stand to get that perfect shot. Maybe you just can't get close enough. (Those darned security guards…) Maybe you shot the picture as a landscape, and then found out you could sell the middle part as a magazine cover.

There are easy solutions for making the subject of the picture bigger, changing its orientation, getting rid of the junk at the edges, and generally improving the composition. And you'll learn them in this hour.

In this hour you will

- Remove unwanted parts of an image
- Change the size of an image
- Enlarge the working canvas
- Rotate an image

Cropping

Cropping is the artistic term for trimming away unwanted parts of a picture. You can think of it as a specialized kind of selection, which is probably why the people who created Elements put the Crop tool in the same toolbox section as the Selection Marquees (see Figure 9.1).

Crop tool

Crop tool
options

FIGURE 9.1

You can use the Crop tool to remove unwanted parts of an image.

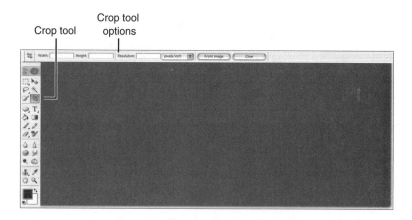

To crop part of an image, click the Crop tool. You can specify the width and/or height of the final image and its resolution by entering those values in the Options bar. To enter the values of the current image so that the final cropped image will use the same dimensions, click Front Image. Then click in the image and drag downward and to the right to select the area you want to crop. When you've selected the part of the image you want to keep, the Options bar changes, as you can see in Figure 9.2.

If needed, click Shield on the tool Options bar to make the uncropped area go dark, so that it's easier to see what will remain. You can adjust the color and opacity of the shield using the Options bar. Drag any of the boxes (handles) located around the edges of the selection to adjust the size of the cropped area. Rotate the selection by moving the mouse pointer outside the selection and dragging. You can also click in the middle of the

selection to adjust its position on the image. To crop the image, click the button labeled
with a check mark.

FIGURE 9.2

After cropping, the
Option bar changes.

You can also crop by making a selection with the Rectangular Marquee and
then choosing Image, Crop to trim the picture.

Task: Crop a Picture

To crop a picture, open any image and follow these steps:

1. Select the Crop tool from the toolbox or press **c** on the keyboard. (It looks like two
   overlapped pieces of L-shaped matboard—the same tool artists use to help compose paintings.)

2. Starting at the top-left corner of the selection, drag your mouse down and to the
   right, across the picture, while holding the mouse button down.

3. Notice the small boxes at the corners and midpoints of each side. These are *handles*. Drag the handles on the cropping box to make the box smaller or larger and
   fine-tune the selection. Click in the middle of the selection and move it around on
   the image. Rotate the bounding box. The area outside the box will be dimmed.

4. After you have the cropping box placed where you want it, double-click inside it
   to delete the area outside the box.

Remember, if you crop too much of the picture, you can undo what you have just done. If it's too late to undo because you have already done something else, just go back to the Undo History palette and click the uncropped picture. You can also choose File, Revert to go back to the last saved version of your picture. As long as you don't close the file, you can keep cropping and undoing it as much as you want.

Thinking About Good Composition

I can talk for days about what makes good composition, but I'll try to keep it to only a few minutes. By the way, you can see the photos that I'm talking about in this section in the color insert in the middle of the book. Please check them out.

Composition is what makes the difference between a merely good picture and a great one. Composing the picture correctly means making sure that the viewer sees the same scene that you, the artist, see. This should be important to you, because as an artist your task is to capture and share your unique vision of the world around you, whether it's the smile on your baby's face, the magnificence of the Grand Canyon at sunset, or a stormy day at the beach. How do you do this?

First of all, think about what you're seeing. If it's the smiling baby, where is he or she in relation to the camera? If she's halfway across the room, the real subject of the picture, which is the smile, is going to be lost in space. So, rule number one: Get close to small things. If you fill the frame with a baby's face, you'll get the full effect of the smile: flashing eyes, chubby pink cheeks, and those first few teeth peeking out. Use your zoom lens, if you have one, to come close without actually sticking the camera up the baby's nose. That would get rid of the smile in a hurry. Otherwise, crop the picture tightly.

Suppose, now, you are trying to get a shot of the Grand Canyon that expresses how big it is. You're standing at the railing at one of the many "scenic overlooks," staring downward a mile or so to the canyon bottom, and across to the other end of the canyon. It's a great view, but a lousy picture. Why? Well, when you're standing there, you can feel the space around you. You can look down at your feet, and then keep looking down and outward just a little, and the next horizontal surface is a long way down . If you're like me, you find yourself hanging onto the fence. If the picture is going to work, you need to find a way to provide some sense of "out there, back here." In other words, perspective.

To help give a sense of perspective, sometimes I bring a tree branch when I go out to shoot landscapes. My husband or a friend can hold it right at the edge of my shot. That helps define the difference between "here" and "there." (It's cheating, of course, but it works.) Because I didn't have a branch with me on this particular trip, I moved on to the next overlook. This one had a patch of snow on the ground, and a nice old tree right next to the fence, with a nice collection of distant rocks blazing with color as the sun started to go down. The tree gave me the sense of perspective I wanted, and the colors on the rocks were an additional bonus. Rule two: if your subject is space, keep it in perspective. Rule two and a half: Be patient.

The ancient Greeks brought us the third, and final, rule of composition. They called it the "Rule of Thirds" (being Greek, they pronounced it rather differently). It works by applying geometry to discover the ideal placement of the center of interest within a picture. If you divide the shape of the picture into thirds horizontally and vertically, you'll have four spots where the lines intersect (see Figure 9.3).

FIGURE 9.3

These four spots are where your eye naturally goes.

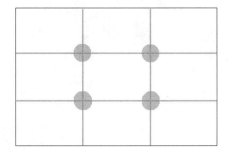

Open any of your best pictures and check them out. Chances are good that if the subject isn't centered, it's touching one of these four spots. I've superimposed this grid on one of my own favorite shots in Figure 9.4, and the upper right dot hits the pussycat right in the ear. (Actually, she's a Siberian Lynx and would not be amused at anyone bopping her in the ear or elsewhere.) You can see her without the grid in the color insert.

Your eye is naturally drawn to certain objects more than others. From the moment he's born, a baby seeks to identify faces, his mother's first, and then others. That remains true for the rest of our lives. We also look for contrasts: a man-made object against natural ones, something radically different in color from its surroundings, anything that seems "out of place." Psychologists have tested this over and over again, theorizing it's a survival skill of some sort. The tests also prove that we first look in the four intersections of thirds, and then in the middle of a page. They've found this to be valid about 75% of the time. And I'm not going to argue with a psychologist.

FIGURE 9.4
Pretty darn close to the magic spot.

Resizing

Elements make it easy to change the size of the picture, or of anything in it. This is often necessary. For instance, say you import pictures from a digital camera and accidentally set them to import at 72 dpi. If you have one of the current multi megapixel cameras, your picture can easily be 14×17 inches or more.

You have two options: resizing the image or resizing the canvas. Resizing the image makes the picture bigger or smaller. Resizing the canvas makes the picture *area* bigger, while leaving the image floating within it. You'd do this if you need more space around an object without shrinking the actual image.

Resizing an Image

In Hour 3, "Starting and Saving Your Work," I talked about changing resolution. The resolution of an image is measured by the number of pixels it contains per inch. Obviously, the more pixels per inch, the more data, and the clearer the image. Resolution and size are tied together. If you increase the resolution of an image, shrinking the pixels so that there are more of them per inch, the image's size is shrunk as well. If you want to have your cake and eat it too (that is, increase the resolution of an image [the number of pixels per inch] while maintaining its size), Elements has to come up with more pixels per inch than actually exist. It does so through a process called *sampling*—educated guesswork, as it were.

To resize an image, open the Image Size dialog box (shown in Figure 9.5) by choosing Image, Resize, Image Size. Here's where you decide whether or not you want to resample—that is, add more pixels to an image based on the colors of the neighboring pixels. Resampling typically results in a loss of clarity, or general fuzziness, but you have to weigh that against your intentions. If you want a higher resolution in order to get a better printout, but the printout will be no good to you if the image is 2 inches by 2 inches, you'll have to resample. But if you don't care about the final dimensions of an image and you just want good quality, don't resample.

After opening the Image Size dialog box, turn on or off the Resample Image option as desired. Resampling, by the way, will either enlarge or reduce a file's size, depending on whether the image size increases or decreases. If you turn on Resample Image, select the type of resampling you want Elements to use—see Hour 3 for a complete description of each option.

In this dialog box, you can see the pixel dimensions in pixels (logically) or percentages, by choosing the appropriate option from the pop-up menu. If you turn off the Resample Image option, however, the Pixel Dimensions area becomes grayed, because you won't be changing the total number of pixels. Regardless of whether you're resampling or not, you can still enter the desired image print size (in the Document Size section of the dialog box) in inches, centimeters, points, picas, or columns; you can also set percentages by selecting that option from the pop-up menus. As I mentioned earlier, if your desire is to change the resolution and not bother with the resulting image size, you can adjust the Resolution value instead. Of course, if the Resample Image option is turned on, changing either the image size or its resolution will result in a change in the total number of pixels (and the file size).

The easiest way to enlarge or reduce the image is to make sure that the Constrain Proportions option is checked at the bottom of the dialog box, and then simply enter a value in any one of the fields and click OK. As if by magic, the other numbers will change to give you the correct matching values. Changing the percentage to 200% doubles the size of the picture, for example. Unfortunately, if you choose to also resample in order to maintain the current resolution, it more than triples the file size.

As you make changes in the Image Size dialog box, Elements will automatically update the file size at the top of the dialog box so you'll know before you commit to a change how that change will affect your file's size.

9

FIGURE 9.5

The Image Size dialog box allows you to resize your image.

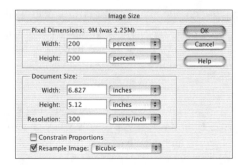

If you resample an image and it looks fuzzy, try using the Unsharp Mask filter (described in Hour 11, "Removing Red Eye, Dust, and Scratches") to bring it into better focus.

Resizing a Canvas

Resizing the canvas to a larger size gives you extra workspace around the image; it does not change the size of the image. Because resizing uses the current background color to fill in the added space, be sure that it's a color you want. I always resize with white as the background color. Resizing the canvas to a smaller size is another way of cropping the picture by decreasing the canvas area. It's not recommended because you can accidentally lose part of the picture and not be able to recover it.

To resize the canvas, open the Canvas Size dialog box by choosing Image, Resize, Canvas Size and specify the height and width you want the canvas to be (see Figure 9.6). You can specify any of the measurement systems you prefer on the pop-up menu, as you saw in the Image Size dialog box earlier. Photoshop calculates and displays the new file size as soon as you enter the numbers. If you turn on the Relative option, you can enter the size of the border you want. For example, if you enter 2 inches in the Width box, the edge of the canvas is set 1 inch from the sides of the image (for a total of 2 inches). Enter the same value in the Height box, and you have a nice, even border around the image that you can fill with color or pattern to create a frame.

Use the anchor proxy to determine where the image will be placed within the canvas. Click in the middle to center the image on the enlarged canvas, or in any of the other boxes to place it relative to the increased canvas area. When you're ready, click OK to change the canvas size.

FIGURE 9.6

By adding an inch to the size of the canvas, I've given it a 1/2-inch border all around.

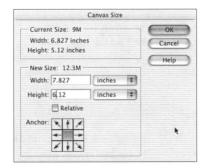

Resizing a Portion of an Image

You can also resize a portion of any image. To do so, first select the object or a piece of an image to be resized, using the most convenient Selection tool. With the selection marquee active, choose Image, Resize, Scale. This places a bounding box that looks like the cropping box around your selected object (see Figure 9.7). Drag any of the corner handles on the box to change the size of the object/image within the selected area while holding down the Shift key to maintain its proportions. If you drag the side handles of the box, you'll stretch the selection's height or width accordingly. If you don't like having to hold down the Shift key as you drag, you can click the Maintain Aspect Ratio button on the Options bar to maintain the proportions of the image/object within the selection. You can also enter a percentage in the Width and/or Height boxes on the Options bar to resize the selection without dragging.

FIGURE 9.7

Remember to keep the Shift key pressed to retain the proportions.

You can resize everything on an entire layer if you choose Select, Deselect to deselect everything first, then activate the layer you want to resize, and choose Image, Resize, Scale.

Rotating an Image

Under the Image, Rotate menu shown in Figure 9.8, you've got more ways to turn things around than you're likely to ever need. However, if you have a scanned picture or a digital camera image that should be vertical but opens as a horizontally oriented picture, you'll need these rotation options to straighten things out. Actually, this is a common occurrence when you use a scanner because it's usually quicker to scan with the picture horizontal, regardless of its normal orientation.

FIGURE 9.8

More flips than a gymnast....

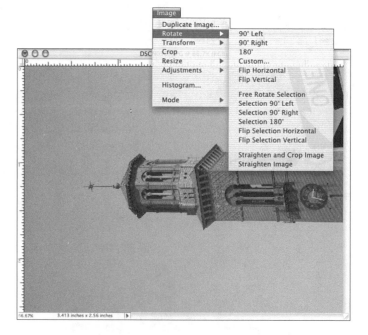

Choose 90° clockwise (right) or counterclockwise (left) to straighten up a sideways image, or 180° if you somehow brought in a picture upside down. Until I realized that my new scanner worked backwards from the old one, I did that a lot.

Flipping Images

Flipping is not just for pancakes. The Flip options on the Rotate menu allow you to flip an image vertically or horizontally, as if it were a piece of paper. If you have a picture of a girl facing left, for example, and you flip it horizontally, she'll face right. This might come in handy if you need her to look at some text or something on a page that's located to the right of her image. If you flip the image vertically instead, she'll stand on her head!

Sometimes you need to flip an image before you print it, so it will read correctly. For instance, suppose you're making a sign printed on acetate, which is transparent. If you simply print it as is, the ink can come off when anyone touches the sign. If you flip the text horizontally first, then print it on the back of the acetate so that the text is read through the acetate, the ink is protected by whatever you have mounted the sign on. You can even sponge off the fingerprints left by those wise guys who try to scratch it and fail.

If you want to print to a T-shirt iron-on, as shown in Figure 9.9, the image actually gets flipped twice, once in Elements before you print it and again as it is ironed face down on the shirt. When you are finished, it reads correctly.

FIGURE 9.9

Sometimes you have to flip images.

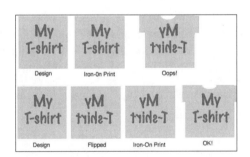

You can rotate and flip a selection or layer instead of an entire image if you want. Just select the area/layer you want to flip or rotate, then choose one of the flip/rotate selection commands from the Image, Rotate menu. Remember this feature. It will come in very handy when you start making composites of elements from several different pictures. For instance, you can make a quick reflection of an object by copying it onto a second layer and then flipping the copy (the layer) vertically. You can create a cool reflection effect by using a combination of flipping and skewing type. See Hour 10, "Straightening Skews and Leveling Horizons," for details. The Free Rotate Selection/Layer option is also discussed in Hour 10.

Rotating by Degrees

To rotate the image by something other than a right angle, choose Image, Rotate, Custom to open a dialog box such as the one shown in Figure 9.10. Enter the number of degrees to rotate. If you're not sure, guess. You can always undo or reopen the box and rotate more, or even change the direction if needed. Click the radio button to indicate the rotational direction: right or left. Then click OK to perform the rotation.

FIGURE 9.10

You can even rotate by fractions of a degree.

Straightening Images

The last two items on the Rotate menu are the Straighten and Crop Image command and the Straighten Image command. You might use one of these commands to straighten an image that was scanned in rather crookedly, but you should be careful when using them. I don't know what criteria Adobe's creative department used to determine whether an image is straight. These two commands are "automatic" and just happen while you wait. However, they don't seem to work very effectively. If repeated often enough, or if your horizon's just a tiny bit tilted, the Straighten Image command might eventually get you flattened out, but it works in very small increments. One trick that helps is to increase the canvas size first, so that Elements has a better idea where the edges of the image are.

Still, it's much quicker and easier to do the job yourself. In the next hour, you'll learn how.

Summary

This hour talked about cropping, resizing, and rotating your images. When you crop, you actually trim away the unneeded parts of the picture. Cropping can make a big difference in the composition, by encouraging the viewer to look at what you want her to see. You can also convert a picture by careful cropping from landscape to portrait orientation, or to a square, a long rectangle or another shape. Resizing the image makes it bigger or smaller on the screen and for printing. Resizing the canvas enables more room around the image, so you can add other things to it as well. Finally, you learned how to rotate an image or a portion of it when needed, to correct errors or to create interesting effects.

Q&A

Q Is there a difference between rotating 180° and flipping vertically?

A Yes. Imagine a playing card with a dot painted on the upper-left corner. If you rotate it 180°, the dot goes to the lower-right corner. If you flip it, the dot ends up in the lower-left corner (and you'll be looking at the back of the card).

Q How can I deselect *part* of a selection before I rotate it?

A The easiest way to do this is to press Option (Mac) or Alt (Windows) with the Selection tool active. You will see a small minus symbol next to the Selection tool. Select the part of the selection to deselect, and it is removed from the selection and added back to the picture.

Q I added an inch to the height and width of the canvas. Why did I only get a half-inch border around it?

A The image stayed centered, so half of the inch you added went to each side. If you wanted a one-inch border, you'd have had to add two inches, one for each side.

Workshop

Take a few moments to tackle the short quiz on cropping and image composition and check your answers to see how you did. Then work on the activity for extra credit.

Quiz

1. To crop a picture
    a. Use a selection tool, and press Delete.
    b. Use the cropping tool to drag a bounding box around the area you want to keep, and double-click inside the box you've placed.
    c. Use a selection tool and choose Image, Crop.

2. What do you look at first in a photo?
    a. Faces
    b. Colors
    c. The horizon

Quiz Answers

1. b. or c.

2. a. if you believe the psychologists.

Activity

Most pictures can be improved by careful cropping. Try this experiment. Cut two L-shaped pieces from a sheet of white or neutral gray paper or cardboard, and lay them on top of one of your printed pictures, as shown in Figure 9.11.

FIGURE 9.11
How to make a cropping frame.

Use these pieces as a cropping frame and look at your snapshots or at pictures in a magazine to see how different cropping affects the picture. Try finding long, narrow compositions, square ones, and rectangles.

Hour 10

Straightening, Skewing, and Distorting an Image

You've probably seen hundreds of snapshots of buildings that look like they could easily tip over and horizons that appear to run downhill. It happens, and most of the time it's unavoidable. The photographer may have been standing on the deck of a bouncing boat, or on the side of a hill. The "tiltin' Hilton" effect is caused not by shoddy construction but by wide-angle lenses that make vertical objects at the edges of the photo lean toward the middle. What separates pros from amateurs is that pros know how to fix these little details, and they never show off their work without doing whatever it takes to make the picture perfect.

In this hour you will

- Level your horizons
- Straighten selected areas of an image
- Skew and distort images
- Change your perspective
- Put an image in a blender

Straightening the Horizon

The crooked horizon line is one of the most common problems, and one of the easiest to fix.

Open an image that needs straightening. Figure 10.1, my example, can be downloaded from this book's page on the Sams Publishing Web site.

FIGURE 10.1
The horizon should not run downhill.

1. With an image that's right up against the edges of the window like this one, it's typically easier to change the zoom level (and thus the size of the image in the window) to give you room to work. To do this, change the zoom percentage to a smaller number, drag the window border outwards, or simply maximize the window.

2. Choose Image, Rotate, Free Rotate Layer. You'll be asked if you want to change the layer from a background layer to an ordinary one; click OK. Click OK again to finish the job.

3. Now you're ready to straighten the image. Move the pointer off the image and onto the canvas, and it will change to the rotation pointer, which is curved almost in a circle. Drag in the direction you want the image to move, until the part that should be horizontal (in this case, the horizon) is parallel to the top of the screen.

4. When you're happy with the results, click the check mark button on the Options bar to commit your change.

5. With the Crop tool, crop away any revealed edges or other leftovers, as in Figure 10.2. You should now have a nice photo in which the ocean doesn't look as if it's falling off the Earth.

FIGURE 10.2
When we're done with this, you won't get sea-sick looking at it.

10

If you try this with an image of your own, you'll need to get the photo off the background layer just as we did in the example, because Elements can't straighten a background. Sometimes, you can simply choose Image, Rotate, Free Rotate Layer, and Elements will ask if you want to move the image from the background to a layer (as it did in our example), but if that doesn't happen to you and the Free Rotate command is unavailable, simply drag the image from the layer palette into a new file, which causes Elements to place the image on its own layer (and not a background layer). If your image has multiple layers and you want to straighten them in one step, link them by clicking the bottommost layer in the palette, and clicking the icon immediately to the left of each layer you want to link.

Remember that you can always attempt to straighten an image (even if it's on the background layer) with the Image, Rotate, Straighten Image command. It works in a lot of cases, but as I mentioned last hour, sometimes it makes things worse.

Use this same procedure any time you have to fix something that's out of kilter, vertically or horizontally. The same trick was applied to a steeple in Figure 10.3. If you have trouble telling when it's straight, add a layer to the picture and draw a line across or down as needed. Use a brush about 3 pixels wide and a nice, bright color; hold down the Shift key as you draw the line so it stays straight. When you're finished, just drag the layer with the line onto the Trash button at the bottom of the Layers palette. Don't flatten the image until you have gotten rid of the line.

FIGURE 10.3

The green line gives me something to line it up against.

Straightening an Image

Frequently, you need to straighten just part of the picture. It might be a perspective problem, or perhaps the furniture really *is* crooked. Antiques frequently lean a little. In the example below, I love the effect of the wide-angle lens on the car, but not on those brass posts holding up the rope around it. My choices are to get rid of the posts and the rope, which would be a lot of work, or to straighten the posts. Being lazy, my course is clear. I'll just fix the posts. Figure 10.4 shows the basic car.

FIGURE 10.4
The brass posts don't look right.

The posts lean in different directions, so I'll have to fix them separately. First, select one. The magnetic lasso is ideal for this job. After tracing carefully around the post, I can use the Image, Rotate, Free Rotate Selection command to make it vertical. Figure 10.5 shows this step.

Now all I need to do is fill in where it was. The Clone Stamp tool is a good choice for this job. I cover it in more detail in Hour 11, "Removing Red Eye, Dust, and Scratches," so here I'll just gloss over the details so you can get the idea of how I used it to fix my photo. Two preparations will help you use the Clone Stamp tool. First, zoom in close enough to see what you are doing. This sounds obvious, but many people forget about the magnifying glass and just squint or leave nose prints on the monitor. Press Z to select the zoom tool and click the part you want to see close up.

FIGURE 10.5
Just a little kick to the left and it's straight again.

When you need to work in close quarters replacing a background, as you often do when using the Clone Stamp, a second trick for making your work easier is to select the area you need to work on. Use the Magic Wand and click in the open area to select. Once the area is selected, it's as if you'd masked everything around it: You can stamp like crazy and only the selected area will pick up the color. Figure 10.6 shows the selection trick applied to a zoomed-in section of the car.

FIGURE 10.6
Working only on the selection is much easier.

On the car image, if I crop off the tilting signs and the other post on the far left, I can forget about the red velvet rope and leave the rest of the photo as is, at least for now. Figure 10.7 and the color section both show the final picture.

10

FIGURE 10.7
The picture is all done and much less distorted.

Skewing Images

A certain amount of confusion surrounds skewing, distorting, and changing perspective. Which is which? Skewing allows you to tilt any side of an object, selection, or entire layer. For example, you can use skew to tilt a building to the left, and create your own Tower of Pisa. Distortion allows you to pull at the corners of a shape, selection, or layer, and stretch it in that direction. Use distortion to really twist a shape. If you use distortion on the bottom of our building, you can make the bottom seem really wide or really skinny. If you use distortion on a person's face, you can create the kind of effect you typically see in carnival mirrors. When you change an object's perspective, you change where it appears in 3-dimensional space. With perspective, you can make a building seem to fall toward you or away from you. You can make a building that was shot straight on seem as if you're viewing it from a corner across the street.

Figure 10.8 compares these three techniques on a simple rectangle. You can apply the skew technique to text as well. To distort or change the perspective of type, you must simplify the layer it is on, which of course makes the type uneditable. To do this, select the type layer and choose Layer, Simplify Layer. For more fun with text, see Hour 6, "Adding Type," for tips on how to warp text within a shape.

FIGURE 10.8

Skewing, distorting, and changing perspective are very similar, yet different.

Select what you want to skew: shape, selection, or layer. Then choose Image, Transform, Skew. A bounding box appears, with small handles along its sides. *Do not touch any of the corner handles, because that will distort the image instead of skewing it.* To skew, drag any one of the middle handles along the side. If you select a building, for example, you can click the handle in the middle of its top side, drag it to the left, and tilt the building toward its left side. To apply the setting, click the check mark button, double-click inside the selection, or press Enter/Return.

Task: Create Text and Its Shadow

Let's combine the flip techniques from last hour with the skew techniques to create some text and its reflection. Start off with a new image, using the default size, white background, and RGB.

1. Use the Horizontal Type tool to type your name in whatever color you like. I chose Times New Roman, 72 pt, red type.

2. Create a duplicate of the type layer by choosing Layer, Duplicate Layer.

3. With the Move tool, move the duplicate type away from your original so you can see it. Because it will serve as the shadow, move the text directly below the original.

4. Choose Image, Rotate, Flip Layer Vertical to flip the text upside down.

5. Darken the shadow text a bit by clicking the Text tool and choosing a darker color from the color picker on the Options bar.

6. Now you're ready to skew the shadow text to make it look more like a shadow. Choose Image, Transform, Skew. Click the middle handle on the bottom of the text selection (the top of the text letters), and drag it to the right, tilting the shadow text in that direction. The result should look something like Figure 10.9.

FIGURE 10.9

Me and my shadow.

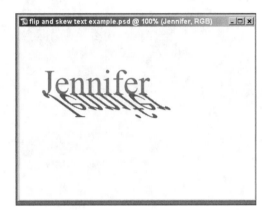

10

7. Name your file My Name.psd and save it. We'll do some more work on it later in this hour.

Distorting Images

Distortion, as I explained in the last section, lets you pull the corner bounding boxes in any direction, and even cross over the other edge to put a twist in the object. Distorting can also help you put someone on an instant diet or—if you're mean—add a bunch of pounds.

In Figure 10.10, the woman is as she was. In Figure 10.11, I used the Distort command to shrink her down a size or two and also retouched her chin. Because I selected her before doing the distortion, the background remained the same. I just moved her back on top of it when I finished shrinking her.

To apply distortion, select a layer, shape, or area, then choose Image, Transform, Distort. The bounding box appears; drag a corner handle to pull the image in that direction, distorting it. I pulled the two corner handles at the top of the selection of the woman inward, to make her head skinnier. I pulled in the two lower corners as well, but not as much, so that the shape was a sort of triangle with a flat top. Then I touched up her chin using techniques you'll learn in upcoming hours. Of course, if I had pulled the corners of the selection outward or inward by a large amount, or twisted them over each other, I could have really distorted the features of her face, but I was trying to achieve something more realistic, so I went slowly and made minor adjustments.

FIGURE 10.10
This is before...

FIGURE 10.11
...and this is after.

Changing the Perspective of an Image

Changing perspective is a way to salvage some of those unfortunate pictures that the camera just couldn't handle. In Figure 10.12, I was obviously standing much too close to the building I wanted to photograph. This image can still be saved, believe it or not. I just need to put it in perspective.

To change the perspective of a selection, shape, or layer, select it, then choose Image, Transform, Perspective. The bounding box appears again. Drag a corner handle, and this time, the perspective changes (the opposite handle moves in the opposite direction). When you're through, click the check mark button on the Options bar.

> You can skew, distort, and change the perspective of a selection, shape, or layer in one step by choosing Image, Transform, Free Transform. You can also rotate and scale (resize) the selection, shape, or layer while Free Transform is turned on.

10

I'm going to use perspective and rotation to fix my photo. In case you'd like to work along, the original photo is at the book's page on the Sams Publishing Web site.

FIGURE 10.12
Is the building falling over backward, or am I?

Task: Fix Perspective

1. The first step is to correct the perspective so all the columns are pointing the same way. Zoom out, as I have, so you will have some elbow room. Select the entire picture, and then select Image, Transform, Perspective. You'll be asked whether you want to convert the layer; you do, so click OK twice. When the bounding box appears, drag a lower corner inward until the columns are more or less parallel. See Figure 10.13.

FIGURE 10.13

When I drag one corner, the opposite one moves with it.

2. Then, simply switch to Free Transform by choosing Image, Transform, Free Transform, and rotate it until it's vertical. You'll have some corners showing, as in Figure 10.14.

FIGURE 10.14

When you rotate a picture, blank corners are almost inevitable.

3. Either crop them out or do as I did, and fill them in with the Clone Stamp tool (a tool that copies surrounding pixels to fill in gaps—you'll learn to use it in Hour 11). Figure 10.15 shows the final, much-improved version.

FIGURE 10.15
Special cameras made for shooting architecture let you make these corrections when you take the picture by tilting the film. This is easier.

Liquify an Image

It's cheating a little bit to put this one here instead of with the filters, but Adobe used to list it in the Image menu in Photoshop 6, so I'm going to stick with tradition and include it here. Besides, it's so much fun, you shouldn't have to wait another eleven hours to try it. A *filter*, by the way, is a series of commands that, when applied to a layer or selection, change its appearance in some manner. If you look at a person's face through a sheer yellow cloth, for example, that person's face looks fuzzier and a bit more yellow. That's essentially what a filter does.

You can select from any of the filters in Elements to produce a wide range of interesting effects.

Liquify is similar to a program that was popular several years ago called *Goo*. It lets you distort things, not geometrically, but pixel by pixel, exactly as if you were dragging your finger through wet paint. And it has a few other tricks up its sleeves as well. Let's look at Figure 10.16.

FIGURE 10.16

Liquifying can put your image through a blender, or just scrunch it a little. It's up to you.

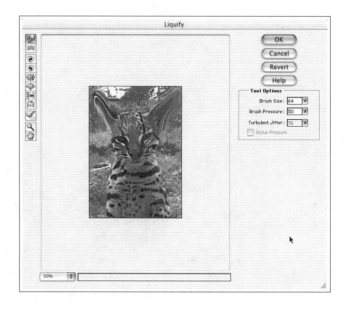

To start, select the layer or area you want to liquify. (To liquify a text layer, you must simplify it first using the Layer, Simplify Layer command.) Then choose Filter, Distort, Liquify. The Liquify interface, shown in Figure 10.16, takes over your screen for the duration. For demonstration purposes, I just created a simple squiggle, but you can liquify anything or anyone. Liquify has its own toolbox with shortcuts that are the same letters used for different tools on the Elements toolbox, which might be confusing. For example, *W* opens the Magic Wand tool in Elements, but it gets you the Warp tool in Liquify. Figure 10.17 shows the Liquify toolbox with its tool names and shortcuts. Note that tool options for changing brush diameter, pressure, and turbulence jitter are also present.

FIGURE 10.17

Be careful with the shortcuts or just click the individual tools to select them.

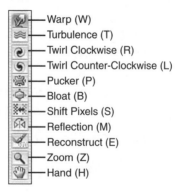

The Warp tool is the easiest to master. It works by pushing pixels forward as you move the mouse. Its effect depends not only on brush size and pressure, but on how quickly you move your mouse or tablet stylus. To set the brush size and brush pressure for any of the tools, adjust the appropriate value in the Tool Options section, located on the right. Larger numbers get you a bigger brush/more pressure. In Figure 10.18, I used the Warp tool with the same brush size but (from left to right) moved fast, slow, and very slow. You can easily see the difference.

FIGURE 10.18

Don't try this with a trackball. It's too frustrating.

10

With a bigger brush size and the Warp tool, you can gently push out the sides of buildings, puff up a kid's cheeks as if he's about to blow out a candle, or draw interesting swirls. Using a smaller brush, you can create smaller effects such as a gentle ripple in a patch of water on a sidewalk, or a little more fullness in someone's hair.

Turbulence is unpredictable. Ask a pilot (or anyone who's flown into Denver airport, home of bouncy landings). Use the turbulence tool to blend surrounding pixels, creating misty effects such as fire, clouds, ocean waves, and smoke. The effect reminds me of mixing melted chocolate into cake batter—it takes a lot of mixing to thoroughly blend the two. To lessen the blending effect, lower the Turbulent Jitter value in the Tool Options area. Using this tool to blend pixels depends not only on speed, but also on direction—whether you're going in the natural direction of the image, or across it. You simply have to practice with it. Fortunately, when experiments go awry, Liquify has a Revert button that will take you right back to the beginning of your adventure.

Let me stop here to make a quick plea for you to get yourself a graphics tablet. I highly recommend any of the Wacom line, but your best bet is to go to your local computer store and try out everything on display. That's what they are there for. Of course, when I do that, I always go back and check prices online to see if I can get a better deal on the same item. Still, I've never walked out of CompUSA or MicroCenter without buying something. Too many toys, too little time …

Twirls are fun. After selecting one of the Twirl tools, simply place the mouse where you want a twirl and hold the button down. Watch as it slowly twirls pixels clockwise (when you use Twirl Clockwise) or counterclockwise (when you use Twirl Counter-Clockwise). Release the mouse when you've had enough. The trick here is to hold still if you want an even twirl. Dragging with a Twirl tool softens the twirls, making them almost mushy. Figure 10.19 shows the effect of using both Twirl tools on my line.

FIGURE 10.19

The Twirl tools swirl the pixels at the point where you click.

Puckers and bloats also work best if you hold the mouse still. Preset the brush to the size of the bubble you want for a bloat or pucker, then hold the button down and let it happen. If you use the Pucker tool, Elements moves pixels towards the click point, like your skin when you pucker your mouth. You can drag the Pucker tool down a section of an image to shrink it into itself, but drag slowly. These changes take a while, especially on older or slower computers. It might not look like a big deal on the screen, but a whole lot of math is going on. If you drag the Pucker tool along a person's cheek, you can make her face thinner. Bloat works the opposite way; pixels are pushed away from where you click, like your skin when you puff your cheeks. Drag the Bloat tool along a person's cheek, and her face will appear larger and more bloated.

The Shift Pixels and Reflection tools are even less predictable than turbulence. Shift Pixels pushes pixels away from the drag path, in a perpendicular direction, to the left or upwards. If you press Cmd/Alt while dragging, they'll move to the right or downward. The Reflection tool copies pixels to create a reflection. Drag in a direction perpendicular to the item you're trying to reflect. For example, to reflect a child onto a mirror above him, drag above his head. To reflect that same child onto an imaginary mirror to his left, drag on his right side. To cast the reflection in the opposite direction (down or to the right) press Cmd/Alt when dragging.

Earlier, I mentioned that you can completely remove the effects of Liquify by clicking the Revert button. To remove an effect from part of your image (either partially or totally), use the Reconstruct tool. Simply drag over the area you want to affect—drag slowly to remove an effect more completely. To completely remove all effects in a direct line between two points, click at the beginning and then Shift+click at the end. On the other hand, if you like what you've done, click OK to close the Liquify dialog box and apply your changes.

Like so many tools, Liquify can seem intimidating. But if you start with something simple, you can end up with something not too scary. If you start with something complex, you can end up with the most amazing results. If you like abstract art, this is a great way to use up some of those pictures that didn't come out right the first time around. Figure 10.20 shows what happened when I "melted" a photo of a bowl of gumdrops with the Warp tool and added a couple other familiar objects. In Figure 10.21, I took the same art and went many steps further. Please see these, and a couple other liquify examples in the color section.

FIGURE 10.20

Melted gumdrops, a pocket watch, and a fifty cent piece.

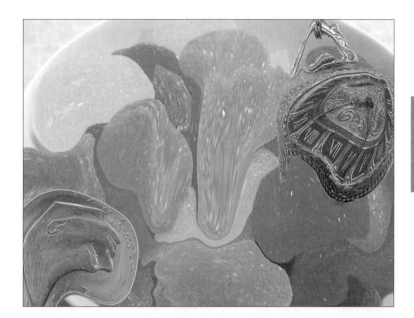

10

FIGURE 10.21

Now the objects are almost unrecognizable.

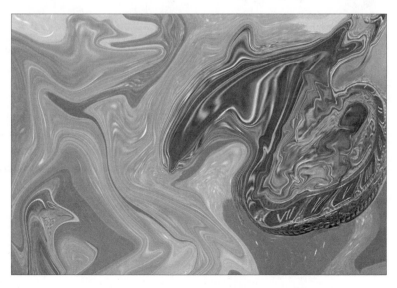

Task: Reflecting Text

Now that you've learned a bit about the Liquify filter, we'll use it to change our earlier text and shadow example to an example of text reflected in imaginary water.

1. Open the My name.psd file you created in the task titled "Create Text and Its Shadow."

2. Select the shadow text layer.

3. Choose Filter, Distort, Liquify. You'll be asked whether you want to simplify the layer. Click OK to continue.

4. Click the Warp tool. Because our text is so small, set the brush size to 1. Set the brush pressure to 50.

5. Drag the mouse through the text in a swirling pattern until you get the effect you like, and then click OK to save it.

6. Your image probably looks something like the one shown in Figure 10.22.

FIGURE 10.22

Text reflected in a "pool" of water.

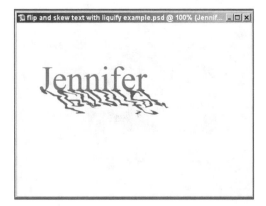

Summary

This has been a warped and twisted hour. First, you learned to straighten horizons, roofs, poles, or anything that should be horizontal or vertical and isn't. You learned about the Skew, Distort, and Perspective commands and how to apply them to both objects and entire images. You also saw what they can do for type. Then, sticking with the theme of distortion, you learned how to use the Liquify filter.

Q&A

Q **The thing I need to straighten isn't straight. It should be at a 45° angle. I just can't seem to rotate it the right amount. Any ideas?**

A Do you know you can draw a line at precisely that angle? Hold down the Shift key, and drag a line at approximately that angle. It will magically snap between 45°, 90°, and 180°. If you are using it as a guideline, be sure to keep it on a separate layer that you can hide or discard.

Q **How can I use Liquify to make a swirling, Art Deco kind of background?**

A Start with a gradient with the appropriate colors. (You'll learn about gradients in Hour 22, "Creating Art from Scratch.") Then, select Filter, Distort, Liquify; select a big brush, and swirl with either of the Twirl tools until you like what you have.

10

Workshop

Take a few moments to tackle the short quiz on straightening, distorting, and perspective below and check your answers to see how you did. Then work on the activities for extra credit.

Quiz

1. Before you straighten an entire photo, what should you do?

   a. Save it.

   b. Zoom out so you have room to rotate it.

   c. Copy it to a new layer.

2. To make something straight when you rotate it, line it up with

   a. The edge of the computer screen.

   b. The edge of the frame

   c. The edge of the bounding box

   d. A guideline you've already drawn.

3. You can liquify one layer and leave the background "normal."

   a. True

   b. False

Quiz Answers

1. b. But a. is never a bad idea, either.

2. b. or d. Either works.

3. a. True. Liquify affects layers one at a time, or merged, depending on what you hope to achieve.

Activities

1. Time to play. Take a colorful picture and liquify it until it's just pure colors. Have fun, but pay attention to what the tools are doing. Work on a copy, of course, so you don't lose your original. While playing around, use the Reconstruct tool to remove an effect.

2. Take a picture with a deliberate perspective problem, such as standing too close to a tall subject, tilting the camera while shooting, or shooting an object from very far away with a zoom lens. Then import the image into Elements and use what you've learned this hour to fix it.

HOUR 11

Removing Red Eye, Dust, and Scratches

Good photos can suffer from a host of easily fixed problems. Dust and scratches are most common on old pictures, and particularly on scans of them. Red eye is seen mainly on pictures taken with a flash camera, but it can happen at any time, if the subject's eye catches the sun or an indoor light. And nearly every picture needs a little bit of cleanup, especially outdoor shots that can be spoiled by litter on the ground, dead leaves, or whatever is there that shouldn't be. If you didn't have the foresight, or a flexible assistant, to remove the "schmutz" before you took the picture, you can still take it out in Elements. All you need is patience and a steady hand.

In this hour you will

- Clean up small problems on photos
- Get the red eye out
- Remove dust and small scratches from photos

Making Basic Cleanups

The basic cleanup should be your first step when working on any picture. Study the picture. Ask yourself some questions:

- Would cropping help improve the composition? If so, see Hour 9, "Cropping and Resizing Your Pictures," for help.

- Is it crooked? Do you need to straighten the whole picture or just a piece of something? Jump between Hours 9 and 10, "Straightening, Skewing, and Distorting an Image," for solutions.

- Is there something in there that doesn't belong? If the unwanted element in your picture is large, skip to Hour 19, "Creating Art from Scratch," to learn how to use the Eraser tools to remove it. If it's a small item that's wandered into the background, stay tuned to this hour, where you'll learn how to remove it with the Clone Stamp.

- If it's a scanned photo, was the glass in the scanner clean? You can pick up dust, pet or human hair, and all sorts of scuzz in your pictures if you don't keep the scanning surface clean. Find out how to remove dust, hairs, and similar small items in this hour.

Here's a photo I just scanned for these examples (see Figure 11.1). It was shot about eight or nine years ago when the Tall Ships came to Boston. This is the training ship Esmeralda, a four-masted schooner from Chile.

FIGURE **11.1**
At close to 370 feet long, I barely got her in the frame.

As you can see, this is definitely in need of some cleaning up. First, I'll crop out the black edges from the scanner. It looks pretty straight, so we won't mess with rotating it. However, if you look carefully, you'll see that the black speck between the two middle masts is a helicopter. It's not big enough to see clearly, so we'll take it out with the Clone Stamp (I'll show you exactly how to do so in a minute). Figure 11.2 shows this step completed.

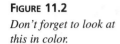

Figure 11.2

Don't forget to look at this in color.

Removing Small Objects with the Clone Stamp Tool

When small objects wander into your photographs uninvited, use the Clone Stamp to get rid of them. The Clone Stamp works by copying the color of nearby pixels onto the pixels you drag over with the tool. So to fix my photo, I used the tool to copy the colors of the sky nearby, and to paint with those colors over the image of the helicopter, thereby removing it.

To use the Clone Stamp tool, zoom in on the area you're trying to fix, then select the tool from the toolbox. Choose a brush from the drop-down list. Typically, a soft-edged brush is best, because it will soften the effect and make it less obvious. Next, select a brush size. Choose a brush that's large enough to cover the telephone wire, tree branch, or stray dog you want to remove, but not too big. Select a blending mode and opacity. For this kind of repair, I usually leave these set to Normal, 100%. Turn on the Aligned option if you want to copy colors from nearby pixels. Turn it off if you want to copy the colors in one area of the image to several different places. If you want to "mix your paint" using colors from all layers, turn on the Use All Layers option.

After setting options, press Cmd/Alt and click in the image to take a sample of the colors there. Then click and drag to begin painting. Short strokes are best. If the Aligned option is turned on, you'll paint with colors taken from a spot that's roughly the same distance from the mouse pointer as the original spot and the place where you first began painting. The spot where your colors are coming from is marked with a big *X*. If the Aligned option is not on, your paint color will come from the place where you first clicked to take a sample.

To get rid of the offending helicopter, I zoomed in, clicked the Clone Stamp tool, selected a relatively small soft brush, sampled some sky, and used one short stroke to remove the helicopter from the sky.

Removing Small Objects with Copy and Paste

The cluster of little boats just at the stern of the ship, under her flag, is a distraction. Fortunately, it looks like there's enough water at the bottom-left edge to cover them up. For this, I'll start by copying some water and pasting it into a new layer over the boats.

When you want to cover something in an area of your image that should look like another area of the image, why not simply copy the good section and paste it over the bad? You can fix large areas with a single click using this method. Of course, you'll have to soften the edges of the pasted area, but that's not a problem.

To remove those distracting boats from the left side of my photo, I copied a small piece of water from below them, then pasted it back into my image. Elements automatically creates a new layer for the pasted data, which is placed exactly above the spot on the image where I copied it. This makes the pasted area a bit tough to see, so I temporarily hid the image layer by clicking its eye icon in the Layers palette. Then I used the Move tool to position the patch as carefully as I could. I repeated this process a few times, because I needed several different patches of water to cover the boats. When I was done, I merged all the layers by selecting Layer, Merge Visible. Then I used the Clone Stamp to sample the correct water color nearby, and paint it over the edges of my patches, hiding them. Follow the horizon when you drag with the Clone Stamp, in order to imitate the ripples in the water (see Figure 11.3).

FIGURE 11.3

Zoom in so you can see what you're doing.

With my careful copying and pasting, and some help from the Clone Stamp, the little boats are gone in no time. Now I'm ready to go on to color corrections, lighting changes, and any other major changes. I might try applying a watercolor filter (which makes the photo appear as if it were painted with watercolors), Chalk & Charcoal (which simulates that artistic effect), or Spatter (which spreads out the colors in a spattered pattern). On the other hand, I might just leave it as it is, which isn't bad. See this in color in the color section.

Fixing Red Eye

You've seen it a thousand times—that "devil eye" look that spoils pictures of everyone from grandma to the new baby, puppy, or cat. Usually the eerie glow is red, but it can be green, blue, or even yellow. It's caused by light reflecting back to the camera lens from the inside of the eye, which can only happen if the pupil of the eye is open—as it would be in a dimly lit room, or outside in full shade. Red eye appears red in humans because of the network of blood vessels back there. Our four-footed friends are more likely to display green or yellow eye, although normally blue-eyed Siamese cats eyes will also glow fiery red. Figure 11.4 shows an especially awful example, with both eyes affected.

FIGURE 11.4
He's really a very gentle cat.

11

A Pound of Prevention...

The easiest way to cure red eye is to prevent it in the first place. Most cameras with on-board flash, both digital and film cameras, have an anti–red eye flash mode. It uses one or more quick pre-flashes to decrease the size of the subject's pupils before the main flash goes off. The intention is to narrow the pupil enough to miss the camera lens entirely. It's usually at least partly successful.

The second way to avoid red eye is to increase the ambient light. Turn on all the room lights, rather than relying on the flash. Brighter lights will narrow your subject's pupils and also allow the use of a lower flash setting to dim the reflex.

A less common problem is alcohol/drugs, though certainly alcohol and its results have affected a great many wedding pictures. Both alcohol and narcotics will further dilate the users' pupils, and that will make red eye even worse. Besides, there's nothing attractive about being blotto.

Try having your subjects look away from the lens. It might help, but it also might make the composition a little strange, unless you can also show what they're looking at. Sometimes, just a few degrees are enough to make a difference. If you know you've got a red eye problem, start by having the subject look at your shoulder instead of the camera, and increase the head turn if necessary. Get closer to your subject to widen the flash-subject-lens angle and thereby avoid the reflection. The longer the camera-subject distance, the greater lens-flash distance must be to avoid red eye.

If your camera can sync to an external flash (not all models can), use an external flash positioned at least three feet away from your camera lens to change the angle of the light entering the eye. You can also bounce the flash off the ceiling or a white card or reflector before it reaches the subject to redirect the reflection away from your lens.

A Couple of Cures

Either your attempts at prevention failed, or these are old pictures, shot before you learned that red eye is sometimes avoidable. Anyway, you've got it bad. Now what can you do? Elements has an "automatic" red eye repair tool called the Red Eye Brush tool. It's in the toolbox, shown in Figure 11.5 along with its Options bar.

Red Eye Brush tool

FIGURE 11.5

Pay attention to the Options bar settings.

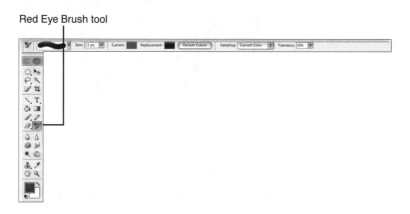

The brush isn't exactly automatic, but the accompanying directions will walk you step-by-step through the process of using it. To find them, look in the palette well on the Shortcuts bar, or under the Windows menu for How To and locate Remove Redeye (see Figure 11.6).

FIGURE 11.6

It's simple when you have the recipe in front of you.

 Whenever you are using a palette, drag it down the screen to disconnect it from the toolbar. Otherwise, it will automatically close whenever you click somewhere else on the screen.

From there, you simply follow the directions, which tell you to do the following:

1. Select the Red Eye Brush and choose a brush tip from the drop-down list. By default, it's a soft-edged brush, and I typically don't change it.

2. Next, set your brush to roughly the size of the pupil. (If the area is small, zoom in to see clearly.) Don't worry if the pupil you need to fix is partially covered by an eyelid; you'll only be changing the bad color (called the Current color) to a good color (known as the Replacement color).

3. Set the Sampling option to First Click. This tells Elements to sample the color you want to replace from the area under the brush when you first click on the image. Alternately, you can choose Current Color from the Sampling list, which tells Elements to use the color shown on the Current swatch. To set this color to the default (dark red), click the Default Colors button. This also sets the Replacement color to black, which is the other default. You can click the Current swatch and use the Color Picker to select a unique color of your choice.

4. Change the Replacement color if needed by clicking the swatch and choosing a color from the Color Picker. It's unlikely that you'll need to do this, though, because the color is set to black by default, and that's what most pupils should be.

11

5. Adjust the Tolerance level as desired. A lower value tells Elements to replace pixels that are really close to the Current color (If you selected First Click in step 3, the Current color will be set to the color of the pixel you first click on.)

6. Center the brush crosshairs over the red part of the eye, and click, as in Figure 11.7.

FIGURE 11.7
One click just about does it.

7. Drag the brush as needed over the red areas to remove them. Because you selected a brush size that matches the size of the pupil, you won't have to drag much. Don't worry about "coloring outside the lines." The color will only change where it should, unless you drag across something else the same color, like the cat's nose in this case.

That's the official Elements way to do it. It's quick, easy, and somewhat effective. Figure 11.8 shows the final result, as does the corresponding color figure in the color section. It works fairly well in grayscale, but I'm not very happy with the color result. It's unnaturally gray, as if the poor cat has cataracts. After selecting the "wrong" gray part of the eye, I can add a Hue/Saturation adjustment layer and darken it by moving the Lightness slider to the left, or I can start over and do the job differently. (An adjustment layer lets you isolate part of an image and make changes to just that part. Adjustment layers also let you try out effects on an entire image without committing to them. You'll learn how to use them in Hour 20, "Making Composite Images." You'll learn about adjusting Hue/Saturation for an entire image in Hour 12, "Too Light/Too Dark: Adjusting Brightness, Contrast, and Color.")

FIGURE 11.8
The recipe didn't do enough.

Task: Fixing Red Eye from Scratch

When the official Elements method doesn't do it, here's another way that's almost as easy, and generally more effective. Just follow these steps:

1. Zoom in to make the eyes as large as possible. (You can work on one eye at a time.) Use the Magic Wand to select the off-color parts of the pupil. Usually, they are the same color or close to it. (Adjust the Tolerance value as needed to select as much as you can.) Leave the small white circles in the middle of the eyes. Those are "catchlights" from the flash. See Figure 11.9.

FIGURE 11.9

Select as much of the red as you can.

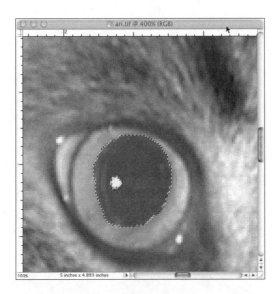

2. Press Ctrl+Shift+U (or select Remove Color from the Enhance, Adjust Color menu) to desaturate the selection. Now the incorrect color is gray. Saturation, as you may recall from the discussion on color systems in Hour 7, "Printing Your Pictures," is the intensity of a color. By removing it, you take out the color hue, and reduce the selection to gray tones similar to what you might see in a grayscale image. The lightness and darkness are still there, just not the color. You'll learn other ways to play with saturation in an image in Hour 12.

3. Make sure the foreground color is set to black or very dark gray. Switch to the Brush tool (located in the toolbox), select a large soft brush from the drop-down list, and click the Airbrush icon on the Options bar (it's on the far right). Set the blending mode to Darken and the opacity to no higher than 20%. Although we'll

cover blending modes in Hour 20, I can tell you now that the Darken mode will darken only the pixels that are lighter than the foreground color. Pixels darker than that color are not touched. Brush in layers of black, letting the color build up naturally. Because you turned on the Airbrush function, you'll be spraying only bits of color each time you drag over the eye. Continue until it looks right, zooming out to see it in context. If you make a mistake, you can use the Undo History palette as shown in Figure 11.10.

FIGURE 11.10
Use the Undo History palette to step backward if you go too far.

4. Repeat with the other eye. Figure 11.11 and the corresponding color plate show the final result.

FIGURE 11.11
Now he looks quite normal. Pity he doesn't act it.

Removing Dust and Scratches

Here's another case where prevention beats cure. Always try to clean your scanner and photos before you start scanning. A soft cloth and some careful work with a paintbrush might have saved a lot of work on the example you are about to see. If it doesn't come clean, though, you can clean it with Elements.

Using the Dust & Scratches Filter

The Dust & Scratches filter can be a tremendous time-saver when you're doing basic cleanup on a photo, particularly an old scanned one. If you're not careful, though, it can ruin the picture by overcompensating for the spots and losing detail. The filter works by adding a slight blur, which you can carefully adjust to produce a good compromise between spots and sharpness. To use it, choose Filter, Noise, Dust & Scratches.

Figure 11.12 shows the filter's interface, applied to a very detailed scan of an old photo. As you can see, there are large chunks of dirt, as well as smaller bits of dust and at least one hair running through the picture. But it's a good, clear scan, and worth the time it will take to clean it.

FIGURE 11.12
Gloucester Harbor, circa 1908.

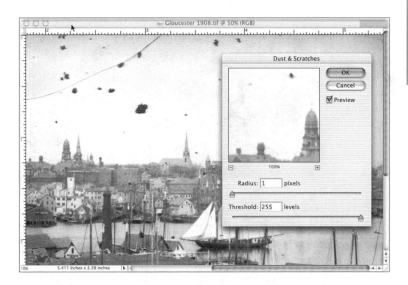

The filter has two sliders, one for the radius of the area it examines for differences, and one for how much different in color or value the pixels in that area must be in order to be noticed and removed. You want to keep the radius value fairly low to avoid over-blurring your image. Also, keep in mind that the Threshold range of 0–128 seems to work best for the majority of photos. You can set the Threshold to 100 and select a small radius, and then lower the Threshold value gradually until you achieve a balance between removal and sharpness.

Using this filter to remove the large pieces of dirt in this particular image would require such a degree of blur that you wouldn't be able to see the details of the picture. In Figure 11.13, I've raised the radius of the particles slightly (increasing the individual areas to be examined for differences) and lowered the threshold a good deal so that more pixels will qualify for removal, and now, just as we begin to see some differences in the spottiness, the detail is rapidly disappearing. One way to compensate for this is to isolate the area you want to change. Because most of the scratches, dust spots, and so on are in the sky, I could select the entire sky and use the filter on it. Or I could try a completely different method—applying the Despeckle and Unmask filters.

FIGURE 11.13

Compare the large picture with the previous one. A lot of sharpness is gone.

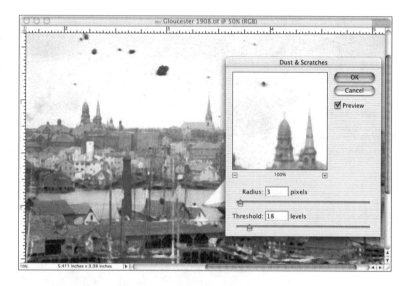

Using the Despeckle and Unsharp Mask Filters

So, perhaps the Dust & Scratches filter is not the right tool for this job. Unfortunately, most of the time the only way to tell is to try it. Still, the picture certainly needs cleaning up. What other options might we have? Despeckle? It's just above Dust & Scratches on the Filter, Noise submenu. The Despeckle filter looks for areas in the image where sharp color changes occur, such as the areas you might find in our sky dotted with dust. Then it blurs the area, but not its edges. This helps to preserve the sharpness in a photo, while removing dust and dirt. The filter is also helpful in photos that have banding—visible bands of contrast that often appear in digital captures and scans of magazine photos and other slightly reflective material. To try the filter, choose Filter, Noise, Despeckle. There are no options, so Elements applies the filter right away. If you don't like the effect, click Undo to remove it. Applied several times to our photo, it had no visible effect, so let's try something else.

The Unsharp Mask filter (Filter, Sharpen, Unsharp Mask) definitely did some good, as shown in Figure 11.14. Not only did it remove some of the smaller dust spots, it added contrast and sharpness to the photo, making it even more worthwhile to take the time to remove the dirt by hand.

FIGURE 11.14

Unsharp masking is going to help a lot.

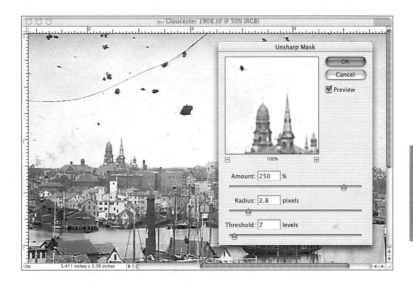

The Unsharp Mask filter is one of the most useful, and most misunderstood, filters in the bunch. Unsharp masking is a traditional technique that has been used in the printing industry for many years. It corrects blurring (sharpens the edges) in an original image or scan, as well as any blurring that occurs during the resampling and printing process. The Unsharp Mask filter works by locating every two adjacent pixels with a difference in brightness values that you have specified, and increasing their contrast by an amount that you specify. Because it perceives the dust spots as very slightly darker blurs, you can manipulate the settings so that it removes the smallest spots. At the same time, it does tend to accentuate the larger ones, sometimes even placing a white band around a particularly large black spot. That's actually not a problem, because we'll be using the Clone Stamp tool to cover the big ones—and their "halos."

Start by setting the Amount value, which tells Elements how much to increase the contrast of the pixels that qualify. Typically, a number between 150 and 200 is about right (One and a half to two times their original brightness).

The Radius control sets the number of surrounding pixels to which the sharpening effect is applied. I suggest that you keep the radius fairly low—around 2–3. The Threshold setting controls how different the pixels must be to be sharpened. The lower the setting, the more similar the pixels can be and still be affected by the filter. The higher the setting, the greater Photoshop's tolerance of difference will be. A value less than 20 usually works best. Of course, as always, feel free to go wild and try all the settings. That is the best way to learn. Be sure that you check the Preview box so that you can see the effect of your changes. When you like it, click OK.

Removing Dust and Scratches with the Clone Stamp

The best way to cover all the spots, tedious though it may be, is to stamp them out. Switch to the Clone Stamp tool, select a large, soft-edged brush, and be sure to press Alt and click in the sky as close to the spot as possible, because sky tones can vary quite a lot, and you want to copy a good one (see Figure 11.15). Be sure you have not checked Aligned. Though it's helpful when you need to copy something, it's not right for this kind of cover-up job. Figure 11.16 shows the final photo, looking pretty darn good for something nearly a century old.

FIGURE 11.15
The Clone Stamp tool at work.

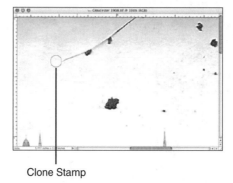

Clone Stamp

FIGURE 11.16
Don't try to catch every little spot. If it's too perfect, it doesn't look authentic.

Summary

This was a short but very important hour. You learned the steps for basic photo cleanup, something you should do with every image you open, before you get fancy by applying filters, changing colors, or using any of the hundreds of tricks Elements can do. You learned to remove small objects that might distract from the subject of your photo. You learned all about red eye, in both people and critters. We discussed what causes it, how to prevent it, and two different ways to remove it. Then we talked about some ways to remove dust and scratches from your photos. You learned about the Dust & Scratches and Despeckle filters, and that they don't always work. You also learned about the Unsharp Mask filter, and how it can help with a dusty scan while adding extra sharpness and contrast.

Q&A

Q How should I clean my scanner? There are smudges on the glass.

A There should be cleaning instructions in the scanner manual. In most cases, though, all you need to do is wipe the glass with a lint-free cloth or paper towel, using a few drops of window cleaner or rubbing alcohol to take off anything sticky or greasy, like smudges or fingerprints. Be careful not to scratch the glass.

Q Can I clean the lens on my camera the same way?

A Absolutely not! Camera lenses are delicate. Go to your local photo shop and buy a package of lens tissue and a bottle of lens cleaning fluid. There are no substitutes for these. Take a sheet of tissue. Tear it in half the long way, roll it up tight, and use the torn edge as a brush to remove any dust or grit from the lens first. If there are visible fingerprints on the lens, apply a single drop of fluid. Wait a minute so it can work, then using your tissue brush clean from the center of the lens to the edges. If you actually pick up dirt or grit on your "brush," discard it and make a new one. While you are at the camera store, buy a lens cap, if your camera didn't come with one. Use it, or at least keep your fingers off the lens.

Q My daughter's face broke out the day her school pictures were taken. Can I use the Clone Stamp to hide the spots as you did with the old photo?

A Sounds like a good plan. If you have trouble, try changing the tool's blending mode on the Options bar to Lighten. Then you'll affect only those pixels that appear darker than the surrounding skin (the color of the sample spot where you first press Cmd/Alt and click).

11

Workshop

Take a few moments to tackle the short quiz on removing imperfections and check your answers to see how you did. Then work on the activity.

Quiz

1. Why crop first?

    a. Because you might be able to cut off things you'd otherwise have to retouch

    b. Because it looks better

    c. Because the computer can work faster on a smaller picture

2. Red eye can only be red.

    a. True

    b. False

3. The Dust & Scratches Filter will also _____ your image.

    a. Sharpen

    b. Blur

    c. Colorize

Quiz Answers

1. All are true.

2. b. False

3. b. Use it carefully.

Activity

Find some pictures you haven't worked on yet, or go out and shoot a half dozen or so. Put them through the basic cleanup. Straighten and crop as needed. Fix any red eye, and remove any dust. Remove, by hiding, anything that doesn't belong, such as litter on the street, stray branches, or power lines.

HOUR 12

Too Light/Too Dark: Adjusting Brightness, Contrast, and Color

Digital cameras generally give you good, accurate color, but a lot depends on the amount of light available. Pictures shot outdoors toward the end of the day often take on an orange tone, as the sun goes down. Rainy day pictures might be drab as the weather itself. Indoor photos can pick up all kinds of color casts depending on the lighting in the room. Scanning photos can add color shifts caused by the scanner. Or maybe you've scanned old, faded prints in hopes of saving them in Elements. You'll be amazed at what you can do by just making some small adjustments to an image's brightness, contrast, and color.

In this hour you will

- Fix certain image problems automatically
- Adjust other problems by eye
- Make adjustments to color in a photo
- Play tricks with color

Using the Automatic Correction Tools

Being somewhat lazy, I always start to fix a problem image by trying anything that says Auto. Elements offers three: Auto Levels, Auto Contrast, and Auto Color Correction. All are on the Enhance menu, along with the other color correction tools we'll be looking at later this hour. Remember that all these corrections can be applied to the entire image, to a selection, or to one or more layers.

Auto Levels

It's certainly worth a click. Auto Levels automatically adjusts the tonal range and color balance in your photo, to make sure that there is a range of values (shadows, midtones, and highlights). It defines the lightest and darkest pixels in an image, and then redistributes the intermediate pixel values proportionately. If Elements doesn't think the levels need adjusting, it won't change anything. If it does, the screen will blink and your image will reappear, looking better (hopefully). If you don't like the changes, click Undo.

If you don't like the result of Auto Levels, but you agree that the picture could use some tweaking, choose Enhance, Adjust Brightness, Contrast, Levels to open the Levels dialog box, shown in Figure 12.1, and do it yourself. What you're looking at is called a *histogram*, and it's essentially a graph of the number of pixels at each level of brightness from 0 to 255. (Stop and read the upcoming sidebar to learn more about histograms.) The image this represents in Figure 12.1 has a good spread all the way across the spectrum— just enough light and dark spots, and not too many boring middle tones.

FIGURE 12.1

Levels aren't hard to adjust.

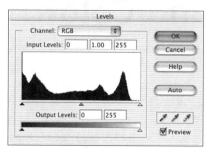

There are several ways to use the Levels dialog box. The easiest is to move the Input Level sliders (up arrows) just under the histogram until you like the result. Just be sure that you have checked the Preview box, so you can see the effect of your changes on the picture.

More scientifically, you can drag the sliders to the points at either end of the scale where the histogram begins to rise steeply. Typically, these will have numerical input values somewhere between 0–30 and 225–255. Then, move the middle slider, which represents the midtones, to about halfway between the two. This remaps the values; narrowing the range increases the contrast while widening the range decreases it.

Drag the Output Level sliders at the bottom of the dialog box to adjust the range of shadows and highlights. This increases or decreases the amount of contrast and brightness in an image.

You can also use the eyedroppers to adjust the levels. Click the Set White Point eyedropper (on the right) and click the lightest part of your image. Then click the dark-tipped eyedropper (Set Black Point, on the left) to select it and click the darkest point on the image. If you have an area in the image that seems to be right in the middle, click it with the midrange (Set Gray Point) eyedropper (in the middle).

There's a menu command in the Image menu called Histogram. It doesn't actually *do* anything, but if you learn how to use it, you can save yourself lots of time.

If you've ever taken a course in statistics, you already know that a histogram is a kind of graph. In Photoshop Elements, it's a graph of the image reduced to grayscale, with lines to indicate the number of pixels at each step in the grayscale from 0 to 255.

You might wonder why this is important. The main reason is that you can tell by looking at the histogram whether there's enough detail in the image, so that you can apply corrections successfully. If you have an apparently bad photo or a bad scan, studying the histogram will tell you whether it's worth working on or whether you should throw away the image and start over. If all the lines are bunched up tight at one end of the graph, you probably can't save the picture by adjusting it. If, on the other hand, you have a reasonably well spread-out histogram, there's a wide enough range of values to suggest that the picture can be saved.

The Histogram command has another use, which is to give you a sense of the tonal range of the image. This is sometimes referred to as the *key type*. An image is said to be *low key*, *average key*, or *high key*, depending on whether it has a preponderance of dark, middle, or light tones, respectively. A picture that is all middle gray would have only one line in its histogram, and it would fall right in the middle.

All you really need to know is that, when you look at the histogram, you should see a fairly even distribution across the graph, if the image is intended to be an average key picture. If the picture is high key, most of the lines in the histogram are concentrated on the right side with a few on the left. If it is low key, most of the values will be to the left with a few to the right.

12

You can also adjust levels by color. The Channel pop-up menu at the top of the dialog box gives you access to the three color channels—red, green, and blue. You can use this feature to adjust the amount of a single color in the image, and to keep shadows and highlights from getting muddy or developing a color cast.

Auto Contrast

Auto Contrast works in a similar manner, but doesn't attempt to adjust color channels separately, so it often gives a different (and in my experience, more satisfactory) result (no color cast). It also doesn't seem to over-correct, as Auto Levels can. But, of course, a lot depends on the image to which you're applying it. Some images need more careful tweaking than any "auto" adjustment can make. To try out Auto Contrast, choose Enhance, Auto Contrast. Again, if you don't like the result, click Undo.

You can also adjust brightness and contrast in an image by using the Brightness/Contrast dialog box shown in Figure 12.2. Choose Enhance, Adjust Brightness/Contrast, Brightness/Contrast. Just move the sliders to the right to increase the amount of brightness and/or contrast, or to the left to decrease them. Experiment until you like the result. Remember that you can apply any of the corrections discussed in this hour to a selected area of your image. To lighten or darken areas of an image, you can also use the Dodge and Burn tools described in Hour 14, "Repairing Black-and-White Pictures."

Figure 12.2

Be sure the Preview box is checked.

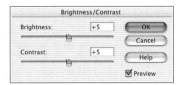

Auto Color Correction

I like really bright, saturated color. The person who wrote the algorithm for Auto Color Correction apparently prefers a more subdued palette. I'm seldom really happy with the results of Auto Color Correction, but—as they say—your mileage may vary. It might be just right for the image you're working on, so don't hesitate to try it by choosing Enhance, Auto Color Correction. We'll cover various ways you can adjust color levels yourself in just a minute.

Just for fun, in Figures 12.3, 12.4, 12.5, and 12.6, I've taken the same picture and applied each of the three auto corrections to it. (They're also included in the color plate section.) Judge for yourself which worked, and which did more harm than good.

FIGURE 12.3
The original photo.

FIGURE 12.4
Auto Levels applied.

FIGURE 12.5
Auto Contrast applied.

12

FIGURE 12.6
Auto Color Correction applied.

Adjusting by Eye with Color Variations

Sometimes if you want something done right, you have to do it yourself. This applies to color correction as much as to any other endeavor. Figure 12.7 shows the Color Variations dialog box. You can find it in the Enhance, Adjust Color submenu. Use the Color Variations command to add or remove red, blue, or green to or from the shadows, midtones, or highlights in an image; lighten or darken the shadows, midtones, or highlights; and increase or decrease the intensity (saturation) of color.

FIGURE 12.7
See this in color in the color plate section.

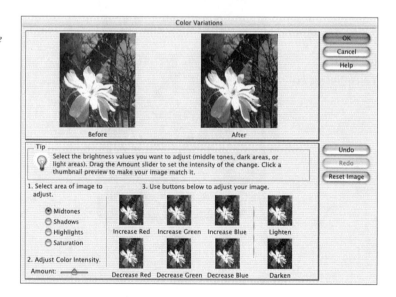

To use it, first decide whether you need to correct the shadows, midtones, or highlights, or the color saturation, which will affect all three equally. Move the intensity slider if you think you need more or less correction, and finally, choose the small image that looks most like the kind of adjustment you want. (You might want to use a magnifying glass. Because the previews are so small, subtle changes are hard to see.) If you like the direction it's going, but need more correction, just click the same image again. You can undo as many changes as you like by clicking the Undo button more than once. The Reset Image button removes all changes.

Adjusting Color with Color Cast

Color cast is the term experts use when an image has too much of one color in it. Sometimes an image will get a cast from poor lighting, bad scanning, or as an aftereffect from some other adjustment such as Auto Levels. The Color Cast Correction dialog box, shown in Figure 12.8, removes color casts by having you locate a point in the picture that should be pure white, middle gray, or black, and then adjusting the color so that it actually is white, gray, or black. To adjust the target color (and thus, the other colors in your image), Color Cast adds the color opposite the target color on the optical color wheel to cancel out or neutralize whatever color is too strong in the black or white or gray. For example, if the target color is magenta and it should be black, Color Cast adds green (magenta's opposite on the color wheel).

To use Color Cast, choose Enhance, Adjust Color, Color Cast. Then use the eyedropper to click a point in your image that should be pure white, pure black, or medium gray.

FIGURE 12.8

Just click on something in the picture that should be white, black, or neutral gray. Elements will do the math and change the colors.

If you don't like the result the first time, try a different black or white spot, with or without clicking Reset first. The results will vary according to the color strength of the pixel you select.

Adjusting Color with Hue/Saturation

The Hue/Saturation dialog box is the most complicated of the lot, mainly because it has three sliders instead of two. Display it by choosing Enhance, Color, Hue/Saturation. As you can see in Figure 12.9, it also has a pop-up menu that lets you adjust a single color rather than all of them at once. (This is also the only place in Elements where you can do anything at all with cyan, magenta, and yellow, the key components of the CMYK

12

color model.) However, I'd suggest sticking with Master until you start to understand how the algorithm works.

FIGURE **12.9**

The Hue/Saturation dialog box.

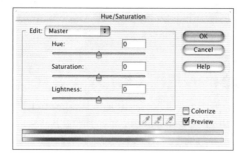

As always, check Preview so that you can see the effects of your changes in the picture you're working on.

There are three sliders: Hue, Saturation, and Lightness. The Hue slider moves around the color wheel from color to color. With Master selected, you can move all the way from red (in the middle of the slider), left through purple to blue or blue-green, or right through orange to yellow and green.

The Saturation slider takes you from 0% in the center, to 100% saturated (pure colors) on the right, or 100% unsaturated (no color, or essentially a grayscale image) on the left. When you move the slider from right to left, the colors opposite the image colors on the optical color wheel are added, so the image colors move toward gray.

The Lightness slider lets you increase or decrease the brightness of the image, from zero in the center, to +100 on the right (pure white), or –100 (pure black) on the left.

As you move these sliders, watch the two spectrum strips at the bottom of the window, as well as the image itself. The upper strip represents the current status of the image, and the lower one changes according to the slider(s) you move. If you move the Hue slider to +60, for example, you can see that the reds in the picture turn quite yellow, and the blues turn purple. Also, the reds in the upper spectrum line up with the yellows in the lower spectrum. In effect, what you are doing is skewing the color spectrum by that amount. If you move the Saturation slider to the left, you'll see the lower spectrum strip become less saturated. If you move the Lightness slider, you'll see its effects reflected in the lower spectrum strip as well.

If you select a color instead of selecting Master from the pop-up menu, the dialog box changes slightly, as you can see in Figure 12.10. The eyedroppers are now active, enabling you to select colors from the image, and the adjustable range sliders are centered on the color you have chosen to adjust. You can move these sliders back and forth to focus on as broad or narrow a range within that color as you want. This might not seem like a big deal, but it's really very powerful. For example, I was trying to adjust a picture of a girl wearing a dark magenta shirt. Her skin seemed too pink to me, but the shirt seemed almost right. So I selected Reds from the Edit list, and moved the sliders to narrow my definition of "red" so that it fit her skin tone but not her purplish-red shirt. Then I adjusted the saturation level to remove red from her skin, leaving it a more natural color.

I could have used the eyedroppers to be more precise in selecting my range, by taking samples of color from various points on her skin. To do this, you start with the first eyedropper on the left. Click on a point on her skin that's a middle-tone color, not too light and not too dark. Then use the middle eyedropper to add other samples to the range, lighter and darker. Use the eyedropper on the right to remove colors from the range, such as the red in her shirt.

FIGURE 12.10

This tool could make your brown eyes blue.

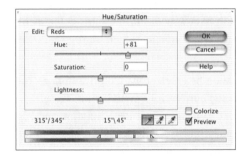

Suppose I want to change a single color within a picture. Let's say I want to convert some of the yellow flowers in Figure 12.11 to some other color. All I need to do is select the two flowers I want to change, open the dialog box, and choose Yellows from the pop-up menu at the top. Then I can move the Hue slider around until I find a color I like, maybe a nice turquoise. Because I'm working on a selection, only the selected flowers will change color. However, these flowers have a brownish center that is included in the Yellow range, so when I change the Hue to turquoise, the brown centers take on a bluish cast. Since that's not what I want, I set the sliders back to the center and start over. This time I subtract the brown centers from the range by first dragging the left slider to the right, eliminating oranges, and clicking on various spots within the brown centers using the third dropper. Look at Figure 12.11 in the color section to see the effect.

12

FIGURE 12.11
Why not blue daisies?

You can create a neat effect by using the Hue/Saturation dialog box to colorize a photo, essentially turning it into various shades of the same color such as red or blue. You can use this technique on a grayscale image as well, if you first convert it to RGB by choosing Image, Mode, RGB.

In the Hue/Saturation dialog box, select the Colorize option. The colors in the image are changed to variations of the current foreground color. To select a different color as your base, move the Hue slider. You can adjust the Saturation and Lightness levels as well, if you like. This is a nice technique to "dull down" an image to make it suitable for use in Web backgrounds, stationery, business cards, and so on. Try it sometime!

Removing and Replacing Color

Remove Color is easy to understand and easy to use. When you select it from the Enhance, Adjust Color submenu, it simply removes all the color from your picture, converting it to grayscale, but without changing the color mode to grayscale, too. Why is that important? Because, having turned the picture to grays, you might want to paint back some colors, perhaps different ones, or paste things in color on layers over it, or…who knows? It's your picture. By the way, you can use the Remove Color command on a selection, removing color from just an area of an image. You might select the background and remove the color from behind a person, for example, to make her stand out in an interesting way. This technique is used in advertising all the time to draw attention to products.

Replace Color, on the other hand, is—in my opinion—the least comprehensible dialog box in any form or version of Photoshop. You can use Replace Color to replace one color in an image with some other color. For example, you can change all the yellow roses in a photo into red ones, or try out a new paint color on your house. Still, the dialog box is a bit intimidating. I've taught you an easier way to do it, but in case you really want to try out Replace Color, the following task will show you how.

Task: Replace Color

1. To make the change apply to every instance of the color you're replacing, make sure nothing is selected. If you only want to change a single flower, area, or object, select it.

2. Choose Enhance, Adjust Color, Replace Color. You'll see the dialog box in Figure 12.12. You can work in Mask mode (Selection) or Image mode. In Mask mode, a black mask appears over the areas of the image that you don't want to replace. Partially masked areas indicate those regions that will be only partially replaced with the new color. The unmasked areas (shown in white) indicate the parts of the image that match the foreground color to the degree you specify. At any time, you can remove the mask and look at the entire image by clicking Image. This helps you verify that all the areas you do not want to affect are masked.

FIGURE 12.12

The mask covers the areas that won't be affected.

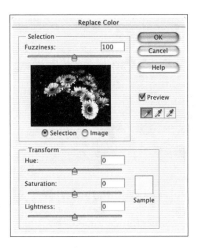

12

3. Using the first eyedropper, click in the document window on the color you want to change. The mask in the sample window changes to mask just the areas that don't match the color you clicked on. If the sample is not the midrange of the color you want to change, try again.

4. Use the plus eyedropper to select additional colors or shades of the same color to change. Elements adjusts the mask based on your selections. Use the minus eyedropper to deselect colors you don't want to change.

5. You can use the Fuzziness slider to control the sensitivity of the range of colors masked, in the same way you'd use Tolerance to control the sensitivity of the Magic Wand. As you move the slider, you'll see more or less of your mask. Higher Fuzziness numbers are more tolerant.

6. When you're ready to replace the unmasked areas with another color, move the Hue slider right or left to locate the new color. You'll be able to see it in the sample swatch. Modify it with the saturation and lightness sliders until it's just what you want. Click OK.

7. The new color will replace the old one in the areas you have selected.

Well, okay, maybe it's not all that complicated. I think I'd use my method for changing a single selection, and Photoshop's method for globally changing, let's say, all the yellows to pinks. For the most realistic look, go through the process several times, changing some of the yellows to pinks at each pass, but each time selecting slightly different ones. Figure 12.13 shows my final daisies, gone from yellow to red-orange.

FIGURE 12.13
Be sure to look for this in the color plate section.

Compensating for Lighting Mistakes

When light comes from behind a subject, it can make the subject a bit dark. But it can also make for a strong contrast between your subject and its background. If you adjust the exposure so that the subject is properly lit, you risk making the background overexposed. To compensate for washed-out skies, sun-kissed lakes, and other light backgrounds in your images, use the Adjust Backlighting tool. It adjusts the midtones in the image, darkening the background without lightening the subject too much.

You can select an area if you want your changes to affect only that portion of the image, then choose Enhance, Adjust Lighting, Adjust Backlighting. Drag the Darken slider to the right until the background is no longer washed out, then click OK.

The Fill Flash tool has almost the opposite effect; it adds light to the subject, just as a camera flash would. Again, in backlit situations, a subject can become too dark and lose detail. This tool helps to compensate for that. Select an area to affect if desired, then choose Enhance, Adjust Lighting, Fill Flash. Drag the Lighter slider to the right until you can see some detail in the subject. Because this effect might wash out the subject too much, bring up the colors by adjusting the Saturation levels. When you're satisfied, click OK.

Using the Quick Fix Dialog Box

The Quick Fix dialog box gives you access to the most-used correction tools with one or two clicks. With it, you can adjust the brightness, color, sharpness, and alignment (straightness) of your image. If you're going to do your own corrections from scratch, this is a good place to start.

To use Quick Fix, choose Enhance, Quick Fix. Select the type of adjustment you want to make: Brightness, Color Correction, Focus, or Rotate. In the second column, select the specific adjustment you want to make. A set of controls relating to that adjustment type appears in the third column; use these controls to make the actual adjustment. If the adjustment is an automatic one, click Apply to let Elements apply the adjustment.

If you like what you see but need to make other changes, change any option in the first two columns; new changes will build on the first one. If you don't like a change, click Undo to remove it. You can click Undo more than once to remove multiple levels of adjustments. If you click Reset Image, you'll remove all the changes you've made in the Quick Fix dialog box. When you're through making changes, click OK.

Remember that with automatic adjustments, you can click the Apply button as many times as you want. Each time you do, the selected correction will be applied again. For example, if your photo improves with Auto Levels, but not quite enough, try it again by clicking Apply a second time. Also, remember that you can affect just a selected portion of your image if you like, by making a selection before you open the dialog box.

12

Task: Fix a Badly Overexposed, Very Blue Photo

The photo shown in Figure 12.14 has a lot of things wrong with it. It actually looks as if the flash didn't go off, or someone tried to shoot in the dark without one. It's too dark and its colors are too washed out. It needs more saturation to bring out the colors, and it needs more light. It's also too blue. Let's try fixing it. In case you want to work along, you can find the picture (titled "Bridesmaids") at this book's page on the Sams Publishing Web site.

FIGURE 12.14

You can't put it in the wedding album looking like this. (Photo courtesy of Judy Blair)

1. Open up the Quick Fix dialog box by selecting Enhance, Quick Fix.
2. The first step is to lighten this a little. Let's see what Auto Contrast can do for us. Choose Brightness from the first list, Auto Contrast from the second, and click Apply. It certainly increased the contrast, but I was looking for something more.
3. Choose Auto Levels from the second list, and click Apply. This makes a big—and helpful—difference, as you can see in Figure 12.15.

FIGURE 12.15

That was a good first step.

3. Because increasing the contrast seemed to help a little, we'll move down to the Brightness/Contrast Adjustment and do some more tweaking there. Select the Brightness/Contrast option from the second list. In the third column, set the Brightness to +38 and the Contrast to +8. That perks it up some more.

4. Now that the contrast and brightness seem to be about right, let's start working on the color. Select Color Correction as the Adjustment Category. We'll do this ourselves, so choose Hue/Saturation from the second column. I shifted the hue just a tiny bit to warm up the skin tones, and added a tiny bit more saturation and some lightness. To duplicate this effect, set Hue to –1, Saturation to +1, and Lightness to +12. The changes, shown in Figure 12.16, seem to help.

FIGURE 12.16

When all you need are subtle changes, alter the settings by one number at a time.

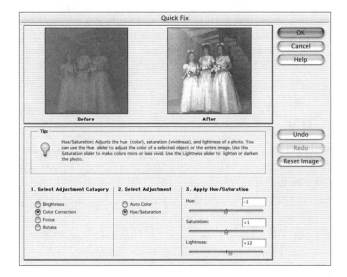

5. What about focus? Because the picture has ended up looking grainy, adding a little blur will smooth it out. The Blur filter applies the opposite effect of the Unsharp Mask and the other Sharp filters—instead of increasing the crispness within an image, this filter softens it. Select Focus from the first column, and Blur from the second column, then click Apply. This is the equivalent of applying the Blur filter once.

6. We're done. It's not a great photo, but compare the final version in Figure 12.17 to the original in Figure 12.14. Be sure to look at these in the color section, too.

12

Figure 12.17

This looks much better than before.

> As you are making any of the adjustments that require dragging sliders on the Quick Fix dialog box, make sure you stop and release the mouse button before you attempt to judge the result of your change. For some reason, Elements doesn't make those changes while the mouse button is down. This is not a problem in the individual tool windows, only in Quick Fix.

Summary

You learned a lot about color in this hour. You learned about the auto color correction features in Elements, and that they don't always work as you'd hoped. So, you learned how to make the same changes yourself. You found out all you need to know about histograms, and how to use the Levels dialog box. You mastered fixing contrast, and learned to use color variations to fix off-color pictures. You learned about color cast and how to cancel it out. You learned how to use the Hue/Saturation dialog box for maximum control, and finally you learned how to remove and replace colors.

Q&A

Q Why do some old photos get such weird colors? I have a batch of prints made from slide film in the early 1960's and they are *all* purple.

A Well, it *was* the 60s. I seem to remember a certain purple haze myself…. But seriously, it could have been bad processing, or a bad lot of printing paper, or that the pictures were stored somewhere too hot. All those things can cause color shifts. If you still have the slides somewhere, see how the color is. Otherwise, scan that purple print and fix it!

Q How do you use the histogram to tell whether there's detail in the shadows?

A You look at the peaks and valleys. If there's a good cluster of lines in the area representing darks, you're all set.

Q. If I screw up my adjustments in one of these dialog boxes, is there anyway to revert, rather than just canceling and starting again?

A. You can always undo one step backward within a dialog box. If you press the Option/Alt key, the Cancel button changes to Revert and brings you back to the status when you first opened the dialog box.

Workshop

Take a few moments to tackle the short quiz on adjusting lightness, contrast, and color and check your answers to see how you did. Then try the activities.

Quiz

1. The photo is too green. What should you do?

    a. Open Color Variations and choose Decrease Green

    b. Say you took it in Ireland

    c. Use Remove Color and then add back some lighter green

2. Increasing saturation does what to colors?

    a. Darkens them

    b. Lightens them

    c. Makes them more intense

    d. Removes them

3. How do I lessen the degree of change in the Variations dialog box?

    a. Press Shift+Control+F6 while you click the thumbnail.

    b. Use the Amount slider.

    c. You can't do that.

Quiz Answers

1. a. Color Variations is under the Enhance, Adjust Color submenu.

2. c. Saturation is a measurement of how much pure pigment is in a color.

3. b. Always look for the easy way.

12

Activities

1. Find a photo with a person in it, and change him to a Martian by changing his skin tones to green.

2. Find some pictures that need help with their color, and fix them up. Try the Auto corrections first, and then try doing it yourself.

HOUR 13

Using Repair Recipes and Tutorials

Adobe has made many of the complicated photo rescue and enhancement procedures much easier for you by supplying easy-to-follow "recipes" for them. If you follow a recipe, your results are pretty well guaranteed to be good. What other software would make that promise? For that matter, what cookbook would?

If you need more help than a simple recipe provides (or you can't find a recipe to fix the problem), try out one of the tutorials, or get help online from people who have been there and know how to get back.

In this hour you will

- Discover the How To palette
- Follow a recipe and avoid disaster
- Learn the tricks of the trade with a tutorial
- Use the Internet to get help

Using How To/Recipes

The only hurdle to overcome in using recipes is finding them. For reasons known only to Adobe, they live on a palette called, not Recipes, but How To. When you first start Elements, the How To palette presents itself and opens in the work window. If for some reason it doesn't, or if you've already closed it to make room to work, you can open it by selecting How To from the Windows menu, or by clicking its tab in the palette well on the Shortcuts bar, if that's active. (By the way, you can also activate the Shortcuts bar, or shut it off, from the Windows menu.) The How To palette is shown in Figure 13.1.

Palette well

FIGURE 13.1

You'll find the recipes in the How To palette.

How To palette

After you open the How To palette, use the drop-down menu to locate the kind of recipe you want, and then click on the recipe to open it (see Figure 13.2).

FIGURE 13.2

The Recipes pop-up menu.

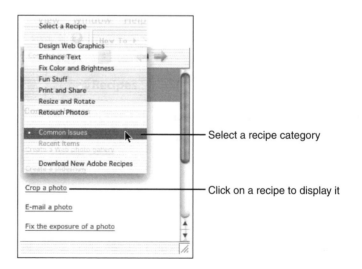

Select a recipe category

Click on a recipe to display it

There are several different recipe categories, and more will undoubtedly be added as they are written. Here's a list of the recipe categories you might find:

- Design Web Graphics—In this category, you'll find recipes creating Web buttons and adding polish with bevels, shadows, or glows. You'll find out how to create Web animations and banners for the top of your pages.

- Enhance Text—This category is filled with recipes that enable you to do neat things to type, such as adding a bevel, filling it with a gradient or image, and adding a shadow.

- Fix Color and Brightness—Look here for quick ways to fix problems with color and light in a photo.

- Fun Stuff—When you feel confident with Elements, explore this category and learn some neat techniques, such as colorizing a black and white photo, creating a coloring book page from an image, and creating a collage of photos.

- Print and Share—This category is full of recipes for printing and sharing your images in a Web gallery, attached to an email message, or with a slideshow.

- Resize and Rotate—Learn how to crop, resize, and straighten a photo using the recipes in this category.

- Retouch Photos—Use these recipes to repair torn photos, remove red eye, clean up scratches and dust spots, and repair other common problems.

- Common Issues—If you have a question or problem, chances are good that someone else has had it too. Adobe has assembled recipes that solve the most common problems, and placed them in this category.

Once you have opened the recipe that you want, be sure to drag the palette down the screen a little, away from the Shortcuts bar. As long as it remains docked, it will disappear as soon as you do something else. This is true, incidentally, of all Elements palettes. You must cut them loose from the bar by dragging them if you want to keep them visible.

Read the recipe. Make sure it sounds as if it will do what you want. Prepare the image to which you want to apply it or, if it's something that will stand alone, start a new page in Elements.

13

With some of the steps in a recipe, you may find a Do This Step for Me link. Clicking here tells Elements to complete the step for you. This is good to use when a step is confusing to you, and you want to see how it's done before trying it yourself.

At the bottom of some recipes, you'll find links to related recipes. Click one if you wish to view that recipe. Go back to the previous recipe and eventually to the category list—the list of recipes for that category—by clicking the left arrow. Go forward to recipes you've viewed in that category by clicking the right arrow. The Home icon takes you back to the category list.

Task: Create a Text Panel Using a Recipe

Just for fun, let's try following a recipe. "Create a Highlighted Panel for Type" sounds interesting. By following the recipe, you'll highlight some text by muting the background behind it. This is a particularly effective technique to use when you want to make text that you've placed on an image more noticeable and a bit easier to read.

1. To display the recipe, select the Enhance Text category, then click on Create a Highlighted Panel for Type. If needed, move the How To palette to an area of the screen where you can read all of its text while you work. Resize the palette as needed.

2. Given that the recipe asks you to start by dragging a marquee, it clearly assumes there's already an image or at least a blank page open. (It's always a good idea to read through the recipe before you do anything else, so you can get a sense of the assumptions it makes.) Open any image you have, and save it with a new name if you don't want to make permanent changes to it. If you don't have a photo available to use, start a new image and use the Paint Bucket tool to fill the background with your favorite color. Now you're ready to use the recipe to create a highlighted panel that will make the text you'll add later stand out against your background.

3. The first step in the recipe instructs you to select the Rectangular Marquee tool. If you click the Do This Step for Me link, Elements opens whichever marquee tool was last selected, even if it was the circular one. Just to be sure, select the Rectangular Marquee tool yourself.

4. Follow the next step and drag to create a rectangular box that will hold your text later. You don't have to be all that precise, because you can always change the size of the box if needed.

5. Follow the next step in the recipe by choosing Layer, New Adjustment Layer, Brightness/Contrast. This step inserts a new layer that you can use to make the chosen adjustment (brightness and contrast) to part of your image. In this case, you'll adjust the brightness and contrast within the selected area for any layers below the adjustment layer.

Because you only have one layer in your image at the moment, the adjustment layer will not change anything else. But if you had already typed your text on top of your image, you'd have two layers because text is always placed on its own layer. So, to avoid lightening the text with the background, you would need to activate the background layer first, before performing step 3 of the recipe.

6. The New Layer dialog box appears; click OK to create the adjustment layer.

7. The Brightness/Contrast dialog box appears. Step 5 tells you to make sure that the Preview option is on so you can see the changes you're making. Select it if needed.

8. In step 6, the recipe tells you to adjust the brightness and contrast levels until you get the result you want. Drag the Brightness slider to the right to lighten the background in the selected area. Adjust the Contrast as well if you want.

9. When you've lightened the background sufficiently to make text placed on top of it easily readable, click OK as instructed in step 7.

10. The next step, of course, is to add some type. Click the Horizontal Text tool, select a font and font size, then click in the lightened area and type some text. My result appears in Figure 13.3, and in the color section.

FIGURE 13.3
The light background really draws attention to the text.

This technique also works in reverse—darkening the selection so you can add light type or use a color that otherwise wouldn't have enough contrast against the background. I think I'll go for the gold. Figure 13.4 shows the result.

FIGURE 13.4
The letters pop right out.

13

There are, of course, several ways you could do the same thing on your own. The easiest would be to add a layer over your photo, draw the block with a shape tool, pour paint into it, and then reduce the opacity of that level until you have the effect you want. Then, put your type on top of everything else, and merge the layers when you're done. The advantage to doing it this way is that you can use a color instead of black, and some other shape instead of a rectangle. And you can style the type, maybe make it gold embossed with a pale yellow glow. It's up to you. Are you a recipe-follower, or do you like to improvise? If you can't cook without a rack of spices, a handful of fresh herbs, and a cabinet with exotic oils and vinegars, you aren't going to be satisfied for long with Adobe's recipes. The best solution is to master the tutorials included with Elements, and then improvise your own recipes. Unfortunately, you can't save them as recipes in Elements, but if you decide to upgrade to Photoshop, you'll be able to write and save as many as you want. Photoshop calls them Actions, and you can have one for every step you take in fixing a picture.

Looking for New Recipes

At the bottom of the Recipe pop-up menu in the How To palette is the Download New Adobe Recipes option. If you have an active Internet connection, clicking this will do one of two things, depending on your operating system. If you're using a Mac, you'll see the dialog box shown in Figure 13.5. A list of product updates, along with new recipes, will be displayed. The View menu lets you decide whether to display just new updates, or all updates, even if you've already downloaded them. Select the ones you want and click Choose to select the location to which you want to download them. You don't need to click the Tell Me More button, but if you do click it, you'll see a page on Adobe's Web site that gives a general explanation of what updates are. Finally, click Download to download the updates and new recipes to your computer. You'll need to restart Elements to view them.

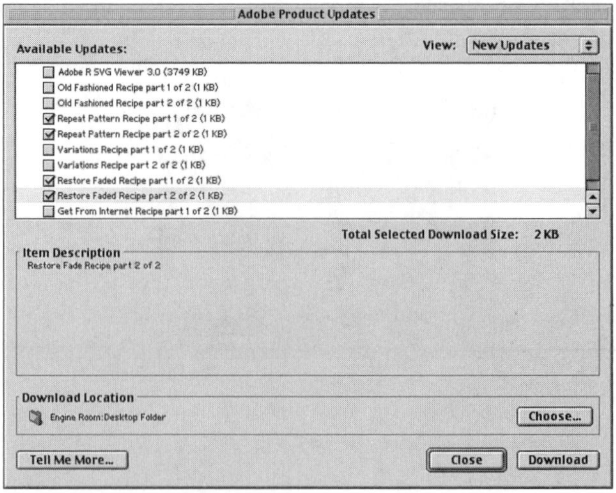

FIGURE **13.5**

Check Adobe often to see what's cooking.

If you use Windows, Elements will display the Online Services Wizard instead. It will scan for new recipes that you don't have, and display them. Simply choose the ones you want by pressing Ctrl and clicking. Click the Download button to begin the download. After the download is complete, you'll see a message telling you to click Finish. The new recipes are available for use right away; simply select Recent Items from the recipe category list in the How To palette.

By the way, if you click Back in the Wizard dialog box, you'll display the Online Services main screen, where you can download program updates, or upload images to Shutterfly, which can then print them for you on high-quality paper.

Following a Tutorial

Sometimes you'll need to create an effect for which there's no recipe and no shortcut. The best way to master the techniques that will eventually make you a great photographer or digital graphics artist is to go through the Elements tutorials, which you probably installed along with the program. Assuming you did an Easy Install, they'll be in a folder called Tutorials, inside the main Elements folder. To open a tutorial, go to the Help menu and choose Photoshop Elements Tutorials, as shown in Figure 13.6.

FIGURE 13.6

Tutorials are hidden here.

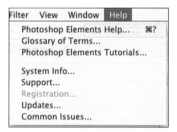

When you select the Photoshop Elements Tutorials option, a browser window like the one in Figure 13.7 will open with a list of what's available. Choose an interesting topic from the pane on the right, and click to open it.

13

FIGURE 13.7

These tutorials, and the entire Photoshop Elements help system, actually run in your browser.

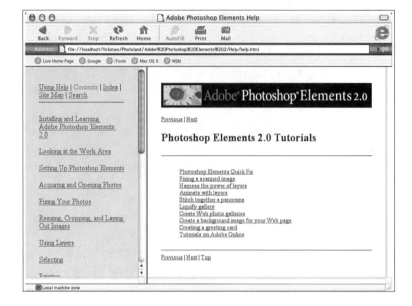

Tutorials are longer and more conversationally written than recipes, and come with the image files you'll need to follow along. There are no Do It for Me links, so you'll have to read carefully and follow the directions closely. Figure 13.8 shows a typical page from a tutorial. This one, called "Harness the Power of Layers," happens to be all about layers, and if you're still having trouble using them, I recommend it.

FIGURE 13.8

Tutorials take you through specific exercises, unlike recipes, which work with your own pictures.

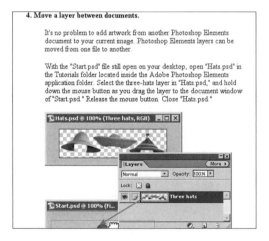

Going Online for Help and Inspiration

There are more tutorials at Adobe Online, along with many other useful things. This is also where you'll go—automatically, if you choose—to look for updates, bug fixes, and enhancements to make Elements run better. The quickest way to get to Adobe Online is to click on the yellow flower at the top of the toolbox. You may see a screen asking you whether you want to check for updates. Click Yes, and you'll see the screen in Figure 13.9. Click the Updates button to download any current updates or software fixes. They'll be installed automatically where they are supposed to go. Click the Preferences button to indicate whether you want Elements to automatically look for updates and download them for you, and if so, how often.

FIGURE 13.9

Updates can happen automatically, or only when you choose to go looking.

If you're looking for help rather than updates, click the Go Online button. Your browser will open, if it's not already open, and you'll be transported to Adobe Online, directly to the Elements home page shown in Figure 13.10. Here, you can find all kinds of interesting stuff including more downloads, a user forum, the latest news from Adobe, tryouts of other Adobe products, and more. The user forum is a good place to get questions answered. The people who actually write these programs read and respond to letters there frequently, and the help you get from them is reliable and actually helpful. And, of course, there are more tutorials, listed under Training & Events.

The tutorials here are good ones. More are added periodically, so keep checking back. You can also find ideas you can use in the Photoshop tutorials section. Of course, Elements can't quite do everything that Photoshop can do, so be prepared to look for workarounds for things such as placing guidelines on a page. (You've already learned this one…. Add a layer, draw lines on it, and trash the layer when you're done with the guidelines.)

13

FIGURE 13.10

Tutorials are listed under Training & Events.

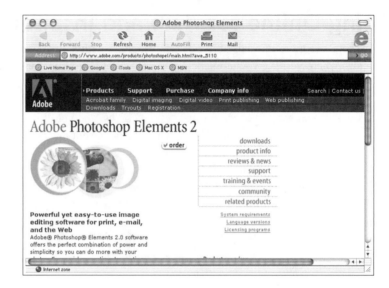

Web Sites for Ideas and Help

Naturally, you'll start at Adobe for help with Adobe products, but that doesn't mean you should stop there. If you do a Web search for Photoshop Elements tutorials, you'll find literally hundreds, perhaps thousands (I didn't stop to count) of references. Even weeding out the ones in Japanese, Italian, and other languages I don't speak, there were far too many to chase down. But I did find some good ones, and even some that were specifically dedicated to Elements, rather than Photoshop. However, you shouldn't ignore the Photoshop sites, especially the ones that offer downloadable free filters and plug-ins. Any plug-in that works with Photoshop also works with Elements.

Check out some of these Web sites for more help and ideas:

- Jay Arraich's Photoshop Elements Tips—Jay's a longtime photographer and Photoshop user, and was one of the beta testers for Elements 2. His tutorials are excellent; they're easy to follow and interesting.

  http://www.arraich.com/elements/psE_intro.htm

- myJanee.com Graphic Creations and Photoshop Resources—Excellent Photoshop tutorials in a well laid out, accessible Web site. Most of Janee's tutorials apply to Elements as well as to Photoshop. This site also has a very good question and answer section.

  http://www.myjanee.com/

- Tutorialengine.com—Over 1,000 tutorials on all kinds of programs, including a good Photoshop section. I found many items here that I had never seen elsewhere, and most appeared to be doable in Elements.

  http://www.ascenvia.net/engine/

- Phong.com—Phong's tutorials are a little more complex, and a little more off-the-wall than most, but they are fun to read, and will definitely give you ideas about what to try in Elements.

  http://www.phong.com

- The Photoshop Guru's Handbook—The guru is pretty good. His tutorials are divided into three levels, for beginning, intermediate, and experienced users.

  http://photoshopgurus.info/

- Planet Photoshop—Last, but far from least, is this excellent site for all things Photoshop. In addition to a daily tutorial—which actually changes several times a week, if not daily—there's a news section to keep you up to date with the latest in tools, industry gossip, and more. There are downloads, user forums, a resources list with loads of great sources for filters and plug-ins, and so much else that I'm sure I haven't discovered it all yet. It's a commercially run site, so there are ads, but even those are all related to graphics and digital photography.

  http://www.planetphotoshop.com/

Joining the National Association of Photoshop Professionals

Don't be put off by the name. This group welcomes beginners, too, and has a lot to offer. Your dues ($99 U.S.) bring you access to the association's members-only Web site (www.photoshopuser.com), with job listings, discussion groups, weekly live chat, discounted training videos and seminars, and a member gallery where you can post your own work and see what others are doing. You get 8 issues of *Photoshop User Magazine* (not available by subscription otherwise), discounts on all kinds of hardware and software, and access to the Help Desk, a confidential Q & A service run by my good friend Pete Bauer. And you get a discount on tickets to the PhotoshopWorld Expo, plus an invitation to the members-only Saturday night party. You can also find discounts on car rentals, travel and hotels, and access to Smart HR, a one-source solution for human resource issues (health insurance, 401(k) & Section 125 plans, payroll and payroll taxes, employee manuals, and unemployment paperwork to name a few). Whew! I'm sure there's even more that I haven't even mentioned.

It's worth joining just for the magazine. I write a Beginners' How To column for them in each issue, demystifying some aspect of Photoshop, and a column of easy tips for faster, more creative work. Check the magazine out at www.photoshopuser.com, and sign up for a free sample issue.

13

Summary

The theme of this hour has been "learning how and where to learn." First, we looked at resources inside Elements. You learned how to find and follow a recipe. You saw how to download new ones. Then you learned about tutorials, which are more detailed and less automated than recipes. The purpose of a tutorial is to teach you to use the tools yourself instead of clicking a Do It for Me link. First you learned about Adobe's tutorials that come with the program. Then you learned how to go directly to the Adobe Web site to see more. Then we looked beyond Adobe to see what else is on the Web. You learned about some excellent Web pages dedicated to Photoshop and Elements, and about the National Association of Photoshop Professionals.

Q&A

Q Why don't the recipes have buttons for each step?

A Some of the steps require your creative input. There are buttons to choose a particular tool or to open a dialog box, but the software doesn't know how big a box you want to drag, or what words you want to put in it.

Q Where can I find more filters?

A Start with a Google search for "Photoshop Filters." That will give you hundreds of places to look. Also check the resources section at the sites I listed. Many have direct links to filter sources, including commercial filter demos.

Workshop

It's all part of the learning process. Take a few moments to tackle the short quiz on recipes and tutorials and check your answers to see how you did. Then have fun with the activity.

Quiz

1. How do you save recipes in Elements?

    a. Save them as text files, and add the extension .rcp.

    b. Put them on 3×5 cards and keep them near the computer for future use.

    c. You can't.

2. Tutorials are opened from the _____ menu.

    a. Image

    b. Help

    c. Recipes

    d. How To

3. *Photoshop User* is published by *MacWorld*.

    a. True

    b. False

Quiz Answers

1. Choice c is correct, but b works, too.

2. b. They're part of the help system.

3. b. It's published by the NAPP.

Activity

Go to one of the sites listed earlier in this hour. Find a tutorial that doesn't use paths or channels, and try it in Elements. If you get stuck because there's no tool that does what you need, try to think up a workaround. Keep going, and if you can't do it their way, do it your way.

13

PART III
Photo Rescue

Hour

HOUR 14

Repairing Black-and-White Pictures

Why is it that the pictures you care about most are the ones that inevitably fade, get wrinkled, get chewed up by the dog, or fall prey to so many other disasters? It probably has some relation to Murphy's Law—whatever can go wrong, will.

The good news, though, is that you're not totally stuck when your kid smears peanut butter on the only decent picture of great-grandma, or the cat thinks your parents wedding photo is a new cat toy. First, as soon as you discover the damage, wipe off any residual cat slobber or other foreign substances, if you can do it without damaging the photo any more. The second thing is to scan it into your computer.

Of course, you should have already done that with all the most important family photos and documents, making two CD-ROM copies, and giving one to a friend or distant family member for safekeeping. Floods, fires, and peanut butter happen. If you've protected your most precious memories, you can always make new prints.

Depending on the size of the photo, scan it same size. If it's a tiny snapshot, size it larger—you might as well be able to see what you're doing. 300 dpi is plenty for most uses, especially if it's an old photo. The film grain will be about that size, too.

In this hour you will

- Add contrast to an old photo
- Lighten and darken specific areas of a photo with the Dodge and Burn tools
- Paint over small marks on a photo
- Repair serious damage to an old photo
- Add a sepia look to a black-and-white photo

Easy Fixes

Some pictures need a little help; others need a lot. Let's start with things that can be easily fixed. The little girl shown in Figure 14.1 is badly exposed, and it appears as if this picture, and two others that were sent with it and shot the same day, were taken with a camera that leaked light. That explains the dark streak in the same place on all three. Still, there's a lot of hope for this one. It just needs some contrast.

FIGURE 14.1

Little girl, circa 1950? (Photo courtesy of Judy Blair)

The first step, as always, is to straighten and crop. She looks as if she's about to tip over backward, and whether the camera was crooked or she was, it's an easy fix that might as well be made. Cropping will not only improve the photo, but will take away some of the stuff we'd otherwise have to retouch, saving us some time and effort. Look for tips on how to crop and straighten your old photos or scans in Hour 9, "Cropping and Resizing Your Pictures," and Hour 10, "Straightening, Skewing, and Distorting an Image."

Now that the girl's standing straight up, let's examine another obvious problem—lack of brightness and contrast. To do this, choose Image, Histogram. Looking at the histogram (Figure 14.2) tells us that there's plenty of detail (lots of pixels) in the middle darks, and that's what we need to work on, so we're good to go. I'll use Levels (Enhance, Adjust Brightness/Contrast, Levels) to remap the gray scale. As you can see in Figure 14.3, I've moved the black and white points (the triangles at either end, just below the histogram) in toward the center of the scale, to the points at which the graph indicates more activity. Then, I moved the middle gray point to the place where there's the steep rise in darks. This spreads the lighter grays over a greater area of the graph and compresses the darks, giving the photo more light grays and increased contrast. For help in making this type of adjustment, see Hour 12, "Too Light/Too Dark: Adjusting Brightness, Contrast, and Color."

FIGURE 14.2

The histogram shows good detail in the darks.

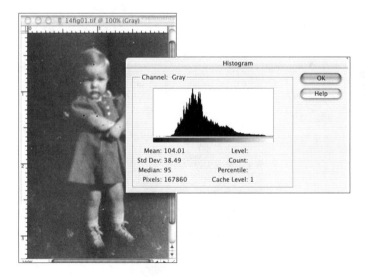

14

FIGURE **14.3**
Use Levels to improve the contrast.

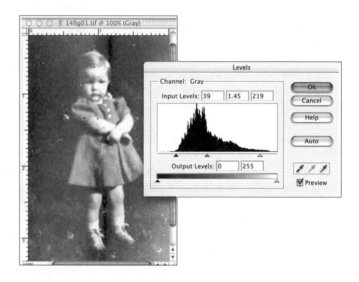

As a last step, I'll get rid of the dust with the Clone Stamp tool, choosing a brush just big enough to cover the spots, and setting the blending mode to Darken for the light spots and to Lighten for the dark ones. That way, the surrounding areas aren't changed. And there she is, in Figure 14.4, nearly as good as new. If you need help using the Clone Stamp, see Hour 11, "Removing Red Eye, Dust, and Scratches."

FIGURE **14.4**
The little girl, looking much better.

Lack of Contrast

As you saw in the picture of the little girl, lack of contrast is one of the most common problems with older photos. They fade over time, of course, but many didn't have much contrast to start with. That's obviously the case with Figure 14.5, shot in bright sun and looking very washed out. This, by the way, is part of the same set as the previous example. Again, notice the black streaks down the middle, probably caused by light leaking into the camera. We'll have to try to lighten them or hide them, too.

FIGURE 14.5

This photo is too light to see details.

As before, first we'll crop, and then look at the histogram to see what we've got to work with. This histogram, shown in Figure 14.6, is unusual in that it's shifted so far toward the light shades. There are very few darks, but there seems to be plenty of detail in what's there, so we should be able to improve this photo.

FIGURE 14.6

This histogram shows that we still have something to work with.

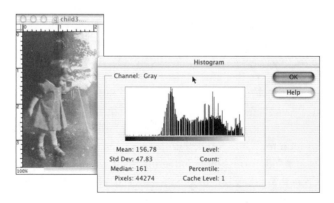

14

We'll start with Levels (Enhance, Brightness/Contrast, Levels) again, and shift the black and white points to where the action begins on the histogram. This time, though, I'll use the eyedroppers to set the black and white points. First, I click the white eyedropper up in the sky (a part of our photo that should be white) to set the white point. I chose the upper-right corner of the picture for this because it seems to be the lightest area. Then, I click the black eyedropper on the darkest spot, which is behind the child, in her shadow. That sets the dark point. Now, I can slide the midpoint back and forth until I find a middle gray point that looks right to me, and reveals as much detail on the child's face as possible. After all, she's the subject, and although it's nice to have detail everywhere, it's most important there. Figure 14.7 shows my settings, and the result.

FIGURE 14.7
Better, but not there yet....

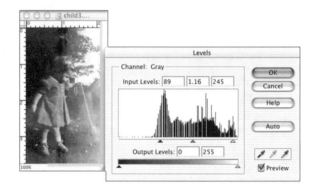

Dodging and Burning

There are still a few more tricks we can use. The Dodge and Burn tools are based on dark room photography techniques that have been used for 100 years or more. Dodging means putting your hand, or some sort of dodging tool, in between the enlarger light and the printing paper while you're making the exposure. This blocks the light from hitting the paper and leaves that area of the print less exposed, and therefore lighter. You have to keep the dodging tool in motion, so you only block some of the light and not all of it. Otherwise, you'd simply have a white spot. The usual dodging tool is a cardboard circle on a flexible wire handle, which looks like a lollipop. Not surprisingly, it's also the Elements icon for the tool. The burning tool has the opposite effect. You can use a sheet of cardboard with a small hole in the middle, or simply hold your hand so a small beam of light gets through, while the rest is blocked—again, this is just like the tool icon. Burning is done after the initial exposure of the paper, and means turning the enlarger lamp back on and giving additional light to a part of the picture, darkening the area you reexposed.

To use the Dodge tool to lighten or the Burn tool to darken, select the one you want to use from the toolbox. Both tools have the same options. Select a brush size that's appropriate for the area you want to affect—you can change the brush style too, but I find that the soft round brush, which is the default, typically works well. Next, select the tonal Range you want to affect: highlights, midtones, or shadows. Then select the amount of exposure you want. For the most subtle changes, I typically use a large soft brush that I can sweep through my photo in a quick motion. I also set the exposure to a low level, and select a tonal range opposite of what I'm trying to add. For example, if I want to darken an area, I choose the Burn tool and select the highlight or midtone range. I choose the shadow range to have the quickest effect. When using the Dodge tool, I choose the shadow range for the most subtle changes.

I can use the Dodge and Burn tools to even out the exposure on this photo. I'll dodge behind her to lighten the trees, and burn around her face to darken that area and increase the detail. Figure 14.8 shows the final version of the photo.

FIGURE 14.8

Still not perfect, but much better. Compare it to the original.

Task: Using the Dodge and Burn Tools

Before we go on, let's practice with the Dodge and Burn tools.

1. Open a new page in Elements. Make sure it has a white background. The default size is fine.

2. Click the Brush tool. Choose a medium large paintbrush from the drop-down list, and set Mode to Normal and Opacity to 100%. Select a paint color by clicking the Foreground swatch on the toolbar. Use middle gray or a medium value of any color you want. Click on the image and drag to make a squiggle of paint across the page, as in Figure 14.9.

14

FIGURE **14.9**

You can use a blank image for practice.

3. Select the Dodge tool. Because it uses brush shapes, choose a large soft brush and set the Range to Midtones and the Exposure to 50%, as shown in Figure 14.10.

FIGURE **14.10**

Setting the dodge tool options.

4. Hold down the mouse button as you move the tool a few times up and down across the line. Each time you go over an area it lightens more. In Figure 14.11, I've nearly erased a piece of the line.

FIGURE **14.11**

The tool only works when it's moving.

5. Now switch to the Burn tool, keeping the same options. Drag it over a different piece of the line. See how each pass darkens the line. (It's actually increasing the saturation of color, which has the effect of making the line look darker.) Figure 14.12 shows what this looks like.

FIGURE **14.12**

The rule to remember: Burning darkens; dodging lightens.

6. Practice with both the Dodge and Burn tools. See if you can put back the area you dodged out, and lighten the burned area to match the rest.

Painting Over Small Blotches

Some pictures need touching up with a brush. The girl shown in Figure 14.8 looks very good, but there are a few distracting dots around her feet. There are several ways to fix such problems—you can use the Clone Stamp to paint nearby colors over a rip or a large splotch, as we will on a badly damaged photograph later in this hour, but you can simply paint over small dots or blemishes.

Using the Brush tool, which you'll learn more about in Hour 19, "Creating Art from Scratch," is not terribly difficult. Select a brush style, size, and color, then drag over the area you want to paint. When trying to brush color onto a photo to cover a small blotch, the hard part is picking a color that matches the one that missing. Do you know how to select the right color to do the touch-up? You probably can't do it from the Color Picker. Perhaps one person in a hundred thousand is good enough at color recognition to select a perfect match for a given color. And even then, it would be as much luck as knowledge, because every pixel on the Color Picker is slightly different from its closest neighbors. Instead, select an exact match with the Eyedropper. Look at the picture and find an area with the exact shade you need. (Usually, it will be immediately adjacent to the damage you're going to repair.) Figure 14.13 shows this step. Then, just click it with the Eyedropper to make it the foreground (active) color. If you press Option/Alt as you click, it will instead become the new background color. You can then use the brush to touch up spots of uneven or missing color.

FIGURE 14.13
Choosing a foreground color.

Preparing an Old Photo for Repair by Removing Sepia

One of the characteristics that really distinguish old photos is the brownish tone they have. It's called sepia, and it comes from dipping the finished print in a bath of squid ink and water. Sepia toning was done to give the print a rich, warm quality rather than the original drab gray. This process also had the effect of stabilizing the print, making it last longer.

I find it harder to work on sepia-colored pictures, so I always remove the color before I start editing them. It's easy to replace it afterward. You'll learn how later in this hour, when we talk about duotones.

There are several ways to remove color. Probably the easiest is to use the Remove Color command that we discussed in Hour 12: Enhance, Adjust Color, Remove Color, or Cmd/Ctrl+Shift+U. You could also convert the picture to grayscale, which would have the same effect, but doing so would require you to convert back to RGB mode if you wanted to add back the sepia when you finished. Another option is to open the Hue/Saturation dialog box, and move the saturation slider all the way to the left to completely desaturate the picture, again removing all color. All three methods produce the same results; I typically use the Remove Color command if I plan to restore the sepia later, change to grayscale if I don't intend to use the sepia again, and use the Hue/Saturation command to put the sepia back (although you can use this command to remove the sepia as well).

Removing color also can get rid of coffee and tea stains, colored ink smudges, and many of the other things that get spilled on a photo. Even if it leaves a gray blob; that will be easier to cover.

Repairing Serious Damage

So far, all the pictures we've looked at have been easy to fix. Let's try one that is more difficult. Take a critical look at Figure 14.14. This one's much too dark, and the sepia is turning sort of greenish. It's also scratched and torn, and needs some spotting. You can see these problems more clearly if you look at the photo in the color plate section.

FIGURE 14.14

*This one's been seri-
ously beaten up and
damaged. (Photo cour-
tesy of K. Rudden)*

First Steps

This will actually be easier than it looks. First, I'll remove the color by choosing
Enhance, Adjust Color, Remove Color. Then, I'll crop away as much of the damage as I
can. Then, I'll reset the levels using the Enhance, Adjust Brightness/Contrast, Levels
command. Just these small adjustments improve it a lot, as you can see in Figure 14.15,
but we still have corners missing, and cracks and scratches to cover. The perfect tool for
this job is the Clone Stamp tool.

14

FIGURE 14.15
*We're already at least
half done.*

Repairing Tears

You learned how to use the Clone Stamp tool in Hour 11, but let me remind you of a
couple of things. First of all, make sure you are using the right size brush. One that's too
big will cover too much of an area, possibly leaving a smooth spot or color that doesn't
quite match. Using one that's too small will make you go over and over the same spot,
building up dark bits wherever the stamps overlap. When repairing a small tear, set the
brush size to just cover it. With larger tears, you'll want to go more slowly, with a smaller
brush. Also, make sure that it's a soft-edged brush for most general purposes.

For this repair, do not check the Aligned option. If you use that option here, you might
accidentally copy the folds of her dress or the edge of her sleeve to someplace where
they don't belong. Better to copy the colors you want, and paint them onto the places
where they belong.

When you're using any of the brush-related tools, go to Preferences, Display
& Cursors and make sure that the Painting cursor is set to show brush size. It
will help a lot in placing the stamp if you can see where its edges are.

Remember that you can zoom in on small areas to make them easier to see. In Figure 14.16, I have come in close on the lady's sleeve to show you a trick. Here, there's a crack running through a seam. I can go above it, to where there's an untouched piece of seam, and copy it as a source. Then, when I move the stamp tool down over the damage, I'm replacing it with a good piece of the same seam. As long as I am careful to stay centered on the seam as I move the stamp, the original and the repair will stay aligned and the seam will look right, as it does in the After view.

FIGURE 14.16
Before and after stamping.

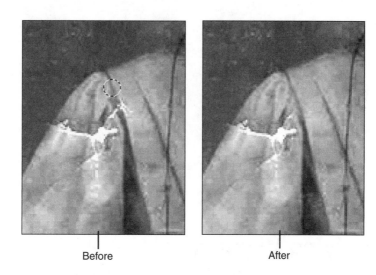

Before   After

After cleaning the picture up with the Clone Stamp tool, we can use the Dodge tool with a very light pressure, to lighten the woman's face. If you look back at Figure 14.15, you'll see that her face is too dark, but the man's face isn't. With the Dodge tool, I can lighten just the area of her face. I've also applied the Despeckle filter (Filter, Noise, Despeckle) at its lowest settings, to suppress some of the dust. A filter, you may recall, applies a series of changes in a single step—]for instance, the Unmask filter sharpens all the edges. As you learned in Hour 11, the Despeckle filter (Filter, Noise, Despeckle) is a handy tool for removing dust and dirt from an image. It works by looking for areas of sharp contrast (such as dark spots on a light background), and then blurring such areas into their surroundings, without blurring edges.

Figure 14.17 shows the final, much-improved version. But I might not stop there; I might use the Burn tool to darken the bottom of her dress and the top of the man's forehead, which both seem unnaturally light to me. And I might work a bit more on her sleeve, but I don't want to do too much, or I'll remove the charm of this old photograph.

14

FIGURE 14.17
This photo is close to 100 years old.

Applying Vignetting

Vignetting was a technique frequently used in the early days of photography to make up for deficiencies in both the camera lens and the glass plates used for negatives. Not much was understood about the art and science of lens grinding, except that the lens tended to be sharpest in the middle and the focus would fall off rapidly as you moved from the center to the edges of the resulting photo. Photo plates were prepared by brushing plain glass with a solution of gum Arabic or some other colloidal (sticky stuff) and silver nitrate. (Chemists, don't come after me. I'm sure there was more in the mix, but those were the important elements.) The gunk seldom went on evenly, especially near the edges of the plate, so the edges of the photo would be correspondingly messy. Today, that messy edge look is considered a special effect, and is frequently seen in black-and-white digital photography. I'll tell you how to do it in our final hour.

Anyway, both of these factors resulted in pictures that were okay in the middle and both fuzzy and messy at the edges. Soon, the better photographers figured out a way to disguise the bad parts, while making it look like an extra fancy effect. They invented the vignette. It's simply a mask that fades from the edges of the picture toward the middle, so that the photo appears to be fading out at the edges.

I have an old photo of a friend's grandmother that's a perfect candidate for a vignette. Grandma Fish appears in Figure 14.18.

FIGURE 14.18

This picture needs some help. (Photo courtesy of Peggy Ogan)

Old vignettes were typically oval, so that's what we'll apply here. But with Elements, you can use this technique with any shape.

Ordinarily, we'd start by cropping, but we'll be vignetting this one and we'll want the extra space for the vignette mask. Thus, we'll ignore that step, and just remove the yellow color (with the Replace Color command) and the dust and spots (with the Clone Stamp). Correcting the levels and adding some contrast (Enhance, Adjust Brightness/Contrast, Levels) helps, too. In Figure 14.19, I've started the vignette process by placing an oval marquee where I want the frame to start. To make marquee placement easier, click the Elliptical Marquee tool, select Fixed Aspect Ratio in the Style pop-up menu on the tool Options bar, and designate a ratio. I prefer W = 2, H = 3 for a tall oval frame. To make a vignette marquee, I find that it's often easier to drag outward from the middle, rather than from the edges in. So, press Cmd/Ctrl and click on the center of her face (the location of the cross in Figure 14.19) and drag the oval outwards until you've selected the area you wish to feature with the vignette. Then, invert the selection (Select, Inverse, or Cmd/Ctrl+Shift+I). That means that the edges are selected instead of the area in the middle.

14

Figure 14.19

It's easier to drag the marquee from the center outward.

We also need to feather the selection by about 25 pixels. (I could have done this when I dragged the marquee, but I wasn't sure at the time how much edge I would need.) We want a soft edge on the vignette, but not too soft. To create such an edge, choose Select, Feather, type 25 as the amount, and click OK. Next simply double-check to make sure that the background color is set to white, then press the Delete key and the background disappears. Figure 14.20 shows the finished portrait.

Figure 14.20

Here it is, a less cluttered, more interesting portrait.

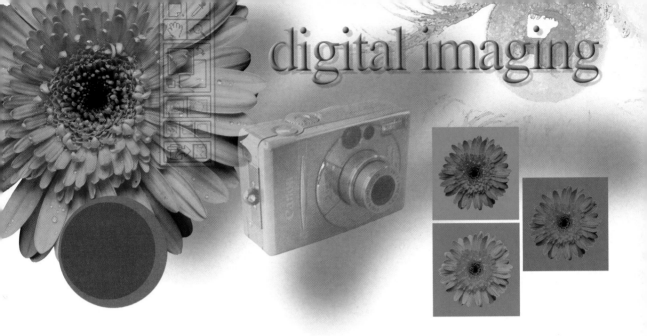

COLOR GALLERY

FIGURE 2.15

The lower the number of levels, the more simplified the drawing becomes.

Hour 2, page 28

FIGURE 6.6

Don't be afraid to experiment.

Hour 6, page 97

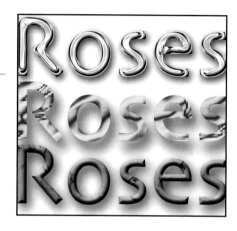

FIGURE 6.7

I added a glow to help define the letters.

Hour 6, page 98

FIGURE 8.7

Choose colors that harmonize so they won't distract the reader from the real message of the page.

Hour 8, page 136

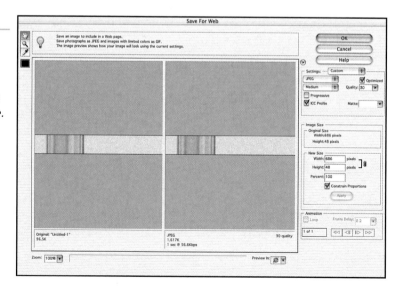

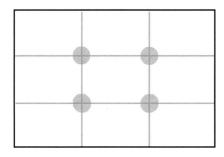

FIGURE 9.3

These four spots are where your eye naturally goes.

Hour 9, page 149

FIGURE 9.4

Pretty darn close to the magic spot.

Hour 9, page 150

FIGURE 10.7

The picture is all done, and much less distorted.

Hour 10, page 165

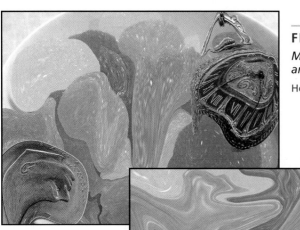

FIGURE 10.20

Melted gumdrops, a pocket watch, and a fifty cent piece.

Hour 10, page 175

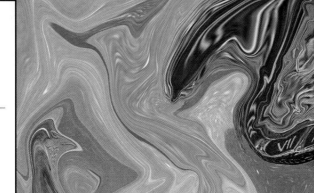

FIGURE 10.21

Now the objects are almost unrecognizable.

Hour 10, page 175

FIGURE 11.2

Once you've removed the helicopter, you're ready to take out the small boats.

Hour 11, page 181

FIGURE 11.3

Zoom in so you can see what you're doing.

Hour 11, page 182

FIGURE 11.8
The recipe didn't do enough.
Hour 11, page 186

FIGURE 11.11
Now, he looks quite normal. Pity he doesn't act it.
Hour 11, page 188

FIGURE 12.3
The original photo.

FIGURE 12.4
Auto Levels applied.

12.3-12.6
Hour 12,
pages 199-200

FIGURE 12.5
Auto Contrast applied.

FIGURE 12.6
Auto Color Correction applied.

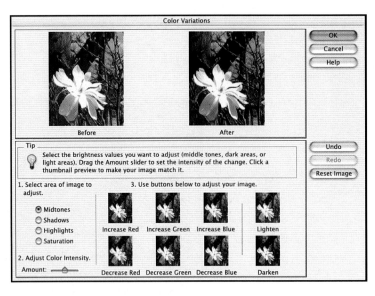

FIGURE 12.7

Adjusting color by eye sometimes produces the best results.

Hour 12, page 200

FIGURE 12.11

Why not blue daisies?

Hour 12, page 204

FIGURE 12.13

Here I've changed all the yellow daisies to pink.

Hour 12, page 206

FIGURE 12.14

You can't put it in the wedding album looking like this.

Hour 12, page 208

Photo courtesy Judy Blair

FIGURE 12.17

This looks much better than before.

Hour 12, page 210

FIGURE 13.3

The lighter background really draws attention to the text.

Hour 13, page 217

FIGURE 14.14

This one's been seriously beaten up and damaged.

Hour 14, page 239

Photo courtesy K. Rudden

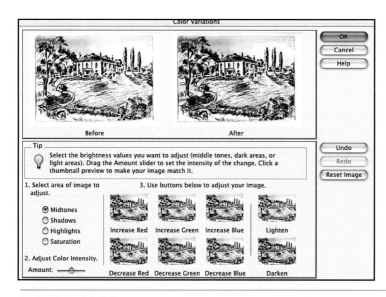

FIGURE 14.25

Even though there's no color in the picture, Variations tries to add some.

Hour 14, page 247

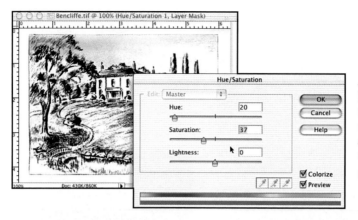

FIGURE 14.26

When you check Colorize, Elements automatically adjusts the saturation to 25%.

Hour 14, page 248

FIGURE 15.1

Can this one be saved?

Hour 15, page 252

FIGURE 15.3

This is better, but not there yet.

Hour 15, page 253

FIGURE 15.6

Our much improved color photo.

Hour 15, page 255

FIGURE 15.10

A little work with the Sponge tool can save a rainy day photo.

Hour 15, page 259

Before   After

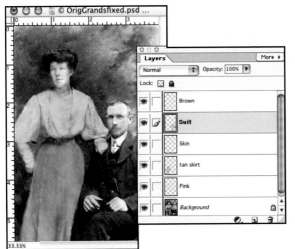

FIGURE 15.17

Don't get bogged down in details. In a picture of this size, you wouldn't see eye color or small details such as the man's suit buttons.

Hour 15, page 263

FIGURE 17.8

Now the sand looks better, and the gull doesn't get lost in the texture.

Hour 17, page 288

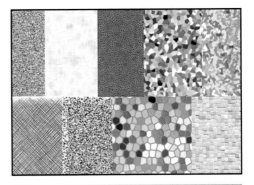

FIGURE 17.20

By changing the amount of noise, you could change each of these to something quite different.

Hour 17, page 296

FIGURE 18.1

Hampton Beach, NH.

Hour 18, page 310

FIGURE 18.8

This definitely looks painted.

Hour 18, page 314

FIGURE 18.10
The result of using the Underpainting filter.

Hour 18, page 315

FIGURE 18.12
The results of the Paint Daubs filter.

Hour 18, page 317

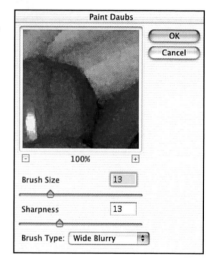

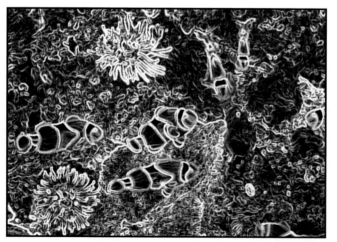

FIGURE 18.23
We've created neon clown fish!

Hour 18, page 325

FIGURE 20.9

Normal—This is the default mode. The blend color replaces the base color.

FIGURE 20.10

Dissolve—A random number of pixels become the blend color. Gives a splattered or "dry brush" effect.

FIGURE 20.11

Dissolve—Applied with a normal brush to second layer @ 50% opacity.

FIGURE 20.12

Darken—Evaluates the color information in each channel and assigns either the base color or the blend color, whichever is darker, as the result color. Lighter pixels are replaced, but darker ones don't change.

FIGURE 20.13

Multiply—Multiplies the base color by the blend color, giving you a darker result color. The effect is like drawing over the picture with a Magic Marker. Where the background is light, you see the original blend color.

FIGURE 20.14

Color Burn—Darkens the base color to match the value of the blend color. This effect is very subtle.

FIGURE 20.15

Linear Burn— Darkens the base color to reflect the blend color by decreasing the brightness. Blending with white produces no change.

FIGURE 20.16

Lighten—Evaluates the color information in each channel and assigns either the base color or the blend color, whichever is lighter, as the result color. Darker pixels are replaced, but lighter ones don't change. This is the exact opposite of Darken.

FIGURE 20.17 *Screen—Multiplies the base color by the inverse of the blend color, giving you a lighter result color. The effect is like painting with bleach.*
The hearts were drawn with the brush set to Wet Edges.

FIGURE 20.18 *Color Dodge—Brightens the base color to match the value of the blend color.*

FIGURE 20.19 *Linear Dodge—Brightens the base color to reflect the blend color by increasing the brightness. Blending with black produces no change.*

FIGURE 20.20 *Overlay—Evaluates the color information in each channel and assigns either the base color or the blend color, whichever is darker, as the result color. Lighter pixels are replaced, but darker ones don't change.*

FIGURE 20.21 *Soft Light—Darkens or lightens depending on the blend color. The effect is said to be similar to shining a diffused spotlight on the image. With a light blend color, it has very little effect.*

FIGURE 20.22 *Hard Light—Multiplies or screens the colors, depending on the blend color. The effect is similar to shining a harsh spotlight on the image.*

FIGURE 20.23 *Vivid Light— Burns or dodges the colors by increasing or decreasing the contrast, depending on the blend color. If the blend color (light source) is lighter than 50% gray, the image is lightened by decreasing the contrast. If the blend color is darker than 50% gray, the image is darkened by increasing the contrast.*

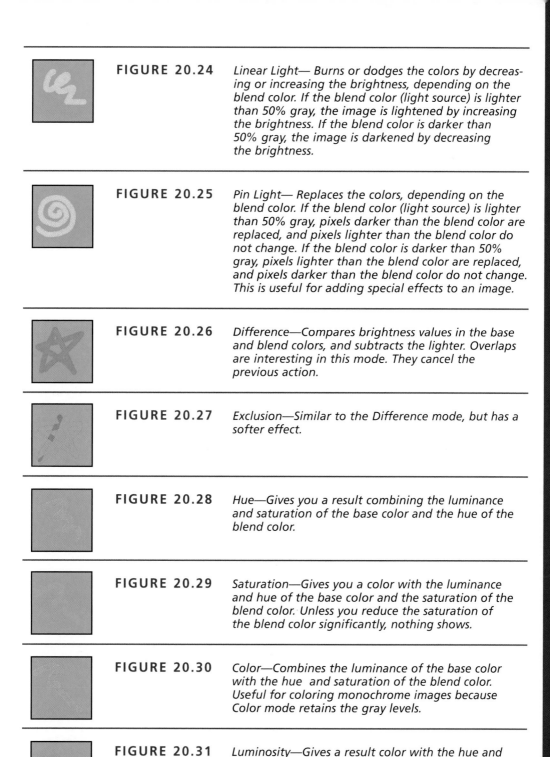

FIGURE 20.24 Linear Light— Burns or dodges the colors by decreasing or increasing the brightness, depending on the blend color. If the blend color (light source) is lighter than 50% gray, the image is lightened by increasing the brightness. If the blend color is darker than 50% gray, the image is darkened by decreasing the brightness.

FIGURE 20.25 Pin Light— Replaces the colors, depending on the blend color. If the blend color (light source) is lighter than 50% gray, pixels darker than the blend color are replaced, and pixels lighter than the blend color do not change. If the blend color is darker than 50% gray, pixels lighter than the blend color are replaced, and pixels darker than the blend color do not change. This is useful for adding special effects to an image.

FIGURE 20.26 Difference—Compares brightness values in the base and blend colors, and subtracts the lighter. Overlaps are interesting in this mode. They cancel the previous action.

FIGURE 20.27 Exclusion—Similar to the Difference mode, but has a softer effect.

FIGURE 20.28 Hue—Gives you a result combining the luminance and saturation of the base color and the hue of the blend color.

FIGURE 20.29 Saturation—Gives you a color with the luminance and hue of the base color and the saturation of the blend color. Unless you reduce the saturation of the blend color significantly, nothing shows.

FIGURE 20.30 Color—Combines the luminance of the base color with the hue and saturation of the blend color. Useful for coloring monochrome images because Color mode retains the gray levels.

FIGURE 20.31 Luminosity—Gives a result color with the hue and saturation of the base color and the luminance of the blend color. Opposite effect to Color Blend mode.

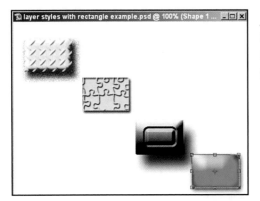

FIGURE 20.2
Which style do you like best?
Hour 20, page 355

FIGURE 20.5
The advantage to working this way is that you can control the amount of the adjustments you apply to each part of an image.
Hour 20, page 360

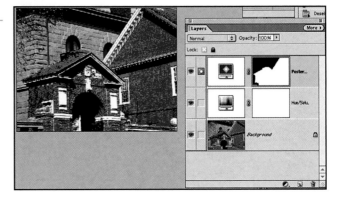

FIGURE 20.35
From left to right, Overlay, Color Dodge, and Saturation.
Hour 20, page 372

FIGURE 21.2
This Posterization was done with four levels.
Hour 21, page 389

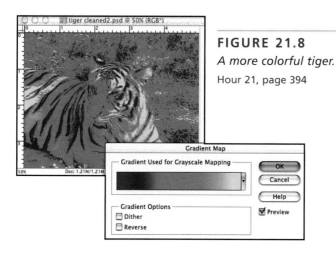

FIGURE 21.8
A more colorful tiger.
Hour 21, page 394

FIGURE 21.14
I probably shouldn't have patted the duck.
Hour 21, page 397

The Midas Touch

A lotta brass...

FIGURE 21.15

*Brass is duller than gold.
Hence the noise.*

Hour 21, page 397

Copperplate

FIGURE 21.16

Copper should shine.

Hour 21, page 397

FIGURE 22.12

Wish I was there....

Task: Cleaning Up a Picture, Step by Step

This task is going to require that you use just about everything you've learned about working with Elements. The photo in Figure 14.21 dates back to about 1906, and it's had a hard life. There are a couple of stains, and someone or something chewed on an edge, leaving holes. It has dust. It's faded and needs more contrast. It's crooked, too, or else the porch was. And the sepia toning has taken on a greenish cast. Download the picture called Grandmas, 1906 from this book's page on the Sams Publishing Web site and follow along.

FIGURE 14.21
The original Grandmas photo, circa 1906.

1. As usual, we'll start by cropping and straightening. As we did in Hour 12, we'll straighten first, then crop. Use the Image, Rotate, Free Rotate command to rotate the picture until the porch is horizontal and its posts are vertical. Remember that you can draw guidelines on a disposable layer to help you level the image.

2. Once that's done, use the Crop tool to select the area to keep, removing the chewed up edges, but keeping as much usable area as possible. Jump back to Hour 12 if you need a refresher course on straightening or cropping.

3. Next, use the Enhance, Adjust Color, Remove Color command to get rid of the faded sepia and the pink stain. Figure 14.22 shows the result of these steps.

FIGURE 14.22
It's too bad we can't crop out the holes.

14

4. Next, open the Levels dialog box (Enhance, Brightness/Contrast, Levels) and work on the contrast. As you can see in the histogram in Figure 14.23, all the grays were bunched in the middle of the range. Resetting the black and white points enables us to spread them out more, while making black really black and white actually white, resulting in much better contrast throughout.

FIGURE 14.23

It's looking better already.

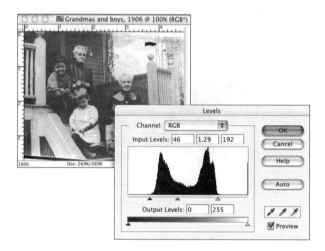

5. Now we need to do some Clone Stamping. We can add back the edges we lost when we straightened the picture (look at the top right and bottom left), and get rid of those holes. The dust can go, too. Don't forget to zoom in when you need a closer look at what you're working on.

6. As almost the final step, use the Dodge tool on all three of the boys' faces. I tried the Despeckle filter (Filter, Noise, Despeckle) on the photo, but it added an unacceptable amount of blur, so I canceled it. Give the brightness and contrast a final tweak in the Brightness/Contrast dialog box we discussed in Hour 12 (Enhance, Adjust Brightness/Contrast, Brightness/Contrast), and then we're finished. Figure 14.24 shows the final image—a major improvement over the original.

FIGURE 14.24

I like the picture better without the sepia, but you can add it back, if you want.

Use these same techniques to restore your old photos. They might work on other photos too, even ones that are not so old! Just remember that you can always undo changes that you make using the Undo button. To undo a series of changes that simply didn't work out, use the Undo History palette. As a safeguard, I always back up my originals to CD, so that any changes I make will never be irreversible no matter what I do. Of course, if you like the result of your changes, back up the updated file as well.

Another technique we haven't talked much about yet is adjustment layers, which let you make specified adjustments to parts (or all) of an image. If you don't like the changes, you can always delete the adjustment layer. You'll learn more about adjustment layers in Hour 20, "Making Composite Images."

Applying Tints

Working with strictly black-and-white images can get boring. Sometimes it's fun to turn the black into a different color, especially if the image is a drawing, map, or other line art. Here's a quick trick I often use on grayscale images, using the Color Variations dialog box we discussed in Hour 12. First, change the color mode from grayscale to RGB. (Image, Mode, RGB) Then, choose Enhance, Adjust Color, Color Variations, as I have in Figure 14.25. (Be sure you look at this in the color section.)

FIGURE 14.25

Even though there's no color in the picture, Variations tries to add some.

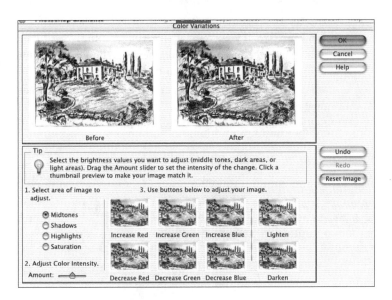

14

With the Midtones option selected, choose any one of the thumbnails that you like. I chose Decrease Green, which gave me a sort of purple-toned image. You can also lighten or darken the picture if necessary. Click OK to save the change. The result is a line drawing with a "color look."

The capability to create duotones isn't included in Elements, although it is in Photoshop. A duotone adds a color to black, or combines any two colors, giving you a much richer-looking image. It's commonly used to replace sepia in a corrected black-and-white photo. In Hour 12, I showed you one way to re-create that sepia look using the Colorize option in the Hue/Saturation dialog box. Here's a way to get a duotone effect in Elements:

1. Open the black-and-white photo and convert it from Grayscale mode to RGB color mode. Select the entire image (Select, All or Cmd/Ctrl+A). Then, use Edit, Copy or Cmd/Ctrl+C to copy it, and immediately choose Edit, Paste or Cmd/Ctrl+V to paste. The copy of the image will appear on a new layer. Rename this "color layer" by double-clicking its name in the Layers palette and typing a new name, if you think you'll forget which is which.

2. With the color layer active, go to the Layer menu and choose New Adjustment Layer, Hue/Saturation. Be sure to check Group with Previous Layer. Click OK to open the Hue/Saturation dialog box. This step adds a new layer for adjusting the hue and saturation levels of the grouped layer, which in this case is the "color layer" we added. Our adjustments will not affect the original layer.

3. Use the Hue/Saturation dialog box to add color to the image. Check both Colorize and Preview, so you can see what you're doing. (See Figure 14.26) The Hue slider will change the basic color, and the Saturation slider will make it more or less intense. Be careful about using the Lightness slider because decreasing lightness will turn the background "paper" dark, along with the image. A small increase (less than 6) in lightness, however, will make your "paper" look whiter without substantially affecting the image. When you like what you see, click OK.

FIGURE 14.26

When you check Colorize, Elements automatically adjusts the saturation to 25%.

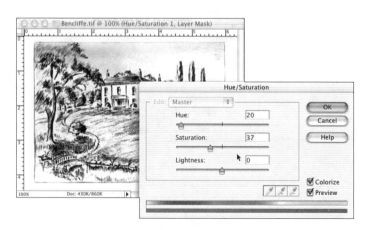

4. Go back to the color layer, and adjust the opacity of the layer using the slider at the top of the Layers dialog box to somewhere between 50% and 75%. This allows the black to show through and combine visually with the color to give the effect of the duotone. Be sure to see the final image in the color section.

Summary

This has certainly been a busy hour. You learned about black-and-white retouching. First, you learned to make simple fixes. You learned how to read a histogram, and how to set levels on a black-and-white photo. You learned about dodging and burning and how to use these effects. Then, we looked at more complicated damage. You learned to use the Clone Stamp tool to replace dust, scratches, and other damage with a good piece of the picture. You learned about removing color to get rid of sepia toning and spilled coffee. You learned to use the Eyedropper tool, and how to make a vignette. Finally, you learned a couple of ways to put back color. You learned how to imitate a duotone, and how to colorize a drawing. That's a lot for one hour, so be sure to practice your new skills before you move on.

Q&A

Q I have some very old pictures that appear to be printed on glass. Can I scan them?

A Those are daguerreotypes. If they are in fancy pressed brass frames, as most are, carefully remove the frame first, and then do your scan. The closer the image is to the scanner glass, the more in focus it will be.

Q Do vignettes have to be oval?

A Not necessarily. You can vignette any shape you can draw with the Selection tools, or you can use the Selection Brush and any of the hundred-plus shapes in the Elements shape library. A heart-shaped vignette might be nice for a picture of a baby or a bride.

Workshop

Restoring old photos is not only fun, it's a way to make money with your computer—when you're good at it. So, practice, practice, practice!

14

Quiz

1. To remove a color cast from an old photo, _____.

   a. Change the mode to Grayscale

   b. Reduce the saturation to zero

   c. Press Cmd+Shift+B for Bleach

2. When using the Clone Stamp tool, if you check Aligned, which of the following will happen?

   a. The stamps will be placed in a straight line.

   b. The stamp source will move in relation to the position of the stamp.

   c. The stamp you place will be on top of the source.

Quiz Answers

1. either a or b, depending on whether you'll want to add back the color when you're done. You can also use the Enhance, Adjust Color, Remove Color command.

2. b. It's handy if you need to copy something to another part of the picture.

Activities

1. To see what perfect contrast can do for a picture go to `http://www.royaltyfreeart.com/ansel/ansel/browse.html` and check out the work of Ansel Adams. One of the greatest black-and-white photographers of all time, Adams perfected what he called the Zone system for assigning black and white points in an image in such a way that there would always be a full range of grays between them.

2. Find and restore some of your family's oldest photos. Start with cropping and contrast, and then make any needed repairs.

Hour 15

Making Color Repairs

Color repairs are apt to be easier than black-and-white repairs, for several reasons. First, the pictures aren't as old, so they are somewhat less likely to be physically damaged. The paper tends to be heavier, and with its glossy coating, is sturdier and less prone to tearing. Very old sepia-tinted photos get brittle with age in a way that pictures printed after about 1950 never do.

The single biggest problem I've seen with color photos from the late 40s and 50s is color cast, or in its more severe form, color shift. When this happens, the entire photo can take on what looks like an overdose of a single color (often pink or purple, but any color can be affected). It's generally blamed on heat or exposure to sunlight, but having seen it happen to pictures that were tucked away in an album or used as a bookmark, I don't think that's necessarily the case. The dyes used back then just weren't stable. Bad processing or letting the film sit in the camera outdoors on a warm day were enough to throw off the color, perhaps not immediately, but as the photos aged.

Of course, bad things can happen to recent pictures too. The sun ducks behind a cloud just as you shoot, and the colors look washed out. The flash doesn't go off as expected. Nothing is immune to spilled drinks, dog/cat/kid damage, and all the other perils of daily life.

You can't save them all. Some are just too far gone, or the data (color, detail) was never there in the first place. But with Elements, you can pull off some pretty amazing rescues.

In this hour you will

- Remove a shift toward a single color
- Fix a flash that didn't work
- Make your brown eyes blue and carry out other selective color changes
- Add sharpness and definition
- Adjust saturation in a selected area
- Smudge the colors in an image
- Flip objects that face the wrong way
- Hand-color an old photo

Correcting Color Cast

Elements makes color cast correction pretty nearly automatic. Figure 15.1 shows an old photo that's so badly yellowed, it's almost brown. Be sure to look at this example in the color plate section.

FIGURE 15.1
Can this one be saved?

I typically start by straightening and cropping an image. The ground seems to be higher on the right than on the left, and we can greatly improve the photo by cropping around the central image of mother and child, and getting rid of the border and that big chimney on the right. After using the Image, Rotate, Free Rotate Layer command to level the

15

ground and the Crop tool to crop the image down a bit, we're ready to begin color correcting.

To correct this kind of color cast, choose Enhance, Adjust Color, Color Cast. You probably remember this command from our discussion in Hour 12, "Too Light/Too Dark: Adjusting Brightness, Contrast, and Color." Figure 15.2 shows the very simple Color Cast Correction dialog box. This tool evaluates the amount of color in what ought to be a black or white pixel. It then applies the same amount of the opposite color on the color wheel to cancel out the overdone one. In this case, the color cast is yellow, so Elements adds an equal amount of blue. If the color cast turned the picture red, it would add cyan. If the cast were green, it would add magenta, and so on.

FIGURE 15.2

Try to find the darkest black or the whitest white.

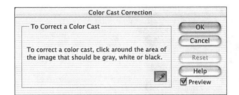

As I mentioned in Hour 12, this command doesn't always do the best job of correcting color cast. To help Elements judge the "correctness" of its first correction, click on any part of the picture that should be either pure white, pure black, or medium gray. To judge whether the correction has worked or not, find part of the picture that's critical, colorwise. Flesh tones are always a good benchmark. I didn't think that the flesh tones looked very good, so I clicked on several areas that I thought should be white, and most seemed to make things worse instead of better. When I tried the baby's dress, though, the flesh tones looked right, even though the picture still needed a lot of work. So I guess the rule for using this dialog box is to keep clicking until you find the right benchmark for Elements to base its corrections on. Of course, if nothing works, click Cancel to undo its attempts to remove the color cast. In Hour 12, you learned about alternatives you can use to remove the color cast manually. The command worked for me, however, as you can see in Figure 15.3 and the corresponding color plate.

FIGURE 15.3

This is better, but not there yet.

Using Fill Flash

Even though the picture was shot in bright sun, there are shadows on both faces because the sun was coming from the side. We'll use Fill Flash to correct this before we finish color correcting. After all, it's the faces that are the most important part of the photo. To open the dialog box shown in Figure 15.4, select Enhance, Adjust Lighting, Fill Flash. As you can see, I have just moved the sliders up a little, to lighten the picture and increase the overall color saturation a small amount.

FIGURE 15.4

If the photographer had used a fill flash, we wouldn't need this step.

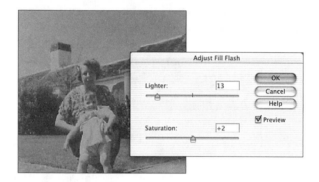

Making Selective Color Adjustments

Nothing we've done so far has had an effect on the sky. It's still brown, and the only way we are going to turn it blue is to select it and force the change. So that's what we'll do. We can select the sky with either the Magic Wand or the Lasso tool, or a combination of both. Because the sky is mostly one color, the Magic Wand is the best tool for selecting it. Using the Lasso tool might prove more difficult because of the irregular edges of the sky area. So I clicked with the Magic Wand tool on a representative part of the sky. Just adjust the Tolerance value so that when you click, most of the sky is selected. Then hold the Shift key down or select the Add to Selection button and continue to click on unselected spots to keep on adding to your selection. If you select a piece that you don't want, immediately Undo (just once) and the rest of the selection will remain selected. You can also click the Subtract from Selection button and click the area you don't want. With the entire sky selected, I can open the Hue/Saturation dialog box (see Figure 15.5) by choosing Enhance, Adjust Color, Hue/Saturation, and make the sky as blue as I want it. In this case, because the rest of the colors are quite subtle, I'll resist the urge to improve the weather and go with a pale blue.

FIGURE 15.5
"Blue skies, smilin' at me...."

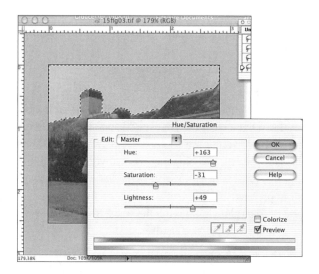

That worked so well, and looks so good, I'll do the same thing with the grass, turning it green instead of blue, of course. Figure 15.6 shows the final image, but you really need to go to the color plate section and compare it to what we started with.

FIGURE 15.6
Our much-improved color photo.

Image Correction Tools

The Elements toolbox has several image correction tools, grouped together on the tool-bar. If you look at the third section of the toolbox, you'll see a pair of focus tools: Blur and Sharpen. Blur looks like a drop of water. Sharpen looks like the tip of a pencil or some other sharp instrument. Below them are the Sponge tool, which looks like a natural sponge, and the Smudge tool, a hand with an extended index finger. (Considering the millions of smudged fingerprints I've wiped up over the years, this is a very appropriate icon.) The last two tools in the group, Dodge and Burn, were discussed in detail last hour.

Blur and Sharpen

If you spill a drop of water on a watercolor painting or an inkjet print, the colors will run together and blur. That's what the Blur tool does. (Well, more or less. It actually blurs individual pixels by lowering the contrast between them and their adjacent neighbors.) Using brush shapes, sizes, and blending modes, you can design a blur to hide a background, to remove graffiti from a fence, or to make faces in a crowd less obvious. When you're trying to pretend your subject is out in the forest, you can blur the cell phone tower and power lines showing though the trees. You can blur the gum wrappers and soda cans in an otherwise pristine landscape.

To use the Blur tool, select it in the toolbox. Choose your brush tip from the drop-down list, and set the brush Size. Choose an Effect Mode (essentially the blending mode—the various types are described in Hour 20, "Making Composite Images"), and then set the strength of the blur. You can drag the Blur tool over a hard edge to soften it or over an image area to eliminate detail.

In the image of two street performers in Harvard Square (see Figure 15.7), the background was very distracting. With the Blur tool set to a large, soft brush at 75% strength, I was able to put most of the background out of focus with just a few swipes of the tool. When I reached the area around the younger man's face, I changed to a very small, hard-edged brush so I could move in close and blur right next to his face, without the risk of removing his nose.

FIGURE 15.7

What a difference a softened background makes.

Before   After

The Sharpen tool is theoretically and literally the opposite of the Blur tool. Instead of decreasing the contrast between adjacent pixels, it increases it. The additional contrast has the effect of making the image appear sharper. To use the Sharpen tool, follow the same steps as before: Select the tool, choose a hard or soft brush tip, adjust the brush size, select an Effects mode (see the discussion of blending modes in Hour 20), and adjust the strength of the sharpening effect. Then simply drag over the part of your image you want to sharpen.

Figure 15.8 shows a nice but rather ordinary picture of some flowers. I think that if one of the bundles of flowers were better defined, the picture might be more interesting. This is definitely a case for the Sharpen tool, with a fairly small brush and medium strength.

FIGURE 15.8

Right now, there's no real center of interest. Sharper flowers would create one.

The one thing to watch out for when you use this tool is that you don't overdo it. Figure 15.9 has two examples: first, the flowers correctly sharpened, and second, the flowers oversharpened. As you can see, when you oversharpen, the image eventually breaks down to a random pattern of black and white, as the tool keeps on increasing the contrast until nothing else is left.

The fun doesn't stop here; there are other ways to blur and sharpen an image, as you'll learn in Hour 17, "Using the Improvement Filters."

The Sponge Tool

The sponge represents a piece of photographic history. Darkroom photographers often kept a clean sponge next to the jug of developer. When the picture in the developing tray wasn't "coming up" fast enough, they'd grab the sponge and the jug, and slosh some fresh chemical on the paper. The combination of fresh developer and the friction from the sponge rubbing it in were generally enough to darken the image and save the print. In your digital darkroom, the Sponge tool does much the same thing. Because this sponge works in color, rather than merely darkening whatever it touches, it changes color saturation. Unlike the sponge in the darkroom, though, it can desaturate as well as saturate, making colors either less intense or more intense. If the image is grayscale, the Sponge tool will increase or decrease the contrast as it raises or lowers the intensity of the gray pixels.

FIGURE 15.9

Here's proof that you can have too much of a good thing.

To use the Sponge tool, select it and choose a brush tip and sponge size. To increase color/gray value intensity (saturation), choose Saturate from the Mode list. To tone down colors/gray values, choose Desaturate instead. To control how much the tool adjusts saturation, change the Flow value. To smudge all visible parts of the image rather than just the current layer, turn on Use All Layers.

By the way, if you're looking for a way to make an image look as if it had been painted with a sponge, try the Sponge filter. You'll learn more about it and the other Artistic filters in Hour 18, "Using the Artistic Filters."

Task: Adjusting Saturation

Figure 15.10, which you can download from the book's Web site, was shot on a rainy day, and looks like it. Let's see whether we can put some sun back in the sunflowers. (If you don't download this and work along, at least be sure you see the before and after versions in the color plate section.

FIGURE 15.10

These colors even look washed out in black and white.

1. Open the Hue/Saturation dialog box, and add a small amount of saturation and lightness to the picture. I used 9 as the setting for both. Because no two monitors are quite alike, your best settings may be different.

2. Select the Sponge tool. On the tool Options bar, set the mode to Saturate and the Flow to 50% or less. Choose a soft-edged brush in a size that's comfortable for working with the yellow flowers. Hold down the mouse button as you drag the Sponge over the yellow parts. See how the color intensifies? Now try it on the purple flowers, but be careful not to overdo.

3. Change the mode to Desaturate, and choose a smaller brush if necessary. Then remove the pale blue from the flowers in the upper-left corner, leaving them white.

The Smudge Tool

It's easy to get the Blur tool and the Smudge tool mixed up. They sound as if they might do the same thing, but they don't. The Smudge tool picks up the pixel(s) where you click, and moves them where you drag. If you imagine dragging your finger through wet paint, you'll get an idea of the effect that the Smudge tool reproduces. In Figure 15.11, I have drawn a line with some sharp up *V*'s and down *V*'s using a hard-edged brush. On the left, I've blurred the two *V*'s at 50% strength using the Blur tool. On the right, I've smudged the two other *V*'s at the same strength using the Smudge tool. There's quite a difference.

To use the Smudge tool, select it and then choose a brush tip and size. Choose a blending mode (again, because blending modes are a pretty advanced topic, I've left them until Hour 20.) Adjust the Strength to control the effect—a lower value creates less smudging. To smudge all visible parts of the image rather than just the current layer, turn on Use All Layers.

FIGURE **15.11**
*There's a big differ-
ence between using the
Blur tool and using the
Smudge tool.*

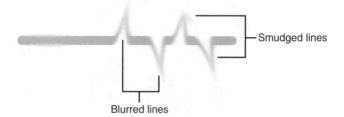

Smudged lines

Blurred lines

The Smudge tool also has a setting called Finger Painting. It places a brush full of paint
(the foreground color) on the screen, and then smudges it as you drag. The effect you
get when using the Smudge tool is a combination of brush size and softness, and the
Strength setting. Higher Strength numbers drag a longer tail behind the brush. Figure
15.12 shows the effects of using the Smudge tool on a photo.

FIGURE **15.12**
*Smudging can give
you interesting effects.*

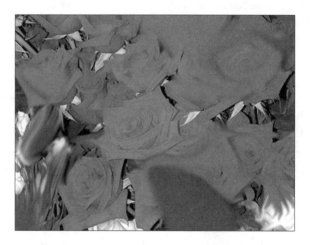

Making Repairs When Nothing's Really Wrong

Every now and then you'll come across a photo that looks technically fine. The exposure's correct, the colors are okay; but you know there's something that's just not right.
It could be better, if you could only figure out what's wrong with it. Figure 15.13 shows
an example, taken on a trip through one of those animal safari parks. There's something
about this picture that bothers me. It's not the zebra poop, though I'll certainly clean that
up before I print. No, it's that zebra with his back to the group.

FIGURE 15.13
It's that darned non-conformist zebra....

Well, there's only one thing to do—turn him around. Fortunately, the background is very generic, so I don't even need to select him carefully. I'll just draw a selection box loosely around him with the lasso, and then cut and paste him to a new layer. Then, I can apply Image, Rotate, Flip Layer Horizontal from the Elements menu bar to turn him around. Figure 15.14 shows that step. When I position him, I just have to be careful to line up the top of the fence behind him.

FIGURE 15.14
About, face!

A little work with the Clone Stamp to fill in the gaps, and he's almost where he belongs. I do, however, still need to move his shadow back so it lines up with his front hooves, just as the other zebra shadows do. Using the Clone Stamp in Aligned mode is ideal here. I can copy the shadow and when I run out of shadow, I'll simply be placing grass where the old shadow is. In Figure 15.15, the circle represents the stamp and the crosshairs are the current source. I simply selected the Clone Stamp tool, turned on the Aligned option, and pressed Cmd/Alt as I clicked on the grass just behind where his shadow was. Then I moved the mouse over, and clicked at his feet. Dragging to the right copies his old shadow to its new location in front of his feet.

FIGURE 15.15
FIGURE 15.15
Using the Clone Stamp in Aligned mode to copy the zebra's shadow.

As a final touch, I'll clean up the piles of zebra doo-doo. It's so much easier with the Clone Stamp than with a bucket and shovel. Now what? Should I tint each pair of striped pajamas a different color? No, but I could…. Figure 15.16 shows the final photo.

FIGURE 15.16
Now he's just one of the gang.

Hand Coloring a Black-and-White Photo

The art of hand-coloring or hand-tinting photographs dates back to the 1920s, or perhaps even earlier. A black-and-white or sepia-toned print would be painstakingly hand-colored with a very thinned out wash of either oil paint or watercolor. Oils were preferred for their longer working time. Watercolors would dry on the paper before they could be properly spread, but they were used nonetheless.

The main characteristic of a hand-colored photo is that the colors are very transparent. There is little or no attempt to paint in detail, as that comes through from the underlying photo. You can achieve this effect in Elements. Start with any black-and-white photo that lends itself to this technique. Though this technique is generally used on portraits, a hand-colored landscape might be interesting.

You'll paint with the Brush tool, which is explained in full detail in Hour 19, "Creating Art from Scratch." Choose light colors for the effect (change brush colors by changing the foreground color) and set the brush opacity to 20% or less. Always paint on a new layer (Layer, New Layer), not on the background. That way, if you go outside the lines, you can simply erase your mistake and continue. I like to keep each color on its own layer so I can adjust the opacities individually, using the Opacity slider on the Layers palette. For instance, if I have chosen a shade of pink for a lady's blouse and then find it's too pink, I can set the opacity to 12% instead of 20%, making it paler, and not have to redo the color. Figure 15.17 shows a colorful couple. I haven't collapsed the layers yet, but I have added about all the color I'm going to use. If it's not subtle, it doesn't look right. Be sure to flip to the color plate section to see this one.

FIGURE 15.17

Don't get bogged down in details. In a picture of this size, you wouldn't see eye color or small details such as the man's suit buttons.

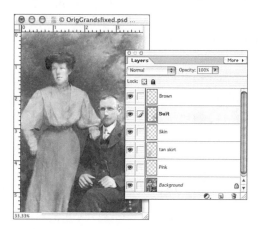

Summary

We spent this hour on color. We focused mainly on color photo restoration, but also on working with hand-colored photos and using the color selection tools. You learned all about color casts—what causes them and how to remove them—and about selective color correction. We improved a photo by coloring the grass and sky, fixing the brownish color cast, and lightening the shadows. You learned how to use the Blur and Sharpen tools to work on small parts of a picture, and how to use the Sponge to change saturation. We talked about how to use the Smudge tool to gently soften a line, and how to use it in Finger Paint mode to really push pixels around. You learned about fixing composition problems in a color image. Finally, we covered hand-coloring, and how to apply it so that it looks right.

Q&A

Q My inkjet printer uses CMYK inks. Why can't I work in CMYK color in Elements?

A Color modes are one of the features that Adobe chose to simplify in Photoshop Elements. But don't feel as though you've been cheated. You couldn't actually work in CMYK anyway. Your computer screen only displays colors in RGB mode. Today's home and office printers make the translation from RGB color to CMYK automatically, and very effectively.

Q I think I could greatly improve my photo by making the background less obtrusive. How can I do so?

A You can try several different techniques. In this hour, you learned how to blur the background with the Blur tool. You can smear it with the Smudge tool, reduce its intensity with the Sponge tool, or darken it with the Dodge tool. If you move your subject to its own layer, you can use the Liquify filter discussed in Hour 10 to warp and twirl the background, remove color from the background as discussed in Hour 12, or experiment with one of the many filters we'll talk about in upcoming hours. The possibilities are endless.

Q If you oversharpen, can Blur bring back the picture?

A Unfortunately, no. Your only hope is to undo, or to back up in the Undo History list to some point before you used the Sharpen tool.

Workshop

Without color, the world would be a very dull place indeed. Color *your* world with these activities.

Quiz

1. Who or what is Roy G. Biv?

    a. The inventor of Photoshop

    b. An acronym for the order of colors in the spectrum

    c. A famous photographer

2. Color cast affects _____.

    a. Just faces

    b. Only the white or light parts of the photo

    c. The whole picture

3. Sponging changes what aspect of the image?

    a. Focus

    b. Saturation

    c. Contrast

15

Quiz Answers

1. b. Red, Orange, Yellow, Green, Blue, Indigo, Violet.

2. c. It even colors the margins.

3. b. Remember that you can use it for both saturation and desaturation.

Activities

1. Locate a color photo in need of repair, and have at it. How much better can you make it look? Which techniques seem to work? Which ones don't?

2. Find an old portrait and hand-color it. Remember to use a different layer for each color.

HOUR 16

Removing and Replacing Objects

It's easy enough to use the Clone Stamp to hide small objects in a picture, but what happens when the object is a large one? You can't use the same tools and techniques on something big. Fortunately, there are other ways to get rid of unwanted parts of the picture and replace them with something else, even when they're right in the middle of it.

In this hour you will

- Copy existing sections of a photo using drag-and-drop copying
- Remove people or objects you don't want to see
- Make the subjects of your photos kiss Tom Cruise, snuggle with Harrison Ford, and dance with Fred Astaire
- Cover large holes, tears, or other missing areas

Drag-and-Drop Copying

The simplest way to hide something is to cover it up. The trick I'm about to show you is an easier method of hiding something than the one we used in Hour 11, "Removing Red Eye, Dust, and Scratches," to hide the small boats. I call this trick drag-and-drop copying. You simply select something that has the right color and shape to cover up what you want to hide. Then, you select the Move tool and press the Option/Alt key. This tells Elements that you want to copy and move the original selection instead of simply moving it. Thus, when you drag the selection with the Move tool you're actually dragging a copy of it, so the original stays where it was, and the copy fits nicely over the object, person, or whatever you wanted to hide. Figure 16.1 shows a simple example. If the edges of your copy are obvious, undo the dragging, and feather the edges of the selection (Selection, Feather) by a few pixels before you move it, to help hide them.

FIGURE 16.1

I lassoed some grass and dragged it over the sleepy student.

Maybe it's me, but I don't like the sloppy kids in Figure 16.2 either. Removing them will be a lot more difficult because there's a lot going on behind them that we'll have to patch up.

I'll start with the feet. Dragging a sort of boot-shaped piece of brick sidewalk and concrete background, I align it using the line between brick and concrete near the kid's leg, and get rid of one leg very quickly. Figure 16.3 shows a close-up of this move.

16

FIGURE 16.2

The baggy shorts look may be "in" this year, but by next year it will be laughable.

FIGURE 16.3

A little more work, and he won't have a leg to stand on.

Using pieces of the sidewalk and the next granite post, I can hide his other leg, and rebuild the post. Note the tiny shadow at the bottom right of the post in Figure 16.4. I copied that with a small Clone Stamp. I then copied some of the concrete pavement to cover his upper leg, as shown in the figure.

Now I'm going to have to improvise. I have one end of the bench behind our guy. This time I'll have to do something different, though. Instead of dragging a selection, I'll copy and paste it, and then flip the copy, as I did with the zebra last hour. Remember that when you copy and paste, the pasted object will appear on a new layer, directly over the old one. This sometimes causes confusion because it looks as if nothing has happened. Take the Move tool and drag it over the copied and pasted area. You should be able to drag the copy off the original. If not, check the Layers palette to make sure it actually copied. After flipping the bench and putting it back, so the sign legs line up with the right side of the sign, I can do a little Clone Stamping to cover some more of the student. Figure 16.5 shows the end of this step.

FIGURE 16.4

The body is trickier. I don't know where the bench ends or what's on the sign.

FIGURE 16.5

I still have work to do.

I can use the same copy-and-flip technique to replace most of the sign. Figure 16.6 shows a close-up of the photo.

Some final rubber stamping, and he's completely gone. Figure 16.7 shows the final version of this one. What about that other kid? Don't worry, you'll find out his fate at the end of the hour, in the "Activity" section.

FIGURE 16.6

Not much more to go with this guy.

16

FIGURE 16.7

All gone, and good riddance.

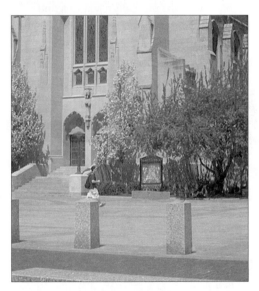

Removing a Person

It seems as though every time a group gets together to take pictures, there's bound to be a wise guy. Or maybe someone steps into the photo who doesn't belong there. Maybe it's your daughter's green-haired boyfriend, or your former spouse who you'd like to see out of the picture, both literally and figuratively. There's no reason that you can't remove him or her.

Figure 16.8 is a typical group photo, with the groom's brother behaving like a typical wise guy. If I can lift him out, this will be a nice shot of the bride and groom with best man and matron of honor.

FIGURE 16.8

Most of our family photos have the same pose.

I'm going to remove the guy second from the right, and move the other one over to fill in the space. I will also clean up the rest of the picture, straightening the pillars of the gazebo and brightening up the color. The first step, of course, is to get the wise guy brother out of the way. In Figure 16.9, I've used the Clone Stamp and some cutting and pasting near the groom to get his brother's right hand out of the picture. When using the Clone Stamp in this situation, you'll probably want to avoid using the Aligned option, so you can paint with the exact color you want and not accidentally copy parts of the bride's veil or the groom's lapel. Also, if you copy and paste first, and then switch to the Clone Stamp, deselect any selected area or the tool will only work in that area.

FIGURE 16.9

Be careful to keep the stamp in line when you're filling in something vertical.

This next piece is even easier. I'll simply cut the side of the picture with the young man we're keeping, and slide it over the other one. Notice that I've kept the entire gazebo pole. Architecturally, it might not make sense, but it should look okay anyway. And it will save me tons of time. Figure 16.10 shows the picture before and after sliding him over.

In bringing the guy from the far right over toward the groom, I've also brought part of the wise guy's shoulder. That's OK, because it almost matches the groom's shoulder. After a little more stamping to paint the post back in and to remove what remains of the wise guy, we're done. The fixes took only a couple of minutes, and the result (Figure 16.11) is a photo the guys' mom is a *lot* happier with. I know. They're my sons.

FIGURE 16.10

All gone. Now we just have to fill in the gaps and remove the stray finger from the groom's ear.

16

FIGURE 16.11

Mom likes this version much better.

Replacing a Face

When it's not possible to cut somebody out of the picture, you might consider replacing him or her. Instead of your ex-husband, maybe you could sit next to Tom Cruise or Matt Damon or even your current husband, in all those old family photos. You could turn your ex-wife into Julia Roberts or Granny from the Beverly Hillbillies, if you can find a photo to work with.

The difficult part of replacing a face is finding the right one to put in its place. You need to find another head shot with more or less the same lighting conditions (shadows falling in the same direction) and at the same angle, though the angle is not as critical. You can always do a 180-degree flip, if you need to, and then rotate the head so it's straighter or more tipped, as necessary. Figure 16.12 is a photo of Josh and Melissa. What if Melissa had married Tom Cruise instead of Josh?

FIGURE 16.12
The happy couple....

I got lucky and found an Internet fan page with a picture that works. It's facing the wrong way, and is not quite the right size, but those are easy problems to solve. The more difficult problem will be matching skin tones, but even that can be managed with the Color Variations dialog box (Enhance, Adjust Color, Color Variations) and some patience. In Figure 16.13, I've enlarged Tom, flipped him, removed some of the background, and pasted him into the original photo. I still need to rotate him so his nose lines up with Josh's, and then blend him in.

FIGURE 16.13
Don't try to position the replacement perfectly until you've made sure that major features line up. In this case, Tom has to rotate several degrees.

In Figure 16.14, I've moved Tom's face, used the Sponge to desaturate the redness from it, and used Image, Transform, Skew to make his face fit over Josh's face a little better. Next, I will continue with the task of blending him in using the Clone Stamp and the Smudge tools. (I used Smudge to fix his hair so that it looked right after I rotated and skewed his face.)

FIGURE 16.14

From here on, it mainly takes patience and the Clone Stamp.

Because Tom's face is on a separate layer, I can add adjustment layers over him (similar to the Brightness/Contrast adjustment layer we used to create the highlighted banner for text in Hour 13) to make the color corrections more believable. It's really just a question of removing enough red. California summer sun has little in common with September sun in New England. Adding a Levels adjustment layer and setting the Channel so the adjustment only affects the red parts enabled me to take more from the darker areas (which are very red) and less from the lighter areas, which was just what the picture needed. To do that, I moved the left triangle in, didn't adjust the right one, and shifted the middle triangle toward the right a little. In Figure 16.15, you can see the final result. It's worthy of the *National Enquirer*.

FIGURE 16.15

I don't think I'll show this to either one of them.

How Far Can You Go?

You can take people out of the places they've been, or put them into places or situations they haven't been in. You can turn that can of beer in the politician's hand into a harmless can of soda, or vice-versa, depending on your party affiliation. The question at hand is not "can you?" but "should you?"

There are certainly some ethical questions to be addressed if you're altering photographs for public display. It really depends on how the picture is to be used. Reputable newspapers and magazines tend to have strict guidelines about what they'll allow for photo manipulation. The general rule seems to be that, if a change affects the *content* of the photo rather than its appearance, you can't do it. You can lighten a too-dark picture of the politician, but you can't change the soda can in his hand into a beer can (or beer into soda). That would be making a change in content.

Editing a picture to improve the composition seems entirely reasonable if it's a picture for your own use, but this is precisely what got the esteemed *National Geographic* magazine in trouble some years ago. They were doing a piece on Egypt and sent a photographer to get pictures of the pyramids. The art director studied the pictures and decided the composition would be better if he moved one of the pyramids closer to the one next to it. As soon as the issue was published, astute readers began calling and writing to the magazine to complain. An apology appeared in the following issue, but simply knowing that the manipulation was possible raised a red flag for many people both inside and outside the publishing industry. The question has been debated ever since. How much change is okay? How much is too much?

It's clear that you can't always believe what you see. The supermarket tabloids frequently feature pictures that stretch the bounds of believability. Remember the one of the President shaking hands with the space alien? Or Bigfoot carrying off the scantily clad woman? (Why was she dressed like that in the snow, anyway?) On the other hand, if a fashion model is having a bad hair day or her face breaks out, retouching is required and expected. Where do you draw the line?

To me, it depends on what's being done and its effect on communication. If it changes the meaning of the photo, particularly in a way that could get you sued, don't do it. Could anyone's reputation be harmed by it? Don't do it. If it's just for fun and not for public display, go ahead, but be careful that the photos don't end up in the wrong hands or displayed on the Web.

Putting Back What Was Never There

Sometimes you need to hide a large part of a picture, and simply don't have enough material to do so. Maybe the photo got torn too much at the edge, or it has a hole. If you use the Clone Stamp to stamp the same piece of grass, tree, or brick wall over and over, it will quickly take on a repeating pattern that you probably didn't even see in the original. The presence of the pattern sends a clear signal that you're hiding something, but not very well.

So what can you do to avoid this? In Figure 16.16, I have a pair of seagulls. The one showing us his backside really doesn't look very good. Suppose I want to stamp it out?

FIGURE 16.16

He just wouldn't turn around.

16

Even if I choose the most generic piece of grass I can find, there's the pattern, showing clearly in Figure 16.17. What you have to do to avoid this is to clone a little bit at a time and keep changing the stamp source. I did this in the second try, with much better results.

FIGURE 16.17

Sometimes you'll want to keep a pattern, like a brick sidewalk. Mostly, you'll want to avoid them.

Cloning the same pattern over and over is not a good idea.

Here, cloning is less noticable.

If necessary—if there's not enough grass or whatever you need to cover—you can start a new document, stamping a couple of times. Then, select the stamped area, flip it upside down, copy and paste (using the Paste command will place the copy on a new layer). Select it again, and flip sideways, and paste that. When you have a good-sized patch of covering material, flatten the layers, and copy the whole thing or as much as you need back into the original picture.

If you are a person who likes to plan ahead, as I am, you can get into the habit of and photographing things such as sandy beaches, sky, and fields of grass, wheat, or flowers to use as backgrounds or copying sources. I shot that seagull both for the winter grass he was on and for the pose he was in, which seemed like it would combine nicely with a pier and fishing boats (it did). I keep my source files in a folder on the hard drive, so they're ready when I need them. It's like having a couple of emergency meals on the pantry shelf. Saves worry, since I know I'll almost always be able to salvage the picture.

If you don't have specific source files, or don't yet have the one you need, look through your other pictures for something that could work. If you're trying to save a portrait, and all else fails in fixing the background, you can always select and copy the subject and relocate him or her somewhere else. Some years ago my sons asked me to shoot a photo so they could see who was taller. I picked up the closest camera and shot them in front of a wall of messy, overflowing bookcases and office clutter. But the photo turned out to be one of the best portraits I had of the two of them—after I removed them from the scene, and let them stand in front of the Golden Gate Bridge.

The real trick in making any of these "photo saves" work for you is to be creative. Think about what could be removed to make the picture better, and what could be put in. If you start by realizing that nothing is impossible, you have a lot of possibilities to try.

Summary

Not all photo repairs involve fixing color, or cropping and straightening. Sometimes what's wrong with the picture is what's in it that shouldn't be. In this hour, you learned how to edit a photo, how to remove unwanted people or things. You learned about drag-and-drop editing to cover a large area with a piece copied and dragged over the background. You learned to combine different methods to replace a complicated background. Then, you learned how to remove someone from a group by simply cutting him out and bringing the edges back together. You learned how to replace a face while keeping the rest of the picture intact, and then you learned about the problems of Clone Stamping and how to avoid them. Finally, you learned about keeping source files handy for quick photo repair.

Q&A

Q I tried to move some grass to cover a bare spot on the lawn, but it's not a very good match. What can I do?

A Depends on why it's not a good match. Is the color off? Add an adjustment layer coupled to the grass, and make it greener or browner. Did you make the selection too square? Using a freehand Lasso selection usually gives a less obvious selection. Feathering the edges helps, too.

Q My teenaged son saw the Tom Cruise wedding picture and wants a poster of himself hugging Britney Spears. (Thanks a lot!) Now, what do I do?

A Start by having him do an Internet search for her in the right pose with some other guy. Then shoot a picture of him in a similar position. Splice the two together at any convenient point. Or, just tell him it's a copyright violation and you can't do it.

Q I have a full-face portrait of my grandfather, but something's stuck to one side of his face. Can I copy the other side and flip it to replace the bad side?

A It's certainly worth trying, but don't be too disappointed if it doesn't look right. Faces are almost never symmetrical, and it's the differences that give us character. Try replacing as little as possible. If you can leave the eye and the corner of the mouth as original, you can probably get away with replacing the cheek and ear.

16

Workshop

Is it what you put into a picture or what you take out that makes the biggest difference? Answer the following quiz questions and work on the activity for fun.

Quiz

1. When you copy an object and paste it back into the picture, it always goes
   _____.

   a. To the same layer you copied it from

   b. To a new layer

   c. To an adjustment layer

   d. To the background

2. To drag a copy of a selection to a new location _____.

   a. Press the spacebar as you drag with the Lasso

   b. Select the Move tool, and press Option/Alt as you drag

   c. Double-click it

3. When you add an adjustment layer, it automatically applies only to the layer immediately below it.

   a. True

   b. False

Quiz Answers

1. b. Elements will automatically add a layer for you.

2. b. To place additional copies, release the key, move the mouse pointer over the original selection, then press Option/Alt again and drag the new copy wherever you want. This method, by the way, does not create a new layer as the Copy, Paste operation does.

3. b. You have to click the Group with Previous Layer check box inside the New Layer dialog box.

Activity

Download the file BU Students from this book's page on the Sams Publishing Web site. Work through the steps I went through to remove the first student. Then, figure out how you can most effectively remove the second one, and do so.

HOUR 17

Using the Improvement Filters

I'm not sure whether Adobe actually invented the concept of filters, or just took the ball and ran with it. It really doesn't matter. Filters are my favorite Photoshop/Elements tools. Elements has all the Photoshop filters on board, and you can also load third-party filter sets to do everything from framing your pictures in your choice of materials to changing the weather in the scene to creating strange abstractions based on fractal geometry.

In this hour you will

- Sharpen images
- Blur backgrounds and annoying objects
- Simulate motion
- Remove dust and dirt and other defects
- Blur details by adding noise
- Add clouds, spotlights, and lens flare
- Map an image onto a cube, sphere, or cylinder
- Add texture such as stained glass, mosaic tile, or burlap

Working with Filters

Filters are also called plug-ins, or sometimes plug-in filters. You can install them very simply, by copying them into the Filters folder. Elements is compatible with all the third-party Photoshop filters, and with most plug-ins that work with other graphics programs such as PaintShop Pro or Painter. If you already have filters installed in another Photoshop-compatible graphics program, you don't need to reload them. You can designate a second plug-ins folder by going to the Preferences dialog boxes (Edit, Preferences), displaying the Plug-Ins & Scratch Disks options (shown in Figure 17.1), clicking Choose, and locating the folder containing the additional plug-ins you want to use. When you restart Elements you'll see the new ones listed at the bottom of the Filters menu.

FIGURE 17.1

Choosing a second plug-ins folder.

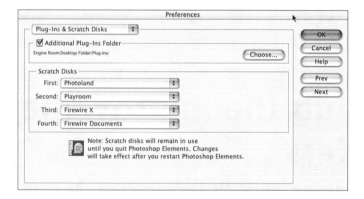

The filters that we're going to be working with in this hour are all "corrective" filters. They are used to change focus, add or remove noise and speckles, and add special effects such as 3-D mapping, clouds, and lens flare.

All the filters in this hour and in upcoming hours will be applied to the current layer, or a selection within the current layer. When using a selection, it's usually best to feather the edge to create a better transition between the affected area and the rest of the image. If your image has multiple layers, you can apply the filter to each layer and blend the effects by adjusting each layer's opacity.

In most cases, if you want to apply a filter, your image must be using RGB mode. (Some filters may be applied to images using Grayscale mode as well.) Filters are found on the submenus of the Filter menu. Some filters are applied without making any selections at all, while others let you make adjustments before applying them. The last filter you used, with the exact settings you selected, will be listed at the top of the Filter menu. To reapply it with those settings, simply choose the filter from there rather than from the submenu.

You can compare filters visually using the Filters palette, shown in Figure 17.2. Change from one category to another using the drop-down list. The filters in each category are displayed in sample thumbnails so you can compare them. To compare the sample original image with the selected filter style, click the List View button at the bottom of the palette. To display thumbnails again, click the Thumbnails button, also located at the bottom of the palette. Double-clicking the thumbnail will open the filter's dialog box, if there is one. If this is one of the filters with no options to set, such as the Blur or Blur More filters that you'll learn about later in this hour, Elements will simply go ahead and apply it.

17

FIGURE 17.2

Browse through the many filters using the Filters palette.

If a palette is open but is still in the palette well, and it takes up too much room on the screen, just click its name tab to hide it. To "roll it up" or hide it temporarily when you've moved the palette into the work window, double-click its tab. Click the tab again to unroll the palette and reveal its contents.

Using the Sharpen Filters

There are four filters in this set: Sharpen, Sharpen More, Sharpen Edges, and Unsharp Mask. You'll find them all on the Filters, Sharpen menu. The first three are very straightforward—there are no options to set. You select them from the Filter menu, and your picture changes accordingly. Sharpen More gives twice as much sharpening as Sharpen, and Sharpen Edges only sharpens areas where there is a lot of contrast between adjacent pixels—such as the edges of the flower next to the dark background, the shadow in the center, and the light-colored stamen. The Sharpen Edges filter treats these contrasting pixels as edges, and increases the contrast between them. It does not increase the contrast everywhere, as Sharpen and Sharpen More do. Figure 17.3 shows some examples.

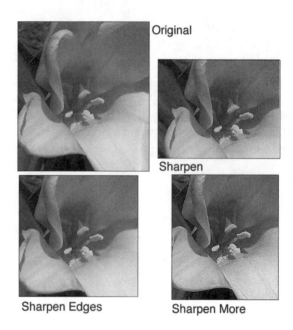

The Unsharp Mask filter is a lot more complicated. It also visually sharpens the photo by seeking out edges and adding contrast to them, like Sharpen Edges, but with the variables involved, it can do a much more selective and therefore better job. Choosing Filters, Sharpen, Unsharp Mask opens the dialog box shown in Figure 17.4.

FIGURE **17.4**
*The Unsharp Mask
dialog box.*

As you can see, there are three settings you must deal with: Amount, Radius, and Threshold. Amount refers to the degree of contrast (sharpness) you'll be adding to the edges of objects in the picture. Radius determines the size of the area that will be sharpened. A large radius sharpens a large area around each perceived edge. A small one sharpens a smaller area. What's best? If the picture has small, delicate detail, you'll need to use a small radius. If not, watch the preview as you increase it. You'll be able to see when to stop. Threshold lets you determine how much of a difference there should be between adjacent pixels before Elements treats them as an edge and enhances them. When you have areas with only minor differences in color, such as sky or skin tones, a very low Threshold setting can make them look blotchy. Still, you want to keep the Threshold as low as you can without letting it add unwanted noise or spottiness to the picture.

Sharpening with any of the filters, and particularly with the Unsharp Mask, should always be the very last thing you do to your picture before saving it. Before you use the sharpening filters, straighten and crop as needed, check for proper tonal level and adjust it, adjust color saturation and remove color cast if present, change the brightness and contrast, and perform the other routine tasks we've already discussed. Then, as a last step, you can add the crispness you want without affecting your ability to make further changes. If you were to sharpen an image first, and then make additional changes, you would probably make the sharpness that Elements put in stick out like a sore thumb.

17

Task: Applying the Unsharp Mask Filter

1. Open an image in Elements and make whatever corrections or alterations it needs. Zoom in or out so the picture is at its full size on the screen. (This will let you see the effects of sharpening, without exaggerating them.) When you're satisfied with everything except the sharpness, open the Unsharp Mask dialog box (Filter, Sharpen, Unsharp Mask).

2. Set the Amount to 500% to start with. This is the maximum, and starting here will help you see and understand what the other two variables are doing.

3. Set the Radius to 1 pixel, and the Threshold to 0. The picture won't look right—it will probably look very grainy, but this is our jumping-off point.

4. If there is obvious grain or noise, increase the Threshold. Start with 2, and then try 5, 8, 12, and so on until the noise disappears.

5. Now, we'll work with the Radius. Increase the Radius until the picture just starts to lose detail, and then back it off a bit. Figure 17.5 shows my image at this stage. (Don't worry about the white halos around edges. We'll lose them next.)

FIGURE 17.5

*We'll lose the halos in
the next step.*

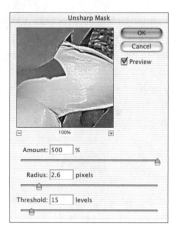

6. Now, reduce the Amount until the picture looks good. You want to get rid of the white edges, but still keep the sharpening effect. You'll probably find that the correct setting for Amount is somewhere between 100 and 250. Of course, it also depends on the amount of contrast and fuzziness in the picture you're working on. If you're not going to use the image onscreen (on the Web, for example) and you're just trying to get the sharpest image you can for printing, you may want to oversharpen the image just a bit.

7. Finally, save the picture and print it or put it on your Web page, or do whatever you'd planned. It's as sharp as it's ever going to be.

Lack of sharpness in either a scanned image or a digital photo is a very common problem, and part of the reason for it is the process. The picture is saved as a series of dots. Inevitably, there are spaces between the dots, and if you have a low resolution scan or a low resolution camera (anything less than 1 megapixel), the spaces will be large enough that the software will add blur to fill them in. That's why the pictures look fuzzy, and why adding contrast at the edges fixes it.

Using the Blur Filters

The Blur filters logically ought to be the direct opposite of the Sharpen filters. Some are. Blur and Blur More have the same global, one amount fits all, method of application. Choose either one of these two filters from the Filter, Blur menu, and the filter is applied automatically, without options. I actually tried a sequence of Blur, Sharpen, Blur More, and Sharpen More on a picture, and aside from some obvious quality loss, I got back to about where I started. However, I don't recommend this as a technique. The image loses some detail at each step.

Blurring, generally, is *not* something you want to do to the entire image. If you are applying a combination of filters for a special effect, Blur could certainly be one of them, but most of the time we want our pictures sharp. Blurring *part* of the image, though, is a very useful technique. When you blur an object against a sharp background, you create the illusion that it's in motion. When you blur a background, you create the illusion of depth of field, where the subject is in focus, but the background is so far away that you can't see all the details. Blur and Blur More are best applied to selections.

Smart Blur

In Figure 17.6, I'm going to use one of the Blur tools to clean up the beach. The heavy shadows on the sand from too many footprints create a texture that nearly hides the seagull. I've selected the sand and everything on it except the gull.

FIGURE 17.6

Before blurring the sand.

Now I'll open the Smart Blur dialog box (Filter, Blur, Smart Blur). Smart Blur has the most flexibility of any of the Blur tools. In its dialog box, which is shown in Figure 17.7, you can set Radius and Threshold, just as you can for Unsharp Masking. You have a choice of Quality settings: High, Medium, or Low. High creates more blur than Low. You also have a choice of effects modes: Normal (which applies the effect to the entire layer or selection), Edge Only (which applies the effect to the edges), or Overlay Edge (which also applies the effect at the edges). The difference between Edge Only and Overlay Edge is the effect—Edge Only makes the image or selection black and the edges white, while Overlay Edge doesn't change the colors in the image, but makes the edges white.

FIGURE **17.7**

*The Smart Blur dialog
box.*

Setting the Radius and Threshold here are the same in theory as setting them for Unsharp
Masking. The Radius determines how much of the area around the perceived edge is
blurred. The Threshold determines how much difference there needs to be between adjacent pixels before Elements will interpret them as an edge, and will apply the blur to the
area.

Some photos are harder to correct than others. This one, because there's so much contrast in the sand, is especially difficult. The solution is to go back and reduce the contrast
and brightness of the sand before trying the Smart Blur filter. I can use the Undo History
palette to move backward to the point where I'd made the selection but hadn't yet added
the blur. Then I can adjust the levels to de-emphasize the difference between light and
dark using the Levels dialog box. This generally means moving the midpoint toward the
darker end of the scale. When there's less contrast, I can use the filter without making
the sand look as if it's been processed. Figure 17.8 shows the final version of this picture. Be sure to see it in color, too.

FIGURE **17.8**

*Now the sand looks
better, and the gull
doesn't get lost in the
texture.*

Gaussian Blur

The Gaussian Blur filter is less adjustable than Smart Blur. Its only adjustment is for Radius. What makes it so useful, though, is that it has a built-in randomness factor that varies the amount of blur applied. This gives it a much more natural look, so you can actually use quite a lot of blur without it being obvious. Gaussian Blur is a wonderful tool for portraits. It evens out skin tones, removes fine lines and wrinkles, and takes years off with a single click.

In Figure 17.9, I've applied it to a picture of a young girl with some freckles and slightly blotchy skin. It doesn't take much blur to make a difference. I've turned off Preview so that you can see the before version on the main Elements screen and the after version in the filter dialog box. When using a tool such as this one, you should wait to apply it until after you've already made any other needed corrections. Use the Clone Stamp to get rid of any major spots, so a small amount of blur will be sufficient to take care of the rest. Too much blur tends to make skin look as if it were made from plastic.

17

FIGURE 17.9

Use the Gaussian Blur lightly.

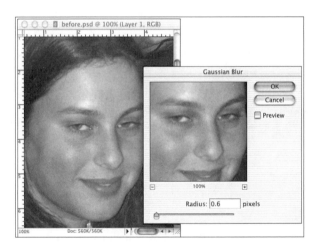

Radial Blur

The Radial Blur filter is just plain fun, especially when you apply it to a round object. The only drawback to using it is that there's no way to preview, so you have to be prepared to do and undo your changes several times until you find the right setting. Figure 17.10 shows the Radial Blur dialog box. There are two different kinds of blur available: Spin and Zoom. Spin simply rotates the pixels around the center point (which you can move). Zoom blurs them outward from the center (again, you can move this spot). Both effects are interesting, if not particularly useful. Figure 17.11 shows examples of both.

The Spin amount was only 10, but the Zoom amount was 50. Zooming requires much more "travel distance" within the image to see the full effect.

To use Radial Blur, select the type of blur—Spin or Zoom—and the Amount of blur you desire. To adjust the center point of the blur effect, click in the Blur Center box and drag the center point.

FIGURE 17.10

The Radial Blur dialog box.

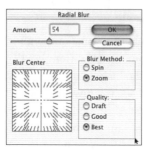

FIGURE 17.11

Three flavors of flower: Original, Spin, and Zoom.

Note the quality settings in the window, too. They determine how quickly, and how carefully, the blur is applied. The Draft setting works very fast, and leaves some rough edges. Good is sort of a compromise between speed and smoothness, and Best, which is noticeably smoother, can take several minutes to apply on an older, slower computer. Figure 17.12 shows all three settings applied to a Zoom blur. There's not much difference in this example between Draft and Good, but Best is definitely best.

Figure 17.12

Here we have the zoom in Draft, Good, and Best.

Draft

Good

Best

17

Motion Blur

When we see lines drawn behind a car, a cat, or a comic strip character, we instinctively know that the subject is supposed to be in motion. Those lines represent *motion blur*, which is actually a photographic mistake caused by using a slow shutter speed on a fast subject. The image's subject appears totally or partially blurred against the background because the subject actually traveled some distance during the fraction of a second that the camera shutter was open.

In the early days of photography, motion blur was a common occurrence, primarily because shutter speeds were slow, and film was not very sensitive. Today, motion blur is unusual, unless the photographer is trying to capture the subject this way on purpose by using the least-sensitive film available or by using a small lens opening (aperture or f-stop) and a correspondingly slower shutter speed. If you want to try to approximate the effect of motion blur, however, Elements gives you a tool that can do it.

The Motion Blur filter (Filter, Blur, Motion Blur) can add the appearance of motion to a stationary object by placing a directional blur for a predetermined distance. In the Motion Blur dialog box, shown in Figure 17.13, you can set both the distance and direction of the blur according to how fast and in what direction you want the object to appear to be traveling. The Distance sets how much of a blur is applied—or how far the original image is "moved." The Angle sets the direction of the blur. To adjust, drag the directional bar in the circle, or enter precise values into the Angle box next to it. The trick is to select the right area to which to apply Motion Blur. To get a convincing blur, you need to blur the space where the object theoretically was, as well as the space to which it has theoretically moved. You don't want to blur the entire image, so you might want to select the area to blur before using the Motion filter.

FIGURE 17.13

Using the Motion Blur filter is tricky at best.

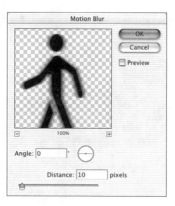

The Motion Blur filter doesn't do much for most photos. After all, the blur caused by the camera shaking is the kind of thing we usually try to avoid—not add. But, for some special effects, and for doing tricks with type, it has interesting possibilities. Figure 17.14 shows one possible use. First, I entered the type and applied the Perspective transformation (Image, Transform, Perspective) to give it some depth. Adding Motion Blur let me walk faster, but I could take this even further.

FIGURE 17.14

You can't run while standing still.

For Figure 17.15, I set the type differently, placing each letter on a separate layer. I then used a different Distance setting (increasing left to right) to each Motion Blur, from 5 pixels on the *W* to 20 pixels on the *K*. The resulting image almost seems to be running off the screen.

FIGURE 17.15

Using layers lets you apply different filters or different degrees of the same filter to an image.

Adding or Removing Noise

The Noise filters have nothing to do with sound. The kind of noise we're dealing with here is electronic noise. It's displayed on a TV screen or computer monitor as a pattern of random dots, usually in color. It's also called snow, and before we all got cable TV, it was common whenever you tried to tune in a TV station that was too far away.

Noise doesn't sound like a useful tool, but rather something you'd like to get rid of. Three of the four Noise filters are, in fact, designed to remove noise. It's fairly obvious from the names what Despeckle and Dust & Scratches are trying to remove, but what about Median? Median reduces noise by looking for individual pixels that are too bright or too dark, and changing them to the median brightness value of the pixels around them. Sometimes you don't want to remove noise, but add it, and of course, that's what the Add Noise filter is for.

Despeckle

Despeckle is the easiest of the filters to use. All you have to do is select it from the menu. It automatically looks for areas that have sharply contrasting pixels, and blurs the "misfits" to blend into the pixels around them. If you have a scan from a magazine that's showing visual banding or other noise, this filter will usually remove it. But be careful about using it on photos with fine detail. The Despeckle filter is likely to blur the detail.

Dust & Scratches

The Dust & Scratches filter, unlike Despeckle, has a dialog box with Threshold and Radius settings. This makes it much more useful, in that you can set the Threshold to the amount of blur you're willing to tolerate, and still get rid of dust, cat hair, and whatever else is messing up the picture. The Radius setting controls the size of the area that's examined for dissimilarities. In Figure 17.16, I have scanned an old photo with many scratches and cracks in the paper.

Finding the right combination of Threshold and Radius settings simply requires patience and a willingness to experiment, but as you can see in Figure 17.17, it is possible to get rid of all but the heaviest scratch without losing too much sharpness. The remaining one can then be easily Clone Stamped out of the picture. Typically, it's best to try keeping the Threshold at the lowest value possible (to avoid losing too much detail) while gradually increasing the area to examine (the Radius). If you can't seem to find a proper balance, try selecting the area that contains the largest amount of dust and dirt, and applying the filter just to that area.

17

FIGURE **17.16**
Can we lose the scratches without losing the face?

FIGURE **17.17**
This sure beats stamping out every line.

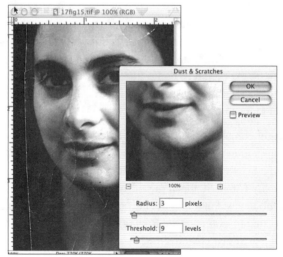

Median

As I mentioned earlier, the Median filter removes noise caused by neighboring pixels that vary too much in lightness or darkness. This filter blurs details even at very low levels, so be careful when using it. I use it sometimes to even out skin tone, reduce freckles, and the like. It seems to work better than applying any of the blur filters, at least when I select a small area, as shown in Figure 17.18.

FIGURE 17.18

Median is useful when removing unevenness in tone from small areas.

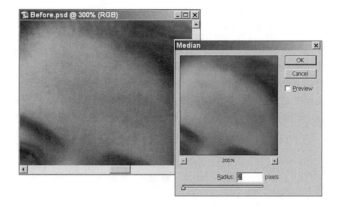

To use Median, select the area you want to affect, then choose Filters, Noise, Median. There's only one option to set—the Radius of the area that's examined for discrepancies. You'll want to leave this set very low, to avoid losing detail. Of course, if you lose some detail, you may be able to put it back in using the Unsharp Mask.

Add Noise

Given that Elements offers you so many tools to *remove* noise, why would you want to *add* any? Actually, noise can be very helpful. I use it a lot when I am creating backgrounds from scratch, as part of the process of turning photos into paintings, or to cover up areas I've retouched a lot. You can apply noise to a picture, as I've done in Figure 17.19. In this case, I want the finished product to look like a hand-colored steel engraving. Adding monochromatic (black) noise and then using the Find Edges filter will give me the look I want, with very little work.

FIGURE 17.19

Choose colored or monochrome noise, and an even or Gaussian distribution.

If you apply noise to a blank canvas, and then apply another filter (or two or three), you can create some beautiful textured backgrounds for Web pages or anything else you might think of using them for. In Figure 17.20, I've used Gaussian colored (non-Monochromatic) noise to put down a layer of confetti (shown here in the upper left), and I've added some other filters to change the original. See if you can identify the Stained Glass, Colored Pencil, Sumi-e, Mosaic Tiles, and Crystallize filters. You'll get to play with these filters yourself in Hour 18, "Using the Artistic Filters." Please don't forget to look at this figure in the color plate section.

FIGURE 17.20

By changing the amount of noise, you could change each of these to something quite different.

Using the Render Filters

The Render filters can create some awesome special effects. You can add lens flare, lighting effects, clouds, and textures, and even map your art onto three-dimensional objects. You'll find these amazing filters on the Filters, Render menu.

Clouds

The Clouds filter is one of the most useful of the Render filters. Quite often, you'll be shooting pictures outdoors and not even notice that the sky is overcast or a very pale blue and essentially featureless. That's when you apply the cloud filter to the selected area of the sky. First, set the foreground and background colors to something appropriate. Use blue and white for a traditional sky, two shades of purple for a storm about to break out, even yellow and green if you're on a different planet. You can pick up some of your existing sky color using the Eyedropper tool if you like. It doesn't seem to make any difference which is the background and which is the foreground color, because the filter uses a random selection of colors between those two to render the clouds. Just choose the colors you want to use, then select Clouds from the Render submenu. If you press Option/Alt while selecting the Clouds command, you'll get a starker, less serene look. There are no options; the filter is applied right away. Figure 17.21 shows some typical clouds acting as a background for the globe. Note that if you choose two colors that are similar in tone (brightness), the cloud effect may be too subtle to see.

FIGURE 17.21
These are ordinary blue and white clouds.

Difference Clouds

The Difference Clouds filter takes the existing colors in the image or selection and inverts their brightness (making light colors dark, and dark colors light) to create a cloud pattern. It then uses the colors opposite from the foreground and background colors on the color wheel to color the sky, giving you strange, dark skies with oddly colored clouds. This is good if you're illustrating a science fiction book…. Again, there are no options to this filter; just select the opposites of the colors that you want to appear and choose Difference Clouds from the Render submenu. If you choose two colors that are already opposites, such as magenta and green, you won't see much difference between Clouds and Difference Clouds, except that the lighter and darker portions are inverted.

Lens Flare

Lens flare is one of those things photographers generally try to avoid. It happens when the sun or some other source of bright light reflects back into your lens and bounces off the layers of glass inside. The resulting circles of light can be an artistic effect, or can ruin the picture, depending on where they happen to land. The Elements advantage is that you can position your lens flare wherever you want it, and also control the brightness and size of the flare.

The Lens Flare dialog box, shown in Figure 17.22, has several settings. The Brightness setting determines the diameter of the flare. If you set it to anything higher than 150, it's likely to overpower the picture so all you'll see is flare. Drag the Flare Center crosshairs in the preview box to position the center of the flare where it looks best. Finally, decide what kind of lens is theoretically causing the flare. Prime lenses, which have only one focal length, cause single flares, while the zoom lens, which has several moveable elements, causes flares with several circles.

FIGURE 17.22

*Lens flares can add
interest to a photo, if
done right.*

Lighting Effects

Lighting Effects is a very powerful filter, with many adjustable settings, and many possible results. What it does is to lighten the picture in the same way that adding a couple of floodlights or a flashlight or any of the other preset lighting patterns would do. Figure 17.23 shows the rather complicated interface. This filter gives you a lot of control, but at a price. You really need to spend a while playing with it to get a sense of what it can do.

First, select a lighting style. Some give you yellow light like that of an incandescent bulb, while others give you white light, which doesn't change the colors in your image. Some styles use multiple lights, others use only one. You can find a complete description of each lighting style in Help, although most of them are pretty obvious. If a lighting style has more than one light, you can reposition and adjust each light separately. To turn off a light, click its center in the preview window, then deselect the On option.

Next, select a light type:

- Omni—Shines a light down onto the image from above. You can move the center of an Omni light by dragging it. To create a smaller or larger circle of light (that is, to simulate the effect of moving the light closer to the image or farther away), drag the handles on the circle.

- Directional —Shines the focused beam of light from an angle that you can adjust. Move the center of the light by dragging it. Change the direction of the light by dragging the handle; you can shorten the line to bring the light closer or make the line longer to pull the light farther away. Adjust the intensity of light within the circle with the Intensity slider.

- Spotlight —Also shines the light from an adjustable angle, but with a flare whose radius you can adjust from wide to narrow, just like a flashlight. Drag the center to move the light focus, and change the angle by dragging the handle. If you shorten the handle, you'll bring the light closer to its focus. If you want to change the angle without changing the light's distance, press Cmd/Ctrl while dragging the handle. To change the size of the light flare, drag a handle on the ellipse; if you don't want to also adjust the angle, press Shift as you're dragging. Adjust the intensity of the light within the ellipse using the Intensity slider. A negative intensity can actually take light away from the image. To control how much of the ellipse is filled with light, adjust the Focus slider.

Figure 17.23

The Lighting Effects dialog box.

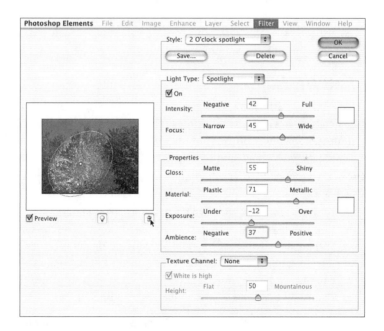

With all the light types, you can set other variables as well. To change the color at the center of the light, click the top color swatch and choose a new color from the Color Picker. To change the color at the edges of the light (the ambient light source, as noted in the following list), change the second color swatch. Here's a description of the options in the Properties area:

- Gloss—Use this option to adjust the amount of light reflection coming back from the image. The available choices are similar to the paper choices for actual printed photos. Matte is less reflective than Shiny.

- Material —Sets additional reflection. Plastic reflects the color of the light, while Metallic reflects the color of the object.

- Exposure —Increases or decreases the amount of light.

- Ambience —Adjusts the light for another light source, such as light from a window or a table lamp. The color of this ambient light is set with the second color swatch, as noted earlier. If you set this value to 100, the ambient light is removed completely; set it to –100 to use only the ambient light and not the light source.

To change how light reflects off particular colors in an image, add a texture. Select the color you want to raise to create the texture from the Texture Channel list. (You can also use the current layer's transparency to create an effect by selecting it from the Texture Channel list.) To raise the light hues of your chosen color, select the White Is High option. Otherwise, you'll raise only the dark hues. Then set the height of those areas to determine how the light reflects off them. If you select Mountainous, for example, expect more shadows, as the light reflects off the areas of the selected color/transparency in your image as if they were mountains.

Texture Fill

This filter is fairly straightforward; it doesn't do any of the fancy tricks its cousins do. Basically, you use the Texture Fill to fill a layer or a selection with a texture. You might do this, for example, to create a Mac/Windows desktop background, some pretty patterned paper, or a special effect within a selected area of your image. To use this command, you'll need a Photoshop/Elements-compatible file (a .psd file). You can create such a file yourself by copying a selection such as grass, hay, fur, or any other textured surface from an image and then pasting the selection into a new file and saving it. You can save color with the texture if you want; it depends on the effect you're going for. You can also create a homemade texture by painting random strokes with the Brush tool in a new file, and adjusting the contrast or applying filters (such as the Find Edges filter) to bring out its texture. Elements has several ready-to-use texture files; you'll find them in the Photoshop Elements 2/Presets/Patterns/Textures folder.

To use the Texture Fill filter, select the area or layer you want to fill. Choose Filters, Render, Texture Fill, then choose the Photoshop-compatible (.psd) file you want to use as a texture, and click OK. The entire layer or selection is filled with the texture. Anything in the layer or selection is completely replaced.

3-D Transform

Using the 3-D Transform filter, you can take an image and convert it into a 3-D object, such as a cube, sphere, or cylinder. You can then manipulate the image using a wire frame, twisting and rotating it as you like. You can change the shape of the 3-D object using the wire frame, creating other shapes such as a wine bottle, hourglass, or baseball bat. You can create multiple shapes and manipulate them together.

To get the best results from this filter, you may want to skew and distort your image so that it fits the rough shape of a cube, sphere, or cylinder. Then, when you're ready to use the 3-D Transform filter, choose it from the Render submenu. The 3-D Transform dialog box appears, as shown in Figure 17.24.

FIGURE 17.24

Create and manipulate a 3-D rendering of your image using these controls.

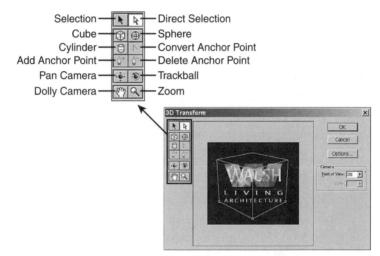

Selection — Direct Selection
Cube — Sphere
Cylinder — Convert Anchor Point
Add Anchor Point — Delete Anchor Point
Pan Camera — Trackball
Dolly Camera — Zoom

17

Start by clicking the button for the shape you want to create, and then dragging in the pane to create the wire frame. Before making any adjustments, click Options to select the options you want to use. Select the Resolution you want; if you select High, you'll wait longer for the rendering to finish, but you'll get better results. Turn on aliasing, which will help make curves in the image smoother. Finally, select Display Background if you want to display the full image behind the 3-D object.

Adjust the wire frame so that it fits the image as well as it can, using any of these techniques:

- To move the frame's position over the image, choose the Selection tool and drag the frame.

- To resize the frame, drag it inward or outward by one of the anchor points (the small handles on the frame).

- To move an anchor point's position on the frame, choose the Direct Selection tool, then drag the anchor along the frame.

- Bend the shape of a cylinder frame by adding anchors. Anchors are added in pairs—one on the left and one on the right. To add a pair of anchors, choose the Add Anchor tool and click on the right side of the frame. The matching left anchor is added for you. After adding a pair of anchors, you can bend the cylinder shape inward or outward at that point by dragging the right anchor.

- New anchor points are smooth, which means that they bend the frame in or out at the point where you add them in a gentle curve. To change the anchor point to a corner anchor point, click it with the Convert Anchor tool. You can convert the anchor back to a smooth one by clicking it again with this tool.

- Remove an anchor point by clicking it with the Delete Anchor Point tool.

While manipulating the wire frame, you may find it helpful to adjust its angle in relation to the image. To do that, drag the Field of View slider. This compensates for the field of view (the angle) originally used to take the picture.

After fitting the wire frame to the image, you can manipulate the three-dimensional object by doing any of the following:

- Moving the object within the window by choosing the Pan Camera tool and dragging it.

- Rotating the object by choosing the Trackball tool and dragging it.

- Zooming the object in or out by choosing any of the bottom four tools and dragging the Dolly Camera slider.

After manipulating the object as you like, click OK to apply the filter. Figure 17.25 shows an image before and after 3-D transformation.

FIGURE **17.25**

As the world turns.

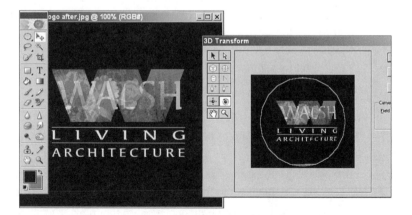

Adding Texture

We've already discussed one way to add texture to an image, using the Lighting Effects filter. There are other methods you can use as well, but none is quite so easy as using the Texture filters. They are all applied to an entire layer or a selection with a similar dialog box, shown in Figure 17.26. All the Texture filters (Craquelure, Grain, Mosaic Tiles, Patchwork, and Stained Glass) allow you to adjust the size of the texture and its effects so you can achieve a look that is either subtle or not-so-subtle.

FIGURE 17.26

Add a stained glass look to your image.

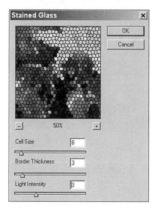

To use any of the Texture filters, select the layer or area you want to affect, then choose your filter from the Filters, Texture submenu. Adjust the size, spacing, intensity, depth, brightness, and other options as desired, using the preview window as your guide. Then click OK to apply the effect.

The Texturizer filter allows you to apply other textures to create your effect. You can apply brick, burlap, canvas, or sandstone, or load any other texture file and adjust its effects using the dialog box. Again, if you use your own texture file, it must be in .psd format. You'll find many premade texture files for your use in the Photoshop Elements 2/Presets/Patterns/Textures folder.

Adjusting the Effect of Filters

In Photoshop, you have the ability to apply a filter and then fade it out by a percentage. Unfortunately, Elements lacks this feature. (For now—the next edition will probably have it.) But you can create a fairly good imitation of the effect by copying the image to a new layer before you apply the filter. Filter the top layer, and then adjust the opacity of that layer until you have just enough of the effect, with the unfiltered background layer showing through and putting back as much of the original image as you want it to. In Figure 17.27, I've applied the Dust & Scratches filter too generously to a copy of the picture.

FIGURE **17.27**

Oops, that's too much blur.

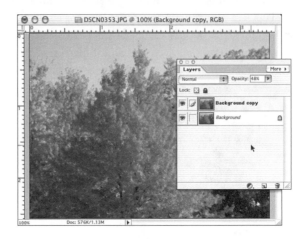

By reducing the opacity of that layer to about 50%, I can get what I wanted—enough blur to wipe out the spottiness of the leaves, but not enough so they're out of focus. Figure 17.28 shows close-ups without the filter, with the filter applied at 100% opacity, and finally, with it reduced to 50% opacity.

FIGURE **17.28**

From left to right: the original trees, the filter applied at 100% opacity, the filter opacity reduced to 50%.

Summary

This hour covered some of the plug-in filters that Photoshop and Elements both use. Filters can be applied to an entire image or to selected parts of it. First, you learned about the Sharpen filters. You learned how to use Unsharp Masking to take the blur out of digital photos and scanned pictures. Then, we looked at the Blur filters. There are several different kinds that do different things to the picture. Blurring is useful for de-emphasizing a background or some unwanted part of the image. The Radial and Motion Blurs give the illusion that the picture, or the part of the picture they're applied to, is moving. Next, we explored the Noise filters. There are three filters that remove noise and one that adds it. You learned that adding noise to a blank page and then using another filter can create some interesting background textures. Then, we looked at some of the Render filters. You learned to make clouds to enhance a drab sky. You learned about lighting effects, and about lens flares. You also learned how to render an image onto a 3-D shape. Finally, you learned a trick to fade the effect of a filter.

Q&A

Q When do you use the Blur filter instead of the Blur tool?

A You can apply the Blur tool to an area as small as a single pixel, because it uses brush shapes. The filter blurs the whole image or any part you have selected. Use the filter for large areas, and the tool for small ones.

Q Why do some filters seem to take a long time to apply? How do I know the computer hasn't just crashed?

A There's an awful lot of math involved in some of these filters. If you have an older, slower computer, it's going to take time. You should see a flashing line under the preview image in the dialog box while the computer's thinking.

Q The cloud filter I applied has the clouds in the wrong place. Is there any way to change it?

A Each time you apply the filter, it calculates new clouds. You may have to try it several times to get a cloud that works with the rest of the picture.

Workshop

Perhaps some of the answers will filter through....

Quiz

1. Sharpen More applies _____ as much correction as Sharpen.

   a. Exactly

   b. Twice

   c. Half again

2. If you use Unsharp Masking, you should apply it _____.

    a. First

    b. Last

    c. After each change you make in the image

3. Prime lenses have more flare than zoom lenses.

    a. True

    b. False

Quiz Answers

1. b. You could also apply Sharpen twice, and ignore Sharpen More.

2. b. Just before the final save.

3. b. Prime lenses have fewer layers of glass, and so fewer reflective surfaces.

Activities

1. Find or shoot a portrait of a friend or family member, and use the Blur and Sharpen filters to improve it. Find and remove wrinkles, eye bags, blotchy skin, and any other imperfections you can find.

2. Try the Lighting Effects filter on the same picture. See if you can add typical "portrait studio" lighting.

3. Use one of the Texture filters or the Texturizer to apply a texture to an image. What effects do you like?

PART IV

Going Creative

Hour

Hour 18

Using the Artistic Filters

One of my favorite activities in Photoshop, and now in Elements, is to turn some of my less spectacular photos into fine art. I am constantly surprised at the effects I can get by combining several filters, or by changing the order in which I apply them. The Artistic filters will enable you to mimic most of the available art media, from oil painting to neon tube sculpture. You can rescue a "bad" picture, or create a real masterpiece from a good one. More to the point, it's fun. One of my sons once told me that he thought Photoshop was "the best video game ever." And that was at least three versions back. He's *really* going to like Elements.

Under the general heading of Artistic filters, I've chosen to also include the Brush Strokes, Pixelate, Sketch, and Stylize filters. Each category includes filters that mimic a specific art style or medium.

In this hour you will

- Paint with watercolors
- Dabble in oils
- Play with pastels, chalk, and charcoal
- Create a neon effect
- Add an eerie glow to an image

Using the Watercolor Filters

Artists who work in other media have a great deal of respect for those who can paint with watercolors. It's arguably the most difficult medium, because you have to work quickly, before the paint dries. But you also have to avoid working with your paint or paper too wet, or else you'll end up with nothing but a puddle. Digital paint is, of course, much neater to work with. It doesn't get under your fingernails or leave a mess to clean up. And, if you take your picture a step too far, you can always undo.

Elements has one specific watercolor filter (Filter, Artistic, Watercolor). It gives you one style of watercolor, which is kind of dark and blotchy. There are ways to make this filter work better, and there are other filters that also create watercolors in other styles, but we'll start with the official one. First of all, let's look at the photo that will eventually be a watercolor. (See Figure 18.1 and the color section). As a photo, it's not very exciting. The composition and focus are okay, and it's well exposed, neither too dark nor too light.

FIGURE 18.1

Hampton Beach, NH.

The Watercolor filter, like most filters, has a dialog box with several options, which are shown in Figure 18.2. You can set the Brush Detail, Shadow Intensity, and Texture. Brush Detail ranges from 1 to 14, with greater detail at the high end of the scale. Shadow Intensity can be set from 1 to 10, again with much deeper shadows as the numbers get bigger. Texture ranges from 1 to 3, but there's not a lot of difference between the settings.

In Figure 18.3, I have applied the filter with a Brush Detail of 11, a Shadow Intensity of 1, and Texture of 1. But, I am not very happy with it. It's too dark. What would happen if I went back to the original photo, lightened it and reapplied the filter? That would change how the filter was applied, and might give me a better result. In 18.4, I lightened the original photo by about half using Enhance, Adjust Brightness/Contrast, Brightness/Contrast, and then applied the filter. It still came out darker than I wanted, so

I went to the Levels dialog box (Enhance, Adjust Brightness/Contrast, Levels) and brightened it there. It's looking much better now, but I think that what I really need is a different kind of watercolor.

FIGURE 18.2

The Watercolor filter dialog box.

FIGURE 18.3

Ugh, it's too dark.

18

FIGURE 18.4

That's better. To make some filters work properly, you often must make changes in the original that you wouldn't accept otherwise.

Dry Brush

The Dry Brush filter (Filter, Artistic, Dry Brush) simulates a watercolor technique that, as the name suggests, uses less water, and more pure pigment. It's good for detail and doesn't darken the picture the way the Watercolor filter does. With this filter, you can set the Brush Size, Brush Detail, and Texture. Brush Size controls the level of detail—with a larger brush, you'll get bigger splotches of color and you'll lose the parts of the image with small areas of color. Brush Detail increases the number of tones, softening the edges. If I set Brush Detail to a high value, for example, I'll see more shades of brown and gray used in the rock areas of my photo. This will also provide more detail than a big spot of gray or brown would. Texture again ranges from 1 to 3, and it controls the level of contrast. The highest setting, 3, makes the areas of individual color more apparent.

In Figure 18.5, I have applied it with a Brush Size and Texture of 2, with Brush Detail set to 9. Because this is so close to the look I wanted, I spent an extra minute lightening the bushes and adding a little extra color to the rocks with the Sponge and Dodge tools. Remember, just because you have used one tool doesn't mean you can't go on and use others. The point is not to master perfect technique with only one kind of filter, but to make a picture that pleases you, no matter *what* you have to do to get there.

Figure 18.5
The Dry Brush filter at work.

Spatter

Spatter is an interesting filter, which can be used for a different watercolor style or perhaps to simulate a gouache painting. (Gouache is a thicker, water-soluble paint, more opaque than typical watercolors.) It is located on the Filter menu under Brushstrokes. The Spatter dialog box has only two settings: Spray Radius and Smoothness. If you imagine that you're using an airbrush, you'll soon get the idea: Spray Radius adjusts the range of the spray, while Smoothness adjusts the density or coverage of the spray, and hence, its smoothness.

Figure 18.6 shows its dialog box, and indicates that we might have a problem using the Spatter filter with this particular subject.

FIGURE 18.6

Spatter makes the water look nice and wet.

The problem that shows in the preview window is that horizons are supposed to be flat, no matter how rough the water is. After all, you can't see the detail of the waves from three miles away, which is about how far off the horizon is if you're at sea level and about 6 feet tall. So, rather than give up on the filter, we'll simply mask the horizon line and let the filter apply to the rest of the image. The easiest way to do so is to drag a marquee along the horizon line, and then to invert, so everything except the horizon is selected. Figure 18.7 shows this step.

FIGURE 18.7

This is the simplest kind of masking.

Now, when I apply the filter, the horizon stays unspattered, and looks much more realistic. The final version in Figure 18.8 is also in the color section.

18

FIGURE 18.8
This definitely looks painted.

Simulating Oil Painting

There are as many styles of oil painting as there are people who paint; all the way from ultrarealistic, tight little brush drawings to big, splashy, abstract swipes of color. Traditional painters begin a new canvas by creating an underpainting, which lays out the scene with a big brush in blocks of color showing little or no detail. When they have the basic underpainting done, they go back with smaller brushes and add detail.

Underpainting

In Figure 18.9, I'm applying the Underpainting filter to the seagull and beach photo we used last hour. To use the Underpainting filter yourself, choose Filter, Artistic, Underpainting. Select a brush size—a big fat brush for larger splotches of color and less detail, or a smaller, finer brush for more detailed work. The Texture Coverage setting adjusts the thickness of the paint and its coverage of the texture you select.

Unlike some of the other filters, which give you only a few adjustments, this one includes resettable textures. The defaults are Burlap, Brick, Canvas, and Sandstone, but you can also load in any texture file (in .psd format) and use it instead. You can size the textures by adjusting the Scaling percentage, and also by setting the Relief or "lumpiness" (higher numbers will make the texture more intense). In addition, you can decide from which direction to have the light strike the texture by changing the Light Dir setting. To reverse the direction of the light quickly, without changing the Light Dir setting, click Invert.

Having done the underpainting with a click, it's now time to actually pick up a brush and start painting. For this, I will use the Brush tool and a very small, hard-edged brush, and I will select colors either from the Swatches palette (which contains a sample of all the colors in the image) or with the Eyedropper (which will change the foreground color to the color I click on).

FIGURE 18.9

I like to paint on sandstone; the canvas is too rough.

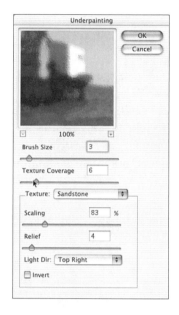

 Pressing the Option/Alt key while any Brush tool is active temporarily converts it to an Eyedropper, for quick color selection.

18

In Figure 18.10, I've been working with the brush for a while, putting back detail and straight lines where the filter has softened the edges too much.

FIGURE 18.10

Be sure to see this in the color section.

Palette Knife

Other oil techniques include painting with a palette knife, with thick brushes, and using strongly directional strokes. When painting with a palette knife, you spread paint over the canvas with the flat side of the knife. The result is a painting with thick, flat strokes. To start, choose Filters, Artistic, Palette Knife. Adjust the Stroke Size—a larger stoke gives you large, flat areas of color, and you'll lose the areas of the image with smaller patches of color. Next, select the Stroke Detail. This controls the number of tones used in areas of similar color, thus reducing or increasing the detail. Finally, select the Softness you want. This adjusts the "edge softness" of the stroke, or the level of contrast at the edge of the stroke. You won't see a lot of difference here between the high and low settings.

In Figure 18.11, I have used the Palette Knife filter, with Stroke Size and Detail of 9 and 3, respectively, and a Softness of 10.

FIGURE 18.11

After applying the filter, I went back and painted in the flowers.

Paint Daubs

The Paint Daubs filter (Filters, Artistic, Paint Daubs), which simulates the look of a painting, either works well with your picture or not at all. It breaks up the image into blobs of color. Its dialog box, shown in Figure 18.12, has a pop-up menu for Brush Type as well as sliders for Brush Size and Sharpness. If you are willing to spend some time experimenting, you can discover combinations that do amazing things to a still life or landscape. However, this is one filter I do not recommend for portraits.

After opening the Paint Daubs dialog box, set your Brush Size. A larger size will give you larger daubs of paint, and less detail. Next, adjust the Sharpness (level of contrast). Finally, select the Brush Type—your choices include a regular Simple brush, a Light Rough brush (which emphasizes the light values in an image), a Dark Rough brush (which emphasizes dark values), a Wide Rough or Blurry brush (which uses wide strokes), or a Sparkle brush (which produces a twirly effect). Figure 18.12, in the color section, shows the results of applying this filter.

FIGURE 18.12
There are six brushes available in the pop-up menu.

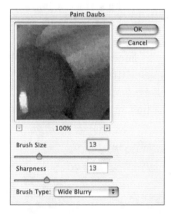

Working with Pastels, Chalk, Charcoal, and Pen

The next category of art media that we'll consider are pastels, chalks, and charcoals. These are all drawing or sketching materials rather than painting materials, so the look is completely different. The image is created from lines rather than blocks of color. Thus, these media lend themselves to pictures with delicate detail rather than areas of flat color. They are good for portraits, because the level of abstraction they provide disguises small flaws and makes anybody look good.

Rough Pastels

It would be convenient if these tools were at least lumped into the same category. Because they aren't, you will have to go hunting for them. The first one we'll try is Rough Pastels, which simulates the look of chalky pastels on a rough surface, such as canvas. With this filter, you'll see more texture in the dark areas than you will in the light. It's on the Filter, Artistic menu. Rough Pastels is one of those amazing filters that make anything look good. Figure 18.13 shows it applied to a photo of a dock cleat.

18

Figure 18.14 shows the interface for the Rough Pastels filter. Start by adjusting the Stroke Length. Pastels are brushed on the surface using the edge of the pastel stick and long, smooth strokes. You can adjust the contrast as well, and make the strokes more apparent by adjusting the Stroke Detail.

Like the Underpainting filter we looked at earlier this hour, the Rough Pastels filter allows you to change the texture of the surface on which the pastels are applied. The background texture is critical for filters like this one because the amount of color added varies based on the perceived roughness of the surface. Choose the one you want from the Texture list, or select a texture file you've created. You can size the textures by adjusting the Scaling percentage; for example, you can set the size of the bricks used in the Brick texture. A higher value creates larger bricks. You can also adjust the roughness of the texture by adjusting the Relief value (higher numbers will make the texture more noticeable). As before, you can adjust the direction of the light source with the Light Dir setting. To reverse the direction of the light, click Invert.

FIGURE 18.13

A cleat rendered in rough pastels.

Smudge Stick

Smudge Stick also looks good on almost any picture. It's smoother than the Rough Pastels and makes the image look as if it has been carefully rendered in soft crayon or pastel, and then the dark areas carefully smudged with a soft cloth or fingertip in a suede glove. See a close-up in Figure 18.15.

FIGURE 18.14

The Rough Pastels dialog box.

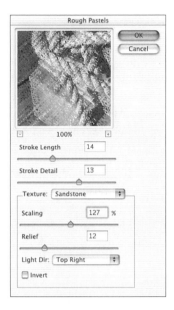

Choose Filters, Artistic, Smudge Stick. A smudge stick is used in a manner similar to a hard pastel, in long stokes whose length you can adjust using the Stroke Length slider. Adjust the range of values to be lightened with the Highlight Area slider. The higher the value, the broader this range of values. To brighten the values defined by the Highlight Area value, drag the Intensity slider.

FIGURE 18.15

Smudge Stick is a nice soft look that reveals textures and details.

18

Chalk & Charcoal

Chalk & Charcoal (Filters, Sketch, Chalk & Charcoal) works with whatever colors you have set as the foreground and background colors. Chalk, the background color, is used to render the light areas of your image. Charcoal, the foreground color, is used to render the dark areas. The medium tones in the image are not rendered, but are displayed as a simulated medium gray paper. Being somewhat traditionally oriented, I usually choose to use a combination of black and white, though you could just as well use pink and green or any other colors you want.

After displaying the Chalk & Charcoal dialog box, widen the range of dark values rendered with charcoal (the foreground color) by raising the Charcoal value. Lowering this value narrows the dark range. Adjust the range of light values rendered with chalk (the background color) by dragging the Chalk slider. Adjust the Stroke Pressure as desired. More pressure leaves more of the foreground/background color on the paper, increasing or decreasing the contrast.

The Charcoal filter (Artistic, Sketch, Charcoal) is not as effective as the Chalk & Charcoal filter unless you're looking for lots of contrast. When rendering your image in charcoal, Elements draws the edges of high contrast with a strong, bold stroke. Areas filled with midtones are drawn with a lighter, diagonal stroke. The color of the charcoal is the same as the foreground color. The paper used with this filter is not a medium gray; instead, it's the same as the background color.

In the Charcoal dialog box, adjust the thickness of the stroke using the Charcoal Thickness slider. The Detail slider controls the range of values rendered in charcoal. By default, only the dark tones in an image are rendered; with a high Detail value, more of the midtones will be rendered as well. Light values are left unrendered, and are filled with the background color. The Light/Dark Balance slider controls how strong a stroke is used—a strong, dark stroke or a light, medium stroke.

Figure 18.16 shows examples of the same image, rendered with both filters.

FIGURE 18.16

On the left, the Chalk & Charcoal filter. On the right, plain Charcoal.

Conté Crayon

I *love* this filter—it's done good things to every picture I have ever used it on. Conté Crayon (Filters, Sketch, Conté Crayon) is a soft, compressed chalk-and-graphite crayon, typically used on medium gray or brown paper in earthy colors.

Like the Chalk & Charcoal filter described previously, the Conté Crayon filter uses the foreground color to render the dark tones in an image, and the background color to render the light ones. For an authentic look, use a dark iron oxide (blood red), black, or sienna brown crayon for your foreground color. As your background color, use white, another earthy color, or a light-toned version of the foreground color.

After displaying the Conté Crayon dialog box, adjust the range of dark values rendered with the foreground color using the Foreground Level slider. Lowering this value narrows the dark range. Adjust the range of Background Level values rendered with the background color by dragging the Chalk slider. You can also change the texture of the background from canvas to something else, in a manner similar to the Rough Pastels dialog box: Choose the texture to use from the Texture list, or select a texture file you've created. Adjust the size of the texture with the Scaling box. Change the roughness of the texture by adjusting the Relief value. Change the direction of the light source with the Light Dir setting. To reverse the direction of the light, click Invert.

18

Figure 18.17 shows my black-and-white cat rendered in Conté Crayon on a sandstone background. I chose black as my foreground color and white as my background color because the cat is black and white, but feel free to use your imagination. Hot pink or lime green could be just what your photo needs.

FIGURE 18.17
Conté Crayon filter applied.

Graphic Pen and Halftone Pattern

These two filters (both located on the Filter, Sketch submenu) do very similar things. Both reduce the image using whatever foreground and background colors you set. Graphic Pen then renders the image in slanting lines, whereas Halftone Pattern renders it in overlapping dots. On the proper subject, the Graphic Pen filter can be very effective, though I can't decide whether it looks more like an etching or a pen-and-ink drawing. Take a look at Figure 18.18 and see what you think. Halftone Pattern, shown in Figure 18.19, looks like a bad newspaper photo.

FIGURE 18.18

It's a drawing. No, it's an etching.

FIGURE 18.19

Create the "high-quality" look of real newspaper!

To use the Graphic Pen filter, set the foreground color to the color of the ink you want to use; set the background color to the color of the paper you want to draw on. Next, choose Filters, Sketch, Graphic Pen. Adjust the Stroke Length as desired. Adjust the range of tones that the pen renders by dragging the Light/Dark Balance slider. If you drag it left toward the light side, the pen will render more light tones; drag it to the right to narrow the range. Finally, select a direction for the pen strokes—choose a direction in which your eye seems to move through the picture.

To use the Halftone Pattern filter, choose it from the Filters, Sketch submenu. The pattern is rendered in newspaper photo style, using dots of various shades of gray. Change the pattern to concentric circles or horizontal lines by selecting that option from the Pattern Type list. Adjust the size of the dots, circles, or lines using the Size slider. Adjust the range of tones rendered by the pattern using the Contrast slider.

> When you're working in Grayscale mode, you notice that many of the filters are grayed out. To get access to these filters again, just change your image back to RGB mode (Image, Mode, RGB Color) and apply your filter. Then, switch back to Grayscale mode and click OK when asked to discard color information.

Sumi-e

Sumi-e is the very old Japanese art of brush painting. It has a loose, free style that can only be achieved by painting with a wide, wet brush. As few strokes as possible are used to convey the subject, which is typically rendered in black ink on white rice paper. A carefully chosen photo should be an ideal medium for sumi-e. You want something that has textures, but is not too complicated (not too much detail, not too many edges) and not too dark. Because a lot of sumi-e art is black and white or uses only muted colors, you might want to adjust the hues in your image (the filter will not replace them). The filter will blur areas of similar color together, while adding dark strokes along edges of different colors, and within dark areas.

Many of the Elements filters, including this one, tend to darken a picture. If I know I'm going to continue working on an image after I've done the basic corrections, I'll often create a light version or one with extra contrast just for the filtering process.

I shot these clownfish (see Figure 18.20) at an aquarium. Fish don't like to pose, so I added a couple of extras when I did the basic clean up on the photo by copying, resizing, and flipping two of them. Can you find which two? The changes produced a better photo, but it still didn't say what I wanted it to about the colors and the joys of life on a coral reef. Although the colors in this photo aren't typically used in a sumi-e painting, the fish seem to be screaming for an Oriental technique.

18

FIGURE **18.20**
Send in a couple more clowns....

As shown in Figure 18.21, the filter softened the shapes, as if a big, wet brush had painted them. It intensified the colors and turned the shapes just abstract enough to make them interesting.

FIGURE **18.21**
Adding the Sumi-e filter produced exactly what I wanted.

To use the Sumi-e filter yourself, choose Filters, Brush Strokes, Sumi-e. Select the width of the brush strokes with the Stroke Width slider. Adjust the Stroke Pressure as well; a greater pressure will increase the darkness of the brush strokes. The Contrast slider adjusts the level of contrast in the image. Typically, you'll want to lower the contrast to achieve the soft look found in sumi-e paintings.

Creating a Neon Effect with Glowing Edges

I saw an interesting art show recently where all the work was done in neon tubing. Some, of course, looked cartoonish, but one artist had mounted her tubing against black velvet, and had used many small pieces in different colors rather than one long single colored line. It occurred to me that the Glowing Edges filter (Filter, Stylize, Glowing Edges) might do much the same thing. Its dialog box is shown in Figure 18.22.

FIGURE 18.22
The Glowing Edges dialog box.

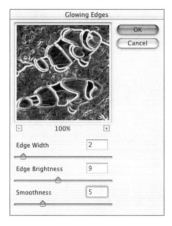

The filter works by looking for edges and placing a white or colored line on each edge it detects. The amount of contrast between the edge and what it's next to determines the color of the line applied to it. The tropical fish did prove to be a good image for this filter. Figure 18.23, and the color section, show the final result.

18

FIGURE 18.23
We've created neon clown fish!

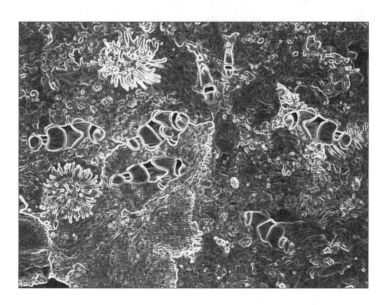

Display the Glowing Edges dialog box by choosing Filters, Stylize, Glowing Edges. Set the size of the neon edging by adjusting the Edge Width slider. Adjust the brightness of the neon glow with the Edge Brightness slider. The Smoothness slider defines the range of contrast that must exist between neighboring colors before an "edge" of neon is placed between them. If you raise this value, only strong, contrasting edges will use neon; if you lower this value, practically every edge in your image will use neon.

Adding a Neon Glow

You can find a filter similar to Glowing Edges on the Filters, Artistic submenu. It uses a combination of the foreground, background, and a neon color you select to recolor your image and add the neon effect. The effect, in this case, is less like neon tubing, and more like a subtle glow, as shown in Figure 18.24.

FIGURE 18.24

Cast a sinister look over a scene with Neon Glow.

First, select the color you want the filter to use when rendering dark tones by changing the foreground color. Select the color to use for midtones by changing the background color. The defaults of a black foreground and a white background are perfect for this filter. The highlights will be rendered by the neon color you choose from the dialog box.

Display the Neon Glow dialog box shown in Figure 18.24 by choosing Filters, Artistic, Neon Glow. Next, select the glow color you want to use by clicking on the Glow Color swatch and choosing a color in the Color Picker. Adjust the range of values rendered by the glow color (the range of values considered to be highlights) by dragging the Glow Size slider. A lower value will narrow the highlight range; a higher value will widen it.

A negative value will invert the range, causing the neon color to replace the dark values, and the foreground color to replace the highlights. Change the Glow Brightness as desired—low values cause the glow color to be used at the edges of its defined area; higher values move the glow farther into its area.

Texturizing with Grain

Although I talked about the Texture filters in general last hour, I want to talk specifically about the Grain filter (Filters, Texture, Grain) in this hour, because it can be used to create the artistic effect of a pointillist painting or a stippled engraving. Basically, the Grain filter adds noise to an image, in a pattern determined by the type of grain you decide to use. As you can see in Figure 18.25, the Grain dialog box has a pop-up menu that gives you a choice of ten different types of grain, from Soft to Clumped to Speckle.

FIGURE 18.25

Use the pop-up menu to choose a type of grain.

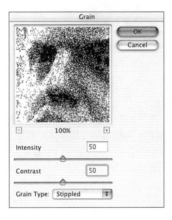

18

Some kinds of grain will retain the original colors of the picture, and some won't. In this case, I chose Stippled, so the picture loses most if not all of its color. The final result is shown in Figure 18.26. It reminds me of granite, and also of stippled engravings. Some of the other grain textures duplicate other artistic media. For example, to recreate the look of a pointillist painting by George Seurat, try the Regular, Soft, or Enlarged grain type. The Speckle and Clumped grain types also add an interesting artistic look to an image. Give them all a try!

Sponging an Image

Before closing this hour, I'd like to mention one more filter on the Filters, Artistic sub-menu: Sponge. With it, you can create a kind of watercolor effect that looks as if it were done with a sponge rather than a paintbrush. This filter blends areas of color, but retains the edges to give some detail to the image.

Open the Sponge dialog box, shown in Figure 18.27. Adjusting the Brush Size slider changes the size of the individual areas of color used to render the image. It correspond-ingly changes the size of the sponge pores, which paint tiny bits of gray all over the image. The Definition slider adjusts the darkness of the paint used on the sponge—from light gray to dark gray. With the Smoothness slider, you can change the amount of blending between the areas of color that make up the image, and the gray spots left by the sponge.

FIGURE 18.27

Sponging creates a blurry, soft effect.

Summary

I hope you enjoyed this hour; I did. Making photos into "art" of various kinds is one of my favorite things, and I like sharing the tricks and techniques I've picked up over the years. In this hour we looked first at watercolors and at several ways to simulate different styles. You learned a quick and easy way to mask a horizon, or any part of the picture that needs to remain a straight line. Then, we took up oil painting. You learned about underpainting, and about going back and adding detail after converting the picture to a painting. You learned about using a palette knife effect, and about the Paint Daubs filter. Then, we did some work with Chalks, Charcoals, Pastels, and Conté Crayon. After that, we got a little more into exotic media, with Japanese brush painting and neon tubing. Finally, we worked with the Grain filter, proving that all art can be taken for granite.

Elements includes many filters, as you've probably guessed from looking at the Filter menu. And, as I mentioned earlier, you can import other filters you might find on the Web. I can't cover the details about every filter, but they work more or less as you've already seen—some apply their effect as soon as you select them, while others allow you to make adjustments in a dialog box. Either way, use a copy of a favorite photo to play with each of the remaining filters. Some of them are pretty amazing. Imagine the situations in which you might use each filter, and make a mental note of the ones you like. They'll come in handy some day—believe me.

Q&A

Q Do the filters I use have to add up to an identifiable style? I've found a couple of nice painting effects, but I really can't tell what kind of paint they are.

A They do add up to an identifiable style—yours! There aren't any rules for this stuff, except that you should be happy with the results of your work.

18

Q How many filters can I use on one picture?

A There's no limit, except that you may eventually lose the original image.

Q How do you decide which filter to try?

A Elements makes it easier for you with the Filters palette. You can look at the thumbnails, and see what looks interesting or what you think might work with a particular image. If you guess wrong, there's always Undo.

Workshop

Put the paint box and easel away. Take off the smock. Digital painting is easier and much cleaner. More fun, too. Test yourself with the following questions, and then have fun with the activity.

Quiz

1. Sumi-e is Japanese for _____.

    a. Raw fish and rice

    b. Ink painting

    c. Photoshop

2. Elements uses only official Elements plug-ins.

    a. True

    b. False

3. Dry Brush is a style of _____.

    a. Etching

    b. Oil painting

    c. Watercolor

Quiz Answers

1. b. It's not sushi.

2. b. Elements can use any plug-in that's compatible with Photoshop or PaintShop Pro.

3. c. You press the excess water out of the brush, leaving pure pigment to paint with.

Activity

Find a photo of a still life, and see which art medium works best with it. Try at least four or five different styles, including Rough Pastels, Dry Brush, Underpainting, Chalk & Charcoal, and Conté Crayon.

HOUR 19

Creating Art from Scratch

Up to now, we've mostly talked about how to correct existing images such as photographs. Sometimes, you need to create your own images, such as logos and Web buttons. Using the painting and drawing tools in Elements, it's easy to create your own art.

In this hour you will

- Explore different methods of choosing colors
- Draw simple shapes
- Select a shape so that it can be moved or resized
- Paint with a brush and draw with a pencil
- Remove all or part of an image

Choosing Colors

The tools in Elements use the foreground color, the background color, or a combination of both. So before you use most tools, you should set these colors. Some tools give you the option of selecting a color for use with just that tool, as you'll see shortly.

The simplest way to select a color for the foreground or background, or for exclusive use with a particular tool, is to click the appropriate color swatch, and then choose a color from the Color Picker (more on this in a moment). You'll find the swatches for the foreground and background colors at the bottom of the toolbox; a separate swatch may appear on a tool's Options bar, and if so, click it to display the Color Picker so you can change the color used with that tool.

Using Color Pickers

You actually have a choice of Color Pickers. Which one you use (Adobe Apple, or Windows) depends on which one you selected in the Preferences dialog box. You can always open the General preferences to see which is selected, if you forget. Adobe's Color Picker, shown in Figure 19.1, is probably your best bet. It gives you the most options.

FIGURE 19.1

Select a color with the Adobe Color Picker.

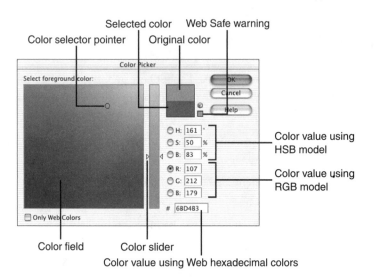

The original color appears in the top swatch on the right; the color you're about to change it to appears beneath. To select a new color, you've got lots of options. To select a color visually, adjust the color slider so that the range of colors from which you want to select appears in the color field. Then just click the color you want, or drag the Color Selector pointer around until the exact color you're looking for appears in the Selected color swatch.

If you'd rather not select a color visually, you can choose a color by entering values into either the HSB or the RGB box, to the right of the color slider. You can also enter the hexadecimal value for the number if you prefer—this is the same number you would enter within your HTML code to specify a particular color. If you're one of those people who can think of colors in terms of numbers, one of these methods is probably for you. If you want a refresher course on the various color models used by Elements, jump back to Hour 7, "Printing Your Pictures."

Notice the warning cube just to the right of the Selected color swatch. It's telling me that the color I've just selected is not one of the Web-safe colors—the 216 colors shared by the Windows and Mac operating systems. If I'm not going to display this image on the Web, I can safely ignore this warning. However, if I want to limit my choices to only Web-safe colors, I can select the Only Web Colors option. This prevents non-Web-safe colors from appearing in the color field.

After choosing the color you want to use, click OK.

Using the Swatches Palette

Another method for selecting the color you want to use is to click it within the Swatches palette, shown in Figure 19.2. The palette, as you can see, looks like a sort of paint box. The Swatches palette helps you build and store a consistent set of colors for use in refining an image. To display the Swatches palette yourself, click its tab in the palette well, or if it isn't there, choose Color Swatches from the Window menu.

19

FIGURE 19.2

The Swatches palette has several different sets of colors, including Web-safe colors and Windows OS colors.

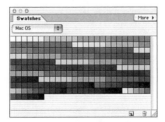

Elements comes with eight different sets of swatches, which you can select from the pop-up menu at the top of the palette. The Default swatch set contains a sample of the most often used colors, but you can add colors to this set or any of the other swatch sets if you'd like. To add the current foreground color as a new swatch to the displayed swatch set, just click in the empty area of the Swatches palette. You'll be asked whether you want to give the new color a name, and then it will be saved for you at the bottom of the palette. If you want to replace a swatch with the current foreground color, press Shift as you click it. To remove a swatch from a set, drag it to the trash can icon at the bottom of the palette.

After opening the Swatches palette and choosing a swatch set to display, you can select a color for use as the foreground color by simply clicking it. To select a color as the background color, press Option/Alt as you click it.

Other Tips for Selecting Colors

If the image itself contains the color you want, there's a simple method for choosing it. Simply click with the Eyedropper tool on the color in the image, and the foreground color will immediately be changed to match. You can click with the Eyedropper in any open image, even if it's not the one you're working on. To change the background color using the Eyedropper, press Option/Alt and click within the image.

If a tool has its own color swatch, you can change its color by changing the foreground color. You can also change the tool color with the Eyedropper. Just select the tool you want, then press Alt as you click in the image. This changes the foreground color and the tool color at the same time. If you want to change only the tool color, you'll need to use the Color Picker method, by clicking the tool color swatch.

If the colors you want to use as the foreground color and the background color are reversed, switch them by clicking the Switch Colors icon, as shown in Figure 19.3, or by pressing X. To set the foreground color and background color to the default colors (black and white), click the Default Colors icon or press D instead.

FIGURE 19.3

The current foreground and background colors appear at the bottom of the toolbox.

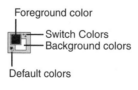

Foreground color

Switch Colors
Background colors

Default colors

Using the Shape Tools

Using the various shape tools, you can create rectangles, ellipses (circles and ovals), lines, polygons (shapes with flat sides such as diamonds), and even custom shapes such as musical notes, dog paw prints, and word balloons. When you create a new shape, it's placed on a new layer by default. You can override this setting whenever you want to place more than one shape on a layer. You might want to group shapes this way to make them easier to format and place within an image.

You can also combine shapes on one layer to create a single shape. Or you can choose to display only the area where the shapes intersect, or to exclude this overlapping area. For example, if you draw a square and then add a second square that overlaps it partially, using the option to display only the area where the two shapes intersect, that intersecting area will be the only portion of the two squares that is retained. If you draw the second square using the exclude option, the only portions retained will be the areas where the shapes *do not* overlap.

To draw a shape, follow these general steps:

1. Click the Shape tool button (the fourth one down on the left; it looks like a blue pillow) and select the specific shape you want to draw, such as Rounded Rectangle, from the left end of the tool's Options bar. You can also select the shape you want to draw by clicking and holding down the Shape tool button and choosing a shape from the menu that appears.

2. Set your options on the Options bar. We'll discuss each of these options in a moment.

3. Drag in the image to create the shape. Typically, I click at the upper left and drag down and to the right to create a shape.

Changing the Style

The preceding steps describe how to draw a single shape using the current settings, which will typically draw the shape without a border, and filled with the color shown in the tool color swatch (which initially matches the foreground color).

But as you can see on the Shape tool's option bar (shown in Figure 19.4), there are many settings you can adjust. Some settings you can change after the fact, as you will see later in this section. But first, let's take a look at the settings you might change before you draw your shape.

19

FIGURE 19.4

Set your options before drawing your shape.

The simplest option to change is whether or not the shape has a different style, such as a border of some sort, a shadow, or a textured fill. You select a style from the Style list (before or after drawing a shape—the Style setting affects the current selected shape, but if none is selected, it affects the shape you're about to draw), which is located toward the right end of the Options bar, as shown in Figure 19.4. Initially, the style is set to None, which means you'll get a shape filled with the tool color, and with no border. Click the down arrow on the Style list to reveal a group of styles, such as the Bevel styles, which add a bevel edge to a shape. You can display a different group of styles by clicking the right arrow at the top of the palette and choosing another set from the menu that appears. To return to drawing shapes without a style, select Remove Style from the menu.

You cannot use the Edit, Stroke command to add a border to a shape, as you can a selection or a layer. That's because the shape is editable. If you first simplify the layer on which you've drawn shapes (Layer, Simplify Layer), you can use one of the selection marquees to select the shape's outline and stroke it. But first try out some of the many style options explained here; you may find exactly what you're looking for, and with less trouble.

Setting the Geometry Options

You might also want to change the geometry options before (but not after) drawing a shape. These options control how a shape is drawn, and can help you draw a shape with more precision. The geometry options vary with the type of shape you've chosen from the left side of the Options menu. To display them, click the Geometry Options down arrow at the end of the shapes group, as shown in Figure 19.4.

The only way to explain the geometry options is to take them one shape at a time. The Rectangle, Rounded Rectangle, and Ellipse tools share similar geometry options:

- When you select Unconstrained, your dragging motion determines the shape.
- If you select Square or Circle, you can determine the size by dragging, but the shape will be drawn as a perfect square or circle.
- Select the From Center option to draw the shape from the center out, rather than from the upper-left corner to the lower-right corner.
- Select the Snap to Pixels option to help you draw a rectangle/rounded rectangle with borders that sit on the pixels' boundaries.
- To constrain the shape to a particular height/width, select Fixed Size and enter one or both values.

- To retain a particular proportion to the shape as you drag, select the Proportional option and enter the proportions in either or both boxes. The resulting shape will be proportionate to the size of the shape you drag to create. For example, if you enter a 2 in the W box and a 1 in the H box, your shape will be twice as wide as it is high.

The Rounded Rectangle tool has one other option on the Options bar itself, and that's Radius. The value you enter here determines the curve at the corners of the rectangle you draw.

The Polygon tool has its own set of geometry options. The Radius value sets the exact distance from the center of the polygon to its corners; by changing this value, you can draw a polygon of an exact size. The Smooth Corners option renders a polygon with rounded corners rather than sharp angles. To draw a star, select the Star option. Then set related options: Indent Sides By sets the angle of the points by forcing the sides to fit the proportion you enter, and Smooth Indents adjusts the angle of the points even further, to lessen the inside angles. The Polygon tool has one other option, displayed on the Options bar but not on the Geometry Options palette: the Sides value. As you may have guessed, this tells Elements how many sides of equal length you want your polygon to have.

As you can see from the geometry options for the Line shape shown in Figure 19.4, you can add an arrowhead at the beginning or end of the line by choosing Start or End, or both. After turning on either arrowhead, set the arrowhead's width and length, which are proportionate to the width and length of the line itself. Curve the sides of the arrowhead by entering a Concavity value other than zero. The Line tool has one other option as well that is not shown on the Geometry Options palette, but appears on the Options bar: the Weight option, which controls the thickness of the line. Fat lines, by the way, are filled with the tool color.

Now that you know a bit about drawing each type of shape, let's discuss the other settings on the Options bar.

Drawing Additional Shapes

After drawing one shape, you may want to draw another. After all, most shapes are actually made up of many ellipses, rectangles, lines, polygons, and so on. To change to a different shape tool so you can draw a different shape, click the shape's button (located at the left end of the Options bar). Then change any geometry options you want, and change any additional settings we've already talked about. You're now ready to click in the image and drag to draw the new shape. Before you do, however, you might want to consider how that shape will affect the other shapes in your image.

19

The shape area buttons on the far right of the Options bar (see Figure 19.5) require a bit of explanation before you use them. The first button on the left is Create New Shape Layer. If this is selected (which it normally is by default), a new layer will be created automatically when you draw the shape. If you choose any other option, you'll draw the new shape on the current shape layer. The next button, Add to Shape Area, dictates not only that the shape you draw will appear on the current shape layer, but that the two shapes will be treated as one shape for the purposes of formatting, resizing, moving, and so on. If you select Subtract from Shape Area, the second shape will not be filled and the area where the two shapes overlap will be removed from the original shape. Think of this option as cutting away part of the original shape with a shape tool.

If you select Intersect Shape Areas, only the intersection of the two shapes is filled. If the second shape doesn't intersect the first, neither shape is filled. The last button, Exclude Overlapping Shape Areas, is the exact opposite; the area where the two shapes intersect is left unfilled, and other non-overlapping areas are filled.

FIGURE 19.5

Use these buttons to control how a new shape affects other shapes.

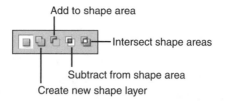

Add to shape area

Intersect shape areas

Subtract from shape area

Create new shape layer

There's one last thing you need to consider before you draw additional shapes: the fill color. When you draw your first shape, it's filled with the tool color shown in the color swatch at the right end of the Options bar. Initially, this color is set to the foreground color, but you can change it before you draw the shape in any of the ways discussed earlier in this hour.

When you're ready to draw additional shapes, *do not change the tool color or the style.* If you do, you'll change the fill color or style of the shape you just drew. Instead, draw the shape, and then, while it's still selected, change the color and/or style as desired.

Creating a Custom Shape

To create a custom shape such as a rabbit, choose the Custom Shape tool from the Shape tools list. On the Options bar, open the Shapes list, and a palette of default shapes appears. If the shape you want to draw is not shown, click the right-pointing arrow to open a menu of other shape groups. To draw a rabbit, for example, click the arrow and select Animals. Then click the rabbit shape in the palette.

After selecting the custom shape you want to draw, set other options as desired, such as the color and shape area options. Then drag in the image to create a shape.

Selecting a Shape

Use the Shape Selection tool (the arrowhead pointer located to the left of the shape buttons on the Options bar) to select a shape so you can move, copy, delete, rotate, or resize
it. Just click the tool and then click on the shape you want to select. Handles (small
squares) appear around the selected shape, as shown in Figure 19.6. Drag the handles
outward or inward to resize the shape. Dragging a corner handle maintains the *aspect
ratio* (the width in relationship to the height). To change only the horizontal or vertical
width, drag a side handle. To resize a shape by a certain amount (that is, to *scale* it),
enter the appropriate values in the boxes on the Options bar. You can enter a value in the
Set Horizontal Scale box, and click the Maintain Aspect Ratio button to automatically
adjust the Vertical value by a proportionate amount. When you're done, click the check
mark to commit the change.

FIGURE 19.6

*Handles appear
around the selected
shape(s).*

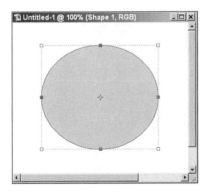

19

Click the center handle (which looks like a cross) to move the shape. If you want to
move all the shapes on a layer together, use the Move tool instead. Click the Move tool,
then click anywhere on the shape layer. Drag the selection to move the shapes as a
group.

You can also rotate a selected shape using the techniques you learned in Hour 9,
"Cropping and Resizing Your Pictures," and skew it as you did in Hour 10,
"Straightening, Skewing, and Distorting an Image."

Task: Create an Umbrella

We'll use the Shape tools to create a small object: an umbrella. Start a new image using
default size, RGB color, and a white background.

1. Select the Ellipse shape tool. Select a bright color for your umbrella, such as blue or yellow. Make sure that the Create New Shape Layer option is selected.

2. Click in the image and drag to create an oval umbrella shape.

3. Click the Subtract from Shape Area option. Then click the Rectangle tool, and use it to cut out the bottom of the oval, flattening it.

4. With Subtract from Shape Area option still selected, select the Ellipse shape again. Draw small circles with the Ellipse tool that cut out portions of the flattened bottom of the umbrella shape, creating its scalloped edge. Your shape should look roughly like the one shown in Figure 19.7.

FIGURE 19.7

Our umbrella is taking shape.

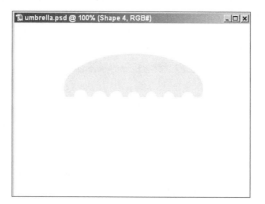

5. Select the Rectangle tool and the Create New Shape Layer option.

6. Draw a small rectangle at the top of the umbrella. Draw a long, thin rectangle at the bottom of the umbrella for the handle.

Remember that you can move a selected shape by dragging it. This will help you get all the pieces of your umbrella in line. To select a shape, click on it with the Shape Selection tool.

7. Select the Ellipse tool, and draw a small circle at the base of the thin rectangle, creating the bottom of the curved handle.

8. Select the Subtract from Shape Area option, and draw a smaller circle slightly above the first circle, creating the upper part of the curved handle. At this point, your image has several layers; that's okay. Your umbrella should look roughly like the one shown in Figure 19.8.

9. Name your file umbrella.psd and save it. You will be refining it later in this hour.

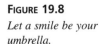

FIGURE 19.8

Let a smile be your umbrella.

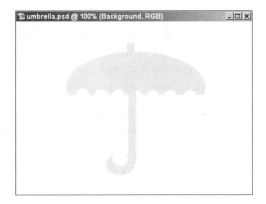

Using the Brush Tool

With the Brush tool, you can paint color on an image with hard or soft brushes of various widths and degrees of opacity. There are also brushes with special tips, for painting with stars, grass, leaves, and other shapes. You can even imitate chalk, charcoal, hard pastels, oil pastels, dry brush, watercolor, oils, and other artistic techniques.

When you paint with the Brush tool, the paint is applied to the current layer, so make sure you change to the layer you want to use before painting.

Also, if you paint on a layer containing text or a shape, that layer will need to be simplified first, which means that the text/shape will no longer be editable. In such a situation, Elements will typically ask you if you want to simplify the layer, and all you'll need to do is click Yes to proceed. If you want to simplify a layer yourself, select it from the Layers palette and choose Layer, Simplify Layer.

Setting Brush Options

To use the Brush tool, click it and then choose the color you want to paint with (the foreground color). Set your options from the Options bar, shown in Figure 19.9. First, choose the brush tip you want from the drop-down list. Adjust the size as needed.

FIGURE 19.9

Set the brush options before you start.

Choose a blending mode and a level of opacity if you like. Blending is rather complex, so it's explained in detail in Hour 20, "Making Composite Images." Opacity, as explained in Hour 5, "Making Selections and Using Layers," adjusts the strength of your paint—with a low opacity, the paint color will not cover any color or image beneath it. A higher opacity creates a more solid paint that covers any color or pattern you paint over.

If you click the Airbrush button, you'll be able to control the flow of paint by varying the amount of time you press the mouse button down and remain in one spot.

After making selections, paint with the brush by clicking on the image and holding the mouse button down as you drag. Release the mouse button to stop painting.

Painting with the Impressionist Brush

The Impressionist Brush doesn't paint, so you won't use it to create art. Instead, you use this brush to change the texture of an image to simulate the look of an impressionist painting or a pastel drawing. The effect is that the brush creates a wet paint–like pattern by borrowing the colors that are already present in the image. This makes the image look as if it were painted using a freestyle technique, as shown in Figure 19.10.

FIGURE 19.10

Give your images the look of a classic painting with the Impressionist Brush.

Because the Impressionist Brush doesn't paint new colors onto the existing image, the current foreground and background colors are set aside. Instead, this tool samples the pixels in the area you define, and then uses a brush tip the size you specify to fill the area with a mix of those sampled colors.

To begin, click the arrow on the Brush tool and choose Impressionist Brush. Select a brush tip and size. A small brush tip works best for me, but feel free to experiment. Set the blending mode and opacity. The blending mode controls how the pixels painted by the brush are blended with the original pixels—again, you'll learn more about blending in Hour 20. If you want more definition in the finished image, set a low opacity value so the brush doesn't completely obscure the sharp edges in the image underneath.

Before you begin painting, click the More Options button to set these options: the Style menu controls the style of the brush stroke, from tight, short strokes to loose and curly strokes. The Area value controls the area of pixels painted by the brush. If you enter a large number, a large number of pixels surrounding the brush tip will be changed. A smaller area provides more control, but requires you to paint more strokes to change a large portion of an image. Finally, set the Tolerance level: With a low tolerance, you'll change only pixels that are very close in color to the ones you brush over. A higher Tolerance value allows more pixels in the designated area to be changed, as long as they are sufficiently similar to the pixels you paint over.

After setting options, drag over the image to change pixels of similar color within the designated area.

Task: Create Rain for Your Umbrella

There are many ways in which you might create a rain effect for an image. We'll use the Brush tool to create a simple effect.

1. If it's not already open, open the umbrella.psd file.

2. Open the Layers palette and make the Background layer active.

3. Select the Brush tool. Choose a 14-pixel Spatter brush tip (You'll find Spatter near the middle of the brush tip list—just rest the mouse pointer on a brush tip style in the list, and its name appears). Use Normal blending mode, 100% opacity. Set the foreground color to a light grayish blue.

4. Draw diagonal lines close together, in the manner of wind-swept rain. Make sure you don't draw rain under your umbrella!

5. Click the Impressionist Brush button on the Options bar. Click the More Options button, and set the Style to Loose Medium, the Area to 20 pixels, and the Tolerance to 0.

6. Drag back and forth over your rain streaks, softening them. Your image will look something like the one shown in Figure 19.11.

7. Save the image and leave it open.

19

FIGURE 19.11

FIGURE 19.11

A little rain never hurt anybody.

Using the Pencil Tool

Using the Pencil tool is remarkably like using the Brush tool. With the Pencil tool, you can draw hard-edged lines on an image in your choice of color.

Setting Pencil Options

Simply click the Pencil tool and select a color by changing the foreground color. Select a pencil tip, adjust the width of the drawn line, set the blending mode, and change the opacity as desired. Then click on the image, hold the mouse button down, and drag to draw a line.

Selecting the same tip with the Brush tool and the Pencil tool produces different results, as you can see in Figure 19.12.

FIGURE 19.12

Although these lines were drawn with the same soft-edged 5-point tip, different tools produce different results.

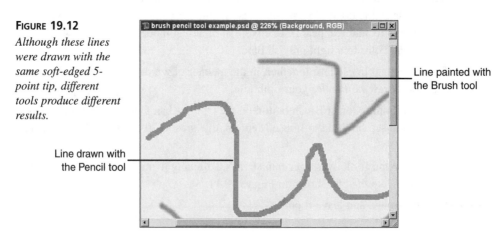

Line painted with the Brush tool

Line drawn with the Pencil tool

Replacing One Color with Another

You can replace one color with another using the Pencil tool and the Auto Erase option. First, change the foreground color to the color you want to replace. Remember that, after opening the color picker, you can click anywhere in the image with the eyedropper pointer to "pick up" or choose that exact color. After selecting the color to replace, set the background color to the color you want to replace it with. Then choose your pencil tip and set your options. Be sure you select the Auto Erase option at the right end of the Options bar. Then draw by dragging over the image. If you drag over an area that contains the foreground color, it will be replaced by the background color. Other parts of the image will remain unaffected even if you drag over them.

Task: Adding Ribs to Your Umbrella

With the Pencil tool, it's easy to add ribs to your umbrella.

1. With the umbrella.psd file open, click the Pencil tool.

2. Create a new layer above the others.

3. Set the foreground color to one that's slightly lighter than the umbrella color, such as a light yellow or light blue.

4. Select the Hard Round brush tip style from the list, set the tip size to 3 pixels, and draw ribs from the top of the umbrella to each of its points. The result is a rather whimsical rendition of an umbrella in the rain, shown in Figure 19.13.

5. Save and close the image file.

FIGURE 19.13

The final version of our umbrella.

19

Using the Eraser Tools

All of the Eraser tools change pixels in your image in a particular way. You've learned that you can replace one color with another by choosing the Auto Erase option and drawing with the Pencil tool. In this section, you'll learn about two of the other tools Elements provides for erasing parts of an image: the Eraser tool and the Background Eraser tool. In Hour 24, "Animated GIFs and Other Cool Tricks," you'll learn how to use the Magic Eraser tool.

Erasing with the Eraser Tool

When you drag over pixels with the Eraser tool, the pixels are removed and made transparent, so lower layers can show through. If you use the Eraser tool on the Background layer or any other layer with locked transparency, the result is different. Instead of erasing pixels and making them transparent, the tool replaces the pixels you drag over with the background color.

To use the Eraser, activate the layer you want to erase a portion of, and click the Eraser tool. Select from one of three Modes: Brush (which provides a soft-edged brush tip), Pencil (which provides the harder-edged pencil tip), or Block (which provides a square blocky tip). If you choose Brush or Pencil, select the exact tip to use from the drop-down list and adjust the size. With the brush or pencil tips, you can also adjust the opacity to limit the strength of the eraser—a lower opacity level causes the brush to erase to only partial transparency or to the background color, depending on which level you are erasing on.

After setting options, click and drag on the image to erase pixels, as shown in Figure 19.14.

FIGURE 19.14

Erase on a layer and let the background shine through.

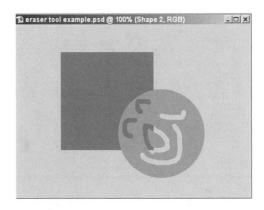

Erasing with the Background Eraser Tool

You use the Background Eraser to erase or remove the background from around an object without erasing part of that object in the process. The theory behind its operation is that an object's color generally differs greatly from the color of the background that surrounds it. As you click and drag the brush over the image, the Background Eraser continually samples the color under the *hotspot* (the small cross in the center of the tool's pointer), and sets that color as the background color. It then erases only colors that closely approximate this background color, over the entire area of the eraser.

You can safely set the eraser to a large size (the pointer will then look like a wide, transparent circle). The large size is safe to use, because the Background Eraser does not erase all the pixels in that circle (under the eraser); instead, it erases only the pixels within the circle that match or nearly match the one under the hotspot. To erase all the background pixels surrounding any object—for instance, a car on a street, or a single flower in a garden—you carefully drag the eraser with its hotspot *near*, but not *inside*, that object. If the circle area of the eraser should fall within the object's border, the object remains safe, so long as the hotspot rests over a color that's substantially different. So if you drag this eraser entirely around an object whose color stands out from its background, you'll erase only the background and leave the object intact.

To use the Background Eraser, click the arrow on the Eraser tool button and select it. Adjust the size of the eraser as desired, and then select one of the two options from the Limits menu. Contiguous erases pixels under the eraser that match the sampled color, and which are touching, or contiguous to, the hotspot itself. If you select Discontiguous instead, any pixel under the eraser whose color closely matches the sampled hue will be erased. You can control how closely pixels must match the sampled pixel by adjusting the Tolerance value. A lower value limits the number of pixels that will match the sampled pixel. A higher value allows you to erase a greater variety of pixels. After setting the options you want, click on the background to sample its color, then drag with the Background Eraser on the image to erase the background, as shown in Figure 19.15.

19

FIGURE 19.15

Use the Background Eraser to separate an image from its background.

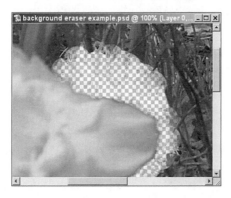

Summary

With the drawing tools in Elements, it's easy to create simple images such as logos and clip art, or to edit an existing graphic so that it suits your needs more exactly. The options for each tool give you control, while allowing you the freedom to experiment as you wish.

Q&A

Q I've tried to cut an object out of a picture, but there seems to be a bit of a halo. How do I get rid of it?

A One way to solve this problem is to remove some of the background first, then cut out the object. To remove the background from around an object, use the Background Eraser.

Q I want to make a photo look more like an oil painting. Any suggestions?

A Why not give the Impressionist Brush tool a try? By softening the hard edges in your photo and blending neighboring colors, you might just achieve the look you want. There are also many filters you can apply that imitate various artistic techniques such as painting with oils or watercolors and drawing with pastels. (You saw how to apply some of the artistic filters in Hour 18, "Using the Artistic Filters.")

Q The shape I just drew is the wrong size, and it's not positioned in exactly the right spot. Do I have to start over?

A Not at all. You can use the Shape Selection tool to select your shape and resize it. The tool can also help you reposition your shape.

Workshop

Take a few moments to tackle this short quiz on drawing and check your answers to see how you did. Then work on the activities for extra credit.

Quiz

1. Each shape you draw is placed on its own layer.

    a. True

    b. False

2. If you want to cover the background with the paintbrush color, you should set the

    a. Blending mode to Normal

    b. Tolerance level to a low value

    c. Opacity to a high value

    d. You can't cover the background with paint

3. To set the color of a shape's outline (border), change the background color.

    a. True

    b. False

Quiz Answers

1. b. A shape is placed on a new layer only if the Create New Shape Layer option is selected. Otherwise, the shape will add to or subtract from the shape on the current layer.

2. c. To completely cover another color with paint, set the opacity level to 100%. If you use a low value, some of the background color will show through.

3. b. You can set the fill color of a shape with the foreground color, but the background color has no effect. If you want to add a border around a shape, you must simplify it first by choosing Layer, Simplify. Then you can select the shape and add a border with the Edit, Stroke command. If the shape is a combination of several layers, merge them into a single layer with the Layer, Merge Visible command.

Activities

1. Find a photo of an object such as a flower or a car and use the Background Eraser tool to remove the background from the image. Then copy a new background into the image.

2. Create some art of your own! Use the various drawing and painting tools to create your own logo that you can use on your Web site, emails, or school papers. Play with some of the texture fills available on the Style menu for shapes; add special touches with the Brush and Pencil tools, add text and apply a text effect to it, and render the final version in 3-D using the 3-D Transform filter. Have fun!

19

Hour 20

Making Composite Images

Whenever you combine elements from more than one source, you're said to be making a composite. The process of creating a composite can include something as simple as adding a gradient, or as complex as making a montage of half a dozen pictures, plus type and effects. How you want to use the technique is up to you. Some people create wonderfully surrealistic photos. Others simply improve the composition by throwing extra sheep in the meadow or fish in the aquarium. Still others use it simply to put a drop shadow behind the type on a title page.

In this hour you will

- Adjust brightness, contrast, and scale in a composite image
- Apply layer styles to layers and selections
- Use adjustment layers to fix problems in selected areas
- Work with blending modes when using tools or layer styles
- Apply effects to an image

- Create your own custom effects and shadows
- Play with reflections
- Use distortions to blend objects
- Create a panoramic photo using Photomerge

Working with Lighting and Scale

When combining images, the two main things to watch out for are lighting and scale. If the shadows and highlights on the imported image don't match those on the original, you might not immediately recognize why the picture doesn't look right, but you'll know that it doesn't. This will happen if the light source for one photo doesn't come from the same direction as the light source in the photo you wish to combine with it. Of course, if the shadows aren't exactly in the right place, you can use the Clone Stamp and the Brush to move them where they need to be, as we did with the zebra photo in Hour 15, "Making Color Repairs." However, this is rather tricky (not to mention tedious) business, so avoid the problem as much as possible by selecting photos that have their sources of light coming from the same direction whenever possible.

Scale is an even trickier question. You *can* create very funny photos by having the family cat cowering in front of a three-foot-high mouse, or some similar scene, but should you? It's a gimmick. It's not art, which is not to say I don't do it myself. My cat Reebok would have sworn the rat shown in Figure 20.1 was at least three feet tall.

FIGURE 20.1

The rat has, of course, been resized, and I've added Gaussian blur and a small drop shadow.

Less exaggerated differences in scale are harder to spot, but you'll probably notice that the picture isn't quite right, even if you can't immediately see why. If you're going to photograph your kids in front of the Golden Gate Bridge, they shouldn't be taller than it is. Nor should they be tiny, or set so far back that they have nothing to stand on. Scaling them to fit is easiest if you put them on a new layer, and select Image, Resize, Scale. Press Shift as you drag on the bounding box to keep the proportions correct as you rescale the image (in this case, rescale your kids so that they look as if they fit in the picture of the Golden Gate).

Using Layer Styles to Create Composites

Layer styles apply a style such as a shadow, bevel, or metallic fill to all the objects on a layer. There are 14 different kinds of layer styles, ranging from Bevels, Glows, and Drop Shadows to Glass Buttons, Patterns, and Wow Chrome. As you learned in Hour 6, "Adding Type," they are most often used with type, to make it stand out from the rest of the image, but you can apply layer styles to any kind of object.

Before I tell you some of the ways you can use layer styles with objects to create composite pictures, let's review what we know about layer styles. A layer style is a special effect, and when you add it to a layer, it's applied to all the objects on that layer—text, shapes, or the outer edge of an image. So be sure to move objects you don't want affected to other layers before you proceed, and if working with an image, make sure you resize it so you can see the edge effect (if any) for the layer style you select. For example, you won't see a drop shadow on your image if that image takes up the entire layer.

Adding a layer style is fairly simple: First, change to the layer you want to affect by clicking its name in the Layers palette. Then, open the Layer Styles palette (Window, Layer Styles), choose a category from the list (such as Drop Shadow, Bevel, or Wow Chrome), and when the palette opens to display a list of the styles in that category, click on the thumbnail of the particular style you want to apply. The cursive *f* appears after the layer name on the Layers palette to remind you that the layer is using a layer style.

You can combine styles if you want. Some styles, you'll find, completely overlay any layer styles you have already applied, leaving few if any remnants of them. Others combine well to create interesting effects. The only way to know which layer styles work well together is to play around with various combinations and make note of the ones you like. To remove all styles from the current layer, click the Clear Style button at the top of the Layer Styles palette. There is no way, unfortunately, to remove one style without removing the rest, unless you want to remove the last style you applied, in which case you can simply click Undo.

20

Here's a quick summary of the various layer styles you can use. Most of them, as I mentioned before, are probably best used with text, unless your idea is to create a rather surreal-looking image. However, you never know what layer style might prove useful, given a particular situation:

- Bevels—Puts a sharp or soft edge on the sides of an object. This edge appears to raise or lower the object above or below the surface of the layer. The emboss styles produce a softer effect than the bevel styles.
- Drop Shadows—Adds a soft- or sharp-edged shadow behind objects.
- Inner Glows—Adds a soft glow to the inner edges of objects, so they seem to glow inside.
- Inner Shadows—Adds a shadow to the inner edges of objects, so they seem to fall below the surface of the layer.
- Outer Glows—Adds a soft glow to the outside edges of objects.
- Visibility—Softens the fill color of objects, or hides them entirely. Click Show to redisplay the fill color at full saturation.
- Complex—Combines several layer styles to create a unique effect. There are too many styles here to list them all, but some of the more notable ones are Chrome—Fat, Molten Gold, Rivet, Star Glow, Diamond Plate, and Paint Brush Strokes.
- Glass Buttons—Fills an object with the color you choose, and makes it appear slightly opaque like glass and raised like a button.
- Image Effects—These layer styles are probably most useful for working with objects rather than text, although they can be applied to either. Here you'll find such things as Fog, Rain, Snow, Water Reflection, Night Vision, and Circular Vignette, which is similar to the vignette technique we used in Hour 14, "Repairing Black-and-White Pictures."
- Patterns—A collection of interesting textures you can apply, including fabric textures such as Batik, Satin Overlay, Tie-Dyed Silk, Blanket, and Denim; surface textures such as Painted Wallboard, Brushed Metal, Ancient Stone, Asphalt, Stucco, Marble, Brick Walk, Dry Mud, and Wood; and unique effects such as Nebula, Abstract Fire, and Smoke. There are too many to mention them all, so be sure to check out this category.
- Photographic Effects—From their name, you can probably guess that these layer styles are especially well suited for working with images. Here you'll find such styles as Negative, Sepia Tone, and Teal Tone.

- Wow Chrome —Applies various chrome textures to objects. I like the Wow Chrome—Shiny Edge the best, especially when combined with Wow Chrome—Reflecting.

- Wow Neon —Adds a neon-like glow in your choice of colors. The neon tubing can appear to be either on or off, depending on your selection. When you apply these styles, the fill color is removed from any objects.

- Wow Plastic —Replaces the fill color with plastic in your choice of colors. This layer style is similar to, but not the same as, the Glass Buttons style.

In the example in Figure 20.2 (which is reproduced in the color plate section), I've applied various layer styles to a simple rectangle shape. I simply created the rectangle on one layer, and then used Layer, Duplicate Layer to copy it several times. After each copy, I used the Move tool to move each rectangle into a unique position within the image so I could see them all. Then I applied one Drop Shadow layer style plus a layer style of some other category to each rectangle so I could compare the effects. How many can you identify? The rectangle I drew was bright yellow. Notice how some of the styles completely replaced the fill color, while other styles look as if they are laid on top of the color.

FIGURE 20.2

Which style do you like best?

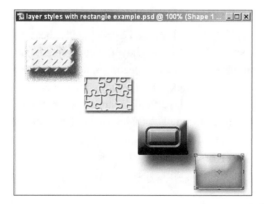

20

As I mentioned earlier, you can add a layer style to text if that text is on its own layer; otherwise, all objects on the layer will be affected. You can add layer styles to shapes as well. You can also create the effect of painting or drawing with a texture layer style if you do the following: First, fill a layer with a textured layer style such as one of the Patterns (Bumpy, Stucco, or Manhole, for instance). Create a new layer above this patterned layer. Select the Brush or Pencil tool, and choose the Clear blending mode. Then paint or draw as usual. You'll notice that instead of painting with the foreground color, you're actually erasing pixels, allowing the texture on the layer below to show through. If you later remove the layer style from the bottom layer, the paint or drawn line will appear in the foreground color you used originally, instead of the pattern.

Using Adjustment Layers to Fix Image Problems

Adjustment layers are used to make particular types of adjustments to the layers below the adjustment layer, or to the layers grouped with it. After I list the types of adjustments you can make, we'll talk about controlling which layers are affected.

With an adjustment layer, you can adjust the levels, brightness/contrast, and hue/saturation. These adjustments correspond to the commands you learned how to use on an entire image in Hour 12, "Too Light/Too Dark: Adjusting Brightness, Contrast, and Color." You can also add a gradient map (a layer that blends one color into another), invert colors (by switching them for their opposites on the color wheel), adjust the threshold (convert the affected layers to high-contrast black and white), or add a posterize effect (which lets you limit the number of tones or shades used in all three color channels, creating a flatter look with less subtlety). You'll learn about the Posterize and Threshold adjustments in Hour 21, "Going Wild with Your Images," and gradients in Hour 22, "Creating Backgrounds and Textures from Scratch."

Adding an Adjustment Layer

To create an adjustment layer, click in the Layers palette, below where you want the adjustment layer to appear. Then choose Layer, New Adjustment Layer and choose the adjustment type from the submenu that appears. The New Layer dialog box will appear; type a Name for the layer and click OK. The adjustment layer will be placed above the current layer and will affect that layer and all layers below it unless you choose the Group with Previous Layer option. The dialog box corresponding to the type of adjustment you selected then appears. (For example, if you're creating a hue/saturation adjustment layer, the Hue/Saturation dialog box appears.) Make the adjustment you want and click OK.

> If you click the Create New Adjustment or Fill Layer button in the Layers palette, you won't be able to name your layer or group it with the previous layer.

After you add an adjustment layer, you'll see it appear in the Layers palette, just above the layer you clicked before you inserted the adjustment layer. The adjustment layer looks like the one shown in Figure 20.3. The first icon on the left tells you that this layer is visible, or in this case, active—the adjustment is being applied. If you click this icon to hide it, the adjustment layer will no longer be in effect. The next icon, the mask icon, tells you that a mask is being used to partially obscure the effects of the adjustment to the layers below. A mask is simply a selection. If you have selected something on the current layer or the layers below the adjustment layer (assuming that you're not limiting the adjustment to a single layer), only the selected area on that layer will be affected by the adjustment. You can actually edit this mask, refining the area you want to affect— more on that later.

FIGURE 20.3

The adjustment layer is listed separately in the Layers palette.

Grouped with another layer

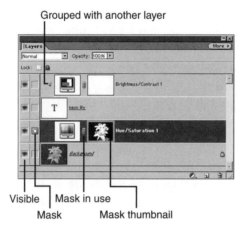

Visible | Mask in use

Mask | Mask thumbnail

 Masks are also used on fill layers, to hide or partially obscure some of the fill.

The next icon, a bent arrow, will only appear if you chose the Group with Previous option. It tells you that this adjustment layer is grouped with the layer below it. Next is the adjustment thumbnail, which depicts an icon that shows you what kind of adjustment has been made. Here, a Hue/Saturation adjustment layer (selected) and a Brightness/Contrast adjustment layer were used. If you want to change the adjustment settings, double-click this icon and the dialog box you originally saw (in this case, the Hue/Saturation dialog box) will be redisplayed. Make your changes and click OK. The next icon, the link, tells you that a layer mask is linked to its underlying layer. The final thumbnail, the mask thumbnail, shows you the shape of the mask that's in place.

If you selected the Group with Previous Layer option in the New Layer dialog box, the adjustment layer is grouped with the layer just below it, and the adjustments affect only that layer. To add the layer immediately below the bottommost grouped layer to the group, press Option/Alt and click the line that separates the two layers in the Layers palette.

20

Editing the Adjustment Layer Mask

Unless you made a selection prior to inserting an adjustment layer, the adjustments will apply to all objects on the affected layers. In such a case, the mask thumbnail on the Layers palette will be completely white, which indicates that the mask is not blocking any part of the adjustment.

To mask part of the adjustment's effects or to adjust a mask that's already in place, click on the adjustment layer in the Layers palette to select it. Then display the mask on the image so you can see it. To display the mask in grayscale, press Option/Alt and click the mask thumbnail. To display the mask in red, press Shift+Option/Alt and click the mask thumbnail. If you started with no mask and you're adding one, the mask will not be displayed because there isn't one to show.

Initially, a mask is white. White areas indicate where adjustments are in effect. Black areas block the adjustment effects, and gray areas block the adjustments only partially, based on how dark the gray is. To add or change a mask, you simply paint with white to expand the area of the adjustment's effects, or with black to mask it. Paint with any tone of gray to partially obscure the adjustment.

When you select the adjustment layer in the Layers palette, Elements automatically changes the foreground and background colors to get ready for any changes to the mask you might want to make. Click the Brush or Pencil tool, choose a brush tip, size, blending mode, and opacity, and paint to create or change the mask, as shown in Figure 20.4. You can also use a shape tool to fill an area with white or black. In addition, you can select an area to work on with any of the selection marquee tools, and then when you paint, you'll only affect that area—this is a nice way of making sure you don't erase parts of the mask you want to keep. When you're done making adjustments, press Option/Alt and click the mask thumbnail to reveal the image again. Elements will update the display and show you the outline of the current mask.

You can use a gradient fill in black and white to create the mask; see Hour 21 for tips on creating a gradient. You can also partially obscure the entire adjustment layer by changing its opacity and/or blending modes (which you'll learn about later this hour). To turn off the mask, press Shift and click the mask thumbnail. Repeat this step to turn the mask back on so that the effects of the adjustment are once again partially obscured.

Here's an example of using an adjustment layer on an image. I shot a picture of an interesting intersection of walls and gates in Harvard Yard. Unfortunately, it was one of those early spring days with a very weak sun and washed-out colors.

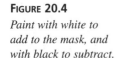

FIGURE 20.4

Paint with white to add to the mask, and with black to subtract.

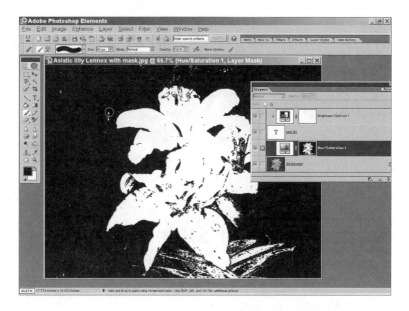

The first thing I want to do to this photo is to brighten up the colors. If I simply call for Auto Contrast, I'll get whatever the folks at Adobe think is an acceptable amount of contrast based on the differences between the darkest pixels and lightest pixels on the page. That might be okay. After all, they're experts. However, this is *my* picture and I'm the expert on what I want to do with it, so the auto correction probably isn't quite right.

I can go back up to the Enhance menu and choose Enhance, Adjust Brightness/Contrast and tweak the sliders myself to get a better, closer correction. But for maximum flexibility, I'll make the correction on an adjustment layer. Then I'll have greater control over the correction—for instance, if I think I've gotten the right brick color but the rest of the image seems too bright, I can reduce the opacity of the layer and thereby reduce the strength of the correction. I can also use the selection tools to mask out part of the area and apply the color correction to the brick while ignoring the granite.

That done, I've decided to add a second adjustment layer, posterizing just the brick buildings by masking out the parts I don't want to affect.

If you look closely at the Layers palette in Figure 20.5, you can see the mask I've placed (the black area) in the mask thumbnail of the posterization layer. Be sure to check out this figure in the color plate section.

20

FIGURE 20.5

The advantage to working this way is that you can control the amount of the adjustments you apply to each part of an image.

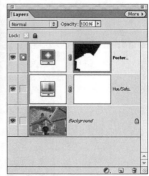

Task: Add Layer Styles and Adjustment Layers to Our Umbrella

To practice what we know about layer styles and adjustment layers, let's edit the image of the umbrella in the rain.

1. Open the umbrella.psd file you created in Hour 19, "Creating Art from Scratch."

2. Change to the background layer. Select a rainy-day medium bluish gray as the foreground color, and use the Paint Bucket tool to fill the background with paint. This will cover over the rain we created earlier, but we'll add it back with a layer style.

3. Open the Layer Styles palette (Window, Layer Styles). Select the Image Effects category, and click the Rain thumbnail. You'll be asked whether you want to make the background a regular layer; click OK to proceed. Type Rain in the Name box and click OK. The image should look like Figure 20.6.

FIGURE 20.6

Rain, rain, go away.

4. Well, not bad. But I'd like to darken the sky a bit without darkening the umbrella. If I use the Enhance, Adjust Brightness/Contrast, Brightness/Contrast command right now, it will only darken the rain layer, and not the umbrella. However, I'd like to prevent the sky *under* the umbrella from getting darkened as well, so let's use an adjustment layer instead. First, select the area under the umbrella using the Rectangular Marquee tool. We don't have to worry if we select any part of the umbrella, because it won't be affected by the adjustment layer anyway.

5. Because any part we don't select will be masked when we create the adjustment layer, choose Select, Inverse to invert the selection and place the marquee around the entire sky except for the area under the umbrella.

6. Choose Layer, New Adjustment Layer, Brightness/Contrast. You can change the name of the new layer if you want, but I think I'll just leave it. We don't need to turn on the Group with Previous Layer option because the rain layer is the only layer below this one, so just click OK.

7. Drag the Brightness slider to the left, darkening the sky so that it's almost night, but not quite. I set my Brightness at –22. Click OK. The result is shown in Figure 20.7.

FIGURE 20.7
Well, at least I'm staying dry.

Understanding Blending Modes

In the real world, when you place a second brush full of paint over paint that's already there, the effect depends on the color of the paint you're applying, how opaque it is, whether the first layer is wet or dry, and so on. In Elements, you can control all these factors by using what are called *blending modes*. Blending modes apply to layers (controlling a layer's effect on the layers below it) as well as to all tools that can draw or paint, including the Brush, Pencil, Clone Stamp, and Paint Bucket, just to name a few. You'll find the tool blending modes on the Mode menu on the Tool Options bar, and the Layer blending modes on a similar menu on the Layer palette, as shown in Figure 20.8.

20

As you can see, there are quite a few different modes. Not all are available with all the tools. Let's take a quick look at the blending modes and what they do.

Suppose that you're working with only two colors. One is the *base* color—the one that's already in place. The second is the *blend* color—the color that you're applying with your tool, or the color on the layer(s) below the one whose blending mode you're adjusting. Depending on the blending mode you choose, you get a third color, a *result* that varies according to how you blend the first two.

FIGURE 20.8

The Tool Options list here shows the Brush blending modes.

Figures 20.9–20.31 show what happens when you choose each of the blending mode options. (The examples were painted with a firm brush in hot pink on a lime green background.)In most cases, the blending mode was applied to the pink brush on a single layer. Where the results of applying the blend to a separate layer are different, I have shown both. Please be sure to see these in color, as it's difficult in some cases to see what's happening in black and white.

FIGURE 20.9

Normal—*This is the default mode. The blend color replaces the base color.*

FIGURE 20.10

Dissolve—*A random number of pixels are converted to the blend color. This option gives a splattered or "dry brush" effect.*

FIGURE 20.11
Dissolve—*Applied with a normal brush to a second layer at 50% opacity.*

FIGURE 20.12
Darken—*Evaluates the color information in each channel and assigns either the base color or the blend color, whichever is darker, as the result color. Lighter pixels are replaced, but darker ones don't change.*

FIGURE 20.13
Multiply—*Multiplies the base color by the blend color, giving you a darker result color. The effect is like drawing over the picture with a Magic Marker. Where the background is light, you see the original blend color.*

FIGURE 20.14
Color Burn—*Darkens the base color to match the value of the blend color. This effect is very subtle.*

FIGURE 20.15
Linear Burn—*Darkens the base color to reflect the blend color by decreasing the brightness. Blending with white produces no change.*

20

FIGURE 20.16

Lighten—*Evaluates the color information in each channel and assigns either the base color or the blend color, whichever is lighter, as the result color. Darker pixels are replaced, but lighter ones don't change. This is the exact opposite of Darken.*

FIGURE 20.17

Screen—*Multiplies the base color by the inverse of the blend color, giving you a lighter result color. The effect is like painting with bleach. I drew the hearts with the brush set to Wet Edges.*

FIGURE 20.18

Color Dodge—*Brightens the base color to match the value of the blend color.*

FIGURE 20.19

Linear Dodge—*Brightens the base color to reflect the blend color by increasing the brightness. Blending with black produces no change.*

FIGURE 20.20

Overlay—*Evaluates the color information in each channel and assigns either the base color or the blend color, whichever is darker, as the result color. Lighter pixels are replaced, but darker ones don't change.*

FIGURE 20.21

Soft Light—*Darkens or lightens depending on the blend color. The effect is said to be similar to shining a diffused spotlight on the image. With a light blend color, it has very little effect.*

FIGURE 20.22

Hard Light—*Multiplies or screens the colors, depending on the blend color. The effect is similar to shining a harsh spotlight on the image.*

20

FIGURE 20.23

Vivid Light—*Burns or dodges the colors by increasing or decreasing the contrast, depending on the blend color. If the blend color (light source) is lighter than 50% gray, you can lighten the image by decreasing the contrast. If the blend color is darker than 50% gray, you can darken the image by increasing the contrast.*

FIGURE 20.24

Linear Light—*Burns or dodges the colors by decreasing or increasing the brightness, depending on the blend color. If the blend color (light source) is lighter than 50% gray, you can lighten the image by increasing the brightness. If the blend color is darker than 50% gray, you can darken the image by decreasing the brightness.*

FIGURE 20.25

Pin Light—*Replaces the colors, depending on the blend color. If the blend color (light source) is lighter than 50% gray, pixels darker than the blend color are replaced and pixels lighter than the blend color do not change. If the blend color is darker than 50% gray, pixels lighter than the blend color are replaced and pixels darker than the blend color do not change. This is useful for adding special effects to an image.*

FIGURE 20.26

Difference— *Compares brightness values in the base and blend colors, and subtracts the lighter. Overlaps are interesting in this mode. They cancel the previous action.*

FIGURE 20.27

Exclusion—*This is similar to the Difference mode, but has a softer effect.*

20

FIGURE 20.28

Hue—*Gives you a result combining the luminance and saturation of the base color and the hue of the blend color.*

FIGURE 20.29

Saturation—*Gives you a color with the luminance and hue of the base color and the saturation of the blend color. Unless you reduce the saturation of the blend color significantly, nothing shows.*

FIGURE 20.30

Color—*Combines the luminance of the base color with the hue and saturation of the blend color. This option is useful for coloring monochrome images because the Color mode retains the gray levels.*

FIGURE 20.31

Luminosity—*Gives a result color with the hue and saturation of the base color and the luminance of the blend color. This mode and the Color Blend mode produce opposite effects.*

It's hard to understand why the designers of Elements bothered with some of these. Others are obviously, and immediately, useful. Spend some time playing with the effects of darken, lighten, and dissolve. These seem to be the ones I use the most.

Applying Effects

Effects are a time-saver. There's really nothing included in the Elements effects package that you couldn't do yourself from scratch, but why bother, when applying an effect is so simple? In all, there are 51 effects on the palette. Figure 20.32 shows some of them.

FIGURE 20.32

A piece of the Effects palette.

In the palette, you can view each effect's result, as it is applied to the sample image marked "Original." To apply an effect, double-click it, or click the thumbnail and then click Apply.

As you browse through the effects list, you'll notice that some of the effects are labeled "(Text)." These effects can be applied to text on a text layer, but not to text created using a text mask. Some effects are labeled "(Selection)," and can only be applied to a selected area. Some are labeled "(Layer)," and can only be applied to an entire layer. Finally, some effects can only be applied to a flattened image. When you choose them, you'll be asked whether you want to flatten your image. Click OK to proceed.

20

To limit the display of effects in the palette, select a category from the drop-down list. Here's a description of the various categories:

- Frames—Adds a frame around the edge of the current layer or a selection (if the effect is marked with the "(Selection)" label).

- Textures —A collection of various textures. The effect is applied to a new layer above the current layer, but it can be partially masked by a selection first.

- Text Effects —Effects suitable only for use on a text layer.

- Image Effects —Effects applied to a copy of the current layer. If you combine several image effects, you may be prompted to flatten the image before proceeding.

Some effects create extra layers; some don't. Adding the Rusted Metal effect to an image makes it look as if it's covered in reddish-orange rust. Actually, Rusted Metal and some of the other image effects simply add a layer filled with color and pattern. If you really want to see your image through the rust, you must go to the Layers menu and change the layer opacity so the image under the effects layer shows through. This is also a really good time to play with layer blending modes. In Figure 20.33, I've applied rust to a picture of rocks on the beach, changed the opacity so we could actually see the rocks, and chosen Overlay as a blending mode. The results are a lot more interesting than either the original or the effect as it was first applied.

FIGURE 20.33
Effects don't turn into art until you work with them.

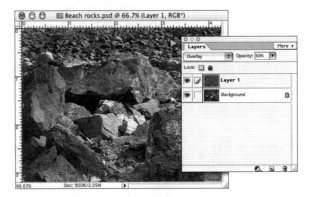

The biggest drawback to using effects is that, with the exception of layer opacity and blend modes, there is no way to customize them. The wood grain in the frame always runs in the same direction and is always the same sort of light oak. The Glass effect is only available in one color combination, and you can't even preview it. However, because a lot of the effects are simply filters or combinations of filters, you may be able to achieve a similar effect with customized results by applying the filters manually. As an effect is applied, you can see the various steps involved, including the names of any filters. So just as you wouldn't buy a "one size fits all" bathing suit, don't feel that you have to be stuck with an all-purpose effect.

Making an Effect from Scratch

Let's see how we can recreate the Rusted Metal effect. First, I'll open the same photo that I used the effect on and add a new fill layer, making it a solid color and choosing a nice reddish brown from the Color Picker. Figure 20.34 shows this step.

FIGURE 20.34

The picture is hidden by the color fill layer.

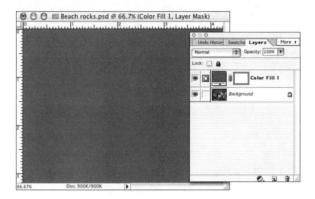

To achieve that flaky rust look, let's try some noise. After opening the Noise filter (Filter, Noise, Add Noise), I can experiment while looking at a preview. It looks to me as if 18% Gaussian noise is about right. It will inevitably be monochromatic because it's applied to a monochromatic source.

Now, I can have some fun with the blending modes. Overlay at 70% provides a nice, brownish cast. Color Dodge at 50% is a very different look, with deep browns and even some greens. Saturation at 75% takes us to another planet. Figure 20.35 shows samples of all of these. The Overlay mode seems to give the closest approximation of the Rusted Metal effect, without darkening the image too much. Be sure to look at this image in the color section.

20

FIGURE 20.35
From left to right, Overlay, Color Dodge, and Saturation.

Task: Painting with Hot Metal

Now that you know how to use the built-in features of Elements, let's try a bit of painting. I've already set up a default Elements image, 5×7 inches with a white background.

1. First, we need a background. Open the Layer Styles palette and browse through the Patterns and Complex categories. They both cover the layer with a pattern, so styles in either category will work here. Click the one you like. Because Elements won't allow you to put a style on a background layer, you'll have to approve changing the background to Layer 0. (Elements automatically suggests an alternative whenever you try to do something unacceptable.)

2. Now you can place the pattern on the background. I chose the Complex style, Purple and Magenta (see Figure 20.36). Just click on it and the screen automatically fills with purple marble.

3. Okay, let's go for the gold. Add a new layer, and choose a comfortably sized brush. Because you're going to be painting with a hard-edged medium (metal), you need to use a hard-edged brush.

4. Paint whatever you like. I'm partial to cats. When the painting is at least partially done, apply the Complex, Molten Gold layer style. The paint will turn to gold. (I sure wish that worked on my bank account.) Use the Brush and eraser as needed to refine the picture.

FIGURE 20.36

My rendition of a favorite feline.

5. The cat seems a little flat. Fortunately, you can access Style Settings (by double-clicking the cursive *f* on the Layers palette or choosing Layer, Layer Style, Style Settings) and make some changes. These will also affect the pattern of light and shadow on the gold. I raised the Bevel Size to 117 and the Shadow Distance to 17. Then I cropped the picture, changed to Layer 0, opened the Style Settings dialog box, and raised the Bevel Size of the purple background to 24. Figure 20.37 shows the result.

FIGURE 20.37

No cats were harmed in the making of this picture.

20

In Figure 20.38, I've assembled a strange collection of stuff, starting with an all-over blanket pattern (the stripes in the background). Then I used a paintbrush on a new layer, and styled my strokes with Paint Brush Strokes, from the Complex collection. I added another layer, and a few strokes with Satin Sheets. Then I drew and filled a bunch of shapes, putting each one on a different layer with a different effect applied.

FIGURE 20.38
Something psyche-delic....

At this point, I have about 20 layers, so I need to stop and flatten them before the file gets too large and too difficult to print. Each new layer adds to the file size, and all of these unrelated objects add to the visual confusion. If you've just started plopping things on a page, without having a real idea of where the picture's going, or what it's about, this is also a good time to weed out elements that don't make sense in the context of the rest of the image.

When you use the layer styles, you have about as much flexibility as you need for most purposes. But sometimes, you'll just want to go a few steps further than Elements wants to take you. Suppose you want an outer glow in chartreuse, or a gray drop shadow instead of black? There's no good reason that you can't recreate any of these effects yourself. Once you see how easy it is to do so, you'll probably make your own more often than not.

Creating Drop Shadows from Scratch

According to my friend Scott Kelby, editor of *Photoshop User Magazine*, type *always* needs a drop shadow applied. Personally, I always try to steer clear of words such as *always* and *never*, but you can certainly improve most type with a little shadow. Here's a quick way to apply a shadow without using a Drop Shadow layer style. (You might not be able to use a layer style in some cases, but this method always works.)

First, set your type. Make a copy on a new layer. (Layer, Duplicate Layer) Slide the duplicate under the original until it's in a good position for a shadow. Reduce the layer opacity to about 20% or whatever looks right to you. Add some blur (Filter, Blur, Gaussian Blur) and you have a drop shadow (see Figure 20.39).

Adding shadows to type is easy. How about adding shadows to objects? That's really not much more difficult. In Figure 20.40, I have selected an object and set my foreground color to gray so I can create a light shadow.

FIGURE 20.39

A simple but effective drop shadow.

Just a shadow, in an alley...

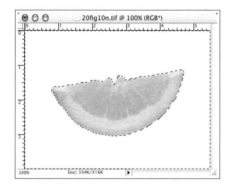

FIGURE 20.40

Select your object first.

I duplicate the layer, then select the background using the Magic Wand and invert the selection so the lemon slice is highlighted. Then I feather the selection by 10 pixels. The next part is a tiny bit tricky. Select the Paint Bucket tool, and make sure your preferred shadow color is the foreground color. Position the tool just outside the edge of the lemon and click once. Figure 20.41 shows the resulting shadow. For a larger one, set the feather distance to a larger number. Although you can add a shadow to an object using one of the Drop Shadow layer styles, you can't get the light directly above an object with the shadows on all sides, as shown here, and you can't change the shadow color. Learning how to create these effects yourself will come in handy some day, believe me.

20

FIGURE 20.41

This time I left the shadow centered on the lemon.

Glows are basically colored shadows, and they usually extend on all sides of an object like the shadow shown in Figure 20.41. To create a glow from scratch, follow the steps you'd use to make a shadow, but choose a light or bright glow color.

Making Reflections

Let's stop and reflect for a moment. Adding a reflection to an object can make it seem more three-dimensional, because, like a shadow, a reflection interacts with the space around the object.

Figure 20.42 shows a very basic reflection. All I did was duplicate the type on another layer and flip it 180 degrees. This makes it look as though the word is sitting on a floor that has a reflective surface. I blurred the reflection a little because my floors are never really clean.

FIGURE 20.42
This kind of reflection is used for water, shiny floors and tabletops, and sheets of ice.

Reflections can face forward or backward, depending on the position of the reflective surface. Sometimes they can do both. The simplest reflections are created by flipping a layer 90 or 180 degrees. More complicated reflections, such as the ones shown in Figures 20.43 and 20.44, are a matter of applying transform, skew, and perspective until you get what you need. See Hour 10, "Straightening, Skewing, and Distorting an Image," for help in making these transformations.

FIGURE 20.43
One reflection in each direction.

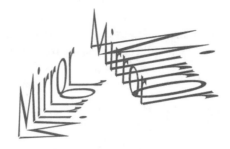

FIGURE 20.44

*And one in both direc-
tions at once.*

FIGURE 20.44

*And one in both direc-
tions at once.*

Using Distortions to Blend Composite Images

Distortions are mainly used when you need to wrap something around something else. You can stretch type around a can of soup or show how a design will look on a mug. This kind of composite is more practical than artistic. If you're wrapping type, you may be able to use the Warp Text button. Otherwise, if you're trying to wrap an image or shape around an object, Distort (or possibly Skew) is what you need. Hour 6 can help you with the basics of warping text, while Hour 10 is the one to check for help with Distort and Skew. Let's try warping some type around a can.

In Figure 20.45, I've drawn a can and set some type to go on it.

FIGURE 20.45

A basic can of beans.

After looking at the available Type Warp styles on the Horizontal Type tool's Options menu shown in Figure 20.46, I realize that I need to choose Arch, rather than Arc, so all three lines will be set on the same curve. (Arc sets them in a fan shape with the bottom line smallest and everything fanning outward.)

When I slide the words into place, the default bend amount is obviously too much. The can has less than a 50% bend. By gradually reducing the bend of the text using the Bend slider in the Warp Text dialog box, and comparing the angle of the top word with the angle of the top of the can, I can get a fairly accurate curve for the letters. Figure 20.47 shows the curved letters.

20

FIGURE 20.46

There are lots of warp choices.

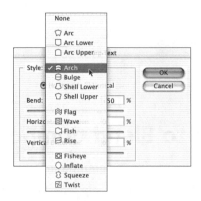

FIGURE 20.47

Align the letters with the top of the can.

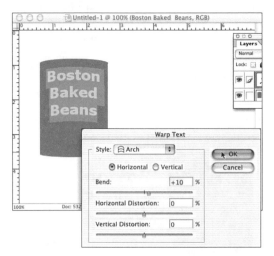

Now, all we need to finish up the job is a little glow around the letters to emphasize them, the company logo (also with a glow), and a gradient on the can to add some more roundness. (You'll learn to work with gradients in Hour 22.) In Figure 20.48, we've put it all together.

FIGURE 20.48

The finished can. It looks good enough to eat.

Putting type on a box is also easy to do by eye. Draw the box. Set the type in two pieces so you can maneuver each piece separately. Align the first piece of type to the lower-left edge of the box using the Skew command. Move it around until it looks correct. Then do the same for the rest of the type. My effort appears in Figure 20.49.

FIGURE 20.49

Remember that the type needs to remain vertical and should be skewed in one direction only.

Next, I'll try a can with an image on it. I could use Distort to twist the image to fit, but because my shape is a can (essentially a cylinder), I can use the 3-D Transform filter (Filters, Render, 3D Transform). The result appears in Figure 20.50.

FIGURE 20.50

Add an image to a can if you can.

Putting Together Stitched Panoramas

20

People have been sticking photos together to create panoramic images for close to a hundred years, with varying degrees of success. The scissors and glue method rarely succeeds. Shooting a panorama all in one photo with a wide-angle lens seems to work, until you notice that the ends of the Grand Canyon are very fuzzy, or the two outermost bridesmaids in the wedding lineup appear fifty pounds heavier than they actually are. Distortion is the main problem. Wide-angle lenses aren't good choices in situations where you want to avoid distortion. The more curve you apply to the front of the lens, the more glass the image has to pass through. Glass adds distortion. The more logical way to shoot a panorama that stays in focus from one end to the other is to take a series of pictures and splice them together. Prior to computers, that was exceptionally difficult, though it certainly was done. Now, thanks to clever software, it's easier than ever to get good results with panoramic photography.

Working with Photomerge

Photomerge is a plug-in that automates the process of assembling a panorama. After you've gone out and taken the photos, you plug your camera or memory stick into the computer and download the pictures. Then you open Elements and Photomerge (File, Photomerge), and tell it where to find the pictures you want to use. The dialog box is shown in Figure 20.51. Click Browse and navigate to the folder in which your separate images are contained, select the pictures you want to use, and then click OK.

FIGURE 20.51

It's easiest if you download your pictures to a single folder. That way you don't have to go hunting for them.

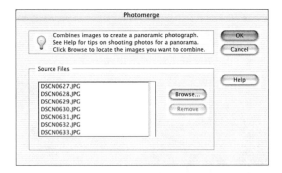

When you click OK, the magic begins. First, Elements opens all the photos you specified, and opens a new image file. Then it arranges them in order, matching the edges where images overlap. It opens a window similar to the one shown in Figure 20.52, so you can watch its progress.

The pictures appear to come in at 50% opacity, so the computer can easily line up areas of major contrast. In this series of pictures, tree trunks seem to be the major point of reference for matching. Pictures that Photomerge can't match are left at the top of the strip, so you can drag them from the box at the top of the window into the work area at the bottom of the window and match them later. When all the pictures have been merged in (see Figure 20.53), Photomerge continues the process by adjusting the brightness and contrast of each pair of pictures so you have a consistent exposure from one end to the other. If the sun has gone behind a cloud and emerged again, as it did for me, you'll have to do some extra tweaking. Apparently, it can only cope with *logical* changes.

FIGURE 20.52
A panorama in progress.

FIGURE 20.53
Processing the exposures.

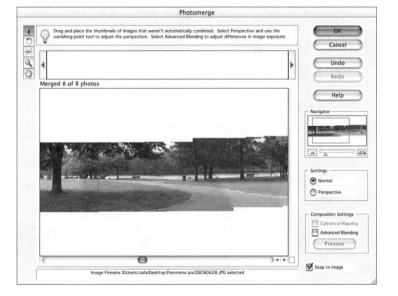

20

You can do some tweaking using the tools in the Photomerge dialog box. Drag a corner of any image in the work area with the Rotate Image tool to rotate it. Move the panorama within the work area by scrolling or by dragging it with the Move View tool. Zoom in with the Zoom tool.

By clicking Perspective in the Settings pane, you can make some other adjustments. To establish which image contains the vanishing point (which image contains the highest point on the horizon, and therefore should be treated as the "middle" image), click that image with the Vanishing Point tool. It will be highlighted with a blue border. The other images will be adjusted in relation to this new vanishing point. If needed, make your own adjustments as well by clicking the Select Image tool and scooting the non-vanishing point images up or down.

There are other options you can choose as well. The Cylindrical Mapping option transforms the panorama as if it were on a cylinder, reducing the bow-tie effect shown in Figure 20.53. This brings the viewer closer and into the panorama a bit, but you'll gain a lot of extra image space for cropping, so it's worth a look to see which view you prefer.

If your panorama has some inconsistencies with brightness and contrast, try the Advanced Blending option. It blends together areas of color, while retaining detail. The effect is a softening of these differences, making the panorama seem more like a whole image rather than a collection of images.

After choosing Cylindrical Mapping, Advanced Blending, or both, click Preview to view the results. Click Exit Preview to return to Normal view. When you're through making adjustments in the Photomerge window, click OK.

The finished product is an untitled file (Figure 20.54) with all the pictures assembled and matched as well as possible. Unfortunately, when you get it, the image has already been flattened, making it difficult to adjust the exposure of one frame that's a little "off."

FIGURE 20.54

The edges suggest that this is more than one photo.

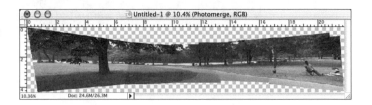

It's still up to you to crop the picture, if you want to. Some photographers argue that the slanting edges and unevenness of the "raw" panorama somehow add to the experience. Others, myself included, prefer to crop. A lot depends on whether, and how, you intend to print the picture. The eight images I assembled for this test of Photomerge produced a strip 4 inches high by 36 inches long. At 300 dpi resolution, that's a 37MB file. I can print it myself if I want to do so; one of my inkjet printers takes banner paper. But I'd prefer to go to a service bureau and come home with a strip 8 inches high by 6 feet long on a nice shiny, heavy poster paper.

Considerations When You Shoot a Panorama

Obviously, the main thing to consider when you shoot pictures for a panorama is that you should hold the camera steady at one height. Don't take it away from your eye while you're shooting. If you get interrupted mid-sequence, start again. Better yet, if possible, use a tripod to keep the camera steady. Remember, digital photos don't waste film. Stay away from the focus and zoom buttons. Autofocus the first picture and let that one dictate the focus for the rest.

Practice the "panorama shuffle." Start shooting with your body aimed at one end of the scene. Take small steps circling to your right as you shoot your pictures from left to right.

Don't use a flash. Particularly, don't use auto-flash, as it will throw varying amounts of light as it sees a need. These make the exposure all but impossible to correct.

Use a normal lens for best results. Set your zoom lens about halfway between zoom and telephoto, and leave it there. Don't use a wide-angle or fish-eye lens. Such lenses defeat the purpose of the panorama, which is to have everything in the same focus and not distorted. Nothing distorts more than a fish eye.

Make sure you have enough overlap between pictures, but not too much. Somewhere around 20% is good. As you pan across the scene, remember what was on the right side of each picture you take, and just cover it again on the left of the next shot.

Take a picture of something clearly different between shooting panorama sequences. That way you won't try to assemble pictures that don't go together. Keep each set of pictures in a separate file as you download from the camera.

Have fun creating your panorama!

Summary

This hour has been about making composite images. Composites are pictures from two or more sources, either two different images or an image plus type. The trick to creating a successful composite is making the images relate to each other. This can be done with reflections, cast shadows or glows, and other tricks that you can apply. You learned how to use layer styles to add a quick glow or drop shadow, and how to use them as part of

20

the image, taking a background pattern or a frame to add to your own picture. You learned about bevels and how to paint with three-dimensional substances such as gold and toothpaste.

You also learned how to create adjustment layers and layer masks to control how particular adjustments affect your image. You learned that blending modes can apply to layers as well as to the brush tools, and some give unexpected results. You learned about the Effects palette, and how to work with it. There are type effects, frame effects, and image effects. Many of these are easy to create from scratch, and doing so gives you much more flexibility. You learned about mirror images, and about distortions. Finally, you learned how to use Photomerge to create panoramic pictures.

Q&A

Q What's the difference between skewing and distorting?

A When you skew, you can tilt an image or section of text in any direction. Press and hold Cmd/Ctrl+Shift as you drag any middle handle on the side of the bounding box to skew. When you distort, you can stretch an object from its corner in any direction. To distort, press and hold Cmd/Ctrl and drag a corner point.

Q Is there a limit to the number of photos I can merge?

A There's a *practical* limit. As you add more pictures, the height to width ratio becomes unmanageable. Start with no more than five.

Q How many layers can I put in a collage?

A As many as you need. Flatten them when you are finished so they won't add to the file size.

Q Does type always need a drop shadow? If so, why aren't drop shadows automatic?

A Type doesn't *always* need a shadow.

Q I'm used to thinking in film terms, where a dissolve is a very smooth transition from one scene to the next. Why are the Elements dissolves so spotty?

A I don't know, and it annoys me too. Maybe if we think of the pixels as being suspended rather than dissolved, it will be easier to understand.

Workshop

Let's see if you can merge the questions and answers, and combine what you know about composites.

Quiz

1. Global light casts no shadows.

    a. True

    b. False

2. Layer styles are _____ effects.

    a. The same as

    b. Different from

3. If blending modes control the way the layers interact with each other, what do they do for brush tools?

    a. Control the interaction of the brush with the background

    b. Control the interaction of overlapping brush strokes

    c. Neither

    d. Both

4. If you change the opacity of the top layer, it will also change the opacity of one underneath.

    a. True

    b. False

Quiz Answers

1. b. It means there's only one light source and all shadows relate to that source, no matter what layer they're on.

2. b. Styles can be adjusted.

3. d. Each stroke will react with whatever's under it.

4. b. Changing opacity only relates to the current layer.

Activities

1. Try out Photomerge. Go out and shoot a four-picture panorama, and see how well Photomerge can handle it.

2. Take any photo, and add an effect over it. Try Gold Sprinkles or Oil Pastels. Reduce the layer opacity to 50% and try out all the blending modes. Take special note of those that do good things to the picture.

20

HOUR **21**

Going Wild with Your Images

Now it's time to emulate Emeril and "Kick it up a notch!" You've seen the good things Elements can do in cleaning up damaged photos and saving the ones that weren't so great. You've learned how to recompose a picture and how to add contrast and brighten up a dull day while keeping things realistic.

Well, a little reality goes a long way. Let's see what happens when we set aside realism. We can reduce the number of colors in the picture to just a handful. We can turn the picture into a puddle of wet paint and play with it until it's beyond recognition. We can turn people green or skies yellow. We can render a scene in brushed copper or polished silver. With a third-party plug-in called Eye Candy, we can also set fire to things or cover them with raindrops, fog, or fur.

In this hour, you will

- Switch colors to their opposites on the color wheel
- Convert to a high-contrast black-and-white image

- Replace colors in an image
- Create metallic text
- Add a neon glow, cover an image in plastic, or add a soft glow
- Put your image underwater
- Solarize an image

Posterizing Colors

Posterizing, in effect, means reducing the number of colors available in the image. You'll find the Posterize command on the Image, Adjustments menu. Instead of pixel-by-pixel full color, you see large flat areas in a photo, making it look rather like a silk screen print. When you posterize an image, the dialog box shown in Figure 21.1 lets you specify the number of tonal levels (or brightness values) for the three channels (red, green, and blue) in the image and then maps pixels to the closest matching level. For example, choosing two tonal levels in an RGB image gives a total of six colors: two shades of red, two of green, and two of blue.

FIGURE 21.1

Start with a small number of levels.

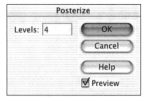

Figure 21.2 shows before and after views of an amusement park that has been posterized. Be sure to see both versions in the color plate section, too.

Note that posterizing can also be applied to an adjustment layer, making it a no-risk method for changing a picture. If you don't like what posterizing does, simply delete the adjustment layer.

Posterization can be applied to both color and grayscale images, of course. Applying it directly to color gives a more random, but usually a more interesting choice. As you play with the posterizing effect, you'll notice that lower numbers of tonal levels are apt to give you more satisfactory results. With too many levels of posterization, you can't really tell that much has changed.

FIGURE 21.2

This posterization was done with four levels.

If you want a specific number of colors in your image, convert the image to grayscale and specify the number of levels you want in the Posterize dialog box. Then convert the image back to RGB mode, and replace the various gray tones with the colors you like.

Remember also that you're not stuck with what you get using the Posterize command. First of all, you can select an area of an image to posterize, rather than the whole thing. You can posterize a single layer, or add a posterized adjustment layer to affect just the layers below it. After posterizing, you can change colors selectively, repaint the sky if it got lost in translation, use the Sponge tool to intensify small areas of color, and add a textured surface to the image. You've already mastered a whole arsenal of Elements tools. Think about what they can do in combination. For example, I love what Posterize has done to my amusement park photo, but the ground seems a little boring now. I could make it more interesting by selecting the ground and applying a Texture filter such as Grain or Mosaic Tile, or a Textures effect such as Psychedelic Strings, Asphalt, or Rusted Metal.

21

Adjusting the Threshold

As you learned last hour, the Threshold command is one of the ones you can use with an adjustment layer. You can also use the command on an entire image if you want. It converts the image into a black-and-white photo with very high contrast. You set the threshold, which determines which pixels are white and which ones are black.

To convert an entire image, choose Image, Adjustments, Threshold. There's only one control in the dialog box that appears; set the Threshold value as desired. Pixels with a lower tonal value than the threshold are changed to white; pixels with a higher tonal value are changed to black. Figure 21.3 shows an image converted to black and white using the Threshold command.

FIGURE 21.3
Use Threshold to convert an image to high-contrast black and white.

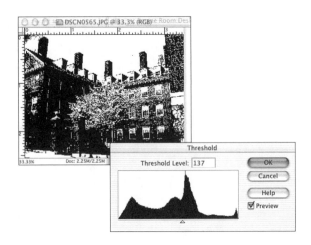

Liquifying an Image

The Liquify filter (Filter, Distort, Liquify) is also fun to play with, though not especially practical. As you learned in Hour 10, "Straightening, Skewing, and Distorting an Image," it distorts images, not geometrically as the Distort command does, but as if they've softened and run together. Salvador Dali would have loved it. By now, you know that you can use the Smudge tool to drag some pixels around, approximating a finger painting. This is different. Liquify gives you tools to warp, twirl, pucker, bloat, shift, and reflect, and a Reconstruct tool for those times when you get carried away. You can apply masks to control what gets liquified. As with other filters, you can apply Liquify to a selection, or the entire layer. Even if you start off without a selection and make the entire layer available to Liquify, you can freeze parts of the image you like by simply not using the Liquify tools on them, and continue to liquify the rest. Liquify is a promising tool for creative photo editing.

I have the most fun with this filter when I start with something really abstract, such as a patterned background. Other people enjoy using it on faces, pets, and so on. In Hour 10, I used the tool on a brushed line and some common objects including a pocket watch and gumdrops. Let's get wild and see what happens when you use the Liquify filter on a human subject.

There are two tools I use most often regardless of whether my subject is living or inanimate: Warp (the hand with extended index finger) and Turbulence (waves). I used Warp to push out the tuba player's cheeks, and to stretch his horn. Figure 21.4 shows the tuba player really blasting one out. His horn is melting!

FIGURE 21.4
Warping in short strokes gives you the most control.

I can use Turbulence to create wind in the picture, so strong that it almost blows his clothes off(see Figure 21.5). To add to the wind effect, I could have pushed his hair out gently with the Warp tool, or twirled it with the Twirl Clockwise tool.

FIGURE 21.5
It's windy out there!

21

In Figure 21.6, I've used Liquify with a picture of two fish. Use Bloat with a very large brush for a fish-eye lens effect, or with a small brush for a fish-eye lens on a fish. You can also use Bloat and a medium brush to make the fish look fatter, while Pucker can make them look thinner.

FIGURE 21.6

There's something very fishy about the fishes' eyes.

Even if a person or other living creature is the subject, you can always use Liquify to create an interesting background. As for using Liquify to create an abstract, nothing could be easier. Start with some color on the page—a photo, or an effects pattern, or even just a good dose of noise—and then use the tools to distort it as I've done in Figure 21.7.

FIGURE 21.7

All you need is something to move. Colored noise is the basis for this image.

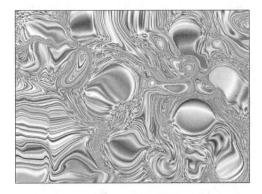

Replacing Colors with Gradient Map and Invert

We looked at a couple of ways of replacing color back in Hour 12, "Too Light/Too Dark: Adjusting Brightness, Contrast, and Color." You learned then about the Replace Color dialog box, and how to shift one color to another. There are some other ways to do it, which you'll find if you go poking around the Image, Adjustments menu.

Using Gradient Map

One of the commands you can use to replace colors in an image is Gradient Map. A gradient, you may recall, is a gradual transition from one color to another—for example, from red to yellow—and all the gradations in between. Some of the preset gradients that come with Elements involve a gradual blending between more than two colors. The Gradient Map command temporarily converts the image to grayscale and maps the grayscale steps in the image to the steps in a gradient you have selected. If you select a red-yellow gradient, shadows will be mapped to the starting color (red), and the highlights will be mapped to the ending color (yellow). Midtones in the image will be mapped to the gradient colors in between.

The Gradient Map command (Image, Adjustments, Gradient Map) is capable of some really awesome effects. In Figure 21.8 (which is reproduced in the color plate section), I have applied a red, yellow, and blue gradient from the presets that come with Elements. To choose a gradient, click the down arrow to display a palette of gradients. Choose one of these by clicking it. To display the gradients in a different category, click the right arrow and select a category from the menu that appears. After selecting a different category, click the gradient you want to use from the new palette of choices. Once you click a gradient, its colors are immediately mapped to the tones in your image so you can see the result.

If you choose the Dither option, you may be able to get rid of any color banding that appears in the image by adding some random noise to the gradient fill. Clicking the Reverse option can bring on some surprising, and often wonderful results, as it turns the gradient around so the darkest shades in the image are mapped to the color at the opposite end. Depending on the colors or shades in the gradient, this might give you a negative look or just an unexpected color shift. It's always worth trying.

21

Figure 21.8

A more colorful tiger.

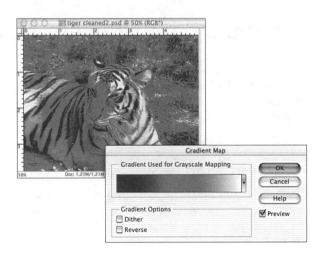

Creating Your Own Gradient

If none of the preset gradients exactly meets your needs, you can create your own.
Display a gradient that's close to what you want, then click it to open the Gradient Editor
dialog box, shown in Figure 21.9.

Figure 21.9

Create your own gradient or modify an existing one.

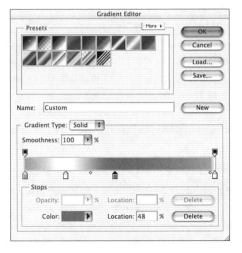

Click the color stop on the left and select the color you want to start with. You can use
the foreground or background color by selecting the appropriate option from the menu
that appears, pick up a color from the gradient bar or the image itself using the
Eyedropper pointer, or click the swatch to select a color from the Color Picker. Define

the ending color the same way, using the color stop on the right. You can drag any color stop along the gradient bar to adjust its value. For example, you can drag the midpoint color stop to define the point where the start and end colors are evenly mixed. Add more color stops to the gradient if desired by clicking below the gradient bar at any point. Select a color and adjust its midpoint as desired.

You can refine the gradient a bit by adjusting its Smoothness value, which tells Elements how smooth to make the transitions from one color to the next. To adjust the opacity of the left and right stop colors, simply click the appropriate Opacity stop (shown above the gradient bar), and enter an Opacity percentage. When you're through making all your adjustments, type a name in the Name box, and click New to save it.

Using Invert

Invert is another color change command in the Adjustments submenu, and although you have essentially no control over it, the results are often worth keeping. It replaces each color in the image with its color wheel opposite. Skin tones turn odd colors such as bluish-green or bluish-gray, though, and some other color pairs don't swap well. Figure 21.10 (check it in the color plate section) shows what happens when I invert a yellow flower. It turns deep cobalt blue against pale violet (formerly green) leaves.

FIGURE 21.10
This could be interesting if combined with some other effect.

Now, if you take the inverted flower and posterize it, or try some of the effects or filters, you might end up with a very interesting piece of art.

Adding Metallic Effects

I think I must have been King Midas in an earlier life. I just love turning things to gold. There are, of course, a lot of ways to do this. The molten gold effect, actually a layer style, has to be applied to the whole layer. Suppose I want instead to pour it over some type or create a golden daisy? It's not very difficult. First, let's gild some type.

21

Task: Creating Gold Type from Scratch

1. Open a new page and set some appropriate type. In this case, *appropriate* means fairly heavy. If you're going for gold, go for lots of it.

2. Set the foreground color to yellow and the background color to light brown.

3. Select the type. Select the Gradient tool and choose the first default gradient, which is Foreground to Background. (See Figure 21.11.) Unlike the Gradient Map, which switches colors in an image, the Gradient tool applies a gradient fill to the current selection or active layer.

FIGURE 21.11

Choose the Foreground to Background gradient.

4. Use the Gradient tool to draw a vertical line over the type, from the top down. You should have nice light-to-dark gold letters, as in Figure 21.12.

FIGURE 21.12

Golden words.

The Midas Touch

5. But I want a bit of texture on my letters. Go to Filter, Texture, Craquelure, and apply it with the settings shown in Figure 21.13.

FIGURE 21.13

Even better....

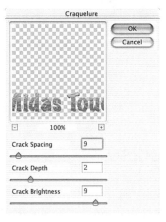

6. Go to the Layer Styles palette to add some depth. I like the look of the Simple Sharp Inner Bevel, so I'll use that, plus a small drop shadow. Figure 21.14 shows the final piece of molten gold lettering.

FIGURE 21.14
I probably shouldn't have patted the duck.

There are, of course, other metals in our arsenal. Brass is very similar to gold, except that the darker brown has a touch of green in it, and the yellow should be lighter and brighter for gradient blending purposes. Adding a small amount of Gaussian noise with the Add Noise filter gives the brass a nice texture, and of course, we'll do the bevel and drop shadow thing, giving us the result in Figure 21.15.

FIGURE 21.15
Brass is duller than gold. Hence the noise.

Copper, shown in Figure 21.16, is also similar, except that the colors tend more toward red/pink. Set the gradient with a dark pinkish brown and a dark reddish brown. Copper tends to be shiny, so no noise is needed. Be sure to see the metallic lettering examples in the color plate section.

FIGURE 21.16
Copper should shine.

Using Weird Effects

Elements has many useful filters and effects. It also has a few that I haven't yet found a use for, and some others that are strange but interesting. Let's take a look at some of the stranger ones.

Neon Glow

The Neon Glow filter (Filter, Artistic, Neon Glow) is guaranteed to turn your landscapes into post-Apocalypse and your in-laws into space aliens. As you probably remember

21

from Hour 18, "Using the Artistic Filters," this filter does not look like neon tubing, but more like a soft glow. The dialog box, shown in Figure 21.17, gives you options to choose a glow color, size, and brightness. When you choose a color such as lime green, hot pink, or purple, the picture can get very strange indeed.

FIGURE 21.17
Why is this building glowing?

Plastic Wrap

Another unusual filter, Plastic Wrap (Filter, Artistic, Plastic Wrap), pours a layer of plastic over your picture. The effect on the building photo in Figure 21.18 is to turn it into something resembling bas-relief. The plastic wrap is actually quite thick, and forms puddles as it goes down, but accents definite edges such as the roof line.

If I wanted to do this picture properly, I'd undo the filter and clear out any obvious texture in the sky before trying again to apply the filter, in an effort to eliminate the gray oatmeal look it has gotten from the filter texture.

The interface, shown in Figure 21.19, is fairly simple. Smoothness determines the degree of shine on the plastic, and Detail determines how closely the plastic follows the contours of the image. Highlight Strength controls the intensity of the light shining down on the plastic, and therefore, the lightness of the highlights.

FIGURE 21.18

Wrapped in plastic, or drowning in it?

FIGURE 21.19

The Plastic Wrap filter dialog box.

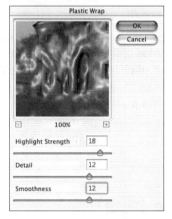

Diffuse Glow

This filter (Filters, Distort, Diffuse Glow) uses the background color and dumps what looks like powder onto the highlights of the image. If it's a light color, it'll look like powdered sugar. If it's dark, it will come closer to mildew. In Figure 21.20, I tried for snow, but got baby powder instead. It's still interesting, just not what I wanted. You'll find as you work with this program that this happens a lot. What you get is not what you wanted, but it's kind of cool anyway.

21

Figure 21.20
A powdered daisy.

Use the Graininess slider to adjust the smoothness of the "powder," from a smooth hazy glow to a noisy rough surface. Use the Glow Amount to control the range of tones that are considered highlights, and thus are replaced with the background color. Higher values widen the range. Control how much the non-highlighted areas are covered with the background colored powder. Higher values narrow the range.

Ocean Ripple

As a longtime sailor, I'd be very afraid if I saw the ocean start to behave like this filter (Filters, Distort, Ocean Ripple). It makes a definite rippling, even bubbly, effect. But it's a lot more like an eggbeater in a bowl of club soda than anything the ocean does unless there's an underwater earthquake. That said, it can be gorgeous on the right subject. In Figure 21.21, I'm trying it on a duck, and it's much like viewing the duck through a sheet of pebbled glass. Because the effect is irregular, unlike the glass filters in Elements, it manages to keep a sparkly quality that the glass filters lose. This filter, in my mind, fits into the "weird but useful" category.

Figure 21.21
A bubbling duck.

You have two settings with this filter. The Ripple Size value controls the number of ripples—with the highest value, you'll get fewer ripples, but of larger size. Ripple Magnitude controls the height (amplitude) of the ripples. The higher the value, the taller the ripples become.

Wave

The Wave filter (Filters, Distort, Wave) is really strange. First of all, you need to be an engineer to understand the interface, shown in Figure 21.22. Its purpose is to create an undulating wave pattern on a layer, making it appear as if the image is underwater. The Sine option gives you the most even undulation, with smooth upside-down U-shaped waves. The Square options create vertical or horizontal rectangular waves of color, like sharp-edged tubes into which the picture has been poured, and the Triangle option creates M-shaped waves with sharp corners.

FIGURE 21.22

A thoroughly confus-ing dialog box.

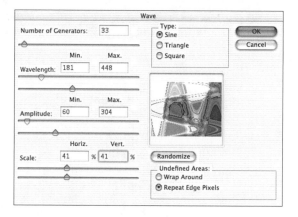

To set the number of waves, use the Number of Generators slider. You can have as many as 999, but lower numbers are less destructive to the image. The minimum and maximum Wavelength values determine their length. Keep the numbers the same or close to each other for symmetry. The Amplitude sliders dictate the wave height. The horizontal and vertical Scale sliders adjust the distortion. If you click Randomize, you will see various wave patterns generated with the same settings.

The Wrap Around option wraps pixels pushed off the canvas by the waves onto the opposite side of the layer/selection. The Repeat Edge Pixels option cuts off the pixels pushed off by the waves, and fills the holes with a color close to the pixels on the edge.

Figure 21.23 shows my original picture and what I ended up with. The next step might be to open Liquify and take it completely abstract. Or I might try ocean ripple or one of the glass distortions.

21

FIGURE 21.23
Before and after making waves.

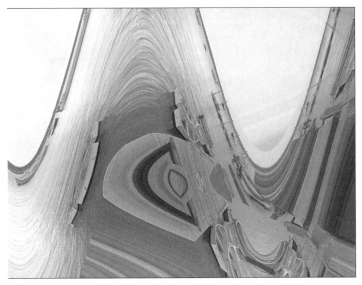

Solarize

The Solarize filter (Filters, Stylize, Solarize) uses a darkroom trick, imported from the film world to the digital world. Solarizing a photo means exposing it to light in the middle of the developing process. The results are usually unpredictable, and often worthless, as the entire picture turns black. But if it's done at the right second, with the right amount of light, you'll partially invert the colors in the picture, with interesting results. With Solarize, the values in the image are changed: the highlights become shadows, and light midtones become dark midtones. The values of shadows and dark midtones are left unchanged. Then colors are swapped for their opposites on the color wheel, producing an interesting effect.

There are no options with this filter. But because solarized pictures can turn dark, you may need to readjust brightness and contrast levels after you solarize. Figure 21.24 is a photo you have seen before, but not like this. I first solarized, and then simply applied auto-levels.

FIGURE 21.24

Solarize inverts the colors in an image.

There are many other interesting filters, and you can pile one strange effect on another until you get something that has artistic possibilities, or until you destroy the image completely.

Summary

We took a different approach this hour, and went poking in some of the darker corners of the Elements menus. We were rewarded with several strange and unusual effects. First

21

you learned to posterize, then to liquify. You learned how to use all the Liquify tools. Then we looked at some special color effects. You learned about gradient mapping and color inversions. We played alchemist, turning things to gold and other pretty metals. Finally, we dug into some strange-looking filters such as Neon Glow, Solarize, and Ocean Ripple. Some of these work by themselves, while others practically beg to be used as part of a set of changes.

Q&A

Q I really like this stuff. Is there more?

A There's always more. In Hour 24, "Animated GIFs and Other Cool Tricks," we'll look at some of the third-party filters, including Smoke, Fire, and Fur.

Q Is there a difference between Solarize and Invert?

A Yes. Solarize only partially inverts the colors in the image, while Invert inverts them all. Try both on the same picture and see for yourself.

Q There's an effect called Ink Blot. What does it do?

A This effect (found on the Effects palette) is strange, even to me. It doubles the size of the picture and puts down a layer of seemingly random black blobs, which are placed symmetrically. You almost can't help seeing something like a fat teddy bear in a tuxedo, or dancing bats. I don't think I'd want to approach this one without tranquilizers.

Workshop

Take another walk on the wild side by answering these questions and doing the activity.

Quiz

1. How many levels can you use in posterizing?

    a. No more than ten

    b. 100

    c. Only two per color

    d. There's no limit

2. What's the difference between copper and brass?

    a. Color

    b. Smoothness

    c. Both

Quiz Answers

1. d. But if you take it to more than ten levels, it's usually hard to see that you've changed anything.

2. c. Copper is pinkish and shiny. Brass is gold with green, and needs noise or texture.

Activity

Open up the metal shop and practice with gold, copper, and brass. Make sure there are visible differences between them. Then try silver. (Hint: Silver contains blue as well as gray, black, and white.)

21

HOUR **22**

Creating Backgrounds and Textures from Scratch

Maybe it's been raining, and you haven't been out with the camera in a while, or maybe you've run out of photos to fix. Or maybe you just want to do something different and creative. Even though Elements was never intended to be a complete graphics program, between the Brush tools, filters, and gradients, you can use it to create backgrounds and textures for all kinds of projects.

In this hour you will

- Create colorful backgrounds and fills with the Gradient tool
- Create a sandy beach
- Learn sources for backgrounds, textures, and other images
- Create backgrounds and textures using filters and effects

Creating Backgrounds with the Gradient Tool

Gradients can be exceptionally useful tools when you're trying to suggest depth or shading or to make a smooth blend between two or more colors. Elements comes with a default set of 15 gradients, plus 8 more sets that you can load from the Presets folder. Of course, unless you are amazingly lucky, none of these gradients will do exactly what you need. That's why you may need to create your own, based on one of the existing gradients.

First, let's take a look at the existing gradients for use with the Gradient tool. If they look familiar, that's because they are—they are the same standard set of gradients you saw when we looked at the Gradient Map adjustment last hour. Unlike the Gradient Map, which exchanges the colors in an image for the colors in the gradient, the Gradient tool fills a layer or a selection with the gradient you choose.

Select the Gradient tool—it's next to the Paint Bucket. You'll want to set your options on the Options bar before using the tool to create a gradient fill. When you click the down arrow next to the currently selected gradient, you'll open the Gradient palette, shown in Figure 22.1. Click the right-pointing arrow at the top-right corner of the palette to display a different category of gradients. If you can't find one that has exactly the right color combination and spacing, don't despair. At the very least you should be able to find one with the right number of colors.

FIGURE 22.1

Choosing a gradient with the Gradient tool.

Suppose you want a three-color gradient that looks like a sunset. There's nothing quite right, but you can edit one. First, you need to select the gradient you want to work with from the palette. This gradient will replace whatever was previously on the Options bar. Now, click that gradient swatch or click the Edit button to open the Gradient Editor, shown in Figure 22.2. This editor is the same as the one we saw in Hour 21, but because gradients are a complex topic, let's review the editor as it relates to the Gradient tool.

FIGURE 22.2

The Gradient Editor dialog box.

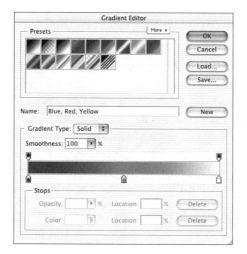

Click the New button to add your gradient at the end of the palette and give it a name. Choose the gradient type from the pop-up menu. Solid makes the three colors change smoothly from one to the next. Noise gives you a random mixture of the three colors. It's an interesting effect, but not at all what you want for a sunset. See both in Figure 22.3.

FIGURE 22.3

Solid and noisy gradients.

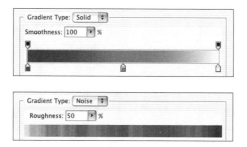

With the gradient type set to Solid, you'll notice tiny swatches with arrows that point to the gradient. They're called stops, and are rather like the stops on a church organ. Just as each stop on an organ adds another dimension to the sound, the stops on the gradient add color or change the opacity. The color stops are on the bottom and the opacity stops are on the top. Their purpose is to let you set the spot where one color changes to the next or where a gradient starts to go from completely opaque to some degree of transparency.

By changing opacity, you can build a gradient that totally covers whatever's under it at one end and is partially or completely transparent at the other end. It's useful for such tricks as adding a metallic highlight to make a shape appear round. You can go back to partial or complete opacity by adding more stops. To add a stop, click the point where you want the opacity to change at the top of the color strip.

To change the amount of opacity, either type a percentage into the Opacity field, or drag the slider. You'll see the swatch inside the stop change from black to gray to white as you turn that section of the gradient from opaque to transparent. In Figure 22.4, I've added a stop (shown above the gradient bar) that reduces the opacity to 25%. I've placed it at 60% of the distance between the two ends of the gradient. You'll notice that the swatch on that stop is now light gray, rather than black. There are also two diamonds, one on either side of the stop. These indicate the midpoint of the gradient change. You can move them by dragging, or by clicking one to select it and changing the percentage in the Location window. Remember that when you select a midpoint, the location indicates the position of the midpoint relative to the two stops on either side, not the beginning and end of the entire gradient.

FIGURE 22.4

You can place as many stops as you need.

To get rid of a stop, simply click and drag it off the color bar. You can't remove the end stops, but you can move them in, if you want a shorter gradient. (That's why distances are measured in percentages, rather than in inches or centimeters.)

Changing and adding color stops works in much the same way. Click on a color stop (located below the gradient bar) to select it. The swatch color will appear below, in the Stops section of the dialog box, as in Figure 22.5. When you click the arrow on the swatch, a menu that allows you to select the current foreground or background color as a component of your gradient appears. The menu also has an option called User Color. Double-click on either the tiny swatch under the color bar or the larger one in the Stops area to open the Color Picker. Choose your color(s) by clicking on the color picker. If there's a shade somewhere in the gradient that you want to use as one of the gradient's base colors, first click on the stop you want to change to select it. Place the cursor on the color within the gradient that you want to use. The cursor then becomes an eyedropper. When you click the color, the stop changes to that color. You can also click with this eye-dropper in the image to pick up a color from there.

FIGURE 22.5

Changing a color stop.

Add more colors to your gradient by clicking below the bar to place additional color stops. If you have selected the foreground or background color from the menu, the new stop will be in that color. If you have selected User Color, the new stop will appear in the color closest to the spot where you have clicked.

Now that you've got precisely the gradient you want, you can save it permanently to the Gradient palette by clicking Save. You can reload the gradient file for use in a later session with Elements by clicking the right arrow on the Gradient palette and choosing Load Gradients. If you just want to use it once, click OK.

To apply the gradient, first select the gradient type you want, as shown in Figure 22.6 (enlarged and rotated so there's room for the labels). The Linear style is your standard blend from the start color to the end color. Although it shows the blend going from the top to the bottom of the layer/selection, you can actually blend from side to side or corner to corner as well. The direction of any gradient (regardless of the style you choose) is determined by a line you draw across the layer/selection—more on that in a moment.

FIGURE 22.6

Choosing a gradient.

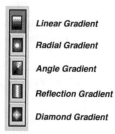

Linear Gradient

Radial Gradient

Angle Gradient

Reflection Gradient

Diamond Gradient

The next style, Radial, blends from the center out, in a circular pattern. If you draw the line from one corner or edge to another, you'll get a half-circle pattern, like a sunset. The Angle style divides the colors in the gradient in half, and then fans them out on both sides of the line you draw on the image to create the gradient. The Reflection style blends from the beginning of the line you draw to the end, and then repeats the blend in the other direction. So with this style, you should draw your line from some point near the center of the layer/selection out to an edge. The Diamond style is similar to the Reflection style, but it reflects the blend four times, creating a diamond in the center. Again, with this style, you should draw your line from the center of the layer/selection to a side or corner. Select the style you want to use by clicking on it, and you're ready to draw the gradient line.

Make sure the gradient that appears in the gradient swatch on the Options bar is the one you want to use, then draw a horizontal line from right to left or from left to right to create the blend, or draw a vertical or diagonal line to make it go in a different direction (see Figure 22.7). As noted earlier, with the Reflection or Diamond styles, you should start at a point somewhere within the layer or selection and draw to an edge. You might want to use this technique with the Radial style as well, so that the circle pattern will be in the middle of the layer/selection. Keep in mind that the start color is placed at the point where you begin to draw the line, and the end color appears at the line's end. For example, you might want to draw from a corner or an edge inward, to lay down the colors in the order you want. You can also reverse the start and end colors by selecting the Reverse option before drawing the line.

FIGURE 22.7

The gradient blends colors in the direction in which you draw.

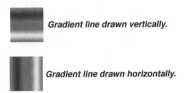

Gradient line drawn vertically.

Gradient line drawn horizontally.

Note that when you draw a gradient line on a page, the gradient will fill the entire layer. If that's not your intention, use the selection tools to draw the shape you want, and then place the gradient within it.

A Gradient can make a handsome background for a Web page or an object you've photographed for a catalog. You can also use gradients to fill shapes so that they look more 3-dimensional, to blend colors in areas where you're making repairs, and to create shadows and other special effects. You can fill type with a gradient if you use a type mask to create it or if you simplify the text layer and select the text. You can fill a shape or any other selection with a gradient as well. As with other aspects of Elements, the best way

22

to learn how to handle gradients is to practice. You'll soon have gradients that make the grade.

Task: Create a Composite Image from Scratch

You've seen in some of the earlier hours that Photoshop can create art from scratch, in addition to editing and altering existing photos. As a final exercise in compositing, let's see what kind of artwork we can make out of nothing. First we'll create a nice looking background, then we'll add something on top of it.

Start with a new image file and apply a gradient as a background. Gradients, as you have seen, can be linear, radial, angled, reflected, or diamond-shaped, and can have as many transparent or opaque colors as you want. To create the gradient we'll be using as the basis of our composition, follow these steps:

1. Select the Gradient tool and look at its Options bar, which is shown in Figure 22.8. We want a gradient that will suggest sky, water, and beach.

FIGURE 22.8

Gradients and the Gradient Options bar.

2. Regardless of which gradient is currently selected, click on its swatch or click the Edit button on the Options bar to open the Gradient Editor. In the Editor, choose the three-color (blue, red, and yellow) gradient from the Default presets. Click it, and its settings will appear in the dialog box.

3. Click the color stop at the lower-left end of the gradient bar. Change its color to the deep blue sky of early evening. (Clicking the block of color at the bottom of the screen opens the Color Picker.) Change the middle color stop to a sort of tropical turquoise, and the right one to sandy beige. The little diamonds indicate midpoints of each color blend. Keeping your goal in mind, slide them left or right as needed to create a horizon and a generous beach. Figure 22.9 shows the gradient in the Gradient Editor. Click OK to use our gradient this one time.

4. Make sure that the Linear Gradient style is selected. Drag the Gradient tool from top to bottom to place it with the blue on top. Your image should look like the one shown in Figure 22.10.

FIGURE 22.9
The Gradient Editor.

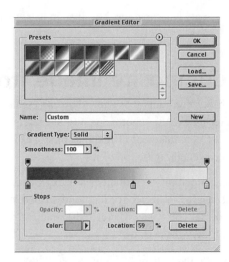

FIGURE 22.10
We've got sky, sea, and sand, but we can do better than this.

5. Now add a cloudy sky to the image. Render Clouds will give you a nice set of clouds. Set the foreground color to the midpoint of the lighter blue and the background to the midpoint of the darker blue. Create a new layer and drag a Marquee selection to define the upper third of the sky. Apply the Clouds filter (Filter, Render, Clouds) to the selection, with the new layer's blending mode set to Color Dodge.

6. Now it's looking like a day at the beach. Let's add some beach grass. Switch to the background layer and remove the selection marquee. Switch to the Brush tool and choose the Grass brush from the Brushes palette, and then move the Size slider to about 45. Set the foreground and background colors to a pale green and pale gold and stamp or paint some grass. The background we've created is shown in Figure 22.11.

FIGURE 22.11
It's a cool background, but it needs a subject. Maybe some boats?

7. Finally, add some sailboats. Change to the Shape tool and select Custom Shape. Open the Shape list and choose the sailboat (it's on the Objects palette). Set the foreground color to white and draw some sailboats of various sizes in the water. Figure 22.12 shows the final result: a fleet of boats in a tropical bay.

FIGURE 22.12
Wish I was there....

Other Sources for Backgrounds and Textures—Working with Stock Photos

Pictures are everywhere. You can download thousands of images from the Web. You can buy CD-ROMs full of photographs and line art. And, of course, you can either scan conventional photos or import pictures from a digital camera into Photoshop Elements.

When you start thinking about combining images, you'll probably realize that some pictures are more suitable than others for this kind of use. You can even classify some as backgrounds, others as objects, and some as the raw materials from which to create special effects. As you browse through your own pictures and look at collections of stock photos, some images will jump out at you, and you'll begin to see possible combinations.

If you're not familiar with the term *stock photos*, you should be. They are pictures that you can use for a fee (a flat fee or sometimes a per-use royalty) to do with as you see fit. You can use them in your reports, in ads, or in practically any way you want, as long as you're not reselling them or using them in any way that's libelous, defamatory, pornographic, or otherwise illegal. Be sure that you read and understand the licensing policies of the stock photo provider before you use them.

Point your Web browser to http://www.comstock.com/ to see some really good stock photography. Alas, you can't use any of the pictures in the Comstock libraries without paying for them. The screen versions download as low-quality JPEGs, but you can get a feel for what's available and how much it costs.

Comstock is typical of stock photo collections. The Comstock collection includes more than 100,000 pictures of everything you can imagine. Figure 22.13 shows a page from the Comstock online catalog. There's no reason you can't use these kinds of images in combination with your own. If you need something basic, such as a beach pier to use as a background, it will be faster, cheaper, and just as effective to use one from stock than to create one of your own using filters, effects, and a lot of sweat, or to take a picture of the same object yourself under perfect lighting conditions (assuming you have easy access to the object, such as the beach pier).

FIGURE 22.13
Stock photos.

Of course, as you wander around town with your digital camera in your pocket, you can start your own stock collection. In fact, this is one of the ways you can make money with your pictures, allowing you to invest the profits in more software and higher-resolution cameras.

22

Creating Backgrounds and Textures

Backgrounds are everywhere, literally behind everything you see. You need to learn to recognize what makes a good one, and how to imitate it, or use the real thing for your own purposes. One way I've done this is to take my camera for a walk. There's a nicely landscaped condo building across the street. It has benches just right for people to sit on, trees to stand in front of, a marvelous brick sidewalk, walls of both brick and concrete, and fresh grass and flowers. When I want to shoot portraits, I walk people over to my "outdoor studio." It's convenient, and always cleaned up, unlike the house. I also shoot there when I have no subject, and I've collected a half dozen good shots of plain grass, the brick, the slatted benches, and so on. I keep these filed on a separate CD-ROM, from where I can retrieve them easily. When I need to "relocate" someone shot against a messy background, I'm all set. I just choose an appropriate piece of real estate and drop them into it.

There's a new store in my town specializing in fancy papers for craft projects. I've already picked out a half dozen sheets to use as backdrops for photographing small objects. Backdrops of this type need to be neutral in color, to go with as many things as possible, but can be textured and/or patterned. Keep them clean and flat in a cardboard folder when you're not using them.

Of course, if you don't have the background you need, you can improvise. Some of the nicest backgrounds are simply based on the Add Noise filter. Take a look at Figure 22.14. Here's 10% monochromatic noise, plus 25 pixels worth of Motion Blur. I used perspective to stretch the bottom out, making it look more like a piece of no-seam paper.

You also have an arsenal of textures hidden behind a filter called Texture Fill (Filter, Render, Texture Fill—see Figure 22.15). Choose any of the grayscale patterns here, and apply it to a new layer for an instant background, or use these patterns as a jumping-off point for further filter experiments.

Another filter called Pattern Fill has some surprisingly nice stuff once you get past the default pattern set. Open the patterns by selecting Layer, New Fill Layer, Pattern. The pattern you see in the window in Figure 22.16 is from a set called "Nature." Eight sets are provided; to switch from set to set, click the right arrow and choose a category from the menu. You can add more patterns as you create them. You'll learn how to do so in Hour 24, "Animated GIFs and Other Cool Tricks."

FIGURE 22.14

Brushed metal texture, from scratch.

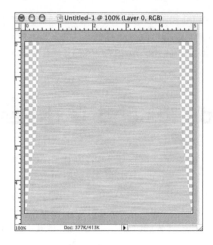

FIGURE 22.15

Texture Fill is found under Render, not Texture. Go figure.

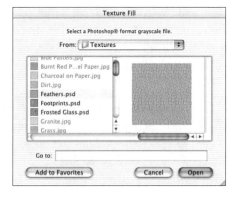

FIGURE 22.16

Create a patterned layer in a flash.

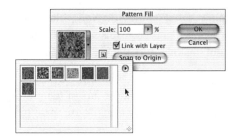

Summary

This was a busy hour. We looked at gradients, and you learned how to design your own with the Gradient tool. You learned about setting stops for color and opacity. Then we used a gradient as a basis for producing art "from scratch." We talked about backgrounds, photographic and otherwise. You learned about paying a fee to use stock photos, and about taking your own stock photos. Finally, we looked at the patterns and fills that come with Elements. There are some very interesting ones.

Q&A

Q How many times can a gradient change color?

A As many as you want, but if you make too many changes it won't be a gradient any more. It'll be stripes.

Q Can I apply a filter to a gradient?

A Yes. It's easiest if the gradient is on a separate layer. Select it and do whatever you want. Sometimes your efforts can produce beautiful results, or at least an interesting background.

Q Once I buy a stock photo is it mine?

A Generally, stock photo providers are selling one-time rights. You can use the photo once, or in one project, but then you may have to pay again if you want to use it again. It's not yours in the sense that nobody else can use it, or even that you have unlimited use. Sorry. Some stock photo providers, such as Comstock.com, have several levels of licensing. You pay once for royalty-free images and you can use them many times. The same is true of flat-rate images, but they are sold as single images only and not in collections. Rights-protected images are sold for a single, clearly defined use, and the fee is based on what you're using the image for.

Workshop

Let's see if you can make the grade-ient with this quiz and activity.

Quiz

1. Elements has _____ different kinds of gradients.

    a. One

    b. Two

    c. Five

2. What's the one thing you have to master to be good at making composites?

    a. Zen

    b. Filters

    c. Layers

3. Stock photos are only for backgrounds.

    a. True

    b. False

Quiz Answers

1. c. Linear, radial, angle, reflected, and diamond.

2. c. You'll need to master layers, but Zen might also help.

3. b. They come in a variety of categories and can be used any way you want.

Activity

Go to the Comstock Web site and look at some of the pictures. As you can see, they are not all great photos. Consider whether any of your pictures would make good stock. When you shoot, think about stock possibilities, and start to put together a portfolio. You can make some money in this business!

HOUR 23

Building Your Own Brushes and Patterns

One of the truly cool things about Elements is that, even though it's considered a beginner-level graphics program, it has all the flexibility of Photoshop, if you choose to use it. Take brushes, for instance. Elements comes with 321 different brush shapes, divided into 13 different categories including Wet Media, Dry Media, Calligraphic, Drop Shadow, Faux Finish, and more. You'd think this would be enough. But no. There's also a brush editor so you can design and save your own custom brush sets.

Elements also lets you create and save fill patterns, swatches, and gradients and keep track of them all with the Preset Manager. When you have photographed or designed a bunch of background textures, it's easy to add them to the Elements menus. You can even make up your own set of custom brushes, adding in the useful ones from the Elements Brush palettes as well as the ones you've designed.

In this hour you will

- Get quick access to brush tips, patterns, and gradients
- Create custom sets of brush tips, patterns, and gradients
- Adjust brush options
- Create new brushes with a shape or selection
- Define new patterns and save them

Using the Preset Manager

Think of the Preset Manager as a sort of librarian that keeps track of all your libraries of brushes, swatches, patterns, and gradients. It can restore defaults with a click, or help you assemble your own library sets of favorite brushes, gradients, and patterns.

Each type of preset library has its own file extension and default folder. For example, brushes end in the extension .abr, and gradients end in .grd. Preset files are installed on your computer inside the Presets folder in the Elements folder.

You can open the Preset Manager by choosing Edit, Preset Manager or by choosing Preset Manager from the menu that is displayed when you click the right arrow at the top of the Brush, Pencil, Gradient, Swatches, or Pattern palettes. Figure 23.1 shows what it looks like.

FIGURE 23.1

The Preset Manager.

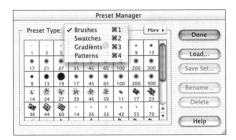

Notice the Preset Type menu. Although the Preset Manager will open in whatever mode you're currently working in, you can reach any of its four functions by selecting them from this menu. I've chosen to talk about brushes here, but all of these actions also apply to the patterns, swatches, and gradients libraries.

To load a new brush set, click the Load button. This will open the dialog box shown in Figure 23.2. Navigate to the Brushes folder, or enter the file path if you know it. Choose a brush set from the list and click Load. If you like having lots of choices, repeat these steps to load as many brush sets as you want. When you're done adding brushes, click Done. The brushes you've selected will now appear in the Brushes list. This saves you the trouble of switching to another category of brushes to access them.

FIGURE 23.2

Load as many brush sets as you need.

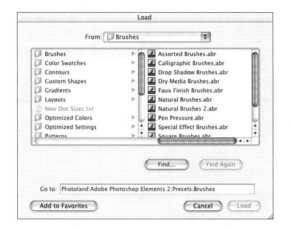

Of course, if you want to switch back and forth between brush sets while you're work-ing, there's an easier way. Just open the Brushes list at the top of the Brushes palette to display a list of brush categories. Figure 23.3 shows this menu. Note, however, that this only gives you access to one set of brushes at a time.

FIGURE 23.3

Pop up the menu and pick the brush you want.

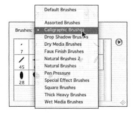

To reset the brushes to the default set, choose Default Brushes from the top of the Brushes menu.

Customizing Libraries

As you work more with Elements, you'll find that there are some brushes, gradients, and patterns that you use a lot, and others that seem useless. Rather than having to pick through the palette to find the ones you want, you can create your own library of favorites.

To make a new brush set, open the Preset Manager and display the Brushes palette by selecting it from the Preset Type list. Load as many brush sets as it takes to display all the brushes you want to put in your personal set. Hold down the Shift key while clicking on the brushes you want to include in the set. You can have as few or as many as you want. Click Save Set, and give it a name. Later, when you realize that "my brushes" isn't a very descriptive name, you can rename it by navigating to the folder in which you saved it (typically Presets) and changing its name just as you would any other file. You can rename any preset (brush tip) in a set by selecting it in the list and clicking Rename. You'll be prompted to enter a new name. You can delete a brush from a set by selecting it and clicking Delete. To delete a set of brushes you've created, again, you'll need to navigate to the proper folder (typically Presets) and delete it just as you would any other file. I'd recommend dragging the brush set file from the Presets folder into another folder, in case you want it again someday.

Elements offers you several ways to view the palettes. You can choose to see large or small thumbnails of the swatches, gradients, patterns, and brush shapes; you can choose text only and see a list (with descriptions that are not very helpful); or you can choose large or small list and have the best of both worlds—swatches *and* descriptions. One more choice, obviously only useful for brushes, is a stroke thumbnail. Instead of showing the shape of the brush, the thumbnail shows what kind of line it draws. Figure 23.4 shows some stroke thumbnails. As a real convenience, the thumbnail example changes if you change the opacity of the brush. To make a selection, click the More button in the Preset Manager dialog box and choose the option you want to use for viewing from those listed. If you're not in the Preset Manager, you can make this choice from a palette (such as the Brushes palette) by clicking the right arrow and making a choice from the menu that appears. You can resize any of these palettes, by the way, to display several columns of brush tips, swatches, patterns, or gradients. Just drag the lower-right corner of the palette outward to make it bigger, or inward to make it smaller.

FIGURE 23.4

I think this is the best way to choose brushes.

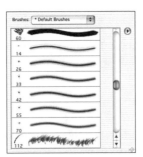

Defining Brushes

Even though Elements comes with 300-odd (some *very* odd) brushes, sooner or later you'll want more. As you learned earlier this hour, you can switch from one set of brushes to another by clicking the right arrow on the Brushes palette and choosing a new category. You can also add brushes to the default list by loading brush sets in the Preset Manager.

Even with all these choices, it's fun and not especially difficult to make your own brush tips. You can also make and save your own gradients and patterns. But let's start with brushes.

For each of the brush tips supplied, there are at least eleven different attributes (such as size, pressure, blending mode, and opacity) that you can turn on or off or adjust, some infinitely. This gives you a lot of latitude in working with existing brushes to customize them. Let's start by playing with the attributes of an existing brush tip. Open a new image file and click the New Layer button at the bottom of the Layers palette to add a new layer.

Select the Brush from the toolbox. Choose the 35-pixel soft round brush from the Default set, as I have in Figure 23.5. Use it to draw a line, with the opacity set to 100%.

FIGURE 23.5
Notice the Mode and Opacity settings.

Reduce the opacity to 50% and draw another line next to the first. Then draw a short line overlapping them. Notice that where the 50% opacity lines cross, they get darker. This doesn't happen with the 100% opacity line, because it's already as dark as it can be. You can see my version of these lines in Figure 23.6.

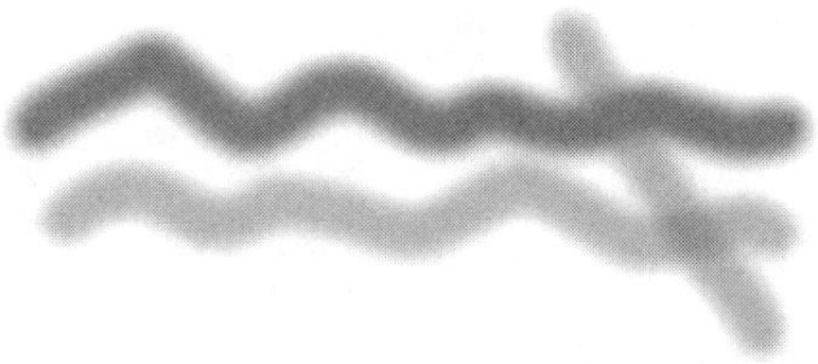

FIGURE 23.6
Brush samples.

Now, let's open the Brush Editor and see why this brush looks like it does. The button to open the Brush Editor is labeled More Options and is at the far right end of the Options bar. Looking at its attributes in Figure 23.7, we can see that this is a very plain brush.

FIGURE 23.7

The Brush Editor.

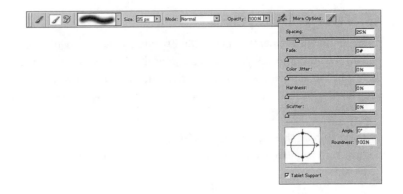

What setting gives this brush its soft edge? Is it spacing? Spacing controls the distance between brush marks as you drag the brush. Close spacing (smaller numbers) gives you a nice even line. As long as the spacing is smaller than the brush width, you won't see spots, but if you make it larger than the width of the brush, you'll draw a polka-dotted line. (Remember this. You can use it to create trails of leaves, hearts, or other little pictures.) Try changing the spacing, first to 5%, and then to 50% (see Figure 23.8) .

FIGURE 23.8

Experiments in spacing.

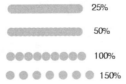

We haven't yet answered the soft edges question. Everything else is set to zero, including Hardness. Hmmm…. No hardness equals—softness! We've found it. Move the hardness slider to 100% and draw a line. Nice firm edges…. That's how we do it. Try moving the slider to different settings and, at 100% opacity, drawing more lines. Now you can change the fuzziness of the brushes.

> By the way, just trash the current layer and start a new one when you run out of drawing room.

Let's try Fade next. It adds realism to your brush strokes by gradually fading the stroke as if you were running out of paint. Figure 23.9 shows some examples. Fade works with an ordinary mouse, but is much easier to control and is more realistic if you use a pen tablet. If you have one, you can check the pressure sensitivity option, called Tablet

Support in the Brush Editor, and control the length of the fade by gradually reducing pressure on the pen, just as if you were using a real one.

FIGURE 23.9
Fading a brush.

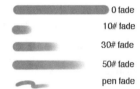

0 fade

10# fade

30# fade

50# fade

pen fade

23

Color Jitter is useful if you want your brush to change color as you paint. It toggles back and forth between the foreground and background colors. With an ordinary brush, this produces a line that looks sort of like a gummy worm. But if you are using a brush that scatters flowers across the page, set up pink and blue as your two colors, and you'll have a colorful garden in a single stroke. Higher values cause the color switch to occur more frequently, while lower values cause it to happen less often. In the example shown in Figure 23.10, you can also see another attribute at work: The Scatter attribute, which places brush strokes at random within a defined area.

FIGURE 23.10
Larger Scatter settings spread spots further.

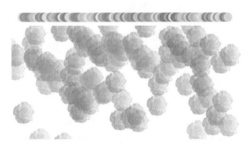

Task: Plant Some Grass with the Grass Brush

1. Start a new image. Choose the Grass brush. It's about three-quarters of the way down the Default Brushes menu. (You can see the names of the brushes if you hold the cursor over the Brushes palette.)

2. Choose an appropriate green for your foreground color and another green for your background color. A combination of light green and dark green works well. Set Opacity to 100%. You don't need to adjust the Color Jitter; it's already set to 100%.

3. Plant grass to make a nice green meadow. If you want, find the Scattered Wildflower brush. (It's in Special Effect brushes.) Change the foreground and background colors to something more flowerlike, and turn on spring. You might want to change the spacing and the amount of scatter. To flip between the foreground and background colors, adjust the Color Jitter value. You know how. Just open the More Options palette and use the sliders.

Your finished picture might look something like Figure 23.11.

FIGURE 23.11
A wildflower meadow.

To put the sky in, I added a layer, then brushed in some blue with a big fat soft brush. Then I moved the sky behind the grass.

Shaping Brushes

Now let's look at the Brush Shape section of the Brush Editor. It's shown in Figure 23.12. By default, the brush is round, but anyone who's been in an art supply store knows that's not always the case. Calligraphy brushes are angled. Many oil brushes are flat. Each brush makes a different kind of stroke. (As they say, "Different strokes for different folks….") It's easy to make your own custom shapes.

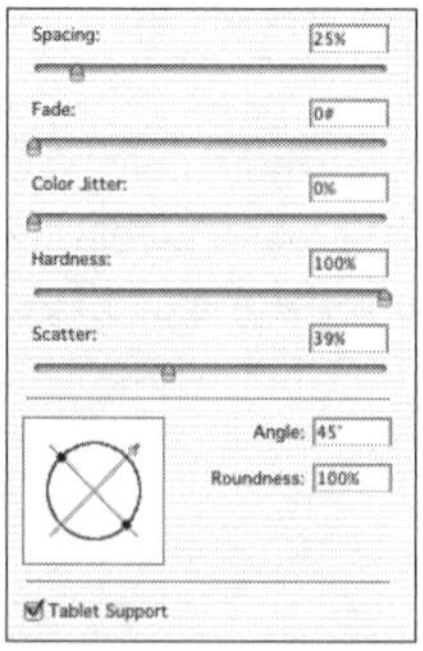

FIGURE 23.12
Use the numbers or drag the shape to change it.

Use the Angle setting to set the slant, if any, of the brush point's long axis. This is a moot point if the brush is round, but as you change the shape of the brush, its angle becomes more important. Angled brushes give the appearance of chiseled strokes. You can enter a value or drag the arrowhead in the angle compass.

Roundness, in this context, is the correlation between the brush's short and long axes. You can either change the numbers or drag on the brush shape diagram to change the shape of the brush. When you're satisfied with the brush mechanics, click OK, and go ahead and use it.

23

Saving a Brush

To save your brush, open the Brushes palette menu by clicking the right arrow with the new brush active. Choose New Brush. Elements will open a dialog box that asks you to name the new brush, and makes a suggestion based on whatever existing brushes are most similar. You can, of course, change this to anything you please.

Creating a Brush from a Shape or Selection

Use the Lasso tool or the Marquee to select a shape from a picture, such as a cat's eye (see Figure 23.13). The shape can be as large as 1024×1024 pixels.

FIGURE 23.13
A cat's eye that I'll turn into a brush.

Paste a copy on a clean layer and give it any needed cleanup. Then choose Define Brush, from the Edit menu. The brush will appear in grayscale in the dialog box preview area, as shown in Figure 23.14. (The brush tip will use the foreground color.) Name your brush, or accept the generic name that Elements supplies for it. Go ahead and use it. It's at the bottom of the active Brushes palette.

FIGURE **23.14**

Saving a brush.

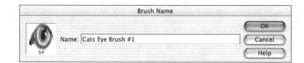

You can, of course, use the same method to save a shape you have drawn as a new brush tip. Don't worry about the background. It's automatically removed, and only the shape is saved.

Defining Patterns

Defining a pattern or texture for use with Elements is very simple, now that you know how to define a brush. Open the image that you want to use a pattern from, select a block of it, and choose Edit, Define Pattern. In Figure 23.15, I've selected a small piece of pink granite from a photo.

FIGURE **23.15**

There are lots of possible patterns in this picture: grass, water, even feathers.

With all of these new patterns to play with, how are you going to use them? One way is to use the Pattern Stamp tool to apply them as if they were regular rubber stamps. To use the Pattern Stamp tool, follow these steps:

1. Select the Pattern Stamp tool from the toolbox. It shares a space with the regular Clone Stamp tool.

2. Choose a brush tip. Drag the slider in the Options bar to change the brush size, if necessary. Specify a blending mode and opacity if you want something other than normal and 100%.

3. Choose your pattern from the Pattern palette on the tool Options bar.

4. Select the Aligned option if you want your pattern to tile automatically each time you stamp it. Leave the box unchecked if you'd rather try a random distribution. The pattern block will be centered on the cursor, so you can place it where you want.

5. Now, start stamping. In Figure 23.16, you can see two examples of my pink granite pattern, one aligned and one not. I think the lower, non-aligned piece looks a little more realistic, but sometimes tiles are what you need.

23

FIGURE 23.16
Using the Pattern Stamp tool.

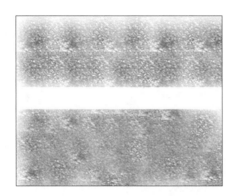

Summary

In this hour, you've learned to work with and manage the brush and patterns libraries in Elements. You probably discovered brushes and pattern sets you never knew you had. You learned how to add brushes and patterns to your sets, and how to create them from scratch.

Q&A

Q How many sets of patterns and brushes and so on can I keep?

A As many as you want, and as many as will fit on your hard drive. For easy searching, give each set a descriptive name, and keep the sets reasonably small.

Q Can I make my signature into a brush shape so I can rubber-stamp it on things?

A Good idea! Keep it small, and use a thin brush or pencil.

Q I just want to clean up some photos. Do I really need to make my own brushes?

A Of course not. With over 300 brushes already available, you can probably find what you need. If not, though, why compromise? It's not hard to change the behavior of a brush.

Q Can I use my brother's Photoshop brush sets? He's on a Mac and I'm not.

A Brush files are cross-platform, and if he created the brushes in Photoshop 6 or 7 and used the .abr filename extension, you should be able to load them. Try it.

Workshop

You might have to "brush up" on brushes and patterns to answer all the quiz questions.

Quiz

1. How many different preset libraries are there?

   a. One

   b. Two

   c. Four

   d. Five

2. Can you use several brushes at once?

   a. Yes

   b. No

3. How do you make a brush paint spots?

   a. Make the spacing greater than the width of the brush

   b. Check Speckle

   c. Add Color Jitter

   d. Tap the mouse

Answers

1. c. Brushes, Gradients, Patterns, and Swatches

2. a. Yes, *if* you assemble them into a new brush first.

3. a. or d.

Activity

Now that you know how, actively manage your brushes and patterns. Make up sets for specific projects, such as retouching tools or oil paint–style brushes. Take the patterns you created in an earlier lesson and incorporate them into your pattern library. Practice with such options as Color Jitter and Hardness.

HOUR 24

Animated GIFs and Other Cool Tricks

After your hard work in the last 23 hours, think of this one as dessert. I'll show you a couple of very cool tricks, and all you need to know about finding and using third-party filters.

In this hour, you will

- Make an animated GIF
- Put type in a circle
- Work some magic with the Magic Eraser
- Learn about third-party filters

Animating a GIF

Animated GIFs are those little bits of art that twirl around, blink, or wave back at you from Web pages and forum signatures on the Web. If they aren't too big and flashy, they can be cute.

Animation is done, as it was fifty years ago, in layers. The difference is that for a GIF animation, each layer must be a complete frame with the entire picture in it. In the old days, you could put the body on one layer and the arms, which moved, on a different layer. Now, because the animation is accomplished by scrolling through the layers, everything needs to be kept together or you will see an armless torso, followed by waving arms.

Figure 24.1 is my animation model, a Japanese Happy Cat. This one, I believe, represents good health. I'm going to make him wave at you in a very simple three-step animation.

Figure 24.1
*This cat will soon
wave his paw.*

The first step is to copy the cat into a new image file. (If you want to work along, the cat is in the collection of images that you can download from this book's companion Web site. See the Introduction if you've forgotten where the downloads are.)

Duplicate the layer twice, so you have three in all. The bottom layer is the "resting" state for the animation, so you don't need to do anything to it. It will be the first frame in our animation. The second layer is the "transition" state and the third layer is the "final" state. You can insert as many transition layers as you need. More steps will give you a smoother animation, and a much larger file. Unfortunately, it may not play well on some computers, or if the Internet is running slowly, as it sometimes does.

Move to the top layer and make the changes necessary to take the picture to the final state. In Figure 24.2, you can see that I have moved the cat's paw to a fully extended wave position. To do so, I cut it loose with the Lasso, rotated it, and filled in the gaps in black and green with a small brush.

Next, move to the middle layer. Because this is a small animation and the cat's paw has to move only a short distance, one middle step is enough. If the paw had farther to travel, we could put in more transitional steps, but the animation will look fine with just one step here. Cut the paw loose and rotate it halfway between where it is on the first and third layers. Again, use a small brush to fill in any gaps. Now your animation should look like Figure 24.3. The "art" part of the job is done.

FIGURE 24.2

The waving cat.

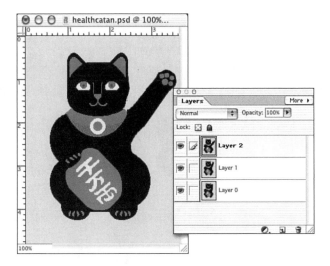

FIGURE 24.3

The cat in mid-wave.

24

The final step in creating an animated GIF is to choose Save for Web on the File menu. You don't need very many colors for this particular example, so you can make it a 16-color GIF with no noticeable change. Be sure to check Animation in the upper settings pane. The picture was too large to fit where I wanted to put it, so I scaled it down to 50%. In the Animation box at the bottom of the window, check Loop if you want it to go continuously. Otherwise, it will run its steps once and stop. (If you want a limited number of repeats, add the additional steps as extra layers on the original animation.) You can add a delay between each frame in the animation by setting the Frame Delay value. Figure 24.4 shows the final settings for the animation.

FIGURE 24.4

Finishing the animation.

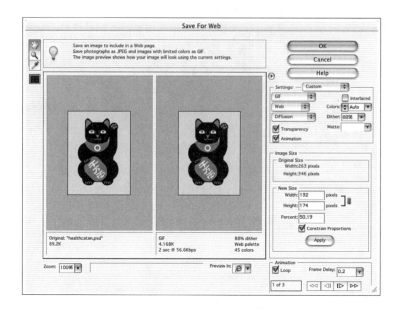

Click OK and save it as a GIF. But before you do, you may want to preview your animation. There are two ways to do so: You can preview each frame using the frame controls in the Animation pane, or select your favorite browser from the Preview In list and click the button. If you choose the latter option, you'll see both the waving cat and the HTML code to put him on your Web page or wherever he's going. By the way, it's a good idea to check out GIFs and anything else for the Web in other browsers as well. After all, you want to make sure everyone can enjoy your work.

Setting Type in a Circle

You've probably heard that this is impossible. You can't even set type in a circle in Photoshop 7, never mind in Elements. Okay, maybe not, but it surely looks like a circle, acts like a circle, and so on. I'd call it a circle.

The workaround, since Photoshop introduced limited type on a path, has been to set two arcs and position them to form a circle. That doesn't really work, though.

When you set type in an arc, it reads left to right, as it should in most languages. Setting the line of type twice, and making one line arc upward and the other arc downward does in fact give you type in a circle, more or less (see Figure 24.5).

FIGURE 24.5

Is it in a circle, or isn't it?

But if you look carefully, you'll realize that the bottom line, although it reads correctly, is upside down with regard to its baseline. It doesn't follow the circle as it should.

However, there is a way to set type, or a string of dingbats, or a painted line, or anything you can imagine as a perfect circle. It's done with the Polar Coordinates filter, one of the most obscure filters in Elements.

Start with a square image file. (This is significant: If your page is rectangular, you'll convert your type into an oval, rather than a circle.)

Place your type, or whatever you're using, from edge to edge near the bottom of the page. Figure 24.6 shows an example.

FIGURE 24.6

Give the type plenty of headroom.

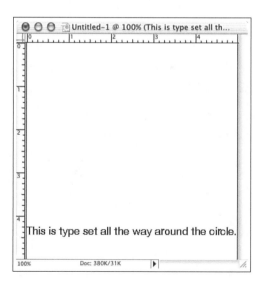

This is type set all the way around the circle.

From the Filter menu, choose Distort, then Polar Coordinates. You'll be warned that you must simplify the type in order to proceed. After you check your spelling, click OK. In the resulting dialog box (see Figure 24.7), select the Rectangular to Polar option. Figure 24.8 shows the resulting circle of text.

The Rectangular to Polar option takes the top of the image, compresses it, and places it in the center. Then it takes the bottom edge of the image and stretches it in a circle until the ends meet. For our example, the effect is perfect. For a rather strange distortion, try this on a photo of a person, landscape, flower, or other object. Just remember that the image or selection should be square for best results.

The other option, Polar to Rectangular, has the opposite effect. It takes the center portion of the image and stretches it across the top of the canvas. It then pulls the left and right sides of the image down toward the bottom edge. It takes the top half of the image, cuts it in half, and pushes it to the left and right across the top of the canvas.

FIGURE 24.7
The Polar Coordinates dialog box.

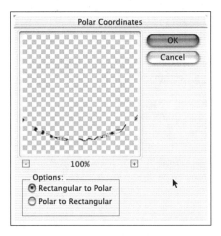

FIGURE 24.8
Voilà! Type in a circle.

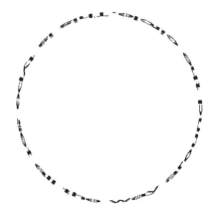

You might notice, however, that the type is somewhat squashed. You can correct this by stretching the type to about twice its height *before* you filter it. Figure 24.9 shows the result with stretched type.

FIGURE 24.9
See how much stretch it needed?

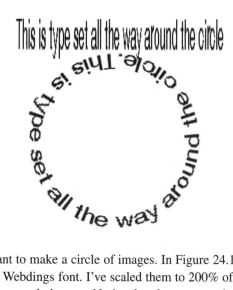

Suppose you want to make a circle of images. In Figure 24.10, we have a row of little people from the Webdings font. I've scaled them to 200% of their original height, so they will remain vaguely human. Notice that they are evenly spaced from one edge of the frame to the opposite edge. This prevents a gap in the line when we apply the filter.

FIGURE 24.10
Some people are ding-bats, some are web-dings.

After applying the filter, I simply inserted one of NASA's awesome photos of our home planet, as shown in Figure 24.11.

Speaking of NASA, did you know that you can download and use any of their photos at no charge? Here's the official word from the NASA Web site (www.nasa.gov): "NASA images generally are not copyrighted. You may use NASA imagery, video and audio material for educational or informational purposes, including photo collections, textbooks, public exhibits and Internet Web pages. This general permission does not include the NASA insignia logo (the blue "meatball" insignia), the NASA logotype (the red "worm" logo) and the NASA seal. These images may not be used by persons who are not NASA employees or on products (including Web pages) that are not NASA sponsored."

FIGURE 24.11

We're all one world, let's stop blowing it up.

Using the Magic Eraser

Magicians have lots of ways to make things disappear. There is an Elements tool that can do a similar kind of magic. It is called, appropriately, the Magic Eraser. It can remove a simple background with just a few clicks, leaving a transparent background for Web use or for layering in a composite. If the layer is locked for transparency, however, the Magic Eraser will replace the pixels with the background color.

To reach the Magic Eraser, click and hold on the regular Eraser to open the menu. The Magic Eraser is the one that has the sparkly part of the Magic Wand tool attached to it (see Figure 24.12).

FIGURE 24.12

The Magic Eraser and the picture we'll use it on.

The background in this photo is fairly plain, with two distinct areas: shadow and plain wall. To remove it, first set a reasonable amount of tolerance on the tool Options bar. Tolerance here works just as it does with the Magic Wand. The higher the setting you give it, the greater the range of pixels it will select with each click. If you overdo the tolerance, you may find yourself erasing part of your subject as well. You may need to experiment with several settings to find the best one.

To erase, simply click *once* on the part of the picture you want to erase. The Magic Eraser erases pixels similar in color (within the Tolerance you set) to the one you clicked. If you turned on the Contiguous option, only matching pixels surrounding the pixel you click will be erased; otherwise, matching pixels throughout the layer will be erased. To leave a few pixels at the edges of the background you're erasing (and smooth the edges there), turn on the Anti-Aliasing option. Adjust the strength of the eraser by changing the Opacity. Figure 24.13 shows the result of one click with a tolerance of 5.

24

FIGURE 24.13
Just one click!

That removed a good-sized piece of wall. Figure 24.14 shows the result after a dozen more clicks. It's not perfect, but a couple of strokes with the regular Eraser will finish the job quite nicely.

By the way, when you make part of a Background layer transparent, as I've done here, the name of the layer automatically changes to Layer 0 and it loses its background status, so you can paste it over another background. (If you don't want the background layer converted to a regular layer, use the Eraser tool instead of the Magic or Background Erasers.) Figure 24.15 shows my subject, out of the studio and into the mountains.

FIGURE 24.14
I never liked that wall color.

FIGURE 24.15
A nicer setting for a portrait.

If you have a photo with a complicated background, Elements has another eraser that will do the job for you. You learned about it in Hour 19, "Creating Art from Scratch." It's called the Background Eraser, and appears on the same menu as the Magic Eraser. Its icon is an eraser coupled with a pair of scissors. Unlike the Magic Eraser, which only requires clicking, the Background Eraser makes you do the erasing by dragging the mouse pointer. However, because the tool samples and removes a range of background colors (instead of pixels that closely match the color of a single pixel), it's practically mistake-proof.

Figure 24.16 shows a cute little teddy bear that I'd like to take out of his box.

FIGURE 24.16

No place for a bear.

First, I'll choose a fairly large brush, just to make the work go quickly. The tool allows me to get in close without erasing my subject, which means that I don't have to be so careful with my often-shaky hand. I'll set the tool options to a fairly low tolerance (about 5). Setting the Background Eraser to Contiguous means that it will only erase matching pixels adjacent to the point that's being sampled. (The sample point is represented by the crosshairs in the center of the brush.) Again, you don't have to be too precise here, just make sure that the crosshairs never move onto your subject, or you'll erase part of it. By choosing a large brush size, you can easily prevent that catastrophe.

Figure 24.17 shows teddy, his box mostly erased in less than a minute. Notice that I can bring the eraser right up to the edge of the bear without losing any of his fur. That's because the contrast in color between the bear and the box is sufficient to fall outside the 5% tolerance.

FIGURE **24.17**
*Now to find someplace
more suitable.*

However, because the tolerance setting is low, the eraser has left the darker lines of the box. I can go back over these with the regular eraser and remove them before I relocate teddy to a new setting (see Figure 24.18).

FIGURE **24.18**
*Even bears need
friends.*

Using Third-Party Filters

Ever since I started using Photoshop—I think it was PS 3—I have loved to play with the program's filters. After a while, though, I began to wish for something even more exciting. I started looking for third-party plug-ins. I found many. Some simply copied Photoshop's own filters. Some were strange, some were just utilitarian, and some were wonderful! Because of the way Elements is designed, almost all Photoshop filters work with it. Let me show you some of my favorites.

Kai's Power Tools

Kai's Power Tools, if memory serves, were the first commercial plug-ins for Photoshop. They've consistently been interesting, useful, and fun to use. There are currently two sets of tools, KPT 5 and KPT 6. Each set has ten different (some *very* different) filters. They are sold separately, through your favorite software dealer or through Corel Corporation (www.corel.com), which bought the rights to these products from MetaCreations. Unfortunately, for us Mac users, Kai's Power Tools does not work in OS X, only System 9. Figure 24.19 shows the menus from both filter sets.

FIGURE 24.19

Menus for KPT 5 and 6.

24

As you can see, the names don't tell you much. You'll need to do some exploring to find out what these filters can do. Frax4D, one of several fractal filters, generates fractals and allows you to change the lighting, environment, and other parameters by just dragging or clicking (see Figure 24.20). Is it practical? Not very, but it's lots of fun.

By the way, the @ sign sort of squished into a button at the top-right corner of the screen takes you to Corel's Web site. The button with the three interlocking rings will open the PDF version of the KPT guidebook most relevant to what you're trying to do. In the bottom-right corner of the screen are two buttons: One's a sad face, the other's a happy face. Sad cancels your changes, and happy applies them as you close the filter screen to return to your photo.

KPT filter interfaces are intended to be intuitive, but most of us need a little help from the included PDF. Figure 24.21 shows a typical KPT screen from KPT6. This filter is called Materializer. Basically, it adds texture, lighting, and a 3-D effect to your image, but does so in a unique manner. As you can see, there are lots of options to set, and lots of possibilities.

FIGURE **24.20**
The interface is similar in most of the KPT filters.

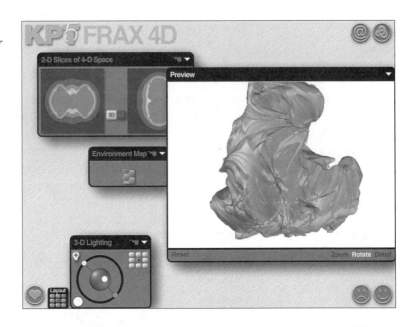

FIGURE **24.21**
Part of the fun is finding out what does what.

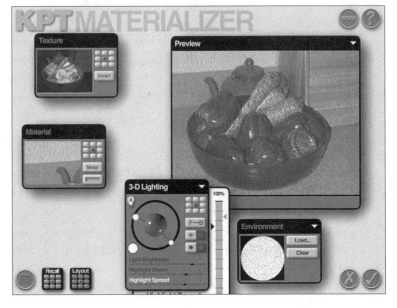

Alien Skin: Eye Candy 4000 and Splat!

Eye Candy 4000 is another compilation of Photoshop filters. As the name of the publisher (Alien Skin Software—www.alienskin.com) suggests, some of these filters are a little out of the ordinary. There are 23 in all, ranging from anti-matter to wood. Some of these, particularly marble and wood, can be used to create very realistic backgrounds or textures. Eye Candy's interface, though it seems complicated at first glance, is really quite simple. Move the sliders to see what each one does. Be forewarned: Some of Eye Candy's filters may take a while to render. Try to be patient, especially if you are using an older, slower computer.

Fire, Fur, and Water Drops are some of my favorites. Fire adds very realistic flames to areas you have selected. By using a couple of layers of Fire and a good dose of another filter called Smoke, you can satisfy your pyromaniac tendencies safely, without ever leaving your desk. Figure 24.22 shows a building going up in flames.

24

FIGURE 24.22

I hope I never see it like this.

Remember that you can use these third-party filters in combination with Photoshop's own filters, and you can use the same filter several times for a stronger effect.

Alien Skin's latest filter set is called Splat! The name makes it sound a little stranger than it really is, but of course, that's Alien Skin's "thing" anyway. (Their sales reps at computer shows all have orange and green punk hairdos, and they hand out little rubber alien figures. If you ever go to any of the "worlds"—MacWorld, PCWorld, PhotoshopWorld—look for them. They're really nice friendly folks.)

Splat! Filters include Border Stamps, Edges, Fill Stamps, Frames, Patchwork, and Resurface. Surround your girlfriend with white roses, or the baby with jelly beans. A lot of the contents are silly, but some are quite beautiful. As a final example, Figure 24.23 shows one of Splat's Resurface filters, Canvas, with a picture I'd already converted to an oil painting. Notice how much realism this adds.

FIGURE 24.23

The cat photo looks kind of like a painting, but the canvas in Splat works better than the one provided in Elements.

Before

After

In Figure 24.24, I've applied the Resurface filter to my cat "painting" using the Alien Skin interface. As you can see, the interface is straightforward and simple to use. And I love how it brings out the texture of the painting "canvas."

FIGURE 24.24

The Alien Skin interface is fairly simple.

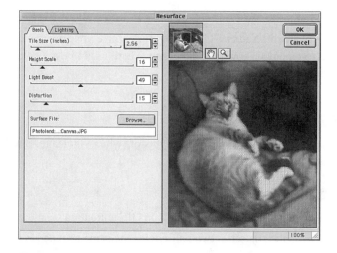

Andromeda Software Filters

Andromeda Software (www.andromeda.com) has several sets of cool filters with a user-friendly interface. There's Prism, which makes your subject appear as it might if you were looking at it through a real glass prism. Funky, huh? And there are a number of photographic filters, plus excellent focus correction. These are well worth checking out.

Summary

This final hour has taught you some useful tricks and, I hope, some fun ones. You learned to make an animated GIF and to set type in a circle. Then you discovered how to use the Magic Eraser to separate objects from their backgrounds in a hurry. You learned about third-party filters and how to use them. The one thing I hope you learned in all 24 hours is that you should experiment. Elements has infinite possibilities. Take advantage of them.

Q&A

Q I know that people in some online forums don't like signatures with animated GIFs. Is there a way to turn them on and off?

A Unfortunately, no, unless you're very good at HTML and can find a way to write in a timer. Just keep them small and unobnoxious.

Q Are there more third-party filters?

A Absolutely. I could only mention a few in the space and time allotted. Do a Google search for third-party Photoshop filters.

Q What's the most important thing to know about Elements?

A Experiment! You can't break anything. Save your most interesting accidents, if you can remember how they happened. There might be a whole new technique hidden in there.

Workshop

Last one…. Sweep up and turn the lights off when you leave. But first, here are a few questions.

Quiz

1. How many layers do you need in a GIF animation?

2. Why isn't type set in two half circles the same as type set in one big circle?

3. Where do third-party filters show up when you install them?

Answers

1. At least two.

2. When you set type in two arcs, the baseline is above one arc and below the other, rather than one continuous line, as it is when you use the Polar Coordinates filter.

3. At the bottom of the Filter menu.

Activities

I have no more activities for you. Now you're ready to do your own real-world projects: restoring old pictures, cleaning up new ones, making art, or doing whatever you bought Elements to do. Have fun!

Index

B

Background
icon, 78
option
New dialog box, 39
Print Preview dialog box, 114
thumbnail, 83
background color, toolbox, 21
Background Eraser, 19, 347, 442
background textures, 318
backgrounds. *See* **gradients**
balance, color balance (photos), 196
Banner option (Web galleries), 140
bars
menu bar, 13
Options bar, 13, 22, 32, 74
Polygonal Lasso tool Options bar, 71
Shortcuts bar, 7, 13
graphics (creating), 16
icons, 14-15
palette well, 16
toggling, 32
Tools Options bar, blending modes, 361
bas-relief, Plastic Wrap filter, 398
base colors, 362
base layers, 86
Best option (Radial Blur dialog box), 290
Bevels layer style, 354
Bicubic command (Resample Image menu), 47

Bilinear command (Resample Image menu), 47
Bitmap (BMP), 43
color mode, 29
option (New dialog box), 39
bitmapped graphics, pixels, 5
black-and-white graphics
fixing, 230
burning, 234-235
cleaning up, 245-247
contrast, 233-234
dark points, 234
dodging, 234-235
dust, 232
gray scale, 231
removing color, 239
sepia, 238
small blotches, 237
tears, 240-241
tints, 247-249
vignetting, 242
white points, 234
hand-coloring, 262
blank spaces. *See* **canvas**
blend colors, 362
blending
composite images, distortions, 377-379
pixels, 293
blending modes, 361-369
Brush tool, 342
Impressionist Brush, 343
tools, 22
Bloat tool, 174
block eraser, 19
Block mode (Eraser tool), 346
blotches, fixing (photos), 237

Blur
command (Filter menu), 286
filters, 286
Gaussian Blur filter, 289
Motion Blur filter, 291-292
Radial Blur filter, 289-290
Smart Blur filter, 287-288
tool, 20, 256
Blur, Motion Blur command (Filter menu), 291
Blur, Smart Blur command (Filter menu), 287
blurring graphics, 287
Blurry brushes (Paint Daubs filter), 317
blurs, strengths (choosing), 256
BMP (Bitmap), 43
color mode, 29
option (New dialog box), 39
bold type, 93
Border option
Modify dialog box, 77
Print Preview dialog box, 115
Border Size box, 140
Border Stamps filters, 448
borders, 115, 336
Bounding Box option (Print Preview dialog box), 114
bounding boxes, 19, 27, 166
boxes. *See also* **check boxes; dialog boxes**
Border Size, 140
bounding boxes, 19, 27, 166
cropping boxes, handles, 147

dots, overlapping (Halftone Pattern filter), 322

Download button, 219

Download New Adobe How To Items command (How To palette menu), 9

Download New Adobe Recipes command (Recipe menu), 218

downloading recipes, 218

downsampling graphics, 46-47

Draft option (Radial Blur dialog box), 290

drag-and-drop copying, 268-270

dragging marquees, 71

drawing

graphics, 335

shapes (vectors), 20

drivers, scanners, 56

Drop Shadow layer style, 354-355

drop shadows, creating from scratch, 374-376

drop-down lists, Preset Sizes, 16

drum scanners, 56

Dry Brush

filter, 312

pattern, 79

duotones, photos, 248-249

Duplicate Image command (Image menu), 25

Duplicate Layer command (Layer menu), 166, 355, 374

dust, removing from photos, 189-192, 232

Dust & Scratches filter, 189-190, 293

dye-sublimation printers, 110

E

Edge Brightness option (Glowing Edges filter), 326

Edge Only effects mode (Smart Blur dialog box), 287

Edge Width option (Glowing Edges filter), 326

edges, soft (brush tips), 426

Edges filter, 448

Edit menu, 24

Edit menu commands

Color Settings, 111

Copy, 248

Define Brush, 429

Define Pattern, 430

Fill, 78

Paste, 248

Preferences, 34, 282

Preferences, General, 8

Preset Manager, 422

Stroke, 78, 336

Undo, 51

editors

Brush editors, 425, 428

Gradient Editor, 409, 413

effects

applying, 369-371

creating from scratch, 371

customizing, 370

filters, 303

Frames (effects), 370

Glass, 370

graphics, deleting, 174

Image Effects, 370

Layer effects, 369

metallic effects, 395-397

Rusted Metal, 370

Selection effects, 369

Text effects, 369-370

Textures (effects), 370

Ellipse tool, 340

ellipsis (…), 23

Elliptical Marquee tool, 71, 243

email

files, sending, 15

graphics, sending, 49

photos, sending, 141

Encapsulated PostScript (EPS), 43

End (geometry option), 337

Enhance menu, 29-31

Enhance menu commands

Adjust Brightness/Contrast, 196, 359

Adjust Brightness/Contrast, Brightness/Contrast, 198, 246, 361

Adjust Brightness/Contrast, Levels, 231, 234, 239, 311

Adjust Color, Color Cast, 201, 253

Adjust Color, Color Variations, 200, 247, 274

Adjust Color, Hue/Saturation, 136, 254

Adjust Color, Remove Color, 187, 204, 238-239, 245

Adjust Color, Replace Color, 205

Adjust Lighting, Adjust Backlighting, 207

Adjust Lighting, Fill Flash, 207, 254

Auto Color Correction, 198

Auto Contrast, 198

Brightness/Contrast, Level, 246

Color Variations, 30

P